EMIL AND KATHLEEN SICK SERIES IN WESTERN HISTORY AND BIOGRAPHY

With support from the Center for the Study of the Pacific Northwest at the University of Washington, the Sick Series in Western History and Biography features scholarly books on the peoples and issues that have defined and shaped the American West. Through intellectually challenging and engaging books of general interest, the series seeks to deepen and expand our understanding of the American West as a region and its role in the making of the United States and the modern world.

EMIL AND KATHLEEN SICK SERIES IN WESTERN HISTORY AND BIOGRAPHY

The Great Columbia Plain: A Historical Geography, 1805-1910 by Donald W. Meinig

Mills and Markets: A History of the Pacific Coast Lumber Industry to 1900 by Thomas R. Cox

Radical Heritage: Labor, Socialism, and Reform in Washington and British Columbia, 1885-1917 by Carlos A. Schwantes

The Battle for Butte: Mining and Politics on the Northern Frontier, 1864-1906 by Michael P. Malone

The Forging of a Black Community: Seattle's Central District from 1870 through the Civil Rights Era by Quintard Taylor

Warren G. Magnuson and the Shaping of Twentieth-Century America by Shelby Scates

The Atomic West edited by Bruce Hevly and John M. Findlay

Power and Place in the North American West edited by Richard White and John M. Findlay

Henry M. Jackson: A Life in Politics by Robert G. Kaufman

Parallel Destinies: Canadian-American Relations West of the Rockies edited by John M. Findlay and Ken S. Coates

Nikkei in the Pacific Northwest: Japanese Americans and Japanese Canadians in the Twentieth Century edited by Louis Fiset and Gail M. Nomura

Bringing Indians to the Book by Albert Furtwangler

Death Of Celilo Falls by Katrine Barber

The Power of Promises: Perspectives on Indian Treaties of the Pacific Northwest edited by Alexandra Harmon

Warship under Sail: The USS Decatur *in the Pacific West* by Lorraine McConaghy

Shadow Tribe: The Making of Columbia River Indian Identity by Andrew H. Fisher

A Home for Every Child: Relinquishment, Adoption, and the Washington Children's Home Society, 1896-1915 by Patricia Susan Hart

Atomic Frontier Days: Hanford and the American West by John M. Findlay and Bruce Hevly

The Nature of Borders: Salmon, Boundaries, and Bandits on the Salish Sea by Lissa K. Wadewitz

The Nature of
BORDERS

Salmon, Boundaries, and Bandits on the Salish Sea

LISSA K. WADEWITZ

CENTER FOR THE STUDY OF THE PACIFIC NORTHWEST

in association with

UNIVERSITY OF WASHINGTON PRESS
Seattle and London

and

UBC PRESS
Vancouver and Toronto

CENTER FOR THE STUDY OF THE PACIFIC NORTHWEST
PO Box 353587
Seattle, WA 98195
USA

UNIVERSITY OF WASHINGTON PRESS
PO Box 50096
Seattle, WA 98145
USA
www.washington.edu/uwpress

UBC PRESS
The University of British Columbia
2029 West Mall
Vancouver, BC V6T 1Z2
Canada
www.ubcpress.ca

Library of Congress Cataloguing-in-Publication Data
can be found in the back of this book.

Earlier versions of portions of this book were previously published in
"Pirates of the Salish Sea: Labor, Mobility, and Environment in the
Transnational West," *Pacific Historical Review* 75: 4 (2006): 587–627;
"Fishing the Line: Political Boundaries and Border Fluidity in the
Pacific Northwest Borderlands, 1880s-1930s," in Sterling Evans, ed.,
*The Borderlands of the American and Canadian Wests: Essays on
Regional History of the Forty-Ninth Parallel* (Lincoln: University of
Nebraska Press, 2006), 299–308; and "The Scales of Salmon: Diplo-
macy and Conservation in the Western Canada–U.S. Borderlands,"
in Benjamin H. Johnson and Andrew R. Graybill, eds., *Bridging
National Borders in North America: Transnational and Comparative
Histories* (Durham: Duke University Press, 2010), 141–64.

Contents

Acknowledgments

HAVING NOW EXPERIENCED THE BOOK PUBLICATION PROCESS from beginning to end, I have new and profound respect for the people who write books and the people who turn manuscripts into monographs. This is hard, detailed work that countless individuals and institutions have helped make happen.

Many archivists helped me navigate their records. The National Archives and Records Administration–Pacific Alaska Region in Seattle has a very knowledgeable and able staff; Susan Karren, John Fitzgerald, and John Ferrell were particularly helpful in my several visits to that facility. I also greatly benefited from the expertise of the staff at the Center for Pacific Northwest Studies at Western Washington University. Chris Friday, who was the center's director when I did the bulk of my research there, has been extraordinarily generous with his time and knowledge over the years. The archivists at the Anacortes History Museum, the Huntington Library, the National Archives and Records Administration facilities in Washington, D.C. and College Park, the University of Washington's Special Collections, and the Washington State Archives in Olympia have all been extremely supportive throughout each stage of this project.

The assistance I received north of the border was also exceptional. The British Columbia Provincial Archives in Victoria, the City of Vancouver Archives, the Library and Archives Canada in Ottawa, the Stò:lō Nation Archives in Chilliwack, British Columbia, and the UBC Rare Books and Special Collections all boast cheerful and skilled staff people. I greatly benefited from George Brandak's command of UBC's Special Collections before his retirement from that facility.

Traveling to these various, far-flung archives costs money. I have been fortunate to receive financial support from a broad range of sources. The American Society for Environmental History, the John and Laree Caughey Foundation, the Center for Pacific Northwest Studies at Western Washington University, UCLA's Graduate Division, the UCLA History Department, the UCLA Institute of American Cultures, and the UCLA International Studies and Overseas Program all provided critical funding in the earlier stages of my research. The Western Historical Association's Martin Ridge Fellowship for Study in Western History allowed me to conduct important archival work at the Huntington Library.

My intellectual debts are just as, if not more, extensive. Barbara Knox got me to college, and Samuel Yamashita encouraged my intellectual curiosity as my undergraduate adviser at Pomona College. Although I ended up changing fields, he taught me the benefits of having a dedicated mentor early on in my academic career. This trend continued in graduate school at UCLA, where I was fortunate enough to work with Steve Aron. Steve has been consistently supportive over the years, and I cannot thank him enough for his keen mind and generous spirit. His insights greatly shaped how this project proceeded, and I have learned much from our conversations. John Agnew and Jan Reiff were both excellent committee members, and I have benefited tremendously from their guidance and expertise.

My luck continued after graduate school. I was fortunate to spend a year as a Native-Newcomer Post-Doctoral Fellow with the University of Saskatchewan History Department. The entire department was incredibly welcoming, and the intellectual community created by Jim Miller, Keith Carlson, and Angela Wanhalla was particularly engaging. Keith kindly let me tag along with him and John Lutz (of the University of Victoria) to participate in their Ethnographic Field School that spring. Students from both the University of Saskatchewan and the University of Victoria come together every other year to work closely with the Stò:lō Nation on projects identified by that community. The combined leadership of Keith and John, the warm reception by the Stò:lō people, and the student group itself made this month an educational and memorable experience.

When I moved on to Stanford the following year, I was able to add David Kennedy and Richard White to my list of mentors. My two years at the Bill Lane Center for the American West were administratively challenging, but, thanks to David and Richard, intellectually stimulating. Thanks also to Emily Brock, Jon Christensen, and Michael Rawson for their thought-provoking discussions. Having the opportunity to engage with the members of that community and with the numerous scholars who visited for various reasons broadened my understanding of U.S. and Canadian western history as well as where this book was headed and how to get it there.

Many other people have helped with this project over the years. The members of my dissertation-writing group WHEAT (Western Historians Eating and Talking) deserve special thanks for reading chapter drafts month after month. Mike Bottoms, John Bowes, Cindy Culver Prescott, Lawrence Culver, Samantha Gervase, Kelly Lytle Hernandez, Rachel St. John, and Allyson Varzally endured very early drafts and helped me better frame the larger story I was trying to tell. I know the dissertation benefited from their comments, and I from their friendship. Dave Arnold, Rob Baker, Tammy Ho, Kelly Maynard, Shauna Mulvihill, and Gabe Wolfenstein have all been supportive friends as I worked on this project. The Nature Nerds—an eclectic, interdisciplinary group interested in sharing work on various environmental topics—offered additional occasions for fun and intellectual exchange. Peter Alagona has been a true friend and intellectual confidant; our many discussions have given me a lot of food for thought. Peter and Rachel, together with Thomas Andrews and Jennifer Price, read revised drafts of chapters at various points in time, and their insights helped improve the end product significantly.

Since graduate school, I have benefited from getting to know other scholars whose work intersects with my own. My thanks especially to Matthew Evenden, Andrea Geiger, Doug Harris, Jen Seltz, and Coll Thrush for their friendship and willingness to talk shop and share ideas. David Igler very generously read my entire manuscript when it was in the early stages of revision. David Wrobel kindly offered suggestions on a revised introduction. Jay Taylor has now read this book more times than he no doubt ever wanted to. His sharp pencil and even sharper mind have pushed me to better articulate and refine my ideas and related arguments; I thank him for his generosity and dedication to ongoing scholarly exchanges. All of these constructive conversations helped me move this project from dissertation to book, which is a challenging process.

The friends who housed, fed, and entertained me during breaks from research deserve special mention. Brian and Angela Oakley as well as Rob Ryan offered me ongoing friendship, places to stay, and delicious meals while I conducted research in Seattle, Olympia, and Bellingham. Thornton Bowman kept me entertained with his good humor and music after long hours in the Seattle-area archives. In Canada, Bob and Corey Mulvihill, Liam Haggerty, and John Lutz all generously offered spare rooms or couches and lively conversation at various points in time.

I was fortunate again to move from Stanford to a tenure-track position at Linfield College in McMinnville, Oregon. The college has supported this project with a faculty development grant, with travel funds for conferences, and most recently with the Allen and Pat Kelley Faculty Scholar Award. The college's recognition of the value of research and writing to my development as both a scholar and a teacher is greatly appreciated. The course releases granted by this most recent award in particular are a true gift—they have enabled me to finish this book and start a new research project. I sincerely thank the Kelley family for funding this important award for Linfield faculty. Reilly Everaert, my work-study student assistant, helped with many aspects of this project, including the all-important process of footnote checking. My colleague Anna Keesey read a chapter and kindly shared her expertise on crafting narrative. My regular carpool members have listened to me muse aloud and complain about this project at every stage but have remained supportive and enthusiastic in spite of that. My colleagues in the history department and in environmental studies have likewise rooted for me as I strove to finish the revisions to the manuscript. I thank them all for their kind support.

The University of Washington Press staff and some other recent acquaintances also deserve thanks. Marianne Keddington-Lang is a wonderful editor and person; because of her, this is a much better book. Her energy and dedication are impressive. Mary Ribesky and Tim Zimmerman have likewise been invaluable throughout this process. The outside reviewers and my copyeditor, Amy Smith Bell, offered much appreciated, constructive feedback on the manuscript. Cameron Suttles, son of the anthropologist Wayne Suttles, has been extremely gracious about granting permission to use material from his father's dissertation and from a later map he helped compile. The University of Washington Interlibrary Loan staff, especially Alan Presley, offered crucial, last-minute assistance on tracking down original copies of maps needed for quality reproductions.

Finally, I would like to thank my family. Sandy and Jerry Wilson, Scott Wadewitz, and Mikel Wadewitz have been very patient with (albeit skeptical about) my decision first to pursue a PhD and then to write a book.

Mikel, in particular, will no doubt be thrilled when I stop talking about pirates and this project. My partner, Tom Mertes, is the most generous and kind-hearted person I know. His support, sense of humor, and knowledge of American history have all shaped this project in myriad important ways. I could not have finished the book without him. I am the lucky one in this gig and am fully aware of that fact. I also want to thank my dad, who passed away many years ago when it was not clear if college, let alone a PhD, was in my future. His job with the railroad did not leave him much time for books or school, but he pursued them nonetheless. I dedicate this book to him.

The Nature of Borders

Pacific Borders

An Introduction

T HE WATER IS DEEP GREEN AND SOMETIMES SHOCKINGLY clear on the ferry ride through the San Juan Islands off of northwestern Washington and southwestern British Columbia. The ferry weaves through hundreds of islands toward Point Roberts, a peninsula that juts out roughly two miles from mainland British Columbia into U.S. waters. The surrounding scenery is a wonderful mix of blues and greens, and the air is sharp, salty, and fresh on a clear day. The San Juan Islands boast more than 350 total miles of coastline, and each island has a distinct shape and size. Some of the larger islands, like San Juan and Lopez, have small, protected bays that offer places to retreat from ocean storms. Orcas Island, also one of the biggest and most centrally located, is shaped like a large pair of lungs poised to pump life into the entire archipelago. Some of the smaller "islands" are really just small pieces of rock that no one could live on. Despite their variations, centuries of offshore gales have left all of the islands with similar wind-swept trees and memories of fishermen lost at sea. The currents shift and swirl, pulling strongly against the side of the boat as seagulls labor into the wind to keep pace with the vessel.

Impressive mountains frame this waterscape, adding to its allure. To the southwest, the snowcapped Olympic range towers nearly eight thousand feet over such small towns as Port Townsend, Sequim, Port Angeles, and Neah Bay that hug the northern shore of the Olympic Peninsula. Slightly taller, volcanic Mount Baker and the North Cascades hover, and the dramatic yet more distant North Shore Mountains of British Columbia sit silently above the forty-ninth parallel. Because of the protection offered by the height and orientation of the Olympics, the sun shines more often on these islands than on the mainland.

It is far more difficult to appreciate the scenery beneath the ocean's surface. Orcas occasionally burst through the waves to remind those above of their complex underwater world. Dall's porpoises or possibly Pacific white-sided dolphins frolic in the waves at the front of the boat. The shimmering green leaves and long tentacles of bull kelp groves undulate with the waves, offering harbor seals places to hide and play. Numerous species of fish also live in these waters and serve as food for animals and people alike. Perhaps the most iconic regional fish that still passes through these waters is the Pacific salmon.[1]

Most Pacific salmon (*Oncorhynchus spp.*) are anadromous—meaning they spend most of their lives in the ocean before determinedly making their way to their natal streams to spawn and die. Because of the distances they travel, these fish have extremely complicated life cycles. After approximately two months of incubation, they are born in rivers or lakes and spend the first few months as alevins (newly hatched fish) hiding in river gravel and living off their yolk sacs. Sacs consumed, they become fry and begin to feed off of small organisms. Some salmon immediately head out to sea, while others remain in freshwater before migrating to the oceans, where they spend their formative years. A few salmon species, such as rainbow trout and kokanee, spend their entire lives in freshwater. When ready to spawn, the fish return to their natal rivers, nose around in the river gravel, and deposit their eggs. Unlike Atlantic salmon, Pacific salmon spawn just once before they die.[2]

Nearly all of the sockeye salmon (*Oncorhynchus nerka*) taken in Washington State hail from the Fraser River tributaries of southwestern British Columbia. The other types of salmon suitable for canning (pink/humpback, coho/silver, chinook/spring, chum/dog) return to rivers on either side of the border. Both countries thus have access to this mobile resource in the waters of the Puget Sound/Georgia Basin, the Strait of Juan de Fuca, and the broader Pacific Ocean. Just over a hundred years ago, when these fish returned to spawn, their thrashing bodies completely filled the region's rivers. Many people who witnessed these runs at their height claimed that it was possible to cross entire waterways on the backs of salmon. Their numbers inspired awe, but such abundance also translated into a false sense of security about their future health.

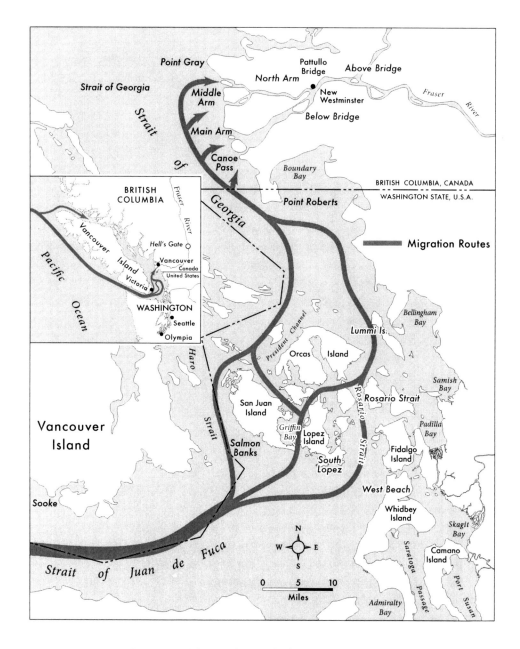

MAP 0.1   Fraser River Salmon Fishery and Salmon Migration Routes. In this western "borderland," nearly all of the red sockeye salmon (*Oncorhynchus nerka*) taken in the Washington fisheries hail from the Fraser River tributaries of southwestern British Columbia, whereas the other varieties of salmon suitable for canning (pink/humpback, coho/silver, chinook/spring, chum/dog) return to rivers on both sides of the border.

The waters of the Puget Sound/Georgia Basin that have nurtured so many species over the years have recently been renamed. In recognition of the connectedness of the entire ecosystem and to honor the region's indigenous* Salishan language speakers, officials in both Washington State and British Columbia have started calling these rich coastal waters the "Salish Sea."[3] For thousands of years, more than two hundred thousand Northwest Indians maintained family, trade, and resource ties across these different bodies of water, and many of these links persist to this day.[4] "By carrying on relations with each other according to precolonial custom," historian Alexandra Harmon writes of this region, Native peoples "have experienced a history that does not fit within jurisdictional lines drawn by non-Indians."[5] This new name celebrates the strength and longevity of these connections at the same time it implicitly recognizes the ecological fluidity of this waterscape.[6]

Looking out over the waves today, it is easy to forget that an international political border has divided this waterscape since the nineteenth century. The Canada-U.S. border—constructed and artificial—is invisible to people, orcas, salmon, and birds, but it is very much there, and it has played a critical role in the history of the Pacific salmon fishery that straddles it. Other lesser-known types of borders drawn by Indians were also important to the evolution of this fishery. This book is thus a study of the nature of these borders—that is, the relationships between political conceptions of space and the ways that people have managed the salmon fishery of the Salish Sea for centuries. The Salish Sea is a perfect waterscape in which to look at borders precisely because both Native and white borders cut across the migratory routes of Pacific salmon. Native borders were created to apply property and access rights to certain fishing locations that, in the pre- and early-contact eras, tended to protect the runs from overexploitation. Indians holding valuable salmon fishing sites limited who could fish when, and they developed social customs and belief systems around the act of fishing, especially early in the season.[7]

This is not to suggest that indigenous peoples somehow innately understood the mysteries of salmon conservation and the rhythms of the natural

---

* Americans and Canadians employ different terminology to refer to Native peoples. I have used "indigenous," "Native," and "Indian" to refer to the first people of North America and their descendants, both to avoid repetition and because these were the words most often used in the time period studied that are still generally accepted today.

world. This stereotype of the "ecological Indian" is not only anachronistic, it is a disservice to Native peoples and their history.[8] Instead, it is important to remember that the pre-contact period stretched over thousands of dynamic years about which scholars know relatively little. The fragility of salmon bones has not helped to clarify the degree to which pre-contact Northwest peoples relied on salmon nor whether they ever depleted their resources.[9] Still, as scant as the available evidence is, it demonstrates that Northwest Indians drew meaningful lines around their best fishing sites to protect salmon from overfishing. Native peoples no doubt experienced famines of their own making, but they also had thousands of years to adjust their management practices for maximum benefit.[10]

Americans and the British approached borders differently. In 1846 diplomats drew a border between the United States and Canada at the forty-ninth parallel and refined that border's water segment in 1872, with no consideration of ecological or biological factors. The Anglo-American border came to signify national jurisdictions that facilitated the emergence of a chaotic, competitive canned salmon industry wracked by ethnic, class, and international tensions. Conflicts among fishermen who used different types of gear and came from different ethnic backgrounds erupted regularly, and their proximity to the forty-ninth parallel soon became critical to Canadians and Americans alike. Legitimate fishermen and fish pirates used their knowledge of the marine environment to break cannery contracts or to steal salmon outright, then slipped across the border to sell their fish for higher prices. The big canners actively sought ways to protect their salmon supplies and urged their governments to appoint more state-sponsored border patrols.

These border crossings did not take place in a vacuum. They had important consequences for transnational salmon conservation efforts and contributed to the growth of a state presence along the forty-ninth parallel. Border manipulations spurred the government to police the border in an attempt to restrict worker mobility, but these actions also fostered mistrust when Americans arrested Canadians, Canadians seized American boats, or one group stole the other's fish. Illegal fish sales and salmon smuggling contributed to fierce infighting among industry players and obstructed efforts to limit overfishing and waste. In short, fishermen and cannery workers—the least powerful players in the fishery—did the most to give the border real meaning, linking border crossings and the border itself to salmon conservation and, ultimately, salmon decline.[11]

How people think about and manage waterscapes, the meaning and effects of work in nature, and the role of local ecological knowledge are all important strands in this story of environmental change and conservation politics. As historian Richard White reminds us, laborers in western extractive industries came to know nature most intimately through their work in the natural world. Western workers learned to read and manipulate the physical characteristics of their workplaces, even as they transformed those environments in sometimes quite radical ways.[12] Workers' knowledge of the natural world was important to their success, but how they chose to use such knowledge could also influence environmental management practices, conservation politics, and the relations between capital and labor.[13] And despite the extensive experience of regional fish workers, environmental conditions still dictated how many of these stories unfolded. Salmon migration routes, weather patterns, and ocean conditions all restricted what workers could do at certain times and facilitated them at others. This book assesses how workers' know-how, their mobility, and their economic and political motivations coalesced in a borderlands environment and with what results for the salmon of the Salish Sea.

The transition from Native to newcomer borders foreshadowed a number of the same challenges that continue to stymie fishery managers today. By the late nineteenth century, Euro-American and Euro-Canadian salmon canners had repeatedly hopped northward up the West Coast in pursuit of more fish. White canners and fishermen—along with miners and loggers—depleted the fish populations of the Sacramento and the Columbia between the 1860s and the early 1900s; the Fraser River/Puget Sound fishery and Alaska were next on the list. By the time those northern industrial fisheries boomed, however, general sentiments about unregulated economic development at any cost were starting to change. Progressive Era concerns about scientific management and conservation of natural resources had become hot topics in the United States and Canada at the turn of the twentieth century, and government managers faced the task of effectively administering those resources for future generations. The Salish Sea fishery presented unique problems for fishery managers precisely because of its transnational character. Government officials had to more explicitly grapple with the mobility of salmon and fishermen and confront the implications of national territoriality for conservation regulations. At the same time, regulators had to cope with the shifting spatiality of the commercial fishery as increasing numbers of fishermen ventured farther out onto the high seas. The history of the Salish Sea salmon fishery marks the beginning of efforts to manage a dynamic, transnational industry that continues to defy regulation in many of the same ways.[14]

This book has been greatly influenced by historians' recent interest in moving beyond the boundaries of the nation-state, venturing across waterscapes, and taking the environmental consequences of border-drawing seriously.[15] "Borderlands history" is no longer shorthand for studies of the Spanish colonial frontier and the region through which the U.S.-Mexico border now runs.[16] Historians have also begun to investigate the complex social, political, economic, and environmental connections among communities that span other borders, as well as coastlines and oceans. This more expansive view of North American history has revealed previously unexamined connections that have added significant complexity to our understandings of national identities, state power, and economic change.[17]

The emerging work of western environmental historians has also shaped this book.[18] In the process of investigating mobile nature, such as weeds and migratory birds, environmental historians have found that different types of borders—and thus different categories of property—present unique challenges for environmental management efforts and have influenced how those efforts have evolved over time. Euro-Americans and Euro-Canadians have been drawing various kinds of borders across the western landscape for decades, and many recent environmental problems involving land and species management have necessitated navigating these land use designations and negotiating with their respective managers or owners.[19]

The Nature of Borders assesses the ecological effects of different types of borders on a water resource. It also shows that both salmon and the water border between the United States and Canada posed specific challenges for fishery managers that influenced the evolution of the commercial canned salmon industry as well as salmon conservation efforts. Both nations quickly discovered that drawing and maintaining an international political border at sea was fraught with social, economic, political, and environmental difficulties. The Pacific Ocean made solidifying the forty-ninth parallel even harder because salmon live much of their lives in both coastal waters and on the high seas. In essence, Canadian and American fishery patrols increasingly had *two* borders that fishermen transgressed: their shared international border and the three-mile territorial limit off the coast. Due to the nature of the marine environment and the behavior of salmon, they failed to solidify either border in the early 1900s. Since the late 1930s, both countries have drawn new managerial borders around this dynamic fishery, but for many of the same reasons they too have proved largely ineffective. The consequences of that failure are evident in the large number of Pacific salmon runs that remain on the endangered species list.

The Salish Sea industrial fishery went bust like the other Pacific salmon fisheries that preceded it, but how that happened and why has much to do with the conditions created by the Anglo-American border before World War I and the proximity of the open ocean. Although border banditry and fish piracy persisted through the 1920s and 1930s, greater efforts to police the border, the decline of regional salmon runs, and the growth of the industry in Alaska all increasingly drove these bandits and pirates northward or into different lines of work after 1918. Pollution, dams, irrigation systems, and habitat destruction caused by the growth of industry and urbanization continued to negatively affect regional salmon populations, even as authorities on both sides of the forty-ninth parallel gradually made more concrete attempts at conservation.[20] A look at salmon diplomacy over the past hundred-plus years indicates that the nature of the Canada-U.S. border has presented a serious impediment to Pacific salmon conservation efforts; this book explains why that happened and how we reached this particular precipice.[21] Ultimately, this book also underscores an emerging intriguing twist: several recent fishery management practices look suspiciously like those of the distant Native past.

Natives and newcomers drew their borders for different purposes, and both had very different consequences for the Pacific salmon fisheries of the Salish Sea. As one travels through this beautiful waterscape, it might be hard to grasp the role of borders in this fishery's history. But look deep into the water of the straits and imagine millions of salmon making their way through these waters after years at sea. That is where this story begins.

The Indians at Nootka had the first extended contact with visiting British and American vessels in the late eighteenth century. This engraving shows the Nuu-chah-nulth seeing off a British boat in 1788. Although this accessibility brought the community many trade opportunities, it also meant that they were more exposed to the diseases that were unwittingly introduced by visiting traders. Engraving by C. Metz. Original image by unknown artist from John Meares, *Voyages Made in the Years 1788 and 1789, from China to the North West Coast of America* (London: Atlas, 1797), plate 25. University of Washington Libraries, Special Collections, NA3963.

James Alden (ca. 1857–1862), an American officer who served as a field artist with the British-American Boundary Commission, painted this picture of the Hudson's Bay Company's Fort Langley in the mid-nineteenth century. The frequency of interaction between the regional Indians and the white fur traders is suggested by the proximity of the Indian encampment on the opposite side of the Fraser River and the large number of canoes pulled ashore, ready for a quick trip across the water to the fort. Courtesy of the U.S. National Archives and Records Administration, College Park, MD [ARC identifier305495].

James Gilchrist Swan, an American, lived in Washington for many years, learned the Makah language, and worked in various government positions, including serving as the Indian agent among the Makah. On a trip to the Columbia River in the 1850s, Swan watched Chinook Indians use one of their most common salmon fishing techniques from the pre- and early-contact era: the beach seine. Requiring three men to operate, beach seines could bring in as many as one hundred fish per haul. The Chinook Indians had a history of preparing the fish in the Indian manner prior to trading them with whites so as to protect their relationship with the Salmon People. From Swan, *Northwest Coast*.

Sketch of Lummi Village, 1868. Government Indian agents attempted to reorder the lives of the Lummi Indians from the 1850s on. The lack of Native people in this image is suggestive of how deserted many of the Washington State reservations were at certain times of the year. Copy of Coleman's sketch. P. R. Jeffcott Papers, #1340. Center for Pacific Northwest Studies, Western Washington University, Bellingham, WA.

Snohomish couple, Puget Sound, Washington, 1905. Regional Indians commonly constructed temporary shelters like these in which to dry salmon during the salmon season. University of Washington Libraries, Special Collections, Seattle, WA, NA710.

Fishing camp at Wing Point on Bainbridge Island, Washington, ca. 1905. Photograph by Webster & Stevens. Museum of History and Industry, Seattle, WA, Negative 1983.10.6950.

Native peoples continued to follow their seasonal fishing and food-gathering rounds well after the designation of the international border at the forty-ninth parallel in 1846. While they initially incorporated working for whites into this annual cycle, the combination of white population pressures and the growth of urban areas made it increasingly difficult for Indians to get work and remain mobile by the 1910s and 1920s. Here a group of Indians are camped on the beach at Port Townsend, 1899. Photo by William Wilcox. Museum of History and Industry, Seattle, WA, Negative Wilcox 5099.

Lummi Island, near Village Point, ca. 1910. Northwest Indians built fish harvesting and preservation sites close to their most productive fishing locations. P. R.
Jeffcott Papers, #1341.1. Center for Pacific Northwest Studies, Bellingham, WA.

Although the exact date and location of this fishing weir are unknown, this is an excellent example of a well-built and well-maintained Native American structure. While there were many variations in practice, the platforms occupied by the people posing for this photo would likely have been owned and heritable fishing locations. *Bellingham Herald*, January 15, 1939, "Ancient Fishtrap Used by Indians." Whatcom Museum of History and Art, Bellingham, WA, x.5914.

Before the arrival of whites, several groups of Coast Salish Indians practiced reef net fishing for salmon off the coasts of Point Roberts and several of the San Juan Islands. Reef net locations technically belonged to individual Coast Salish Native peoples and were heritable properties. When the industrial salmon fishery boomed in the 1890s, however, whites with access to capital increasingly built fish traps atop many of these valuable fishing sites. Photo by Bert Huntoon (1898), Galen Biery Collection, #1330. Center for Pacific Northwest Studies, Western Washington University, Bellingham, WA.

As this small model indicates, reef nets were complex nets that were towed between two Indian canoes out in open water. While the reef net sites themselves were considered a type of individual property, site owners could not fish such complex nets on their own. To alleviate this problem, site owners invited other community members to assist with both fishing and processing activities in return for a share of the catch. Since actual-size reef nets were quite large, the invited participants also contributed small portions of net that were then sewn together by a ritualist to ensure successful fishing. Howard Buswell Collection, #205. Center for Pacific Northwest Studies, Western Washington University, Bellingham, WA.

Fish trap, ca. 1930s. Traps were designed to lead salmon into the interior of the trap, to hold as many live fish inside the trap as possible, and to take up large areas of fishing space. J. W. Sandison Collection, Whatcom Museum of History and Art, Bellingham, WA, 2007.40.124.

By the early 1900s white-owned fish traps like this one blocked Native American access to many of their former salmon fishing locations, even adjacent to the Indian reservations. This was just one of several traps constructed off the coast of Lummi Island, Washington, pictured ca. 1911. Photo by Leslie Corbett. University of Washington Libraries, Special Collections, Seattle, WA, UW26015.

Fish trap, ca. 1919. As fish traps were capable of catching thousands of fish at a time, nontrap fishermen regularly decried their existence, and fish pirates generally found a large supply of fish ready for poaching inside the traps. Photo by Bert Huntoon. Whatcom Museum of History and Art, Bellingham, WA, x.3190.

Because salmon caught inside Puget Sound fish traps generally remained alive until removed, canners could theoretically regulate how many trap-caught salmon were taken to the canneries. Although trap owners did not always succeed at achieving this balance between supply and production capacity, fish pirates exacerbated the situation by removing thousands of fish from the traps and selling them to canneries on both sides of the border. Despite the claims of the trap owners regarding the efficiency and conservation merits of the traps, if too many salmon were contained in a trap at any one time, it was possible for them to suffocate. Bycatch inside the traps was also a concern. Photo by Asahel Curtis. University of Washington Libraries, Special Collections, Seattle, WA, A. Curtis 16021.

In addition to monopolizing fish, fish traps also monopolized salmon fishing space. Fish trap leads extended thousands of feet out from shore, and fish trap owners manipulated the laws regarding trap spacing to take up even more fishing space. They strategically built traps to prevent fishermen using other types of gear from accessing whole coastal areas. Note the reach of the fish trap leads in this view of Point Roberts, Washington. Photo by Edwards Brothers, ca. 1900. University of Washington Libraries, Special Collections, Seattle, WA, UW 8195.

Boundary Bay, 1915. To halt salmon thefts, trap owners began hiring one or two night watchmen to guard their fish traps beginning in the 1890s. However, fish pirates took advantage of the low wages paid these watchmen and often used bribes to convince the watchmen to look the other way while the pirates did their work. Howard Buswell Collection, #712. Center for Pacific Northwest Studies, Western Washington University, Bellingham, WA.

During the boom years of the Puget Sound/Fraser River salmon canning industry, thousands of boats filled the Salish Sea to pursue salmon. These expeditions
often took American and Canadian fishermen across the international border
and into neighboring territorial waters that were technically off-limits. Photo by
Thompson, 1901. University of Washington Libraries, Special Collections, Seattle,
WA, UW5714.

Most Japanese fishermen flew Japanese flags to identify their boats. Non-Japanese fishermen could thus easily identify their Japanese counterparts while out fishing. This may have been particularly significant during the labor disputes of the early 1900s that devolved into violence between ethnic groups in B.C. waters. City of Vancouver Archives, Vancouver, B.C., CVA 371–148.

That these fishermen would pull ashore together in Swinomish Channel near LaConner, Washington, and spend time socializing suggests the extent of social interaction that could take place during the fishing season. Still, friendly relations did not often extend beyond the fishermen's gear-type group; note that this gathering consists solely of gill net fishermen. Photo by Asahel Curtis, ca. 1903. University of Washington Libraries, Special Collections, Seattle, WA, A. Curtis 6812.

MAKAH SALMON FISHING FLEET.
NEAH BAY WASH.
COPYRIGHTED BY P. WISCHMEYER
SEATTLE WASH.
No. 0150

The seeming variety of vessels at anchor in this photograph raises questions about the year in which it was taken and whether or not this was indeed just a picture of Makah vessels. It is possible that this "fleet" consists of a combination of Native American gillnetting boats and the purse seining vessels that grew more common in the early 1900s and 1910s. Purse seiners tended to be European immigrants of Croatian or Austrian descent, and they led the trend among fishermen to fish farther offshore as the years passed. Moving out onto the high seas allowed these fishermen to both reach the fish first and avoid fishery and customs patrols. Howard Buswell Collection, #1848. Center for Pacific Northwest Studies, Western Washington University, Bellingham, WA.

Scows like this one roamed boundary waters to gather fish for delivery to canneries. Some scows were operated independently, and scow owners were known to buy fish from fishermen contracted to different establishments as well as from fish pirates. Undated photo by Corbett. Galen Biery Collection, #1142. Center for Pacific Northwest Studies, Western Washington University, Bellingham, WA.

At the peak of the salmon season, canneries in both British Columbia and Washington sometimes purchased more salmon than they could can before the fish spoiled. In the early years of the industry, it was common to dump dead fish and the fish waste produced during the canning process into local waterways. Photo by Asahel Curtis, ca. 1913. University of Washington Libraries, Special Collections, Seattle, WA, A. Curtis 27678.

Asian labor contractors like Won Toon, pictured here with his wife ca. 1920, tried to control the mobility of their Chinese and Japanese cannery workers. Such contractors appear to have been less successful in these endeavors as time passed. Proximity to the international border gave many Asian workers additional job opportunities and a way to abandon their supposedly binding work contracts. Won Toon worked at the Carlisle Packing Company on Lummi Island. Howard Buswell Collection, #718. Center for Pacific Northwest Studies, Western Washington University, Bellingham, WA.

Northwest cannery crews remained ethnically diverse through the 1910s. The Chinese Exclusion Act and negotiations by the U.S. and Canadian governments to limit the number of incoming Japanese workers gradually translated into smaller numbers of Asian workers inside the canneries of the Salish Sea. Howard Buswell Collection, #1197, ca. 1913. Center for Pacific Northwest Studies, Western Washington University, Bellingham, WA.

In the derogatory parlance common to the early 1900s, the Smith butchering machine on the right was known as the "Iron Chink" because it was expected to replace Chinese cannery workers. Because of the costs involved in purchasing such machinery and the ongoing demand for hand-packed canned salmon, however, the machine, here pictured in 1909, did not become the industry standard for many years. Photo by Asahel Curtis. University of Washington Libraries, Special Collections, Seattle, WA, A. Curtis 16039.

Fraser River salmon canners, ca. 1888. Some Canadian and American canners invested across the border even as they tried to limit workers' ability to cross it for higher wages or salmon prices. Seated from left: D. J. Munn, E. A. Wadhams, A. Ewen, M. M. English, and B. Young. Standing from left: M. Leary, H. E. Harlock, T. E. Ladner, J. A. Laidlaw, and R. Matheson. Royal B.C. Museum, B.C. Archives, Victoria, B.C., D-00540.

1

Native Borders

SALMON MOVED FLUIDLY BETWEEN THE WORLDS OF ANIMALS and human beings in early Northwest Native ethnographies and oral traditions. Salmon and other animals regularly assumed human shape, their ability to blur the line between species demonstrating the strong connections between humans and nonhumans. Salmon People appear often in the stories passed down from one generation to the next. In one Coast Salish account a man and Raven were out hunting on Vancouver Island. Paddling along in their canoe, they suddenly dropped into a hole and landed on the roof of one of the Salmon People's homes. Wanting to be good hosts and currently in human form, the Salmon People took their children to a nearby river and immersed them in the water. The human children immediately turned into salmon, which the parents then cooked and generously offered to their visitors. As they ate, man, Raven, and the Salmon People carefully saved the bones and returned them to the river following their meal. The children were "reanimated and again became humans."[1]

In Katzie (Halqʹeméylem) memory the leader of Sheridan Hill, Swanaset, journeyed to a distant land in search of the Sockeye Salmon People. Once he found them, Swanaset successfully wooed the daughter of the Sockeye Salmon chief, married her, and lived with her family for a time. Each morning, Swanaset watched his mother-in-law return from the beach cradling a sockeye salmon as though it were a child. The family roasted the fish and paid close attention to the bones as they ate. After the meal

Swanaset's mother-in-law took the bones to the beach, gently tossed them into the water, and returned to the house with a young, happy boy. After a while Swanaset's salmon wife accompanied him back to his home village on the Fraser River. Because her relatives promised to visit every summer, she brought Swanaset's people the gift of an annual sockeye salmon run.[2]

Salmon was the skeleton around which Northwest Natives structured their lives. They were children and spouses, they grew in economic significance over time, and they were crucial to the evolution of Indian society. Such intimate connections were not automatic, however. Like any relationship, this one demanded maintenance and care; the region's Indians worked out precisely what that maintenance and care would look like over thousands of years. They transformed their cultural practices, altered their community structures, and drew lines to limit access to important salmon fishing sites. They did these things to ensure that their relationship with salmon remained strong. They did these things to ensure the salmon kept coming. And for the most part, it worked.

LEARNING TO LIVE OFF THE WATER

Twenty-five thousand years ago the Pacific Northwest was covered with ice, inhospitable to both humans and salmon. When the ice started melting around fourteen thousand years ago, the area gradually transformed into more amenable habitat. As environmental conditions stabilized, the salmon population increased in overall abundance. This new availability, together with Native advancements in processing and storage techniques, likely translated into a greater reliance on salmon for food and greater surpluses for trade. By the time white newcomers arrived on the west coast of North America in the 1770s, Native peoples had developed extremely effective and often complex methods for taking salmon. This co-evolution of environment and culture brought salmon to the center of Indian subsistence practices.

The seven species of anadromous Pacific salmon (*Oncorhynchus spp.*) that came to live in Salish Sea waters were impressively adaptable and evolved over millions of years. The Salmonidae family may be a hundred million years old, and the genus *Oncorhynchus* probably emerged between ten to fifteen million years ago.[3] This was well before geologic processes created the Cascade and Olympic mountain ranges sometime between four to seven million years ago. Some older salmonids, like the six-foot-long saber-toothed salmon, did not survive the intense changes in habitat caused by tectonic plate movements and lava flows. However, the modern salmon species that emerged between one to two million years ago proved resilient enough to live through the glaciation of the region.[4] While the rivers feeding the Salish Sea were frozen, these species found temporary homes to both the north and the south. When the glaciers began melting, massive flooding destroyed habitat suitable for salmon reproduction. Gradually, however, rivers found stable beds, and smaller trees and shrubs gave way to Douglas fir, western hemlock, and the western red cedar. As the trees grew in size, they helped root streams and rivers to their channels and provided shade to cool the water. Trees fell across these waterways and created pools. By three thousand to five thousand years ago, the Northwest Coast presented ideal Pacific salmon habitat.[5]

Human beings most likely reached the north Pacific Coast much later than the first salmon. People arrived in the region as early as twelve thousand years ago, but they remained nomadic and dependent on a wide variety of resources.[6] While human beings exploited salmon and developed fishing technologies early on, sea levels, the climate, and other environmental conditions were volatile enough that flexible subsistence tactics remained important for survival.[7] Shell middens—piles of discarded shells, other food remains like bones and antlers, as well as some cultural artifacts—dated between fifty-two hundred and sixty-two hundred years ago suggest that people depended more on near-shore resources and that, on some parts of the coast, food security meant that they tended to move around less than previously. Although these people definitely consumed salmon, they could not yet depend on the fish for their primary food source.[8]

The interwoven environmental and cultural changes that transformed early Northwest inhabitants into skilled fishers took thousands of years. But as of fifteen hundred years ago, many of the region's indigenous communities were well established and had developed subsistence patterns and group territorial boundaries that aligned with their most prized resources. These peoples composed independent local groups, tribes, and occasionally even confederacies, but they do not appear to have had any lasting political unity prior to the arrival of whites.[9] We do not know what these groups called themselves or each other in the pre-contact period, but today it is common to refer to these communities according to their historical language affiliations: the Tlingit, Haida, Nisga'a (formerly Nishga), Tsimshian, Gitxsan (slightly inland), Haisla, Heiltsuk (formerly

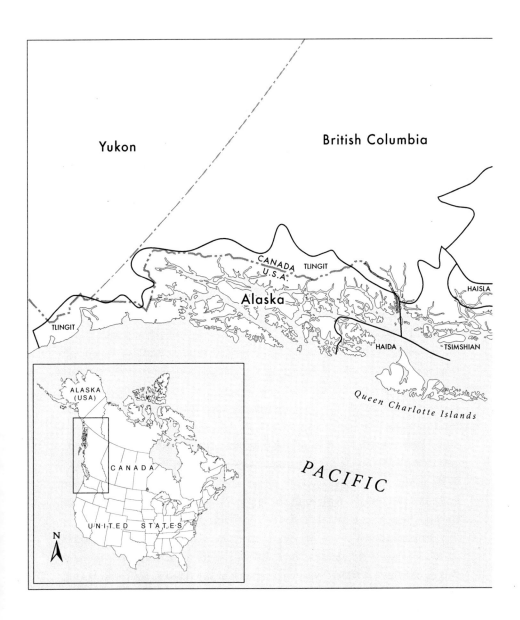

MAP 1.1 Northwest Coast Native Language Groups. Note how the Straits Salish language group's territory spans the international border at the forty-ninth parallel. *Source*: Map redrawn and adapted from Suttles, *Native Languages of the Northwest Coast*. Map adaptation reproduced here with permission of the Suttles Estate and the Oregon Historical Society.

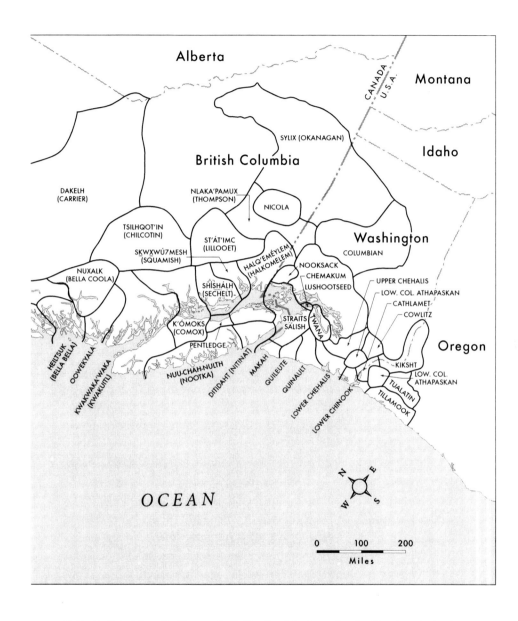

Bella Bella), Nuxalk (formerly Bella Coola), Oowekyala, Kwakwaka'wakw (formerly Kwakiutl), Nuu-chah-nulth (formerly Nootkans), K'ómoks (formerly Comox), Shíshálh (formerly Sechelt), Pentledge (formerly Pentlatch), Ditidaht (formerly Nitinat), Skwxwú7mesh (formerly Squamish), Halq'eméylem (includes the Stò:lō), Nooksack, Straits Salish, Makah, Quileute, Quinault, Twana, Chemakum, Lushootseed, Chehalis, Lower Columbia Athapaskan, Cowlitz, Cathlamet, and Chinookans. Coast Salish territories extended from today's southwestern British Columbia into what is now western Washington State, and so wholly embraced the waters of the Salish Sea.[10]

Although the lush greenery, numerous rivers, and accessible coastlines of the Northwest suggest that people must have had an unlimited abundance of resources before white contact, the reality of food availability was far more uneven and complex.[11] Most Native villages along the coast gradually intensified their dependence on salmon and other marine resources, but each group's immediate environment greatly influenced how they learned to get their food and which foods they depended on most. In fact, local variation in access to resources like salmon could be quite extreme. In Kwakwaka'wakw territory in the northern reaches of today's Vancouver Island, poor salmon access in some areas was a constant problem, while other groups enjoyed surpluses so immense they could not possibly harvest the entire catch.[12] Some groups only periodically suffered scarcity and starvation when a salmon run failed, but other communities had such limited access to productive fishing, hunting, or plant-gathering sites, lean meals were more common. This was particularly true in the far north as the range of food available was less diverse. The availability of resources like salmon, shellfish, and berries thus influenced where groups stopped over or where they settled and so shaped the evolution of subsistence practices and technologies.[13]

Some of the most basic early fishing methods involved hooks, spears, and harpoons, but even such simple pieces of equipment could result in enormous harvests of salmon. John Jewitt, a Bostonian held captive by the Nuu-chah-nulth at Nootka Sound in the early 1800s, later reported that although his captors were not great hunters, "there are few people more expert in fishing." His admiration was born of personal experience: though he tried to mimic Nuu-chah-nulth spearsmen several times, Jewitt was never able to spear a fish, admitting that "it require[d] a degree of adroitness that I did not possess."[14] In the early twentieth century the anthropologist Bernhard Stern observed similar abilities among Lummi spearsmen, who handily caught fish after fish by striking the animal's spinal cord, killing it instantly.[15] The combination of such skill, extremely effective fishing techniques, and abundant regional salmon runs ensured a successful catch. "Such is the immense quantity of these fish, and they are taken with such facility," Jewitt wrote of the Nuu-chah-nulth chief Maquinna's supply in the early 1800s, "that I have known upwards of twenty-five hundred brought into Maquin[n]a's house at once, and at one of their great feasts, have seen one hundred or more cooked in one of their largest tubs."[16]

As time passed, Pacific slope Indians developed increasingly sophisticated fishing devices. Weirs—fence-like obstructions that forced salmon to halt their course upstream—were complex structures that required significant labor to build. Usually set on smaller rivers or streams, weirs made salmon more accessible to dip nets, spears, and gaff hooks. People built weirs on the southern bank of the Fraser River near what is now the city of Vancouver as early as forty-seven hundred years ago, and remains in southeastern Alaska indicate that weirs were used there approximately three thousand years before the present.[17] Fish traps also became increasingly popular along the coast. Traps typically led the fish into an enclosed space from which they could not retreat or escape and so made them easy prey for fishers with nets, spears, or clubs.[18] According to early outside observers, traps and weirs were well designed and impressively productive. John Jewitt reported that the Nuu-chah-nulth caught more than seven hundred salmon in fifteen minutes with their "pot."[19] On Simon Fraser's 1808 trip down the river later named for him, the North West Company's front man described a clever combination of weir and trap that was "a work of some ingenuity."[20]

Fishers also designed effective net-fishing techniques for freshwater and saltwater environments. Many groups used nets to take advantage of both natural and constructed platforms that protruded over the eddies where salmon linger and rest on their upstream journey. Simple, hand-held dip nets were particularly efficient in such spots. Towing nets between two canoes allowed fishers to trawl downstream and capture the salmon working their way up against the current.[21] Indians to the south—especially the Chinook peoples who lived near the Columbia River—frequently used seine nets as well. Long and narrow, the nets encircled up to one hundred fish in one toss of the net, and fishers often dispatched these nets from river banks in a process known as beach seining.[22] Although less commonly used, fishers likewise designed the more intricate and effective gill net, whose precisely measured mesh sizes snagged fish by the gills as they moved through the webbing. When a sizable catch was so entangled, the fishermen pulled them ashore. Because gill nets had to be set in places where salmon were less likely to notice them, their use remained limited until the late nineteenth century.[23]

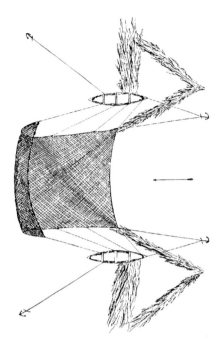

FIGURE 1.1 Diagram of a Straits Salish reef net (c.1888–1889). Drawing by J. W. Collins. *Source*: Originally published in the United States Commission of Fish and Fisheries, *Report on the Fisheries of the Pacific Coast of the United States* (Washington, D.C.: Government Printing Office, 1892), Plate XLV. Image courtesy of the Freshwater and Marine Image Bank, University of Washington Library Special Collections.

The reef net, possibly developed more than a thousand years ago, dramatically increased the catch for Straits Salish people with limited access to riverine salmon fishing sites.[24] The elaborate nets were designed to intercept the Fraser-bound runs of sockeye and pink salmon in the Straits of Juan de Fuca, Haro and Rosario, off the headlands of the San Juan Islands, Lummi Island, and one of the most significant sites, Point Roberts. At its most basic, a reef net was a large willow bark net anchored in position facing the current, which then swept the salmon into the net. Setting the anchors and lines of the net was a major undertaking, but once established, they would often hold for an entire season.[25]

Limited by the tides and generally operated only between July and September, reef nets were amazingly productive fishery devices. In August 1829 the Hudson's Bay Company (HBC) men at Fort Langley on the Fraser River learned of the impressive catches of the reef nets. "Joe," a local Indian, visited Point Roberts, and in the words of one HBC employee, "says that the quantity of Salmon now Caught there is immense and that all the Indians on the Coast to the Southward have resorted to the Point R. village."[26] Decades later, observers in 1900 reported that reef net locations returned catches of between two thousand and four thousand salmon in one day.[27]

Having developed such productive salmon fishing techniques, Northwest Natives had to either eat the fish relatively quickly or process them for their winter's store. Salmon storage capabilities probably emerged between three thousand and thirty-five hundred years ago.[28] While women occasionally assisted with some aspects of the fishing enterprise, smoking and drying salmon was generally their main purview.[29] The ability to preserve the catch was a highly valued skill because improperly dried fish turned moldy and was subject to insect attacks. For thousands of years salmon were consumed in the same general forms: cooked fresh (roasted or baked), dried, and smoked.

Spring and summer marked an intensive period of drying and storing food, as fish and berries demanded attention at the same time. The fishermen delivered the salmon to the women, who hauled them in baskets to the preparation area. The processes for drying salmon varied according to salmon species, but generally the women cut off the heads and tails, split them, and removed the bones prior to hanging the fish on wooden racks to expose them to the sun and wind or over a fire to be smoked. To prevent the drying salmon from rotting and to make sure it stayed soft and pliable, each piece was taken down several times to be bent and twisted by hand. When dry, the precious pieces of protein were folded up and stored in open cedar baskets kept on wall shelves inside the houses.[30]

When environmental conditions stabilized roughly five thousand years before the present, Northwest Native peoples had the capacity to catch and process millions of salmon.[31] They developed sophisticated ways to provide for their communities, but they also recognized the importance of their relationship with the Salmon People. This relationship grew so valuable that it came to influence how the Indians interacted with one another, how they organized their societies, and how they managed their salmon fishery.

BORDER LIMITS

Dramatic changes occurred in Northwest Native communities two to three thousand years ago. Regional peoples began building larger multi-family houses in more permanent villages. Some people began wearing more jewelry and other personal ornaments, and there appears to have been more interest in art objects. Warfare between groups increased, and communities built defensive structures to ward off enemies. All of these cultural changes indicate that some village members found persuasive reasons and viable ways to organize the labor to build those structures, defend those fortifications, and create those art objects. Some people became more influential than others, and these status differences came to be a common aspect of life in the Northwest.[32]

Most regional communities began to divide their societies into distinct categories, and many of them came to include slaves.[33] The Central Coast Salish, for instance, separated themselves into a large upper-class group, a small lower-class group, and a group of slaves.[34] Other societies, such as the Kwakwaka'wakw farther north, split their population according to similar designations of nobility, commoner, and slaves, but they also elaborately ranked each group in turn.[35] Social boundaries determined a person's role in society and came to be closely associated with family lineage, wealth, private knowledge (such as rituals or ways to access powerful spirits), prestige, and access to salmon. What had previously been fairly egalitarian communities began to cultivate and adopt new features of inequality. Why?

The answer to this question may have much to do with who had access to salmon and how restrictive that access had become.[36] A scarcity of salmon could have pushed some families or individuals to assert control over particularly important fishing sites. Archaeologist R. G. Matson has proposed that ownership of resource sites only made sense if the resource in question was localized, predictable, and abundant; otherwise, both managing the site and limiting access would be difficult, if not impossible.[37] Unless a salmon run failed, Northwest Native peoples knew when and where they could obtain this valuable food source, so claiming lucrative locations or preventing others from using them was sensible. Limiting the management of productive fishing locations to a few families or individuals could also make it easier to avoid overfishing. As salmon availability would have been important to the entire village and their relations in nearby communities, it may have been in everyone's interest to surrender management to a small number of people.[38]

Clans, smaller family lines, and even individuals came to hold and strictly guard possessory rights to valuable resource sites at certain times of the year. For instance, over the past two thousand years at Hesquiat Harbor on the west coast of Vancouver Island, each group living there exploited their own local microenvironment. Over time, several distinct households came to use their own exclusive spots within the harbor, possibly in response to population pressures. Shellfish remains at three Ozette village sites in Makah territory also suggest that each house relied on distinct shell beds for subsistence.[39]

Ownership of resource locations meant different things for different communities. At the most basic level, ownership referred to the outright possession of a site when its most valuable resource was available. While several coastal groups practiced this form of ownership, early visitors and ethnographers found ideas about private property to be particularly strong in the north among the Tlingit, Haida, Tsimshian, Nuxalk, and especially the Nuu-chah-nulth and Kwakwaka'wakw.[40] Each significant salmon stream was usually owned by a lineage of local resource holders, and fishing weirs were either the exclusive property of the group or permission had to be obtained to use a weir on the river.[41] "In the numerous bays and rivers," an Indian agent observed of the Nuu-chah-nulth in the 1860s, "the limits of the fishing-grounds, and the ownership of the islands, are strictly defined."[42] Explorer Alexander Mackenzie found similar customs among the Nuxalk during his visit in 1793. Although the community as a whole had contributed to the building of a weir, it appeared that "the chief's power over it, and the people, was unlimited, and without control. No one could fish without his permission, or carry home a larger portion of what he had caught, than was set apart for him. No one could build an house [sic] without his consent; and all his commands appeared to be followed with implicit obedience."[43]

To the south, closer to the Salish Sea, exclusive ownership of a fishing location varied according to production level and related labor requirements. For the Coast Salish, notions of ownership were especially strong with regard to reef net locations. Individuals owned reef net sites, and the properties were esteemed and heritable through both men and women. Yet the reef net was such a complicated structure that the owners of these sites could not possibly build or work them alone. Reef net owners routinely "hired" crews from other families or villages to help build the intricate nets and process the large number of salmon they would invariably catch. Crew members contributed pieces of the massive net that were then sewn together by a ritualist. They provided the muscle needed to haul in these large nets full of fish, and as reward for their labor, were entitled to a portion of the catch. Women then worked together to process both their own family's take and that of the reef net owner.[44]

Well into the late 1700s and early 1800s, several other southern groups developed similar compromises regarding the use of privately held locations or equipment. Village residents often joined forces to build elaborate communal weirs at places owned by the community, although the most productive platforms on the weir were privately owned and heritable properties.[45] In other villages individuals or extended families owned nearby smokehouses but access to the weir itself was unrestricted.[46] Among the S'Klallam (Straits Salish), although the village leader possessed the most desirable fish trap location, he allowed his less fortunate relatives access to the trap during the least active fishing hours. In the process he both maintained his household productivity levels and, through his generosity, his high status.[47]

Fishing tools were expensive to make or obtain and were limited to the wealthy. The labor involved in making nets, for example, meant they were quite costly. Along the coast, Indians made most of their nets of either stinging nettle or willow bark. Net-makers cut and split the nettle, dried and peeled it, then softened and separated it in order to spin it into a two-strand, extremely strong twine. The entire process was very time-consuming. For some groups located farther inland, limited access to net-making material heightened the value of nets, and possessing seine and gill nets was prohibitive simply because of the labor involved.[48] In the early twentieth century, Tom, a Nuu-chah-nulth informant, reminisced about his people's early fishing practices: "Not many [fishermen] had nets. I recall that ten had them when I was a boy. It was the old men who owned nets."[49] The lack of nets during Tom's childhood could also have been related to the loss of labor that accompanied the loss of lives through such diseases as smallpox and malaria.

Owning a fishing location did not always mean having exclusive use of the site, but among most groups there were clear customs for broadening access, particularly when certain fish were in season. According to early firsthand accounts and ethnographies, headmen or site owners usually allowed individuals from both within and outside of the community to fish a specific location as long as they obtained permission first.[50] Among the Nuu-chah-nulth, the chief had to formally open the fishing season before anyone could fish in his territory, and the village fishers often went out together to mark the occasion. Upon their return, each fisherman gave a portion of his catch to the chief as payment, and the chief then allowed him to use the grounds for the remainder of the season.[51] In some villages chiefs opened their locations to other members of the family or community once the immediate household had met their needs, but they might not grant usage of owned, expensive gear in the process. The Twana dip net fishers in southern Puget Sound took a different approach, simply loaning their nets and sites to family or friends; if the catch was large, the community expected those fishermen to share.[52] Many regional groups leased specific resource locations on an annual basis. Because the Cowichan (Halq'eméylem) of Vancouver Island did not have adequate sockeye salmon streams within their home territories, for instance, they arranged to move up the Fraser River to leased sites for the sockeye season. Some of the first ethnographers to visit northern groups discovered that similar rental systems had long been in place there as well.[53]

Having dried salmon available all year influenced the evolution of Northwest Native cultural practices and helped perpetuate the social inequities that had emerged in those communities. Once they knew they had a ready source of food for the winter season, people could stay in one place for longer periods of time and focus their energies on such tasks as woodcarving or basket weaving. The families who produced such goods could then trade them for different types of food or other luxury items, further enhancing the household's wealth. Catching and processing sufficient numbers of salmon for an adequate winter supply also required a significant organization of labor. Well-regarded community members with access to salmon were most likely to have the ability to persuade people to perform this work. The need to quickly process so many salmon may also have been crucial to the evolution of polygamy among many Northwest Native groups. For men, having more than one wife not only denoted high status, it translated into additional labor and thus food and other wealth items. For women, being attached to a high status household may have brought benefits including assistance with chores from other wives and household slaves.

Labor needs probably also contributed to the emergence of slavery among Northwest groups, and the labor that slaves provided to process and sometimes catch salmon further buttressed the social standing of high-status households. Northern groups like the Lekwiltok (part of the Kwakwaka'wakw) engaged in slave raids among the Puget Sound and Straits groups, whereas other groups obtained slaves by purchase or in war. Slaves were usually women and children who had been taken captive and who then had to serve their master in any manner required.[54] Such captives were generally treated well, but because they were valuable property, they were sometimes used to show off their masters' wealth in less humane ways.[55] A slave could be freed only if his or her relatives paid a hefty purchase price or if he or she escaped.[56] Slaves who tried to flee confronted both navigating their escape in unknown terrain and evading neighboring villagers who might capture and return them for a small reward. Some communities considered slaves genderless in terms of the manual labor required of them, but slave women most likely suffered sexual abuse or forced prostitution.[57] Male slaves were often required to perform women's tasks and frequently assisted women in the salmon preservation process.

Many Native peoples—especially the wealthiest community members—used intermarriage to gain access to lucrative fishing locations.[58] There were often strong taboos against marrying within one's own community, and intermarriage between members of separate villages was common. Kwakwaka'wakw family histories show a network of intermarriage and ceremonial relations extending southward to the K'ómoks on Vancouver Island, and many other relationships spanned the reaches of the Salish Sea near the forty-ninth parallel.[59] Similarly, the S'Klallam on the Olympic Peninsula claimed they had long preferred to intermarry with those who lived to the north, especially from Vancouver Island.[60] The Hudson's Bay Company men of Fort Langley witnessed several marriage ceremonies involving people from distant tribes as well.[61] The extent of intermarriage between tribes surprised Indian agent Myron Eells in the 1880s, and he calculated that the S'Klallam "had the blood of eighteen other tribes in their veins; a few having the blood of four tribes," and that "it seems to be a matter of pride to say 'I am half Snoqualmie–half Klikitat.'"[62]

Such unions played a crucial role in realigning entry rights to important resource locations.[63] Among the prestige-conscious Kwakwaka'wakw, the transfer of privileges was often one of the most important considerations prior to acceptance of a new in-law proposal.[64] Although the Nuu-chah-nulth regularly transferred resource sites through intermarriage, these negotiations did not always proceed smoothly. In one early nineteenth-century account, the resource-poor Ahousat group, who owned no noteworthy dog-salmon streams and frequently suffered famine as a result, determined to gain access to their Otsosat neighbors' fishing sites through intermarriage. When the bride's father failed to include access to the fishing grounds in the gift-giving exchange at the marriage ceremony, the two groups became embroiled in a catastrophic war.[65] Intermarriage to acquire access to resource sites was prevalent closer to the Salish Sea as well. The Coast Salish who held rights to reef net sites had a long history of using intertribal unions to expand access to those fishing grounds, as did non–reef netting groups like the Nooksack and the Makah.[66] Intermarriage between groups thus became a way for families to negotiate their community's social borders, capitalize on their status, and gain admission to new resource sites at certain times of year.

Wealthy families with good salmon fishing locations could also use new family connections to take advantage of regional trade networks.[67] By 1750, near present-day Prince Rupert, more than fifty kinds of goods and twenty separate trade routes were used by the ten thousand Tsimshian people of the area.[68] For most regional groups it was considered stingy to sell food to one's immediate neighbors, and wealth and food were two distinct categories within communities and households.[69] Trade of foodstuffs with people outside the immediate community, however, was common and specialized. Large regional trade fairs such as the ones held at The Dalles on the Columbia River drew traders from the entire coast.[70] Depending on the year's surplus, the coastal groups invariably traded significant amounts of salmon and other marine resources with eager interior peoples who lacked them. Many households and communities developed reputations for crafting particular items or for processing specific types of food. The Nuxalk prepared fish eggs in ways that produced a wide range of flavors and textures. The S'Klallam were famous for dried clams and salmon, and they regularly exchanged these foods with their more distant neighbors and interior groups.[71] As a result of this network, Northwest peoples were able to trade for an impressive array of both luxury goods and subsistence items that were either scarce in their own regions or that their families could not produce on their own.

Northwest Indians were astute traders, but they were also known to freely give of salmon in special ceremonies like the potlatch, which bound communities together. Potlatches were large gatherings where high-ranking families invited members of other tribes to witness specific changes in status. The ceremonies involved lavish displays of wealth and distributions of property to guests. Salmon was important because it provided the basis upon which many households managed to host a potlatch in the first place. Potlatch hosts also invariably served salmon to their guests in great quantities, so the fish provided further evidence of the host's status and affirmed his or her access to valuable resources. Potlatches also were an opportunity to mark or celebrate changes in status related to resource site ownership. The attendance of both neighboring and distant groups provided witnesses who, by their presence, affirmed the host's historical right to certain territories or agreed to a change. In this way Native peoples transmitted ownership rights in the presence of the larger community and so averted conflicts or miscommunication over who possessed the rights and when.[72]

Intermarriages, trading, and potlatches together fostered alliances and granted wider access to resources like salmon, but territorial and resource site restrictions also led to conflict. From about thirty-eight hundred years ago, fighting among Northwest coastal groups appears to have escalated and, judging by the rapid rise of defensive fortifications and strategically placed bluff-top villages, spread along the coast by the year 500.[73] Villagers on the Fraser River built tall rock wall fortifications and sheltered lookout points to protect themselves against northern raiders coming from the coast.[74] Territorial expansion and fights over specific resource sites were common reasons to go to war, especially among the more militaristic northern groups. Both oral histories and some archaeological evidence indicate that the Nuu-chal-nulth, Haida, and Tsimshian peoples annihilated neighboring groups to take their lands and fishing locations by force.[75]

More than two hundred years ago, the Lekwiltok drove some Northern Coast Salish peoples from their territory between the Salmon River and Cape Mudge on the eastern coast of Vancouver Island. "We wanted this place because we could get all five species of salmon twelve months out of the year," recalled Lekwiltok Indian chief Harry Assu of his ancestors. "The reason our people moved from the mainland villages to the Campbell River was to secure the fishing grounds here."[76] In the early 1800s the Nuu-chah-nulth Ahousat practically exterminated the neighboring Otsosat in the war that started over access to fishing sites.[77] The Ucluelet, also a branch of the Nuu-chah-nulth, apparently traveled around shopping for the ideal salmon stream. Once they found it, they indiscriminately and repeatedly attacked the owners until they either left or were killed. The people most responsible for this victory then received rights to the best fishing sites procured in the conflict.[78]

Temporary territorial trespassings on restricted resource properties could also cause intergroup conflict, with repercussions for such acts tending to be more severe along the northern part of the coast. The Kwakwaka'wakw site owners strictly prohibited members of outside groups from using their fishing, hunting, and berrying spots and punished trespassers with death. "When a man disobeys and continues to catch salmon," anthropologist Franz Boas recorded, "they fight and often both, or sometimes one of them, is dead." If a conflict erupted over attempts by one fisher to usurp the owned location of another, the legitimate owner of the site was usually victorious, "because the real owner of the fish trap creeps up to the one who steals the place for the fish trap. He just strikes him with a pole, standing behind him. . . . Therefore, generally, the thief is killed, because he does not hear, on account of the noise of the river."[79] The Nuu-chah-nulth strongly resisted encroachments by their neighbors. One Ucluelet chief who longed to own his own salmon river even tried to take one from his own brother-in-law.[80] The Tlingit also strictly guarded their owned sites, but they were more likely to simply break or disable the equipment of the offending parties.[81] Farther south among the S'Klallam, Erna Gunther found that if "the people of one tribe use the fish traps or duck nets of another without asking permission trouble may arise immediately." Killing a resident of a neighboring or more distant village could initiate a pattern of ongoing violence and retaliation.[82]

Although reports of territorial encroachments like these appear in oral histories and ethnographies, there is little evidence to suggest high rates of trespass or fighting over resource sites *within* these stratified communities. Because sharing and redistributing food was such a common practice, there was likely little reason for resource-poor individuals and households to contest the status quo. Although wealth was highly regarded and desirable, it was only meaningful if it was not hoarded unnecessarily; that is, a significant factor in a leader's status was his or her generosity. In fact, all community members were expected to share their food willingly, especially if they obtained more than their immediate household could use.[83] Several early white visitors to the Northwest observed these practices firsthand. According to Indian agent Gilbert Sproat, "The Indians give food ungrudgingly to one another; they have generally plenty and can be free with it."[84] Forfeiting a portion of one's salmon catch to a wealthy site owner, then, was not necessarily a burden, as villagers could expect to partake of a community feast later hosted by that same high-status person.[85] A final important means of community redistribution, especially among the Coast Salish, was trade with certain relatives. A Coast Salish man could take food to his in-laws or cousins at any time and expect to receive payment in return. Such exchanges allowed people to directly convert food into wealth, and these practices acted as a sort of banking system in times of scarcity.[86]

Native people drew social, spatial, and temporal borders around productive resource areas, particularly their best salmon fishing sites. The customs they developed restricted access to such spots and limited the total harvest of salmon. While shifts in the Indians' customs became vital to their approaches to fishery management, the evolution of their beliefs about the physical and spiritual connections between salmon and people further buttressed and justified this regional border system.

SALMON SPIRITS

By the time they had contact with whites, Northwest Native peoples appear to have learned how to protect their salmon fisheries. They clearly understood that sufficient numbers of salmon needed to make their way upriver to spawn, and they developed rules and equipment that ensured proper levels of escapement.[87] They also had intimate relationships with the natural world, relationships that called for respectful behavior and precise rituals. Together with the other customs associated with Native borders and resource sites, these beliefs and related practices, if strictly adhered to, would have helped regulate salmon harvests.

In addition to restricting access to productive fishing sites, the region's Indians took steps to allow female salmon to spawn, regulate when people fished, and limit the amount of salmon caught.[88] Among the Coast Salish, people would not eat female salmon or their eggs during the first half of the salmon season, and they regularly returned those they caught to the river alive.[89] Charley Nowell, of the Kwakwaka'wakw, confirmed the persistence of this practice among his people throughout his boyhood in the 1870s and 1880s.[90] Nuu-chah-nulth people were known to physically prevent other community members from fishing at certain times of the season. Witnessing this, a local Indian agent speculated that it "may not have been so much for his own benefit as that someone should have authority, in the interest of the whole tribe, to prevent the salmon from being disturbed in their ascent up the river."[91] Tlingit and Nuu-chah-nulth chiefs likewise regulated times for fishing and hunting to protect future supplies.[92]

Native groups also designed and used fishing devices to facilitate adequate escapement of the overall catch. Many fish traps were constructed so that high waters granted the fish passage along the sides of the trap, and there was often a hole under each trap that large numbers of ascending salmon easily slipped through.[93] The tidewater traps used by such groups as the Nuu-chah-nulth allowed salmon to pass at high tide.[94] Realizing that weirs were extremely productive, people from throughout the region customarily removed sections of the structure during the day to give the salmon unimpeded access upstream. Furthermore, fishers usually removed all of the weir panels at the end of the fishing season and left only the pilings to mark the site.[95] The Indians had obviously figured out how to diminish their impact on the salmon population.

Spiritual beliefs, rituals, and moral codes also influenced how Northwest Natives treated their most important fish. These attitudes and related customs radiated into respect for all living things and, with regard to salmon, were meant to show appreciation to ensure their return. The First Salmon ceremony, practiced by many Northwest groups, was one of the most important events that attended the opening of the salmon season. The first salmon caught had to be prepared in a particular way, and although the precise customs varied up and down the coast, the bones were usually saved and returned to the river.[96] As man, Raven, and Swanaset learned, saving every single bone was crucial to the salmon's ability to re-form and come again. Numerous taboos determined who could come into contact with the fish and when. Some groups had to keep the river clean, and most villages enforced strict rules against women touching or visiting rivers, fishing locations, or fishing equipment when menstruating, as menstruation heightened powers that might offend the fish or scare them away. The Central Salish Katzie believed the early salmon were supernaturally strong and therefore dangerous, so they refrained from catching sockeye salmon on the Fraser until well after the run had started. While there were undoubtedly instances of noncompliance, every member of the village was supposed to act properly so that the fish would return the following year.[97] These customs were thus not necessarily self-conscious acts of conservation, but they promoted respect for salmon, discouraged waste, and appear to have kept the salmon fisheries abundant.[98]

Native fishing borders and related spiritual beliefs not only contributed to congenial relations between Indians and salmon, they also constituted what appears to have been a highly effective indigenous fishery management system. As time passed and the regional environment stabilized, salmon gradually moved to the center of Northwest Indians' lives. This was the world that white explorers and fur traders descended upon in the late eighteenth century and quite clearly did not understand: a world negotiated for the benefit of both salmon and people.

2

Fish, Fur, and Faith

WHEN GEORGE VANCOUVER'S EXPLORATION PARTY LANDED on the shores of Hood Canal in 1792, they were met by six canoes filled with curious people from a nearby Chemakum village. "On a line being drawn with a stick on the sand between the two parties," Vancouver wrote, the Indians "immediately sat down, and no one attempted to pass it, without previously making signs, requesting permission for so doing." The visiting Europeans may have been in the habit of drawing such lines to manage their interactions with the people they met in their travels. It was a convenient tool: one line on the beach neatly separated the two parties and clearly indicated the spatiality of peaceful relations.[1] For their part, the Chemakum must have recognized the Europeans' concerns and out of economic self-interest and politeness chose to respect the border.

Newcomer attempts at such seemingly simple political division remained as tenuous as that line in the sand for many decades to come. Despite the toll that newly introduced diseases took on the regional Indian population, European, Euro-American, and Euro-Canadian newcomers to the Pacific slope simply could not impose their own spatial or social boundaries on the region's Native peoples. They had to take Native borders and related customs seriously if they wanted to achieve their own economic and social goals. They had to understand the role of salmon in the Indians' worldview. The Indians made sure of that.

ECONOMIES OF SCALE

The captain of the *Boston* did not realize that Maquinna, the Nuu-chah-nulth chief, had accumulated several grievances against white coastal visitors nor that he was concerned about the waning maritime fur trade. As a result, when the New England vessel stopped to trade in 1803, the captain did not hesitate to argue with Maquinna and quickly managed to offend the Nuu-chah-nulth leader. Determined to teach the fur traders a lesson, Maquinna and his men promised to take several crewmembers to a prime salmon fishing spot and so succeeded in separating the men into two groups. "The salmon which they brought us furnished a most delicious treat to men who for a long time had lived wholly on salt provisions excepting such few sea fish as we had the good fortune occasionally to take," crewmember John Jewitt wrote not long after the event. "We indeed feasted most luxuriously, and flattered ourselves that we should not want while on the coast for plenty of fresh provisions, little imagining the fate that awaited us, and that this dainty food was to prove the unfortunate lure to our destruction!"[2] Before the Americans could set their hooks, the Nuu-chah-nulth mounted a dual attack and killed off all but two of the *Boston*'s crew members.[3]

This sort of behavior was not good for business, so it did not happen very often. But the *Boston* crew's interest in catching and eating salmon was indicative of what was to come. From the first tentative voyages of exploration to the later land-based fur trade that prevailed in the region from the 1820s to the 1850s, newcomers soon discovered that salmon were a valuable source of fresh food. While some villages like Maquinna's benefited materially from the growing number of white visitors arriving on the coast, increased contact between Natives and newcomers also exposed those communities to new deadly diseases. Drastic population losses caused by exotic diseases and the growing importance of salmon to incoming fur traders both shaped how Northwest Indians responded to their worlds being turned upside down.

Before 1770, European contact with the coastlines of future Washington State and British Columbia remained negligible, as did their use of local resources. The Spanish made a few attempts to explore the western shores of North America prior to the eighteenth century, but these efforts were neither consistent nor very successful, and early crews hesitated to disembark onto the unknown landscape. The Spanish discovery of the sea otter's rich fur occurred farther south along the coast of Baja California, and in their forays from Acapulco, the Spaniards bought the lush furs from the Natives and introduced them to the Chinese in 1733. It was the Russians who pursued the profitable maritime trade on a large scale in the 1740s, descending on the far north, where they exploited the local Indians in their quest for additional skins. The Russians did not venture farther south until after 1799.[4]

While the 1770s brought ever more visitors to the Pacific Coast, these explorers and traders did not necessarily need salmon or other local food-stuffs because of the availability of other provisions. The Spanish sent several ships north from their base in San Blas, Mexico, in the 1770s, but they had plenty of food on board and in storage at Monterey.[5] Juan Francisco de la Bodega y Quadra's 1775 expedition farther north along the coast found itself short on food because it was an unplanned excursion. Luckily, by trading with the locals and fishing on their own in coastal waters, the crew were able to supplement their meager stores and successfully complete their mission.[6]

The discovery of the Sandwich Islands (Hawai'i) by whites and the islands' emergence as a way station for later vessels making their way across the Pacific also helped curb early white demand for salmon. In his search for the Northwest Passage, the British Captain James Cook visited the Sandwich Islands in January 1778 and restocked his ship's supplies.[7] In May he and his crew anchored near Nootka Sound for over a month to refit their vessel, making theirs the first European group to both set foot on the central coast and to interact extensively with Northwest Natives. Though not particularly in need of food, Cook and his crew still regularly bartered for fish to buttress and diversify their supplies. "Such of the natives as visited us daily, were the most beneficial to us," Cook happily related, "for, after disposing of their trifles, they employed themselves in fishing, and we always partook of what they caught."[8] Due to the season, however, Cook's party apparently did not trade for salmon until they resumed their course northward to Oonalaska. At approximately sixty degrees north (north of present-day Prince William Sound in Alaska), Cook and his men were visited by many Indians whose "company was highly acceptable to us, as they brought with them a quantity of fine salmon, which they exchanged for some of our trifles. Several hundred weight of it was procured for the two ships, and the greatest part of it was split, and ready for drying."[9]

Salmon helped sustain Cook and his crew, but when the men learned of the immense wealth to be made trading sea otter pelts in China, it was the otter that had their attention. Published accounts of Cook's voyage described the trade and conveniently provided navigational directions to prospective fur traders in 1784. And so they came. In the early 1790s twenty-one ships appeared on the coast during one summer trading season.[10]

Many of the early excursions and encounters unleashed diseases to which the indigenous people of the New World had no immunities. Although Captain Cook did not document such diseases, his travels in the northern part of the region were also brief. The journals of Cook's fellow countryman, George Vancouver, indicate that smallpox had hit the Puget Sound region hard sometime before his arrival in 1792. Vancouver wrote haunting descriptions of piles of skulls and bones scattered in former village sites. Many of these areas "had now fallen into decay; their inside, as well as a small surrounding space that appeared to have been formerly occupied, were over-run with weeds."[11] At the southeastern end of the Strait of Juan de Fuca, Vancouver wrote, "the scull, limbs, ribs, and back bones, or some other vestiges of the human body, were found in many places promiscuously scattered about the beach, in great numbers." His ship's officers observed morbid scenes "in such abundance" throughout their survey trips along the coast of Puget Sound that they believed the remnants enough "to produce an idea that the environs of port Discovery were a general cemetry [sic] for the whole of the surrounding country."[12]

Later Puget Sound and lower Fraser Indian accounts also refer to past epidemics, times of significant population losses, and despair.[13] In his 1936 explanation of the Katzie (Halq'eméylem) genesis, a seventy-five-year-old man known as Old Pierre recounted a divinely ordained flood and subsequent snowstorm that punished Native peoples for being too numerous. The most recent major disaster experienced by his people, however, was smallpox that emanated from the east. Old Pierre and his people learned that "a great sickness was travelling over the land, a sickness that no medicine could cure, and no person escape." Approximately three-quarters of the community perished in that epidemic, which occurred before Europeans arrived on the West Coast.[14] In the late 1930s elderly Twana tribal members in southern Puget Sound retold of disastrous incidences of smallpox during both their parents' and grandparents' lifetimes and remembered that the 1800 epidemic from the south had been the most severe.[15] The Lummi Indians (Straits Salish) believed that smallpox arrived in 1792, before Vancouver's visit, and destroyed several of their villages.[16]

Venereal disease afflicted Natives and newcomers alike and contributed to many illnesses and deaths in the early years of contact. Several of the first ships carried men suffering from some form of sexually transmitted disease. The issue was so serious aboard Captain Cook's vessel that he refused to allow his men ashore when they docked in the Sandwich Islands.[17] The Hudson's Bay Company's (HBC) fort journals are likewise replete with references to sexually transmitted diseases and the attempts at eradication.[18] Because some Native men and women seized on the arrival of lonely male fur traders to prostitute their female slaves, efforts to contain sexually transmitted diseases were complicated. Such ventures were so lucrative that demand for female slaves rose rapidly all along the coast in the early years of contact. Venereal diseases often caused infertility in women, and Native birth rates declined in the nineteenth century, further exacerbating population losses.[19]

Even as epidemic diseases spread death and despair through regional communities, a stream of white fur traders in need of salmon and other foodstuffs continued to arrive on the coast. Knowing where to find the Sandwich Islands granted traders a level of security as they crossed the Pacific, but there were still many uncertainties involved in the journey. The length of the trip, the complications attending supply ship arrangements, and the impact of weather on travel patterns could all easily alter a ship's stores. When traveling conditions delayed the *Daedalus*, a supply ship from New Zealand, Vancouver and his crew had to depend on local food sources until their other supplies arrived.[20] Because of these uncertainties and the growing number of vessels visiting the region in the late 1700s and early 1800s, Pacific salmon soon became a vital backup food for the ships' crews.[21]

If crews were low on provisions during the wrong season, newcomer meals could be light ones indeed. When Vancouver met and traded with the Suquamish of Puget Sound (Lushootseed), the lack of food items for sale was a source of concern. "Their merchandize would have been infinitely more valuable to us," Vancouver complained, "had it been comprised of eatables, such as venison, wild fowl or fish, as our sportsmen and fishermen had little success in either of these pursuits." Most likely due to the season, however, the Suquamish had no food to sell.[22] Still, according to one of Vancouver's crew, such a paucity of merchandise was a relatively rare occurrence. Vancouver put his men on just two-thirds' allowance of bread until they could rendezvous with their supply ship, but "this on the

Coast of America cou'd be no hardship," wrote the clerk Edward Bell, "as Fish is always to be got."[23]

As in John Jewitt's later experience, Vancouver and his crew also sought local fresh fish as relief from salted food. One morning, Vancouver noted the welcome visits of the Natives, since they "brought us such an abundant supply of fresh salmon, that we purchased a sufficient number to serve the crew as long as they would keep good; which was a great relief from our salted provisions, being a luxury we had not lately experienced."[24] Although the crew tried to catch their own fresh fish when anchored along the coast, they frequently found it easier to obtain their needed supply by trading with local Indians, a practice that would persist until the late nineteenth century.[25]

Whites traveling overland similarly depended on the Indians and their local waters for sustenance. The North West Company first sent men overland to investigate the future of fur trading in the west and to map viable routes in the late eighteenth and early nineteenth centuries. Alexander Mackenzie worked his way to the northern reaches of British Columbia in 1793, and Simon Fraser explored farther south in 1808. Both men relied on the local people for food, and salmon was frequently the main course. "Examined our salmon—being our only provisions—and discovered we had not enough for a month," observed Fraser in early June as he and his men started westward. "However the Indians say that we shall find plenty from the Natives along the Route."[26] Fraser's journal suggests that he and his party rarely ate anything but salmon.[27] The Indians regularly offered a meal of salmon as a gesture of hospitality, but they also took advantage of the opportunity to trade their fish for European and Euro-American goods.[28] Overall, early white visitors rarely went hungry.

The arrival of maritime and especially land-based fur traders reshaped Native trade networks involving both furs and fish. With the shift from trade in sea otter to land furs in the early nineteenth century, well-connected tribal leaders worked to protect their trade partnerships.[29] Once fur trade forts became established north of the Columbia River from the 1820s to the 1840s, these practices extended into the interior. "Home guards"— that is, Indians who lived near new fort sites and who survived disease— benefited significantly from their affiliations with whites in terms of both material wealth and prestige. The arrival of white traders helped solidify some Native territorial borders as they related to trade privileges, and the new networks invariably affected the barter in salmon. Fur traders not only bought furs from established Indian trade partners, they also increasingly purchased salmon from the same people. Monopolies on the trade of both fur and salmon thus led to increased wealth and status for well-situated regional Native leaders.[30]

With the founding of the first fur trade fort at the mouth of the Columbia River in 1811, salmon became a far more important article of both subsistence and barter for white newcomers. The North West Company bought John Jacob Astor's Fort Astoria in 1814 and renamed it Fort George, but the HBC decided to relocate their operation upriver at Fort Vancouver after the North West Company and the HBC merged in 1821. All of these early ventures relied on salmon for subsistence, and the newcomers consistently purchased or received far more salmon than they caught on their own. Once the HBC built Fort Langley on the Fraser River in 1827, the company had enough on hand to begin marketing salted salmon abroad.[31] The furs were the most lucrative item of exchange, but salmon remained crucial to the traders' physical survival and promised a new source of revenue. Throughout this second, more permanent, phase of contact, the Indians clearly tried to determine how whites interacted with salmon and where they obtained their fish. That Northwest Native peoples were simultaneously undergoing major demographic and territorial changes makes their success in these efforts all the more remarkable.

In the 1820s HBC forts tried to increase their self-sufficiency levels by raising livestock and growing their own produce, but the generally poor agricultural lands of the Pacific slope hindered such progress and probably only increased the traders' dependence on salmon.[32] The residents of Fort Nisqually, for instance, lacked thumbs green enough to make their gardens flourish with any regularity. "Our crop is a complete failure, carrots the size of a goose quill," Nisqually's William Tolmie complained in 1833, the year the fort was founded.[33] "Notwithstanding the great labour bestowed upon it," the garden at Fort McLoughlin in what is now northern British Columbia "has completely failed," John Work reported in 1835.[34] In addition, river flooding, excessive spring rains, poor soil, and periodic thefts by local Indians all limited the success of the forts' agricultural ventures.[35] Fort Langley was conveniently located on the banks of the Fraser River, and its farming efforts were more successful than many others. By the 1830s Langley was supplying other forts with fresh and salted salmon as well as what produce it could spare.[36]

In addition to using salmon in the forts, the HBC's desire to market salmon abroad meant the company purchased even more salmon from local Indians. On his first trip to Fort Vancouver in 1824, Governor George Simpson suggested that the company look into exporting salmon for profit.[37] When the chief factor, John McLoughlin, searched for ways to ease the HBC's strong reliance on imported British goods in accordance with Simpson's wishes, he too saw potential in the overseas salted salmon market. "We can purchase Salmon in the Columbia," McLoughlin proposed to Simpson in 1826, "and I am given to understand it would sell well in New California."[38] McLoughlin further believed it would be possible to salt as many as one thousand barrels of Columbia River salmon per year and noted that the fish was even more abundant on the Fraser.[39]

Although the HBC initially built Fort Langley in 1827 in the hopes that it would serve as the primary depot for the interior forts, its main contribution was its salmon fishery. The proximity of the fort to the Fraser River salmon runs and the Indians who fished them allowed the company to experiment with marketing salmon along the southern Pacific Coast and abroad, but it took several years to promote the trade. The company's first efforts to export salted salmon failed miserably and there was a constant need for additional skilled coopers, but the HBC employees improved their techniques and the business grew increasingly profitable over the 1830s.[40] McLoughlin opposed the company's proposal to move Fort Langley to Whidbey Island in the spring of 1835 because of the economic promise of the overseas salmon trade; the fort's annual rates of production quickly proved McLoughlin's case.[41] An 1839 supply agreement negotiated with the Russian American Company further solidified the fort's role in the company's fledgling international trade network, for Fort Langley produced many of the goods promised the Russians.[42] In that same year the HBC relocated the fort a few miles upriver to increase both agricultural and salmon production. According to HBC official James Douglas, "The Salmon trade must not be sacrificed as it will always yield a more valuable return at less trouble and expense than the farm."[43] The HBC also salted salmon for export at Fort Vancouver, but because Fraser salmon were more popular in the Sandwich Islands and there were more Indians fishing close to Fort Langley, that operation appears to have superseded the one on the Columbia over time.[44]

Salmon dinners could be tasty and fulfilling, especially when caught fresh, but early fur traders were not always thrilled with their lack of meal choices. The first traders at Fort Astoria sometimes complained about the prevalence of salmon rations and, due to the fort's limited menu, scurvy afflicted some of the men.[45] Desertions grew increasingly common for the HBC in the 1830s and 1840s. Fort McLoughlin in particular had ongoing problems with employee retention because the men strongly disliked the pink salmon served there. When John Work issued his men their standard fare of dried salmon at Fort McLoughlin, some complained. The Hawaiian workers especially voiced strong opposition. "The salmon are certainly not good," Work admitted, "but from the superior manner in which they have been fed all along, and knowing that when better is to be obtained they get it, they have no cause to complain, and their complaints were not listened to."[46] So few men agreed to renew their contracts, however, Work was forced to rethink his position on the issue. He finally conceded that "the work is at present but light . . . , but the living is very bad, being principally dry salmon, which from the mode of drying them in smoke, are very bad."[47] Several HBC forts faced more serious problems because of their dependence on salmon. A diet heavy in salmon and lacking vitamin C caused significant health problems at both Fort McLoughlin and Fort Langley, and even seasoned fur traders grew tired of the staple.[48] "Our people never want," Archibald McDonald assured John McLoughlin of his men at Fort Langley in 1830, "still they far from enjoy good health or look well upon it."[49]

A major fire at Fort Langley in the early 1840s slowed production, but the HBC's salmon trade continued to rise in value over that decade.[50] Company officials soon began sending shipments to new markets in California, South America, and London, but they experienced problems with spoilage when shipping such long distances.[51] As a result, the Sandwich Islands became the company's primary market.[52] George Simpson, visiting Oahu in 1841, recognized how important the salmon trade had become to the company's west coast operation and recommended further expansion.[53] In the mid-1840s James Douglas and John Work reported that the salmon fishery at Fort Langley had been "uncommonly productive" and more attention paid to it because "the article has become one of the necessaries of life at the Sandwich Islands." Since each barrel was selling for ten to fifteen dollars apiece in 1845 and the cost of production was about four dollars per barrel, this translated into significant profits for the company.[54] "We shall devote much attention to this fishery, and endeavour to increase our exports of Salmon to 2,000 barrels annually," they assured the HBC committee in London.[55] By 1848 salmon surpassed furs as Fort Langley's most lucrative trade item, and the HBC toyed with building another salmon salting station in the San Juan Islands.[56]

The HBC purchased immense quantities of salmon from the local Natives for both trade and consumption, but the Indians sold fish only when they had a surplus. The dramatic population losses that Northwest Natives experienced throughout the nineteenth century must have reduced the demand for salmon and enabled survivors to sell more to the forts. The Indians often sold thousands of fish per transaction, and it was not unusual for Langley to buy seven thousand salmon in one summer season; they sometimes bought as many as twenty thousand.[57] Ultimately, the relative abundance of fish determined how much salmon local communities were willing to part with. The traders at Fort Astoria, for instance, found that the Indians refused to sell salmon when they did not have a ready supply.[58] "The scarcity of fish among the natives is the only circumstance now which gives us any cause for regret or inquietude," wrote a Langley man in 1827, "as it prevents us from provisioning the People as we could wish, or as they during the present laborious duty would require."[59]

Although each fort generally traded with the same groups for both their furs and salmon, the HBC men viewed their reliance on local Indians for these commodities in markedly different ways. Despite occasional grumblings, the HBC was generally content to rely on the Indians for their furs, but some of the HBC men were deeply concerned about their dependence on Native peoples for their primary foodstuffs. While losing some trade in furs simply meant lower economic returns, a reduction in the salmon trade could have far more serious consequences. Being dependent on Native men might also have simply rubbed the HBC's employees the wrong way. James McMillan, for example, noted that the Fort Langley men's exertions to obtain their own supply of fish—in this case, sturgeon— were "in order to try all ways possible to be independent of the rascally Indians of this place."[60] John Work also was frustrated: "It is to be regretted that we are necessitated to buy their salmon, or we would not take one of them," he asserted, "and when they could not sell them but to us they would have to bring their furs also, or we would not take their salmon. We shall adopt this plan as soon as we get a few fish on hand to make us a little independant [sic] of them."[61]

While the men often yearned to be free of the Indians, the HBC's constant problems with desertions, the need for labor, and the desire to save money cemented the company's reliance on the Native population.[62] Continuing to depend on the locals for salmon, some HBC officials reluctantly admitted, was simply a smart economic decision. Although the Indians manipulated the price of fish according to availability, they generally sold salmon at reasonable rates.[63] Realizing that in years of scarcity procuring salmon would be difficult no matter what, Archibald McDonald mused, "I am *unwilling still* to give an opinion of the Success a fishery of our own would have, but I think . . . that in years of abundance the *Seine* would be quite unnecessary as at the rate we now trade, the expense of our Twine & Agris (*agrès*—equipment) would almost equal the Cost of the Goods we give in Barter."[64] Pride would not trump good business sense.

The heightened contact Northwest Natives had with land-based fur traders and the perpetuation of the maritime trade meant that the region's indigenous population remained vulnerable to European diseases well into the nineteenth century. Smallpox hit the lower Columbia in the early 1800s and raged northward, leaving many villages silent in its wake.[65] A deadly disease that was most likely either smallpox or measles struck the central coast and the Columbia Plateau again in 1824 and 1825, killing from 10 to 20 percent of the population in the affected areas.[66] "Fever and ague"—which scholars are now almost certain was malaria—appeared near Fort Vancouver in October 1830 and reappeared each year throughout the decade. The waves of disease destroyed the Native population living along the Columbia River. Traditional treatments like sweatbaths followed by cold water plunges merely exacerbated the symptoms of the afflicted and hastened their demise. Although extremely difficult to compute, total losses from this last epidemic may have exceeded 85 percent of the total population in the affected area.[67] Smallpox reappeared from 1836 to 1838 in Russian, Aleut, Ingalik, and Tlingit settlements to the north and quickly spread to the HBC's Fort Simpson in Tsimshian territory. HBC officials estimated that the disease claimed one third of the population of the north coast.[68]

Successive epidemics, which killed between one third to 90 percent of the Native population, severely disrupted Indian societies. Communities experienced unimaginable sorrow, significant cultural losses, and shifting territorial claims—including those involving fishery sites. The decimation of villages opened access to fishing areas that had been closed to surrounding groups for a variety of social and economic reasons. The ability of the Cowichan and Nanaimo (Vancouver Island Halq'eméylem) to construct fishing villages on the lower Fraser in the 1820s, for example, was likely due to population losses among the mainland communities.[69] As early as 1824, the Kwantlen (mainland Halq'eméylem) moved several miles up the Fraser into what had been Derby territory after the smallpox epidemics of the 1770s decimated the Derby people.[70] Although they most likely had at least one position on the Fraser already, several Katzie groups also appear to have relocated southward to the banks of the Fraser from their original villages at Pitt Lake sometime before the late 1820s.[71] The Chilliwack (mainland Halq'eméylem) moved northward from the Chilliwack River to the banks of the Fraser in the 1830s to be closer to Fort Langley.[72] While proximity to the fort offered economic opportunities and protections against the raids of the northern Indians, being closer to the Fraser also granted these groups access to the most productive salmon fishing river in the region. The Semiahmoo moved into Snokomish territory (both Straits Salish) and took over their neighbors' fishing and weir sites after nearly all the Snokomish perished in a smallpox epidemic that hit before 1850.[73] Other relocations occurred in the San Juan Islands and on the southern coast of Vancouver Island.[74]

Despite tremendous disruptions and reconsolidations of territorial and fishing borders, Northwest Indians retained control of their salmon fishery and related supplies. Their knowledge of the regional environment and its best fishing sites facilitated their success on this front, as did their savvy trading skills. But how did Native peoples accomplish this as their communities were crumbling around them? And why was it such a priority, given all the other challenges they faced?

From the beginning of their contact with whites, many regional Indians worried about the impact that contact might have on their salmon fisheries. In numerous instances throughout the Northwest, Native peoples articulated their concerns and forced newcomers to abide by indigenous rules regulating how to treat salmon and when the fish could be consumed. The adventurer Alexander Mackenzie was one of the first whites to experience the Indians' convictions on these points. As he journeyed down the Bella Coola River in present-day northern British Columbia in 1793, several Indian groups refused to sell fresh salmon to Mackenzie. At one village, one of his men tossed a deer bone into the river, much to the chagrin of the Natives. A local man immediately dove in to retrieve the bone and then somehow conveyed to the fur traders that salmon might smell the venison, take offense, "and abandon them, so that he, his friends, and relations, must starve." When Mackenzie continued asking after fresh salmon, the man would offer only cooked salmon that had already been prepared and strongly encouraged Mackenzie and his men to continue on their way.[75]

At another village Mackenzie attempted to trade for fresh salmon so that "we might dress them in our own way, but could not by any means obtain that gratification, though there were thousands of that fish strung on cords, which were fastened to stakes in the river." Villagers also refused to allow visitors near the salmon preparation area, and they confiscated Mackenzie's iron kettle to prevent him from using it in the river water. According to Mackenzie, "they assigned as the reason for this precaution, that the salmon dislike the smell of iron."[76] Mackenzie then took out some altitude-measuring instruments that prompted immediate protests from his new hosts. The Natives, again concerned the instruments would scare off their salmon, quickly assembled a canoe and a guide to hasten Mackenzie's departure.[77]

In spite of their reduced numbers, many Indians continued to force whites to abide by rules with respect to salmon consumption and preparation for decades following Mackenzie's faux pas–ridden journey. In 1811, Walaly, a Cathlamet chief who lived near Fort Astoria, refused outright to sell or give any fall salmon to the fur traders "untill [sic] a certain time of the Moon, on account of some superstitious idea." A week later, Walaly relented briefly, but would allow the fort only ten salmon he—or more likely his wife or wives—had prepared and roasted.[78] David Thompson's party repeatedly tried to buy salmon from Natives on the Columbia in the summer of 1811, but they simply "gave us surly looks, and nothing we could offer, would induce them to let us have a single fish."[79]

The Chinook initially brought just a small number of salmon to the traders because they were afraid the whites would cut the fish the wrong way and eat it after dark. Once the newcomers agreed to abide by Indian rules on these counts, the Natives appeared more willing to sell them the fish but still insisted on preparing it themselves.[80] Similar encounters occurred in 1812, when several Chinook accompanied trader Duncan McDougall and his company across the river with a fresh salmon from their village. The Indians had refused to give the fish to their visitors, but instead brought it over themselves for proper processing. "They were unwilling absolutely to deny the fish to Mr. McDougall," one of the men observed, "but it was on these conditions only he could obtain it."[81] Archibald McDonald's attempts to purchase early season salmon near Fort Langley in 1829 also met with little success until the Natives deemed it safe. "Some of the Quaitlines [Kwantlens] Came down & brought us a few raw Salmon being almost the first we have had in this State," he reported that August, "for, the natives here also like those in the Columbia & indeed all over think it Sacrilege to give them otherwise to the Whites at first."[82] William Tolmie had a similar experience near Fort Vancouver in 1833.[83]

In addition to limiting access to the first salmon of the season and requiring non-Natives to consume the fish in very specific ways, there are hints that Northwest Indians may have tried to restrict newcomer contact with salmon-producing streams or particular fishing spots and thus assert the protective power of Native fishing borders. Mackenzie's early journey provides one of the first documented accounts of this behavior. While admiring a complex Indian salmon weir, Mackenzie later lamented: "I expressed my wish to visit this extraordinary work, but these people are so superstitious, that they would not allow me a nearer examination than I could obtain by viewing it from the bank."[84] A few days following the Cathlamet chief's 1811 refusal to sell the Astorians salmon, two fur traders fishing near Walaly's village had their hooks and lines stolen and the chief again refused the whites food.[85] In the spring of the following year, some residents of a Cathlamet village removed two of the company's fishing lines and physically defended the act against the traders' protests.[86]

Similar encounters occurred throughout the region. When Fort Langley's supply ship was delayed in early July 1829, Archibald McDonald sent a party upriver to salt salmon at the main Indian fishery on the Fraser River. The party returned five days later, "having met with a hearty reception from the natives" fishing at the falls, but with few salmon.[87] Although the Natives allowed the HBC men near their fishery, it does not appear that the fur traders actually fished or even succeeded in buying salmon. The few times the fort men tried out their own nets, it was in close proximity to the fort, and there is no record of local Indians having been in the vicinity.[88] Native peoples on the Columbia may also have lied to the Astorians to keep them from catching salmon. On at least one occasion, an Indian visiting the fort mentioned the arrival of a good salmon run on a nearby creek or river, and the fur traders sent a party of men to the destination in pursuit. The group returned empty-handed and from that point forward were more suspicious of such generous "tips."[89] This may have been a way for local Indians to indirectly force the Astorians to buy their fish or to deter white contact with actual salmon-bearing streams.

The newcomers at Fort Astoria/Fort George and the later Fort Vancouver appear to have fished for themselves more frequently than people at other forts. Perhaps the fur traders on the Columbia were better fishermen and had brought good nets with them that had yet to wear out or break. More likely, diseases had killed off so many local people that they could no longer supply the fort with salmon. Surviving Indians in that area also may have been more drawn to the fur trade, and so few Indians were fishing the river by the 1840s that the men at Fort Vancouver were actually supplying the Indians with salted salmon so they would not starve.[90] North of the Columbia, however, the HBC men generally did not catch their own fish because they lacked both fishing skills and the materials necessary to construct their own equipment. While stationed at Fort Simpson, John Work reported that the salmon near the fort were extremely numerous and potentially accessible. "Had we either seines or nets and people that knew any thing of fishing," he lamented, "there is no doubt we might ourselves take sufficient for the daily use of the fort, large as our establishment is, and might salt plenty also."[91] The Fort Langley men attempted to make their own nets that they initially tried on sturgeon, but the fish escaped "from the men knowing nothing of the management of it."[92]

Tellingly, the men at Fort Langley did not procure nets through their trade with the Native population and reported having only homemade nets consisting of imported twine and pieces of old Indian nets sent up from the Columbia River.[93] The company frequently hired Native people for large or labor-intensive projects in and around the forts, and the Astorians actually paid Native fishermen to fish for them on occasion, but there is no indication that the fur traders considered hiring or even approaching Indians to make nets or sell their nets to the forts.[94] These developments are particularly curious given the fact that the HBC employed a number of Hawaiians. Although many of the white HBC traders had no previous fishing experience, some of the Hawaiians may have had some such knowledge from their time in the islands. Still, while the Hawaiians sometimes caught sturgeon, they do not appear to have been especially successful salmon fishermen.[95]

The Indians obviously had an economic motive for not selling their nets or making them for the newcomers. Native peoples benefited materially from their ever-growing salmon trade and so had a vested interest in preventing the HBC from attaining self-sufficiency in fishing. Local

Indians were not dependent on the forts for goods, but the emphasis their communities placed on material possessions and status also must have encouraged their desire to maintain control of the salmon trade. Northwest Natives had two additional reasons not to sell their nets to outsiders: they were valuable tools and the whites were their best customers. Why give them the means to catch their own fish?

Still, based on what we know about the relationship of Northwest Indians to salmon, Native peoples likely also had reasons that were not rooted in economics. It seems reasonable that regional Indians limited newcomer access to fresh salmon and local salmon fisheries because of the importance the Natives placed on honoring and protecting salmon to ensure their annual return. The specific parameters of Native salmon rituals and customs differed slightly along the Pacific slope, but all Northwest coastal groups revered salmon. They were important figures in the Indians' spiritual worldview, and there were very specific rules of behavior regarding their treatment. Locals simply could not trust the newcomers to perform these rituals properly.

The connections that Indians drew between the presence of whites and the diseases that ravaged the Native population were also significant. From the period of first contact, many Native peoples understandably associated the epidemics with the new people in their midst and reacted accordingly. As early as 1790, the S'Klallam (Straits Salish) believed a trading vessel that arrived in the region was Dokwebutl, a spirit that introduced illness.[96] In the north the Haida came to believe in a spirit of "pestilence" sometime in the late 1700s, and both they and the Tlingit explicitly linked diseases with ships. The Tlingit further thought that all who perished from the epidemics were aboard the "disease boats," and, according to ethnographer Frederica de Laguna, "when the epidemic had run its course in one locality, the boat would sail away, perhaps to go to another."[97] Chief factor John McLoughlin, the head of the HBC in the Northwest, discovered that Umpqua Indians located south of the Columbia River blamed fur traders for the diseases that afflicted their community in the 1830s.[98] The Natives near Fort Simpson similarly denounced the HBC for the measles epidemic of 1848. "The ignorant Indians in despair at the loss of so many of their dearest relatives, conceived a suspicion that the disease had been propagated through the Agency of the whites," James Douglas and John Work wrote in December of that year, "and were at one time thinking seriously of attacking the establishment, but their better feelings prevailed over the passion of the amount and they ultimately discovered the folly and absurdity of their groundless fears."[99]

Sometimes whites and other outsiders actually encouraged these perceptions and exploited them for their own purposes. In 1811, Duncan McDougall threatened to unleash smallpox from a bottle at Fort Astoria/ Fort George when he learned some northern Natives had destroyed one of the traders' ships. A Cree two-spirit person visiting the fort at around the same time claimed to have the power to initiate a smallpox epidemic—an assertion that understandably did not endear him/her to the local Native community. Later visitors resorted to similar threats.[100] Although there is some doubt to the story's validity, all lower Columbia oral traditions blame the American trade ship the *Owyhee* for the "fever and ague" that struck the coast in the 1830s immediately after the ship left the Columbia for the Strait of Juan de Fuca.[101] At the HBC's Fort Nisqually, William Tolmie spoke to an Indian in the fall of 1833 who confirmed this story and recounted another about the same American ship captain threatening to initiate an epidemic among the Makah Indians if they did not agree to trade terms.[102] According to a missionary who visited the Makah twenty years after that incident, Captain Dominus of the *Owyhee* had produced an empty bottle and "told them that it was full of 'skin sick' and unless his terms were agreed to he would uncork it and destroy them all; which so frightened them that he had his own way without further trouble."[103]

Most Northwest Native groups would not allow anyone they deemed impure or in possession of unusually strong spirit powers access to their salmon fishery because it could upset the fish and threaten their return. Usually, Northwest Natives associated such powers with puberty, menstruation in women, birth, or death, but it is possible that the connections between whites and disease presented a new threat.[104] And, really, was it worth the risk?

Most regional Indians believed that salmon could take revenge if piqued. The Tlingit and the S'Klallam both tell stories in which salmon inflict death for insults committed against them.[105] Other groups believed salmon, if displeased, could afflict them with illness. In 1896, Charles Hill-Tout interviewed an elderly tribal historian among the Suquamish who told about his tribe's first smallpox epidemics. The disease started with their salmon, which were infested with running sores and blotches, but the people had to catch them and eat them in the winter as they had no other food. Soon everyone had a "dreadful skin disease, loathsome to look upon" and "none were spared." "Camp after camp, village after village, was left desolate."[106] The anthropologist Robert Boyd has interpreted this story as being about a past epidemic experience, but perhaps it was warning of another form of retribution. If Northwest Natives allowed disease-ridden whites to have contact with their salmon fishery, then the offended salmon might bring more epidemics to punish the Indians. Or perhaps the fish would retaliate even further and simply disappear.[107] No salmon could mean the difference between life and death for many of the region's Native peoples.

Fraser River salmon did not appear in 1828—just a year after the establishment of Fort Langley on what must have then seemed eerily quiet river banks.[108] In 1829, Shashia (later Joshua and then Joe), a local Cowichan chief, refused to sell the HBC fort more than a few of his salmon. When a visiting group of Nanaimo broke ranks and sold liberal numbers of fish to the fort, Shashia became angry. He may have blamed the HBC for the previous year's failed runs and tried to convince the Nanaimo of this suspicion, or he may have thought that the HBC offended the salmon in some way and caused the fish to retaliate by not coming back. Perhaps Shashia sought to curb white access to fish. Whatever the case, there were certainly some heated words passed between Shashia and the Nanaimo.[109] Our ability to interpret snippets like these is limited, but we do know that Northwest Natives actively worked to shape the parameters of encounter between white traders and the salmon they held so dear. By paying closer attention to the silences and fleeting glimpses offered by surviving texts and oral traditions, a world in which Native peoples vied for control of their most prized resources comes painstakingly, if incompletely, into view. The more intimate relations that developed between Native women and non-Native men may offer even more insights.

FISH CULTURE: INTERMARRIAGE

Some of the most important and lasting relationships that developed between Natives and newcomers were sexual in nature. By engaging in both short- and long-term romantic unions, male fur traders and Native women frequently crossed both ethnic and social borders during the first phases of contact. Such connections held the potential to ease economic and social exchanges and to extend loyalties between Natives and newcomers. These unions also may have offered Native women opportunities to elevate their status because they gained access to the forts. Still, the marriages that occurred between male fur traders and Native women differed from Indian marriages in important ways.

From the first instances of contact, women played important roles as traders, negotiators, and commodities in Native-newcomer interactions. They propositioned male visitors on their own, and Native men and women also offered white fur traders their slave women for the night or for barter.[110] Stranded among the Nuu-chah-nulth, John Jewitt noted that although all the women worked hard, the main difference between free women and slaves was that slave women were "considered as free to any one, their masters prostituting them whenever they think proper for the purpose of gain." He continued: "In this way many of them are brought on board the ships and offered to the crews, from whence an opinion appears to have been formed by some of our navigators, injurious to the chastity of their females, than which nothing can be more generally untrue, as perhaps in no part of the world is that virtue more prized."[111] Near Nootka, George Vancouver and his crew were met by a large group of Indians who repeatedly tried to persuade the captain to visit their village. "Beside promises of refreshment," Vancouver observed, the local people "made signs too unequivocal to be misunderstood, that the female part of their society would be very happy in the pleasure of their company. Having no leisure to comply with these repeated solicitations, the civil offers of the Indians were declined."[112] Due to beliefs about premarital and extramarital sex, the women who operated independently were likely from the north.[113]

While Native women and fur trade men undoubtedly engaged in sexual relations, the number of actual marriages—in the "custom of the country" or Indian manner—that took place prior to the 1810s is hard to pin down. John Jewitt claimed that he married the daughter of a chief from a neighboring village in the early 1800s. According to Jewitt, Maquinna and his followers valued Jewitt's blacksmithing skills and believed marriage would help him cement ties to the community. Maquinna was thus understandably disappointed when Jewitt broke off the relationship just a few months later.[114] Florence Edenshaw Davidson, a Haida woman born in the late nineteenth century, claimed that her mother's side of the family was extremely fair-skinned because her great-grandmother, Ninasinlahelawas, was married "in the Indian way" to a white ship captain.[115] Many sexual liaisons must have been taking place in the early nineteenth century because the HBC officers made increasingly common references to mixed-blood offspring in the 1820s and 1830s.[116]

Following the transition to the land-based fur trade, intermarriage or intimate relations between Native women and white and Hawaiian male fur traders became more common.[117] Duncan McDougall's 1813 marriage to the daughter of the local Chinook chief, Concomely, was likely one of the first such unions at Astoria.[118] Mr. Manson, the man in charge of Fort McLoughlin, was happily married to a Native woman and, according to William Tolmie, "is much happier with his wife and two pretty children around him than were he a lone bachelor, & leading the sensual life, indulged in by most of the gentlemen, who live in single blessedness."[119] In 1833 another friend of Tolmie's expressed his desire to marry a mixed-blood woman.[120] Fort Langley's George Barnston likewise wedded the mixed-blood daughter of a high-ranking Clatsop (Chinook) woman and an early Astoria fur trader.[121] The chief factor of Fort Victoria, James Douglas, married an Indian woman while at Fort Vancouver, and she remained his lifelong companion.

HBC officers knew that marriages to local Indian women could induce their employees to renew their contracts, help establish friendly relations with the Indians, and, most importantly, facilitate trade relations. While trading furs was the primary goal of the HBC, access to salmon must have become a necessary consideration. The selection of a marriage partner was thus critical to both the individual men involved and the HBC officers charged with feeding their ranks and marketing salted salmon abroad. Langley's Archibald McDonald and some of the other traders had misgivings about allowing these unions, but as McDonald admitted in 1829, "to reconcile the bucks to Fort Langley without Some indulgence of this nature is utterly out of the question—to leave them to prowl about in the Camp would be the worst policy of all—What remains for us then, is to make the best & wisest Selection we Can for every man of them."[122] The best and wisest selection would either initiate or affirm a trade partnership between the HBC and nearby villages. One of McDonald's men, for example, married the daughter of a Kwantlen chief in 1828. Because the Kwantlen were "the principal Indians of the neighbourhood & who at all exert themselves to Collect Beaver, we have thought it good Policy in Mr. Yale to form a connection in that family."[123] When McDonald granted Louis Delenais permission to take a wife, he hoped Delenais would choose a Cowichan woman because it would ease tensions between the company and that community. McDonald's matchmaking ambitions were thwarted, however, when Delenais and another HBC man also married women from the Kwantlen camp located near the fort.[124] While the men's partner selections could have been more politically astute and responsive to McDonald's aspirations, they still likely buttressed the company's access to the local fur and salmon markets.

Having a long tradition of using marriage for soothing or strengthening intervillage ties, the Natives' extension of this custom to fur traders is understandable. Concomely's assent to his daughter's marriage into Fort Astoria/Fort George was probably linked to his desire for ongoing good relations and trade opportunities with the fort.[125] Eager chiefs repeatedly propositioned the young and proper William Tolmie in 1833, but he "respectfully declined them all, declaring it improper for a physician, to have unlawful dealings with the fair sex."[126] Still, while Indians sought intermarriage opportunities to improve relations and increase trade, the fishing privileges that so often attended Indian unions do not appear to have been extended to whites. Native fishery borders remained firmly in place and tightly drawn.

The residence patterns of Indian wives also restricted fur trader access to customary Native male activities and spaces within Indian communities. By moving into or in close proximity to fur trader forts, indigenous female spouses may have improved their standard of living and status in some cases, but they also provided crucial labor to the sparsely populated forts.[127] As salmon grew in importance to the HBC, the women's skills in drying and storing the fish became increasingly valuable. By processing and handling the fish for the forts, Native women simultaneously further protected salmon from white contact or potential insult. Although Indian men did not coach white men in fishing and net-making skills, the HBC fort men did learn fish-drying techniques from their wives. Native women taught newcomer husbands how to process salmon, but it was women's work, and non-Native men were effectively denied access to the meaningful relationships created between men and salmon through the act of fishing.[128]

Intermarriage between members of different Native communities created new permutations of Indian border systems and often opened valuable resource sites for in-laws, but such traditions were not transferred to the fur traders who married Indian women. This may have been a strategic economic move by Native peoples, or perhaps the fur traders simply never asked for the privilege. Still, when considered in light of Indian beliefs about salmon and Native peoples' other efforts to limit white contact with their salmon fisheries, these actions beg further contemplation. While intermarriage between fur trader men and Indian women helped nurture community and trade relationships, Northwest Natives shaped the terms of union to protect their crucial relationship with the region's salmon population. The newcomer threat was simply too great.

Contact with whites initiated tremendous changes in Northwest Indian communities, but the Indians maintained the boundaries necessary to protect their people and their salmon fishery. The fish site ownership and food-sharing practices that the Natives developed over time gave them multiple ways to effectively manage their fishery and keep it healthy. The Indians could not have known, however, that the resilience of their borders and their relationship with salmon would both soon be put to the ultimate test.

3

Remaking Native Space

WAYNE SUTTLES, AN ANTHROPOLOGIST, CONDUCTED DOZ-
ens of interviews with western Washington and British Columbia Native peoples in the 1940s and 1950s. He was interested in
how and where his interviewees had gotten their food before the influx of
whites to the region in the late 1800s. As he talked with people, Suttles drew
maps of the Salish Sea waterscape, carefully identifying the Indians' most
important former resource locations. Simple black lines on white dashes
indicated the range of each community's territory, and a handwritten key
listed out abbreviations for each resource. Suttles painstakingly used this
key to mark crucial food sites and to locate temporary resource camps and
winter villages. The Semiahmoo (Straits Salish), he learned, once fished for
abundant supplies of sockeye, spring, and silver salmon on both sides of
the forty-ninth parallel in what is now called Boundary Bay. The Lummi
(Straits Salish) used resource sites on several of the San Juan Islands and
caught different species of salmon off the coast of Lummi Island and up
the Nooksack River. Local Indians would have known at a glance which
sites were traditionally open to the larger community, which had more
strict access customs attached, and when those rules were in effect.[1]

By the turn of the twentieth century, however, Suttles's maps did not
reflect reality. The Washington State Department of Fish and Game produced a separate set of maps in the early 1900s that makes this clear. The
geographic shapes are familiar, but the hundreds of tiny numbers hugging
the coastlines like a line of marching ants set these maps apart. The num-

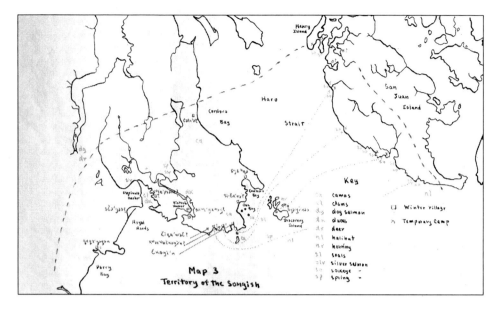

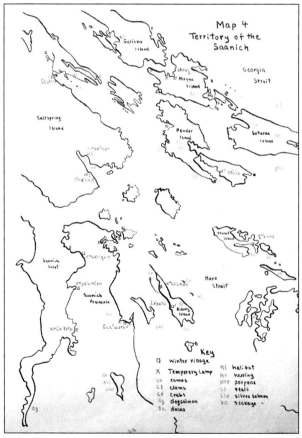

MAP 3.1 Songish Indian resource locations. *Source*: Suttles, "Economic Life of the Coast Salish of Haro and Rosario Straits," 14.

MAP 3.2 Saanich Indian resource locations. *Source*: Suttles, "Economic Life of the Coast Salish of Haro and Rosario Straits," 22.

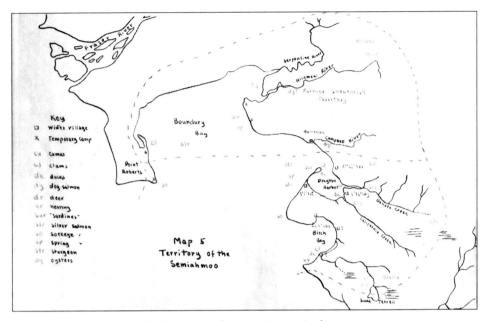

MAP 3.3   Semiahmoo Indian resource locations. *Source*: Suttles,
"Economic Life of the Coast Salish of Haro and Rosario Straits," 28.

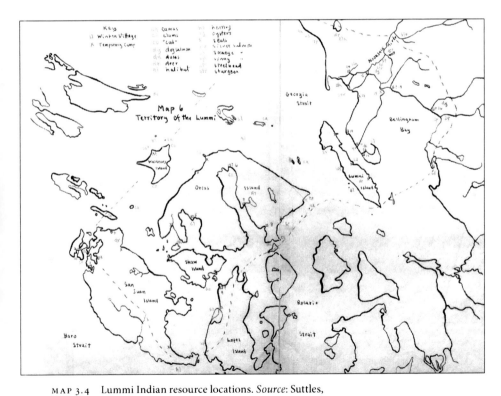

MAP 3.4   Lummi Indian resource locations. *Source*: Suttles,
"Economic Life of the Coast Salish of Haro and Rosario Straits," 34.

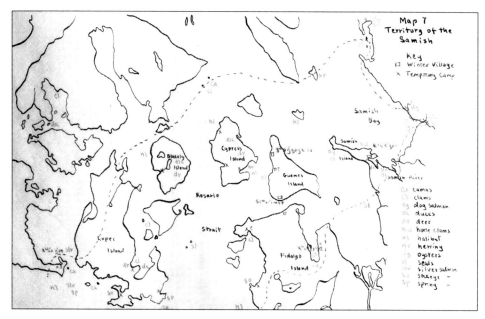

MAP 3.5   Samish Indian resource locations. *Source*: Suttles,
"Economic Life of the Coast Salish of Haro and Rosario Straits," 42.

bers refer to fish trap licenses almost exclusively owned by whites; their placement and prevalence show just how thoroughly the industrial fishery wrested away Native fishing locations in a few short decades.[2] Although they were still hand-drawn, these maps were about commercialization, industry, and, in the minds of whites, progress. Situating these maps side by side reveals a fishery completely transformed for the benefit of white commercial fishery interests and at the expense of the region's Native peoples. By the 1910s white newcomers had commandeered this salmon fishery for their own purposes and, in the process, obliterated many Native borders.

AMERICAN INDIAN RESERVATIONS

The U.S. government was ready to remap its part of the Pacific Northwest by 1846. The Oregon Land Donation Act of 1850 ignored the long-standing federal policy of removing Indians before issuing land titles in new U.S. territory. Between 1850 and the act's expiration in 1855, 529 people had filed for tracts bordering the greater Puget Sound region.[3] Once the immigrant population doubled to two thousand in 1853, Congress carved Washing-

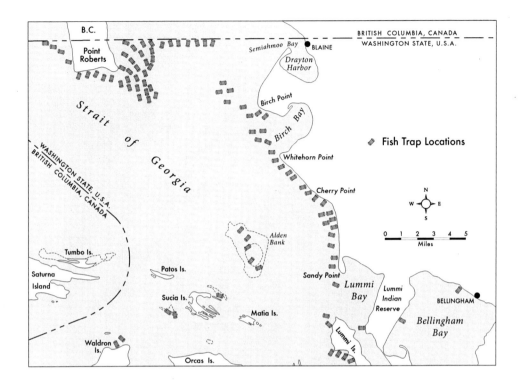

MAP 3.6 Fish trap locations in the vicinity of Point Roberts, Washington, and north of Bellingham Bay in the early 1900s. The large number of American traps that hug the international boundary line prevented many salmon from reaching the few Canadian traps built just north of the border. This proximity to the forty-ninth parallel would also have tempted fish pirates, who could steal fish from American traps and then quickly slip into Canadian waters. The traps built to intercept salmon outside of Lummi Bay and off of Lummi Island would have likewise presented obstacles to Indians fishing in those areas. *Source*: Redrawn from Washington State Department of Fish and Game microfilm records, Washington State Archives, Olympia, Washington (AR64-2-43).

ton Territory out of Oregon Territory and named Isaac Stevens the first territorial governor. Stevens set out to accomplish his duties as governor, railroad surveyor, and superintendent of Indian affairs, but because more white settlers were arriving in the region every day, Native land titles and the location of Native peoples were foremost on his list.

From 1854 to 1857, Stevens concluded a number of heavy-handed and questionable treaties with Washington Indians. The treaties ultimately

MAP 3.7 Fish trap locations near Lummi, Guemes, Fidalgo, and Whidbey Islands in the early 1900s. Wealthy industry players built fish traps directly in front of the Swinomish Indian Reservation and along the outer coast of Whidbey Island, all atop valuable resource locations formerly used by the region's Indians. *Source*: Redrawn from Washington State Department of Fish and Game microfilm records, Washington State Archives, Olympia, Washington (AR64-2-43).

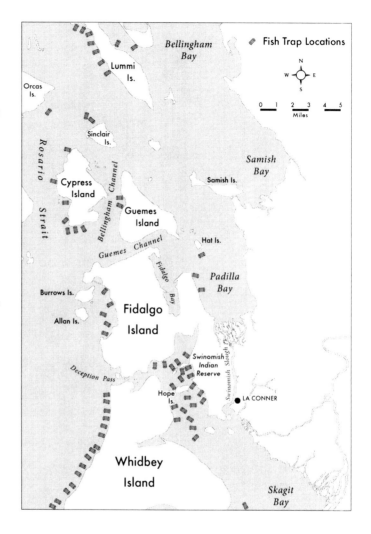

forced Indians to relinquish title to more than sixty-four million acres of land and created reservations to which they were expected to retreat; in return, the government promised the Indians annuity goods. Even though most of the Natives involved were not farmers and the reserved lands were almost entirely unsuited to agriculture, the treaties also guaranteed training and tools for farming. Stevens hoped to make as few reservations as possible to both save money and gain congressional approval, but the scattered locations of Native communities and the lack of clear band representatives soon forced Stevens to create eight smaller reservations, most of which were located along the coastlines of Puget Sound.[4]

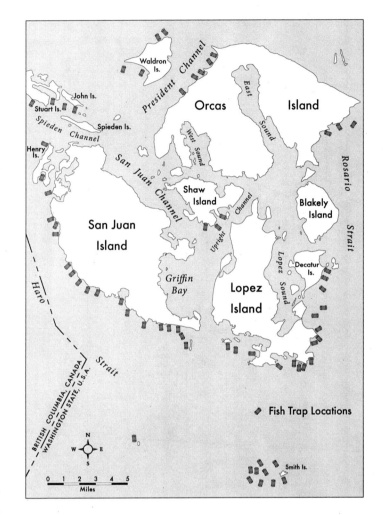

MAP 3.8 Fish trap locations near San Juan, Lopez, and Orcas Islands in the early 1900s. *Source*: Redrawn from Washington State Department of Fish and Game microfilm records, Washington State Archives, Olympia, Washington (AR64-2-43).

Many Indians were unhappy with the treaty provisions, and several Native leaders refused to sign.[5] Because of the introduction of alien concepts of land ownership and the fact that the treaty councils were conducted entirely in Chinook—a trade patois consisting of approximately three hundred words—other Indians who did sign likely did not fully understand the treaty obligations.[6] These documents soon became a source of contention between the territorial government and several local Native groups. In fact, many of the Nisqually and Puyallup (both Lushootseed) were so dissatisfied with their designated reservations that they chose to join the 1855–56 Indian war precipitated primarily by groups living east of the Cascades.[7] Other Indians simply refused to live on reservation lands.

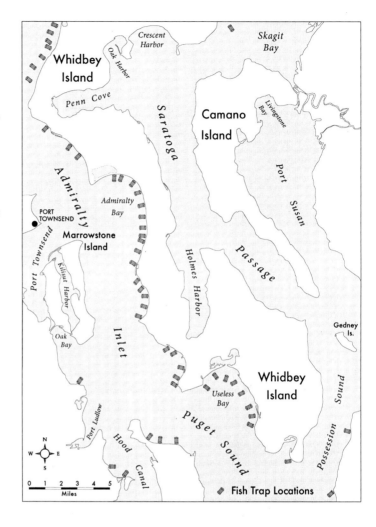

MAP 3.9 Fish
trap locations
near Whidbey and
Camano Islands
in the early 1900s.
Source: Redrawn from
Washington State
Department of Fish
and Game microfilm
records, Washing-
ton State Archives,
Olympia, Washington
(AR64-2-43).

Notably, all of the treaties granted Indians the right to fish "in their usual
and accustomed places," a stipulation that seemingly included places physically removed from the reservations. The porosity of these freshly drawn
borders would shift according to each community's seasonal food-gathering rounds and other economic activities. In addition, lack of financial
commitment by the government and opportunities for wage work further
ensured the new reservation borders remained permeable.[8]

Perhaps encouraged by the results of the Indian war of the mid-1850s,
whereby the government met the demands of the dissatisfied Nisqually
and Puyallup, various groups of local Indians continued to negotiate reservation boundary parameters with the Bureau of Indian Affairs into the

1860s and 1870s. In these discussions the Native people who agreed to live on reservations repeatedly insisted that certain ancestral territories, grazing lands, and especially fishing sites be included within reservation boundaries. In the fall of 1856, for example, the local Indian agent for the Suquamish and Duwamish (both Lushootseed), George Paige, tried to move the Duwamish to a reserve site on the western portion of Puget Sound. When the Duwamish balked, Paige recapitulated and instead proposed a site on the west side of Elliot Bay because it was "a favorite fishing ground of theirs at certain seasons of the year."[9] Perhaps emboldened by their gains following the 1855–56 conflict, the Nisqually demanded more land closer to what the local Indian agent admitted were "excellent fisheries" just a year later.[10]

The Muckleshoot (Lushootseed) went further and refused to move to their appointed reservation because it was too far away from their ancestral homes and fishing sites. The Muckleshoot Indian agent asked for permission to shift the reserve downriver and closer to the fishing weirs where the Indians actually lived. While promises were made in 1862, apparently nothing was done, as an Indian agent repeated the request in 1867. Concerned that the situation would escalate, Superintendent T. J. McKenny decided to grant the Indians the lands they desired. "The reserving of a small tract of land in a country where thousands of acres are open for entry is a cheap and easy way of quieting the Indians and avoiding difficulty," he wrote the local agent. "Many of them are bold daring men who claim that they have been deeply injured," he further cautioned, "and if white men are permitted to take from them their farms and fishing grounds they will be prepared for any desperate measures."[11]

The sad financial state of the western Washington Indian agency influenced many of these negotiations. Well into the 1880s, regional Indian agents complained repeatedly about their lack of funds for personnel, supplies, and annuity payments. "[Given] the total inadequacy of the appropriations," Michael Simmons wrote to his superintendent in the fall of 1860, "I am indeed at a loss how to give satisfaction, or even to do common justice to the Indians." He angrily continued: "The government has violated the treaty by the inadequacy of the amount appropriated that the Indians should take up and defend their rights would be perfectly justifiable."[12] Indians in Washington also frequently expressed dissatisfaction with the delay in the ratification of their treaties and payment for their lands. Often, Indian agents grew tired of apologizing for the government's slow response and despaired that the delays would result in further hostilities between Indians and whites.[13] Agents such as C. C. Finkbonner of the Lummi Reservation paid expenses out of his own pocket for several years but finally gave up and resigned after receiving no compensation from the government.[14]

Due to this dearth of support and the opportunities available elsewhere, Northwest Indians frequently moved off the reservations in pursuit of fish, other subsistence goods, and wage work. In many cases the Indian agent in charge actually condoned this breaching of reservation borders. In the midst of the Indian war in late 1856, for instance, Indian agent Paige tried to persuade a group of Duwamish to abandon their fishing site on the Black River and return to their reserve. William, a headman, insisted on remaining at his fishing location. In Paige's words, the Duwamish "said if they moved down to the Bay they would soon starve, for no food was to be had except the rations given them by the Agents and these rations they said were entirely too short. They could not subsist on flour and molasses they must have fish and at present there was none to be had on the Bay."[15] Like most of the other agents, Paige fed "his Indians" for several months during the Indian war, but as soon as hostilities waned, he reduced their rations and encouraged them to gather their own food off the reservation.[16]

When regional salmon runs failed—as they did in various places in 1857–58, 1862, and 1864—the Indians looked to their agents for the subsistence goods promised in their treaties, but they never received enough to live on for long.[17] Instead, the agents often found themselves encouraging Native fishing—not farming—to alleviate agency expenses. When the Holmes Harbor agent visited "his Indians" at their fishing sites on the Snoqualmie and "Ski-quamish" [Skykomish?] Rivers, for example, he surprised them. "I told them to continue catching and drying salmon so long as they could," agent Nathan Hill reported, because " . . . so long as they lived on their old hunting and fishing grounds they ought not to expect the Department to feed them regularly."[18] Although President Grant's post–Civil War federal Indian policy emphasized farming, the agents in Washington Territory had no choice but to continue to assert the importance of fishing to the Indians under their tutelage.[19] The nature of these new borders thus very much rested on the seasonality and availability of natural resources both on and off the reservation.

The population boom that hit the Puget Sound region after the Civil War and the persistent delays in surveying regional Indian reservations quickly translated into even more permeable reservation borders. Promises of a transcontinental railroad and the potential of a new trunk line connection with Oregon lured immigrants to Washington Territory. The growth rate was striking. Most newcomers gathered in the burgeoning towns around the Sound; between 1870 and 1890 the number of people in Seattle grew from 1,107 to 42,837, and Tacoma—founded in 1868—quickly boasted more than 36,000 inhabitants.[20] As the white population expanded, the need to survey and clearly label the boundaries of the Indian reservations became increasingly acute. Due to government inaction, however, these new borders remained extremely porous and often unidentified well into the 1870s. White settlers staked claims all over the Skokomish Reservation as early as 1861, and the agent at Tulalip reported similar incursions there in 1868.[21] "The defining of the boundaries of these reservations is necessary to preserve peace between the Indians and outside claimants. . . . The want of these surveys," Superintendent McKenny argued to his superiors in 1867, "have given rise to much trouble heretofore which I am desirous to avoid in the future."[22]

Because the early Indian agencies were incredibly short-staffed and their resources limited, whites increasingly pierced reservation borders and encroached on Native lands and resource sites. According to a Skokomish reservation farmer in the early 1860s, the Indians there complained "that the whites are settling their land and occupying their fisheries and that they never received the payment for the same, which was stipulated in their treaty."[23] When Superintendent McKenny learned that a Mr. Webster was interfering with Indian salmon fishing on Tulalip Creek in 1867, he wrote the man a stern letter that appears to have worked.[24] Earlier that year, McKenny actually considered using military force against white trespassers.[25] The frequency of white encroachments by 1870 so frustrated McKenny's successor, Samuel Ross, that he too wielded his pen in defense of Native territory. In a letter to the commissioner of Indian affairs that fall, he complained that a "mania prevails among a certain class of citizens in this direction. I verily believe that were the Snow-crowned summits of Mount Rainier set apart as an Indian Reservation, white men would immediately commence 'jumping' them."[26]

Despite the rapidity with which white encroachments on Native lands escalated, the Indians resisted such challenges to their territories. One such case involved a surveying mishap that mistakenly placed the Puyallups' favorite fishing grounds outside their reserve boundaries in the

1860s. "The Indians are much excited over the matter and threaten any man who may settle on it," reported Superintendent McKenny, "at the same time there are many low white men that will do so as soon as the fact is ascertained, hoping to be bought off by the Government at an enormous price."[27] The dispute apparently continued for several more years, however, as Superintendent Ross reported on further white encroachments of the Puyallup fisheries two years later. According to Ross, "the possession of these lands by the Whites deprived the [Puyallup] Indians of their fisheries, thereby removing one of their most important and valued means of subsistence."[28]

The more frequent white incursions on Indian lands in the territory and the seeming inability of the government to curb such offenses in the 1870s and 1880s caused some Indians to deem allotment of reserve lands as the only solution to white encroachments. "Allotment" entailed the government granting reservation acreage to individual heads of household to be held as private property; allotments theoretically would transform reservation lands into noncommunal, more tightly bordered space. Superintendent R. H. Milroy proposed the allotment of Indian reserves in western Washington a full decade before the government pursued the same policy at the national level. Advocates of allotment believed it would guarantee Indian tenure to the land and instill pride of ownership in private property.[29] For their part—frustrated by increasing white settler trespasses and the federal government's unreliability with regard to reservation surveys, boundary questions, and annuities—some Indian groups considered allotment a viable way to guarantee their exclusive residency and usage of sites that were originally within their reservations.

By the mid-1880s members of the Lummi, Puyallup, Nisqually, Squaxin (Lushootseed), Skokomish (Twana), Port Madison (later known as the Suquamish), Swinomish, Tulalip, and Muckleshoot (all Lushootseed) bands had received allotments on their reservations.[30] As the government delayed issuing patents to many of the plots in question and neglected to grant any patents at all for other areas, however, it became obvious to many reservation residents that allotment would not secure them their ancestral lands and fishing sites as promised.[31] According to elderly Snoqualmie (Lushootseed) tribal members interviewed in the 1920s, when the government dawdled on the allotment procedures, increasing numbers of white settlers moved onto their lands. "They were all feeling bad over that," Susie Kanim remarked about her reservation, "that they could not get no allotment, and not only that, but the white people began to drive them away from their old villages where they were."[32]

Because of the conditions and uncertainties associated with reservation life and the growing opportunities for outside wage work, many Puget Sound Indians refused to move onto the reservations and either squatted on scattered plots or filed their own land claims on nonreservation lands.[33] The most striking example is the S'Klallam (Straits Salish) band. When government authorities assigned the S'Klallam to the same reserve as their age-old enemies, the Skokomish, the S'Klallam understandably declined to remove to the reservation and insisted on inhabiting their former village sites in southern Puget Sound and along the eastern stretches of the Strait of Juan de Fuca. Despite white settler attempts to have them removed to a reservation, the S'Klallam lived in approximately ten of their original villages—Jamestown was the largest—and owned the properties that constituted each town. Each village was close to sawmills and boat docks, as well as to the tribe's best fishing sites.[34] Natives residing in the Skagit River area also defied white settlers and government agents from the 1850s on by chasing away land surveyors, refusing to move to a reservation, and taunting those Indians who abided by white policies.[35] Fed up with Indian agents and failed promises, other Native peoples moved off the reservations as well.[36]

Indians in Washington increasingly experienced affronts to their territories and way of life, but white attempts to confine Native peoples to strictly bounded reservations remained incomplete and ineffective for decades. While reservation borders remained tenuous and their meaning varied over time, they still represented an important step toward a different, predominantly white interpretation of physical space.[37]

CANADIAN RESERVES

James Douglas looked on as American policies south of the forty-ninth parallel degenerated into violent clashes between whites and Natives in the 1840s and 1850s. After the conflicts of 1855–56, he observed that "there must have been some great mismanagement on the part of the American authorities" to have provoked such a response from the Indians.[38] Although Douglas had little patience with his southern neighbors due to their mistreatments and misrepresentations of the HBC and the British, he paid attention to events in Washington Territory because he worried that the Indians might unite to repel whites on both sides of the Canada-U.S. border. Douglas's long history of interacting with local people as a fur trader and the poor Indian-white relations south of the border strongly influenced his approach to Indians in the colonies of Vancouver Island and on the mainland. Despite his experienced and even-handed approach, however, the Native peoples of what would become British Columbia confronted challenges similar to their American cousins within a few short decades.[39]

Douglas initiated land negotiations with Native peoples north of the international border soon after the 1846 boundary treaty was signed.[40] The British government granted the HBC the colony of Vancouver Island in 1849, and Douglas immediately contacted the company's London office about arrangements to purchase Indian lands. Because of British policies on the conditional legitimacy of Native land title, Douglas received authorization to buy only those lands that the Indians had cultivated or upon which they had constructed houses by 1846; all other plots were to be open to white settlement.[41] Starting in 1850, Douglas concluded fourteen treaties with tribes near Victoria, the Saanich Peninsula, Fort Rupert, and what would become Nanaimo. The treaty negotiations were "a troublesome business," he grumbled in a letter to James Yale, an officer at Fort Langley, "but we are getting on very well."[42] Douglas paid the Indians to relinquish their rights to all land except their current villages and fields; and, as with Indians south of the border, they retained the right to hunt and fish. The creation of a greater number of smaller reservations also served Douglas's strategic needs, unlike the policy originally pursued in Washington Territory. Douglas thought it unwise to group all Indians together, as such a move might facilitate cooperation—and perhaps rebellion—among previously unconnected groups.

Both these treaty negotiations and the integrity of the first reserves were put to the test in the late 1850s. Although these transactions were not expensive, the unwillingness of the colonial government to allocate additional funding essentially ended any property negotiations. When mainland Vancouver was made a colony in 1858 also under Douglas's authority, he continued to mark out reserve lands for the Indians and tried to protect them from white encroachments but was unable to undertake treaty negotiations due to lack of funds.[43] Believing that indigenous peoples could assimilate into white society, Douglas also allowed them to preempt land or purchase town lots in the same manner as whites.[44] Still, when gold was discovered on the Fraser in 1858, these attempts to carve out Indian reserves were jeopardized. More than twenty thousand miners arrived in B.C. that summer, and Victoria's population swelled to five thousand seemingly overnight. Douglas proved fairly adept at keeping order in the midst of this chaos, but there were still several skirmishes between gold miners and local Natives.[45]

When Douglas retired in 1864, his successors' desire to promote white settlement in the British colonies had devastating effects on Native people and the range of their territories. Although he possessed the power to approve Indian reserves, the new chief of lands and works, Joseph Trutch, did not acknowledge Indian claim to colonial lands and believed that Indians had no right to sell those lands. Trutch was essentially given a free hand because Douglas's policies were left vague and undefined when he left office.[46] He became convinced that Indians obstructed colonial development, and he was determined to open indigenous lands to white settlement. From 1864 to 1871, Trutch reduced the size of several of the Douglas reserves and forbade Indians from preempting lands on their own.[47]

After British Columbia's confederation with the rest of Canada in 1871, the federal (or Dominion) government assumed control of Indians, already designated Native reserves, and provincial fisheries.[48] Due to an odd clause in the terms of agreement with Ottawa, however, the provincial government controlled all nonreserve lands and thus all future land grants for Indians in the province. Bypassing the touchy issue of Native title to land and the lack of treaty agreements, provincial officials argued that small reserves would encourage Indians to enter the wage labor force and assimilate more quickly. Also, since coastal Indians relied so heavily on fish for their subsistence base and were clearly not farmers, the province held that the Natives did not need large reserves.

Clashes over policy led the provincial and federal governments to appoint a joint commission to assess Native reserve needs in 1876, and the commissioners proceeded to identify and set aside reserves that were important to Indian fishing practices.[49] As historian Doug Harris has argued in his recent study of B.C. reserves, "land followed fish."[50] Thus, in the B.C. context, reserve boundaries quite frequently coincided with seasonal Native fishing sites and might be occupied only at certain times of the year by people with rights to fish that location. Reserve-making based on fishing locations continued through the 1880s and 1890s, even as the Department of Marine and Fisheries (DMF) increasingly restricted Native fishing in favor of the largely non-Native commercial fishery.[51]

As in Washington, however, white encroachments on B.C. Native lands were also common. From the 1860s to the 1890s, Indians from across the province sent protest letters about white tresspasses and their desire for clearly delineated reservations. They also demanded enough land for their farms and livestock as well as protections for their favorite fishing locations.[52] When Indian Commissioner Gilbert Sproat had a meeting with six chiefs in the lower Fraser River Valley in the 1870s, he found that not only did the Natives believe their reserves were insufficient, but that "for several years, white settlers have been coming into the District and, in some cases, have been permitted to take up land which the Indians were hoping to get." Sproat made efforts to alleviate the situation, but the government ignored his report, whites continued to settle unmolested in the area, and the Indians grew increasingly frustrated.[53]

A remarkable meeting in 1874 brought together 109 chiefs from the lower Fraser Valley and more far-flung places such as Lillooet and Bute Inlet on the coast. They drafted a petition addressed to the Indian superintendent complaining about the situation in B.C. and demanding eighty acres per indigenous family. "We have felt like men trampled on," they wrote, "and are commencing to believe that the aim of the white men is to exterminate us as soon as they can."[54] When they received no response from the government, the chiefs at the village of Hope submitted a sharper letter the following year. Upon hearing that the Indian department was planning a celebration in honor of the queen in 1875, Aleais, one of the chiefs involved, wrote the Indian commissioner and warned against further white incursions. "We do not wish to celebrate the Queen's day," he asserted. "She has not been a good mother and Queen to us, she has not watched over us . . . if she is so great as we have been told, she must be powerful enough to extend our present reserves."[55] According to a Musqueam (Halq'eméylem) chief interviewed many years later, the original reserve posts that were installed under Douglas's tenure were moved in response to two reserve reductions in the late nineteenth century. Throughout these processes, however, "the Indians were not notified or consulted . . . and after that three persons came [here] to Musqueam and told some of the Indians that the posts . . . meant nothing at all."[56]

Native peoples on either side of the forty-ninth parallel were confronted with white notions of property and rationalizations about separating whites from Indians beginning in the 1840s and 1850s. Drawing new borders signified attempts to collect and confine Native peoples both domestically and internationally, but Northwest Indians did not always abide by these boundaries and sought to shape them, use them, cross them, or ignore them according to their own desires and needs. Although whites and Indians engaged in reserve and reservation border-making processes on either side of the new international line, both groups simultaneously breached those borders on a regular basis.

FLUID BORDERS

At the same time that whites worked to draw boundaries around the Indians, they also set out to more precisely divvy up their pieces of empire. After years of bickering, the United States and Great Britain finally determined their land border in the western Canada–U.S. borderlands in 1846. How that border would apply to the Puget Sound/Georgia Strait, however, was more complicated and would not be settled until 1872.[57] In that interim the middle of the Strait of Juan de Fuca generally served as the border and the precise line among the San Juan Islands remained somewhat ambiguous. This became a border determined by international politics and understandings of latitude and longitude, not family status, lineages, or salmon availability. The result in the North American West, as elsewhere, was that this border was very much disconnected from Native priorities and uses of space.

Despite its seeming finality and seriousness of purpose, the new international border—like Indian reservation and reserve borders—remained little more than a line on a map for several decades. Whites wanted Natives, especially the dreaded "northern Indians" who crossed into Puget Sound on a regular basis, to abide by the new international line, but regional Indians continued to move around the Salish Sea in search of food and new wage work opportunities. When Native people began working in the canned salmon industry in the 1870s and 1880s, they also quickly learned to traverse the international border for higher fish prices and better wages. Over time, these developments gradually altered how and where many Indians fished for salmon and came to interfere with the smooth perpetuation of indigenous salmon management practices in several areas along the coast.

Northwest Natives maintained strong kinship ties as well as ongoing hostile relations that spanned the forty-ninth parallel well after the initial

Anglo-American delineation of the boundary in the mid-1840s. Because of these relationships, Indians continued to cross the new border to trade, visit with relatives, and raid their enemies' villages as they had before the arrival of whites. As one western Indian agent observed as late as the 1870s, the Indians "are intermarried and visit back and forth continually, and . . . the boundary line of nations has heretofore had but little influence with them or their intercourse with each other; so that to prevent entirely their going on to that side is next to impossible."[58] Nevertheless, recurring and relatively fresh hostilities between Coast Salish bands in the United States and groups from British Columbia collectively known as "the northern Indians" soon extended to white settlers in Washington Territory. Washington settlers claimed innocence in the face of northern Native aggression, but many of the serious skirmishes initiated by the northern groups were actually responses to offenses first committed by whites on the American side.[59]

Because of the violence that attended many of these early border crossings, authorities on both sides of the border sought to limit the crossings of all Native peoples in the 1850s and 1860s. Washington Territorial Governor Stevens built a clause into every 1855 Indian treaty that prohibited Indians from crossing the border for trade purposes, but the Natives ignored it and no one enforced it.[60] Some U.S. Indian agents, such as E. C. Fitzhugh, discovered why. Fitzhugh warned some intimidating Haidas not to land in Bellingham Bay in 1856, but the Haida, living up to their stalwart reputation, stood firm. If prevented from visiting Puget Sound, the Haida assured Fitzhugh, "they will kill every Bostons ['American' in Chinook jargon] they can lay their hands on & destroy all the property they can."[61] Throughout the late 1850s the Indian agent at Port Townsend repeatedly tried to prevent groups of northern Indians from landing, and white settlers there even resolved to shoot any northern Natives who dared come ashore. As most whites feared the Indians and possible retaliation, however, Native peoples generally came and went as they pleased.[62] Although B.C. governor James Douglas was less concerned than American authorities about this issue, he did try to persuade the Indians to refrain from engaging in the violent exchanges that periodically erupted south of the line.[63]

Northwest Natives quickly realized that the whites in their midst imbued the border with specific jurisdictional powers, and they quickly learned to manipulate these to their advantage. Indians living on Fidalgo

Island, at Neah Bay on the Olympic Peninsula, and near the Skagit River all developed successful whiskey smuggling ventures, and by 1870 "British Indians" were hauling dogfish oil to sell at Neah Bay duty-free.[64] By 1878 the U.S. Customs Service was collecting duties on imported dogfish oil, but according to Collector A. W. Bash, the procedures applied to the Makah Indians at that post were fairly relaxed. "This has been done," Bash explained, "to prevent any trouble with the Indians. This tribe being related to the B.C. Indians, have constant communication with British Columbia."[65] Similarly, J. H. Price, a U.S. Customs officer at Neah Bay, noted in his report to collector Bash that the Quileute Indians were given permission to take 150 blankets to B.C. for a potlatch as long as they did not attempt to bring in any contraband.[66] In the 1870s and 1880s "American Indians" also began to slip across the border to escape punishment for offenses committed in U.S. territory, and large numbers of B.C. Indians regularly crossed over for hop-picking jobs around Puget Sound.[67]

The canned salmon industry also beckoned many Indian workers. Salted salmon had long been a fairly profitable trade item for the HBC, but the firm's business in salmon fizzled in the 1850s and 1860s due to problems with storage and spoilage.[68] For their part, Northwest Indians continued to sell their salmon surpluses first to the growing number of white settlers and then to the small number of canneries established by optimistic businessmen.[69] James Syme had canned the first salmon on the Fraser River in 1864, but true working canneries were not established there until 1871. On the American side, William and George Hume and their partner Andrew Hapgood built the first salmon cannery on the Sacramento River in California in 1864, but water pollution problems forced the Humes northward to the Columbia in 1866. Their success spurred other such ventures, and in 1877, Jackson, Meyers, and Company built the first salmon cannery on Puget Sound at Mukilteo.[70] While these businesses all experienced rocky beginnings, they were soon packing larger numbers of fish and earning a profit. By the early 1890s fifteen canneries operated on the Fraser, although there were still just a handful in the Puget Sound district.[71]

Native workers were critical to the success of the early commercial salmon industry of the 1870s and 1880s. At the beginning, canneries arranged to hire Native men to catch fish and their wives to work inside as processors. In the early 1880s approximately twelve hundred to thirteen hundred indigenous men worked as fishermen for the Fraser River canneries, and Native fishermen received the majority of Fraser River gill net fishing licenses from 1880 to the early 1890s.[72] In 1886 the inspector of fisheries reported that Native men and women, as well as some Chinese, provided almost all of the cannery labor in British Columbia.[73]

Until the canned salmon boom of the 1890s, Puget Sound canners employed relatively small numbers of Indians, but they too hired more indigenous peoples as their operations expanded. The Washington State government reported that 108 Indians engaged in fishing for the canneries, and 80 Native women and Chinese men worked inside the plants in 1891. It is possible, however, that this figure overlooked the Native fishermen who only occasionally sold their surplus salmon to the canneries around the Sound. Still, the number of Indians working for the canneries gradually increased, and although statistics are scarce for this early period, Indian department reports suggest that Native fishing was critical to the fledgling industry.[74] According to one agent, the S'Klallam "did a thriving business" in the regional fishery in the early 1870s, and Tulalip agency Natives were all out fishing for canneries at Mukilteo and Muckleshoot and bringing in a good return later that decade.[75] While all of the coastal tribes fished, the Makah tribe at Neah Bay made particularly impressive returns from a wide variety of marine ventures from the 1870s on.[76]

Just as they moved freely through boundary waters to sell dogfish oil, so too did indigenous fishermen follow the best prices for their salmon back and forth across the border. Because there were more canneries on the Fraser River in these early years, the majority of Native border crossings for fishery work were from south to north and Puget Sound Indians began to take advantage of what were often higher fish prices in B.C. "It will be very difficult to prevent English boats from anchoring in Boundary bay, close to the line, and receiving fish from Indian canoes," observed U.S. Customs officer A. L. Blake in 1883. "Nothing but a show of force, would prevent the Indians from selling their fish where they choose."[77] According to U.S. Customs agent Ira B. Myers, the B.C. canneries were naturally drawing all the Native fishermen northward across the border because they paid as much as 50 percent more per fish than their American competitors. A few years later, another Puget Sound Indian told Deputy Collector A. M. White that he generally "finds a better market for fish in Victoria," and Lummi reservation residents were regularly heading to the Fraser to fish as early as 1882.[78]

The incipient U.S. Customs Service and the B.C. Fishery Patrols joined Indian agents and other government officials as witnesses to Native mobility across the border; but as the 1794 Jay's Treaty guaranteed Native peoples freedom of movement across the border and there were no other clear laws against the practice, they were initially unable to prevent Northwest Indians from selling their catch on either side of the line. Many officials (and canners) wanted to assert the power of the state over the region's Native population and force them to sell salmon only to their fellow countrymen, but they remained unsure about the reach of their own authority or their ability to influence Indian behavior. A. C. Anderson, the first fishery official for B.C., reported an American boat fishing over the line in 1883, but he was not convinced that it was something he should be worried about.[79] U.S. Customs agents likewise routinely observed numerous Indians crossing the border to sell their fish. "I suppose *we* have no right to stop them taking what fish they catch at Point Roberts, to the Fraser River canneries, or elsewhere," mused Agent Blake.[80] From his post in the San Juans, Deputy Inspector Myers concurred but then wryly added: "I could hear no complaint but from those who are engaged in the canning business on the American side."[81]

Working in the canned salmon industry complemented some long-standing aspects of Indian fishing practices and so eased their adjustments to the demands of the industrial fishery. From the cannery owners' point of view, Northwest Natives constituted the ideal workforce as they already knew how and where to fish, sometimes used their own gear, and were a relatively inexpensive source of labor. Using Indian leaders to recruit cannery labor and fishermen (known as the "Tyee system"; "Tyee" means "chief" in Chinook jargon) aligned with Native customs regarding the relationships between high status and access to salmon. The gendered division of labor among Indians in the fishery also lent itself to the structure of the new canneries: Native men worked as fishermen, and the women cleaned and processed the catch, just as they had for generations. In addition, because cannery work was seasonal in nature, it initially meshed well with the Indians' other seasonal subsistence and ceremonial rounds.[82] The salmon canneries thus represented a new means for using salmon fishing to create wealth and status in indigenous societies.[83]

Although Northwest Indians quickly learned how to navigate both the new international border and their entrance into the industrial fishery, the transition to the wage labor economy still altered how and where many of them fished and how they managed salmon. For instance, many Indians had to learn to fish new fishing grounds near far-flung canneries. Canneries redefined where these Indians fished and challenged their fishing expertise as they adapted to unfamiliar waters. Some Puget Sound Natives started going to the Fraser River to fish, and others went even farther when B.C. packers opened new plants on northern rivers. The Fraser River canneries drew nearly two thousand Indians from the bands of the Kwakwaka'wakw of Alert Bay and Fort Rupert in the north, the Nuxalk, the Skeena River, Vancouver Island, as well as from the closer lower Fraser River Valley.[84] As one Canadian Indian agent marveled from his New Westminster post in 1886: "There has been a larger number of Indians come to the fisheries this summer from almost all parts of the province than in any former year."[85] These changes, together with the imposition of the reservation system, slowly distanced many Indians from previously established fishing locations for certain parts of the year.[86]

In addition to fishing different physical locales, the emerging industry required Northwest Natives to cross other new cultural and spatial borders. Over time many Indian men began to set aside their canoes and use cannery-owned, planked skiffs or carved-hull Columbia River boats. They also increasingly relied on gill nets (or drift-nets) for their primary equipment, and some Indians became dependent on cannery advances to purchase food and other goods needed during the fishing season. In the early years of the industry many Indians also often bypassed their summer village fishing sites and lived in tent camps closer to the canneries.[87] Transitioning to work inside the plants was a radical shift for Native women as canning methods hardly resembled the techniques that they so skillfully employed in preparing their family's winter stores. In the cannery, white supervisors organized Indian women around tables for gutting, cleaning, chopping, and canning the salmon. Native women also soon came to work alongside Chinese men, marking yet another notable change in how they processed salmon.[88] Northwest Indians continued to adhere to their beliefs about salmon and followed previous customs about fishing for subsistence purposes as much as possible, but as they increasingly worked for distant canneries, they surrendered a certain amount of control over who had access to fish and how salmon were treated once caught. The new industrial fishery forced many men and women to travel and work far from their traditional fishing and processing locations, pushing them away from their management customs and locales more than ever before.

Northwest Indians used white cultural and economic assumptions about the political border to their advantage as they were drawn deeper into the emerging canned salmon industry. Although they likely felt buoyed by the new economic opportunities that attended the rise of the commercial fishery and many of their members continued to fish and manage their time-honored spots as they had for generations, the regional Indian population soon confronted new and more powerful challenges to the nature of their resource border system.

THE TAKEOVER

As the canned salmon industry grew in size, scope, and profitability, the intensity with which Euro-Americans and Euro-Canadians actively usurped Native fishing locations escalated and the international border took on new significance. White commercial newcomers sought to restrict Native mobility and attempted to regulate Indian fishermen out of the fishery. The rise of the industrial fishery in the 1890s soon led whites to physically commandeer Indian fishing locations. Like the early reservation and reserve boundary-making processes, these appropriations were by no means inevitable or uncontested. Yet by the 1910s the commercial salmon industry had remade the Salish Sea fishery in ways that did not benefit Indians.

The canned salmon business of southwestern British Columbia and northwestern Washington State came of age in the 1890s. Because Columbia River packers began to see signs of decline by the turn of the twentieth century, several of them began to look northward to Puget Sound, B.C., and Alaska for their next ventures.[89] Salish Sea canneries grew in number and overall capacity as a result, particularly after the mid-1890s. Although they were not all worked each season, forty-six canneries operated on the Fraser and twenty-three others were sprinkled throughout British Columbia by 1900. Northwestern Washington State had just seven canneries in 1895; that number tripled by 1902. In fact, the value of the canned salmon industry of northwestern Washington exceeded the combined worth of all the other fisheries in the state at the turn of the twentieth century.[90] The amount of salmon canned on both sides of the international border skyrocketed as a result of this expansion. In 1893—a "big year" in the four-year cycle of sockeye salmon—B.C. produced 610,202 cases of canned salmon; Americans produced just 89,774 cases. By 1901—another "big year"—both sides increased their overall pack, but the situation had reversed: British Columbia packed 1,247,212 cases and northwestern Washington canners packed 1,380,590 cases. After 1901 northwestern American canners consistently canned more salmon than B.C. packers until the 1930s.[91]

British Columbia already had established markets in Great Britain for its primary canning fish, the sockeye, but the completion of railroad lines to the Northwest coast and the realization that American fishermen could catch sockeye in boundary waters prior to their entry into the Fraser River spurred the industry's growth south of the forty-ninth parallel. Washington canners and investors then took serious notice of favored Indian fishing locations near the border. Some of these were the same sites that Native peoples had fought so hard to protect and include in their reserves just a few decades earlier. In addition, whites targeted Indian reef net sites that were not adjacent to the reserves.[92] In fact, Coast Salish Indians were still fishing thirty-nine reef net locations throughout boundary waters in the late nineteenth century; several groups of Indians operated between fifteen to twenty reef net gears at Point Roberts alone in the 1880s and early 1890s.[93] Recognizing the fecundity of these Native fishing places, however, industry players with capital sought to take over the sites for their own exclusive use. One of the best ways to accomplish this involved relying on the most efficient method for catching salmon then available: the fish trap.

The fish traps built at the turn of the twentieth century were impressive—and expensive—pieces of technology that lay well beyond the means of ordinary fishermen. A fish trap (also known as a "pound net") was a fixed apparatus made of webbing and wire netting that was held in place by wooden pilings driven into the ocean floor. Built offshore and designed to make the best use of the tides, traps were usually connected to the beach by "leads"—solid walls of webbing and underwater wooden stakes—that guided salmon through several enclosed spaces known as "hearts." As the fish swam forward into the trap, the hearts grew progressively smaller so as to prevent the fish from retreating or turning around. The fish next ended up in another enclosed space known as the "pot." The "tunnel" then ushered the fish from the pot into the final enclosure, known as the "spiller." The fish remained alive in the water until scooped from the spiller and placed on scows for delivery to nearby canneries.[94]

Because the traps were usually built in exposed coastal waters, it took some experimentation to maximize their durability. Some ambitious fishermen toyed with traps on the Columbia River in 1879, and John Waller built the first American trap off Point Roberts in 1880. H. B. Kirby followed in 1883, but his first pound net failed miserably. In 1888, Kirby tried

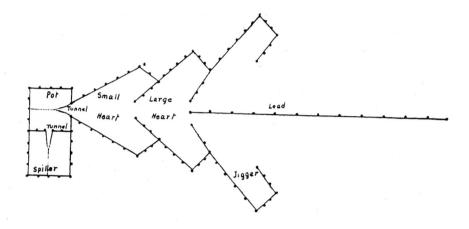

FIGURE 3.1 Diagram of a salmon fish trap. Note how the jiggers extend out into the ocean to direct more fish into the interior of the trap. Source: State of Washington, Department of Fish and Game, *Thirtieth and Thirty-First Annual Reports of the State Fish Commissioner* (1919–1921), 46.

again, modifying his new trap to take advantage of local conditions at Birch Bay Head in the Gulf of Georgia. The success of this trap encouraged others to invest in similar ventures. Once American canners realized they could catch sockeye with fixed structures, traps were suddenly in high demand, especially south of the forty-ninth parallel.[95] In 1893, the first year the Washington State government issued trap licenses, thirteen fish traps were operated in northern Puget Sound waters; though not all were used each year, this number grew to a remarkable 163 in just seven years' time.[96] Canada was much more strict and allowed just a few traps in the 1890s and early 1900s.[97]

Fish trap owners swiftly seized productive Indian fishing locations on both sides of the border. The Songhee (Straits Salish) had long fished reef nets at Macaulay Point, Beecher Bay, and Sooke on the southwestern coast of Vancouver Island.[98] At the turn of the twentieth century, however, the DMF began allowing a small number of traps in B.C. waters, and Canadian canners built some of their very first at Sooke.[99] These traps not only intercepted small numbers of the valued sockeye salmon runs, but they also interfered with Indians fishing on their nearby reserves. Although many Native reserves were created because they constituted critical fishing locations, the DMF would not grant any Native fishermen the exclusive right to fish adjacent to their reserves. The agency would, however, contradict this policy by regularly giving whites exclusive fishing rights to specified trap and seining sites, often in close proximity to these same reserves.[100]

Traps played a more critical role in the dispossession of indigenous fisheries south of the border because Washington State allowed so many traps to be fished each season. An 1895 government drawing shows that a continuous line of fish traps, mostly owned by the Alaska Packers Association (APA), completely blocked Indian reef net sites at Point Roberts

AREA	1901	1905	1909	1913	1917
Point Roberts	5	5	6	6	7
Boundary Bay (U.S. traps)	35	29	29	31	29
Birch Bay[1]	15	10	14	13	14
Lummi Island[2]	3	5	8	10	9
Rosario Strait[3]	1	2	3	5	13
South Lopez	—	—	—	—	5
Salmon Bank	6	4	5	4	7
Haro Strait	2	1	—	3	7
Waldron Island	1	1	1	1	2
West Beach	1	4	4	6	13
Ebeys Landing	—	—	—	1	2
Middle Point	—	—	—	1	2
Strait of Juan de Fuca[4]	—	—	—	—	1
Admiralty Bay and Bush Point	3	5	3	2	7
Oak Bay and Point No Point	1	1	—	—	4
Hood Canal	2	—	—	—	4
Useless Bay and Possession Sound	—	—	—	—	3
Meadow Point and south	—	—	—	—	1
East of Whidbey Island	5	3	3	2	8
TOTAL	80	70	76	85	138

TABLE 3.1 Number of Traps Fishing in Various Localities during the "Big Years," 1901–1917.

[1] This includes Alden Bank.

[2] This includes Bellingham Bay.

[3] This includes Padilla Bay and Guemes Island.

[4] This includes South Side.

Note: Because this data is incomplete before 1915, the total number of traps fished each season remains an estimation.

Source: Rounsefell and Kelez, Salmon and Salmon Fisheries of Swiftsure Bank, Puget Sound, and the Fraser River, 718.

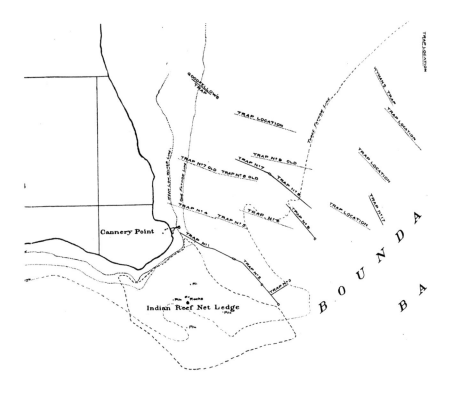

FIGURE 3.2   Trap net locations and Indian reef net sites at Point Roberts in 1895. By the early 1900s Point Roberts was completely surrounded by fish traps, and Indians found it increasingly difficult to operate their reef nets as formerly. *Source*: Rathbun, "Review of the Fisheries in the Contiguous Waters of the State of Washington and British Columbia," insert between pages 302 and 303.

(see figure 3.2). In addition, the Washington State Department of Fish and Game maps further confirm that white-owned fish traps overlay many Native fishing locations throughout western boundary waters by the early 1900s, especially in the San Juan Islands and around Point Roberts (see maps 3.6–3.9).[101] Commercial fishermen caught upwards of 80 percent of their salmon precisely where the Indians used to fish near Point Roberts, in Boundary Bay, and in the San Juan archipelago.[102] According to a Samish (Straits Salish) man, when Native fishermen attempted to continue fishing near these strategically located traps, the trap operators physically defended their newly acquired locations.[103]

Because Indian reservation borders either embraced or were in close proximity to good fishing sites, many of the traps in Washington State soon interfered with Indians fishing on their reserves as well. In 1901 several companies built expansive traps off the east coast of Whidbey Island and up the banks of the Swinomish reservation (see map 3.7). These traps obstructed both Native fishing and transportation routes to and from the reserve.[104] While some of the offending parties agreed to either remove their traps or adjust them so they did not extend above the low-water tidal mark—the technical boundary of the reservation—Pacific American Fisheries (PAF) not only ignored the charge, but one of their employees warned reservation officers away from the trap at gunpoint.[105] Indian superintendent Charles Buchanan wrote a sternly worded series of letters to the company about trespassing and even threatened to bring in the military to enforce the law.[106] The PAF claimed that since the reservation border extended only to the high-tide mark, trap netting in the tidelands was actually not trespassing.[107] The PAF managed to get a federal injunction preventing further physical interference with their trap until the end of the fishing season. In the meantime the PAF continued fishing; the Indians did not.[108]

Despite a state supreme court decision affirming that reservation lands did indeed extend to the low-tidewater mark, white-owned and -operated fish trap encroachments on Native spaces persisted.[109] The PAF operated illegally extended traps in 1903 and again in 1913 (and probably during the years in between), and Indian agents issued several warnings to additional fish trap operators building traps too close to the reservations in other years as well.[110] In a few cases trap operators sought to avoid the wrath of the Indian office and made rental payments to the Indians who lived immediately onshore. Both reservation residents and Indian agents had mixed feelings about such arrangements, however, because many of the proposed traps significantly obstructed Native fishing.[111] As the Indian agent at the Lummi reservation noted in 1914, if the Indian office allowed one white fish trap owner to build a trap adjacent to the reserve, then countless others would "come in and build many mechanical and expensive device of catching fish along Reservation front, which would sure cause complete disadvantage for Indians to catch fish."[112]

Fish traps were not the only threat to Indian fishing by the 1890s and early 1900s. Even as traps grew in popularity, white fishermen using gill nets and purse seines in boundary waters, on the Fraser River, and on other northern B.C. rivers were increasing in overall number. In 1902, 760 men worked on fish traps in Washington State, 672 men worked as purse seiners, and 706 as gillnetters, but the number of purse seiners south of the forty-ninth parallel steadily rose.[113] In British Columbia gill nets were by far the most common fishing method until the 1910s, when purse seining and trolling became more popular. In the mid-1890s B.C. fishers worked approximately 1,700 gill nets, and in 1901 the government issued 4,722 fish-

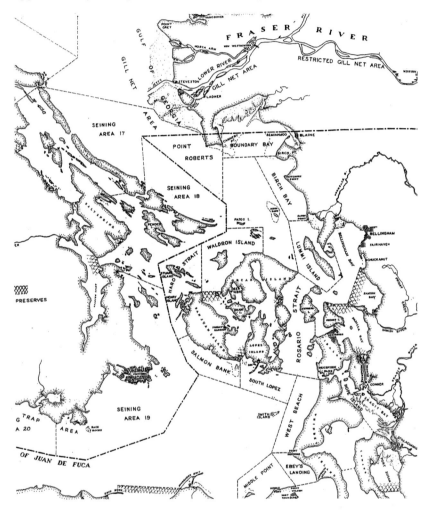

MAP 3.10 The portion of the region from the Fraser River to Point Wilson, showing the different fishing areas. *Source*: Rounsefell and Kelez, *Salmon and Salmon Fisheries of Swiftsure Bank, Puget Sound, and the Fraser River*, inserted between pages 696 and 697.

ing licenses, the vast majority of which were to gillnetters. Using small open boats rowed by a "boat puller," gill net fishermen would string their nets across rivers and other passages and haul them in when full of entangled sockeye, pink, or chum salmon.[114]

The purse seine instead worked more like a traditional net and captured schools of fish like a pouch with a drawstring. As Columbia River Indians had known for generations, seine nets could also be dragged in from the shore.[115] Parts of the modern seine were weighted so it was very heavy and difficult to use without power machinery. In the 1880s and 1890s fishermen set seines from tug-powered scows and skiffs. The crews on the skiffs hauled the net out of the water with oars, an activity that required significant strength. Purse seine crews thus included as many as seven men until the early 1900s. When seining became more mechanized after 1900, it gradually became the favored method among regional fishermen.[116]

In addition to fish traps, white gillnetters and seiners obstructed Native fishing locations and reservation coastlines south of the forty-ninth parallel.[117] The Port Madison Indian agent reported that as many as six to eight seine boats manned by Italians habitually fished directly in front of the reservation, but he was not sure how to respond to their brazen fishing efforts.[118] "This practice of outside fishermen has become very irritating," he grumbled in the fall of 1905.[119] Additional white fishermen trespassed on the Lummi reservation and, according to the acting commissioner of Indian Affairs, were "interfering to a considerable extent with the Indians in their operations in the line of fishing" and simply refused to leave. The commissioner advised the local Indian agent to give the trespassers written notice before forcibly removing them from the area; in this case this course of action appears to have worked.[120] A few years later, officials arrested and fined seventeen white fishermen who were unlucky enough to get caught fishing illegally in Lummi reservation waters.[121]

Clashes between Native peoples and industry fishermen started earlier in British Columbia. Many of the northern tribes were particularly adamant about protecting their traditional fishing locations, with some even demanding payment for fishery access or recognition of exclusive Native rights to specific locales.[122] The situation farther south along the Fraser River developed similarly. As early as 1888, a group of Native chiefs yet again assembled at Yale and drafted a complaint about the large number of cannery nets fishing the mouth of the river. "The supply of fish was unlimited for the use of my people before the canneries erected, when we had no just cause of complaint to make," Chief Sekalim's statement read. "We now pray that some protective measures may be adopted to preserve the supply of fish so vital for our sustenance, and that these obstructions—fishing by nets so close to the Rivers' mouth may be removed."[123] The mid-1890s likewise saw some companies take over former village sites for the construction of new canneries.[124] Many Natives appealed to government officials for additional fishing reserves or other protections, but these efforts met with limited success given the government's goals of promoting economic growth and white settlement.[125]

Finding most government agents unsympathetic, Native peoples in both countries tried to contest the encroachments in white courtrooms, through organized group protest, and appeals through other official channels.[126] One court case in particular highlights the complexities inherent in the transnational, fluid fishery of the Salish Sea. In 1895 the Lummi tribe, through the U.S. government, sued the APA for interfering with their legal right to fish "in their usual and accustomed places." In *U.S. et al. v. Alaska Packers Association et al.*, the Lummi avowed a long history of fishing at Point Roberts and highlighted their status as poor fishermen in need of this valuable fishing location for subsistence purposes. The APA mounted a clever defense that played on white assumptions about issues of national space, the proper place of Indians in a commercial fishery, and the dangers of transborder economic competition.[127]

The APA began by manipulating white ideas about what kind of Indians should have access to the fishery around the Point Roberts peninsula. Nearly all of the APA witnesses repeatedly claimed that mainly "foreign" Indians fished the reef in question. While Point Roberts was a long-standing Native fishing location and a few Lummis might fish there each year, witnesses testified that the Saanich (Straits Salish) or Cowichan (Halq'eméylem) tribes of British Columbia were the primary users of the site. Because "Canadian Indians" had no special legal claim to what was technically American territory, the APA could not be infringing on their fishing rights according to U.S. law.[128] APA witnesses also emphasized that all of the Indians who fished the reef sold their salmon to canneries for significant returns; that is, this was not a subsistence fishery and many of the Indian fishermen were successful farmers who had no real need to consume salmon.[129] This argument cast the Natives as either commercial fishermen in competition with whites or as accomplished farmers who only occasionally fished. Such individuals surely lacked credible claims to "traditional" Native fishing locations.

Several APA witnesses further suggested that because the Lummi sold many of their fish to Canadian processors, allowing the Indians to fish at Point Roberts denied the APA crucial fish supplies and aided their competitors.[130] According to E. A. Wadhams, an APA stockholder, if American white trap operators did not catch salmon at the reef before they entered the Fraser River, their Canadian counterparts would get the fish instead.[131] In addition, the APA argued that their Whatcom County canneries employed whites, bought local Native peoples' salmon, and contributed to the local economy in critical ways.[132] Forcing the APA to remove their traps would allow the Lummi to sell more fish in British Columbia and thus hinder the growth and success of the American canneries south of the line.

Judge C. H. Hanford did not necessarily accept the APA's claims about Point Roberts and the Indians who fished there. Even though he agreed that the peninsula *was* an important Lummi fishing site, he argued that the point was immaterial because the treaty between the U.S. government and the Lummi merely guaranteed an *equal* right to fish in their accustomed places, not an *exclusive* right. Hanford also had no problem with the Native fishermen selling fish commercially. He did, however, believe that forcing the removal of the APA's traps would injure both the local Indians and the regional economy. In the end Hanford ruled against the Lummi and the APA won the suit. The Lummi appealed and tried to take the case to the U.S. Supreme Court; but in 1899, for an unknown reason, the U.S. attorney general advised the Bureau of Indian Affairs not to pursue the case.[133]

In addition to issuing hundreds of permits that allowed fish traps to be built, Washington State regulators also passed laws discriminating against Indian fishing methods and continued to interfere with Native fishing activities. Some of the first state regulations outlawed fixed gear in all tributaries and prohibited fixed gear that stretched across the width of a river or stream. The weirs Indians had been using for thousands of years fell into both categories, and many Native fishers had to adjust their gear to abide by these new restrictions or risk arrest.[134] Requirements regarding licenses also presented challenges for Washington Indians. The state required Indians to buy licenses in the early 1900s but then repeatedly passed laws stating that only U.S. citizens qualified for fishing licenses. As many Native peoples were not citizens, they could not legally obtain a license.[135] Ongoing debates about

Native fishing rights culminated in a 1915 state fisheries code that detailed where and how Indian fishermen could fish. This new code guaranteed Indians the right to fish within a half mile of their reservations in marine waters or within five miles of their reservations in any stream. The law also stipulated the size of both Indian riverine and set nets but did not require the Indians to obtain licenses to fish on their reserves.[136]

The ways that state officials chose to define Indian fishing rights vis-à-vis the laws on the books translated into further difficulties for Native peoples in western Washington. State agents continually interfered with the fishing practices of members of the Lummi tribe, especially in the 1910s.[137] Fishery officials regularly maintained that state laws took precedent over any treaty fishing right, and L. H. Darwin, the fisheries commissioner from 1913 to 1921, vociferously opposed Indian fishing.[138] Although state laws guaranteed Native peoples the right to fish on their reservations, Darwin began arresting Indians for fishing even while on their reserves. Often these arrests were for fishing during the weekly closed period imposed during the season, but the closed-time was determined according to the open-sea, commercial fishery from which the Indians were increasingly excluded by 1915. By the time the fish reached the reservation banks upriver—the only places that the majority of Indians could continue to access salmon—the closed-time was technically in effect and the fisheries department deemed any Indian fishing illegal.

Barred from the open-sea fishery and forced to fish only on their reservations, the Indians could either fish for salmon farther inland and risk arrest or not fish at all. In response to the demands of the powerful sports fisher lobby, Darwin also closed the Nooksack River (adjacent to the Lummi reserve) to net fishing in 1915. An estimated 40 percent of the arrests made in the 1915–16 season were of Lummis for fishing out of season, fishing in closed waters, or fishing without a license.[139] The raids continued despite the vehement objections of the superintendent of the Bureau of Indian Affairs, and they cost the Lummi significantly in time, confiscated equipment, and lawyer fees.[140] "If we cannot make these Indians obey these laws," Darwin complained to the *Seattle Post-Intelligencer* in 1915, "then there will be absolutely no protection for the salmon in the closed rivers and on the spawning grounds during the closed season."[141] Even as Native fishing was increasingly contained, the Indians remained the favorite scapegoats for any shift in the fortunes of the commercial salmon industry or the salmon supply.

Although the Indians of western Washington continued to protest such treatment and tried to legally affirm their fishing rights through the courts, they met with little success prior to World War II. The Lummi filed a protest with the U.S. attorney in 1914 when Commissioner Darwin granted non-Natives a permit to drive a fish trap adjacent to the reservation; two years later they tried to sue Darwin in the state courts to halt ongoing arrests of tribal members, but neither effort went very far.[142] When Lummi John Alexis was arrested for reef net fishing without a license in 1916, he appealed his conviction to the state supreme court and lost.[143] Believing the federal court would be more likely to recognize treaty fishing rights, Alexis and his attorney seriously weighed appealing to the federal court system. When the U.S. Supreme Court ruled that members of the Seneca tribe had to conform to New York State fishing laws in 1916, however, Alexis and his attorneys abandoned the case.[144]

Native peoples north of the border did not fare much better. As the commercial fishery grew in significance, the DMF increasingly restricted Indian fishing and fewer Natives found work in the industry as the years passed. The first regulations in British Columbia were similar to those issued in Washington State. In 1878 the DMF outlawed fishing with nets in fresh and tidal waters as well as using drift nets that obstructed more than one-third of a river; both were common Native fishing methods. Because early fisheries officials recognized a limited Native right to fish, however, these regulations were generally not enforced unless the Indians were in direct competition with whites.[145]

The DMF's changing policies on licensing and on the Indians' rights to fish for subsistence further pushed B.C. Indians out of the industrial fishery. The DMF began to require commercial fishing licenses in 1881, and Native fishermen held six hundred of the seven hundred licenses issued before 1887.[146] In 1888, Dominion officials created the Indian food fishery concept and argued that Indians could either fish commercially with a license or they could fish for food. Native peoples could not sell or trade fish intended for personal use.[147] The DMF's experiment with limited licensing between 1889 and 1892 then led to a serious reduction in the number of licensed Indians fishing on and around the Fraser River, but their numbers rebounded somewhat when the agency abandoned that system. Still, due to an increase of white and Japanese fishermen, B.C. Indians made up just 12 percent of the commercial fishing fleet by the early 1900s.[148] At the same time, fishery guardians began to destroy Native weirs, arrested Indians for selling fish without a license, and tried to control where some Indians fished by refusing them licenses.[149] "The Indians have been barricading the rivers for years and years without molestation," the *Vancouver Province* complained in 1904, "and the wonder is that the sockeye is not memorialized in the national museum as a plaster cast of an extinct migratory fish once plentiful on this coast."[150]

Like their counterparts south of the border, the indigenous people of British Columbia complained, appealed to federal authorities, and sometimes physically prevented fishery guardians from dismantling their fishing structures, but the DMF continued to suppress Indian fishing.[151] After a rock slide at Hell's Gate in 1913 prevented spawning salmon from moving upriver, for example, the DMF prohibited all fishing on the river—even Indian subsistence fishing.[152] In 1918, when word spread that Fisheries Commissioner F. H. Cunningham had declared the Indians were the greatest enemy to salmon on the Fraser, a contingent of Indians from the Chilliwack area traveled to Vancouver to confront him. The problem, they asserted, was not Indian fishing; the problem was the large number of fish traps in Washington State and the net fishermen at the mouth of the river.[153] In fact, while the DMF kept the Native food fishery closed until 1922 as a result of the slide, they placed no restrictions on commercial fishing at the mouth of the river.[154] "The way they [the regulations] are now, our people cannot do anything without violating some law," Cowichan Chief Joe Kukahalt asserted to the Royal Commission on Indian Affairs in 1913. "They cannot get their Grub anywhere without being subject to some law. No matter what they try to take for food they get into trouble about it."[155]

Assaults on Indian fishing locations, rights, and methods occurred on both sides of the forty-ninth parallel as industry players with the most capital vied for control of salmon. Lacking the financial resources needed to remain competetive further hindered Indian participation in the expanding industry. South of the international border, hundreds of fish traps blocked Native fishing sites and forced tribes who once relied on island reef nets and other forms of coastal fishing to the rivers adjacent to their reservations. Even as white and Japanese commercial fishermen moved farther out into the straits and then the ocean to preempt the runs, Indian fishermen were increasingly limited to the interior rivers for their catches of salmon.[156] As one Indian agent noted in 1914: "Many important fishing grounds once owned by [the] Lummi as one body of Indians, are now entirely under control of Fish trap owners, and if Indians were to depend on securing means for consumption from such places, they would eventually starve to death."[157]

In addition to losing their best fishing locations to industrial traps and increasingly well-capitalized, mechanized fishing boats, competition from Asian and white workers in the canneries meant fewer jobs for both Indian fishermen and their wives. A small number of Indians continued to work in canneries for a month or so out of the year, but opportunities for wage work in the industry grew increasingly rare for the Native population surrounding the Salish Sea. Superintendent Buchanan summed up this process of dispossession in a 1914 report: "One by one," the Indians' "richer and remoter fishery locations have been stripped from him while the law held him helpless and resourceless. Driven back to his reservation by the discriminatory operation of the white man's game and fishery laws . . . he is compelled to utilize the fishery locations immediately adjacent to his reservation. Now the aggressive whites are seeking even these and driving him (still under cover of law, perhaps, but none the less certainly) from these."[158] This takeover, largely complete by the early twentieth century, prompted a fifty-nine-year-old Samish man, Sarsfield Kavanaugh, to comment in a 1927 interview: "There is none of the old fishing grounds that I witnessed from my boyhood days that are now used in the same manner that they were used then."[159]

B.C. Natives were able to continue fishing for Fraser River canneries into the early 1900s, but their numbers also declined significantly, especially in the fisheries closest to the forty-ninth parallel. Canadian Indians faced increased hostility from government officials intent on protecting the commercial fishery as well as competition from growing numbers of white and especially Japanese fishermen. According to Indian agent A. W. Vowell in 1902: "The competition which in nearly every field of labour the Indians have to contend against is becoming greater each year; they cannot now, or ever again, expect to make as much money as formerly when they were about the only people available to carry on the limited industries of the country."[160] The numbers are telling: 3,000 people worked in the B.C. salmon fishing industry in 1883, most of them of Native descent; by 1915 the Canadian government issued Fraser River licenses to 1,320 Japanese fishers, 962 whites, and just 295 Indians.[161] Although Native peoples continued to provide crucial labor in the north and on Vancouver Island, in most of the areas closest to the international border, they found it harder to find work fishing.[162] "Whose fault was it that I hadn't sufficient food to eat this year?" Chief Paul Heena pointedly asked the members of a 1914 government land commission: "Who was the cause of our poverty? It is not my fault that today we are poor. I was stopped from providing myself with food. No one should be stopped from providing themselves with food."[163]

Groups from British Columbia that had formerly crossed the border to fish in the San Juan Islands likewise saw their access to long-standing fishing sites jeopardized. "Our people were rich once because we had everything," Dave Elliot of the Saanich related in his 1983 memoir. "When they divided up the country we lost most of our territory. It is now in the State of Washington. They said we would be able to go back and forth when they laid down the boundary, they said it wouldn't make any difference to the Indians. . . . They didn't keep that promise very long . . . and pretty soon we weren't able to go there and fish. Some of our people were arrested for going over there."[164]

The Suttles and the Washington State Department of Fish and Game maps provide snapshots of what the Salish Sea indigenous salmon fishery looked like both before and after it was seized by whites. The images alone offer a mere glimpse of what that momentous transition entailed for the region's Indians. Although Pacific slope Natives adjusted to the formidable changes in their society and remembered their long history of fishing at many locales, the nature of these new white borders—how they were drawn and why—would soon have tremendous consequences for the regional salmon population.

4

Fishing the Line

Border Bandits and Labor Unrest

I N AUGUST 1895, GEORGE WEBBER, THE U.S. CUSTOMS INSPECTOR
at Point Roberts, gazed out at the boundary waters between Washington State and British Columbia and lamented their porous nature. The
Canadian salmon fishing boats that illegally traversed the water border
particularly exasperated him. "If you try to get to them," he wrote, "they
will steam away for a hundred yards across the line and then lay and laugh
at you." The only way to catch them, Webber advised his superiors, was "to
wait your chance, and the first time you can get aboard them in American
waters to make the seizure."[1] Webber's laments echoed repeatedly from
his perch in the salmon-laden waters of northwestern Washington. In his
struggles to uphold U.S. Customs laws and protect this American fishery
from Canadian depredations, he regularly witnessed such illegal border
crossings for salmon. Webber's experiences with the Canadian fishing vessels highlight the critical role the U.S.-Canadian border and the border
environment came to play for the swiftly changing salmon fishing industry and its increasingly non-Native yet ethnically diverse workforce.

As the commercial salmon fishery rose in profitability in the 1890s and
early 1900s, government authorities, canners, and local laborers began to
pay greater attention to the legal and jurisdictional implications of the
Anglo-American border. The 1846 treaty between the United States and
Great Britain had determined that the border ran down the middle of the
Strait of Juan de Fuca, and an 1872 ruling had established the border's cir-
cuitous path through the San Juan Islands. While Native peoples were able

to benefit from initial confusion about their status with regard to the border, government agents soon determined that no Americans could legally fish north of the international line, Canadians could not fish below it, and Asian fishery workers on either side would be met with suspicion no matter what. Fishing over the line might result in equipment and salmon seizures, a fine, or an international diplomatic incident.[2]

Regional fish packers also worried that the growing numbers of white and Japanese fishermen might sell salmon to their competitors on the other side of the border. Because the packers frequently provided boats and gear to fishermen who then signed contracts promising their fish to a specific cannery, the canners claimed that it was a contract violation when fishermen sold salmon to a different cannery. Even the small number of so-called independent fishermen who held noncannery licenses and owned their own gear regularly signed price and delivery agreements.[3] Local authorities generally did not believe such agreements were legally binding, however, so the canners sought other ways to protect their salmon supplies and to direct where fishermen and fish buyers ultimately sold their catch.

Unlike the drawing of Native borders, the imposition of the Anglo-American border was a colonial act completely divorced from issues of salmon conservation and consumption control. Instead, this new border created a spatially, politically, and economically bifurcated fishery that defied easy regulation. Fishery workers who engaged in illegal border fishing and fish sales were undoubtedly interested in fattening their wallets, but other concerns prompted them to break their cannery agreements, breach the forty-ninth parallel, and deliver their fish to whomever they chose. These actions were ways for workers of all ethnicities to take control of some small aspect of their lives, and they embraced it.

THE LINE OF OPPORTUNITY

Once the salmon began running, Point Roberts, an otherwise sleepy, largely uninhabited peninsula that pokes into official Washington State waters just south of the U.S.-Canada border, was transformed as fishers and cannery workers from "up and down Sound" gathered to catch salmon. White, Native, Asian, and a young generational mix of ethnic groups came in hundreds of boats to wait for the salmon. If it was a good year, the sockeye run would fill out by about the middle of July or early August, and the most intense fishing of the season would be under way. The mood, according to one observer, was "very lively" and somewhat frenzied.[4]

The people engaged in the expanding canned salmon industry at the turn of the twentieth century recognized that the international border created two distinct economic, political, and regulatory regimes that could be exploited to their benefit. Many fishers and fish dealers not only freely pursued salmon across the border, they also crossed to get higher prices for their catch despite new and shifting rules against it. Workers of all ethnicities similarly crossed the border if better wages beckoned from the other side. The intense competition among canneries for canning fish and the small number of government agents policing the border led many industry players to embrace the economic possibilities presented by this bifurcated fishery. Had the border been heavily policed and the fishery well managed, it is possible that the Anglo-American border could have contributed to salmon conservation; but instead, the border environment, the lack of effective water patrols, and the border economy facilitated high rates of salmon fishing and movement across the forty-ninth parallel.

Not everyone was a fish thief or a border bandit. Some of the industry players that engaged in border transactions had no desire to transgress the law. Law-abiding buyers sometimes conducted their entire transactions within legal parameters, registering with the relevant customs official and paying the requisite duties on imports and exports. The Canadian steamers *Staffa* and *Fingal*, for example, passed around Point Roberts and anchored in Boundary Bay in 1895. Indian fishers in Washington then filed manifests with the local customs agent before delivering their catch to the waiting vessels. If the B.C. boats were trading honestly, U.S. Customs officers were often willing to be flexible and grant special permits for prearranged pick-ups. As steam scows traveled at extremely slow speeds, agent George Webber allowed those coming into the United States to deliver their fish before reporting to the customs house at Blaine. Forcing the scows to report first, Webber judged, would be a "great hardship" for both the buyers and the sellers and a delay could cause the fish to spoil.[5]

Pacific American Fisheries (PAF), one of the largest packing companies on the American side, prepared extensively for legal purchases from Canadian fishers. Before their departure for B.C. waters, PAF officials and their business partners verified vessel registrations, the necessary customs checkpoints, and the duties on their imported fish. The Pacific Packing & Navigation Company (PP&N) worked with the PAF and advised the canning company to abide by the customs regulations.[6] There were also individual fishers caught crossing the border who did not purposefully break the law. In their quest for salmon, they lost their bearings—especially in thick fog—and found themselves on the wrong side of the line. "Fishermen claim ignorance of the exact location of the boundary line," the *Anacortes American* noted in 1899, "and as fishing grows poorer nearer the Fraser river Canadians are inclined to edge down this way as much as possible and before they really know it, become poachers."[7]

Still, many American fishermen ignored the customs laws and risked seizure or a fine to sell their catch to Canadian canners that offered higher prices. According to one U.S. Customs inspector, such sales were common. He reported that "these fishermen manage to make arrangements with the Fraser River canneries for the disposal of their catch and make a sneak around the point into the Fraser River."[8] Other customs officers witnessed similar exchanges. "The cannerymen of the Fraser river are trying to work Point Roberts for all they can get," Deputy Collector Theodore Spencer observed in 1891. "In consequence of which the cannery people at this place are complaining of them, and I think they have good reasons for it."[9] James Elwood, a cannery operator on the U.S. side, pleaded with one customs officer to prevent the illegal trade. Elwood and his partner J. A. Martin noted: "There is several British Columbia Sloops and Steamers who [are] running from Fraser River B.C. to Point Roberts Wash Ty [Territory] daily for the purpose of getting Salmon and packing them on Fraser River B.C." Because such practices deprived American businesses of fish, they were unacceptable to American canners.[10] Despite the canners' sentiments, American fishermen frequently met interested buyers out on open water and sold their fish across the forty-ninth parallel. "The British Columbia people will try to evade our laws by runing [*sic*] down as far as the line and have the Indians and fishermen bring the fish to them there," Deputy Collector Ellsperman reported in 1895.[11]

Many Canadian fishermen also took advantage of the market competition created by the international line and regularly brought their salmon south to sell to American canners. In an attempt to prevent such sales, B.C. packers successfully pressured the government to periodically place an export embargo on fresh salmon from 1894 on. Fishermen who continued to cross the border were thus willfully breaking both their cannery contracts and the embargo law.[12] Several B.C. canners grumbled to the provincial police about such practices in 1903. An Anglo-British (ABC) Packing

Company representative observed "loads of boats" selling salmon at Point Roberts, and a Fraser River cannery discovered approximately twenty of their boats engaged in similar activities.[13] A few years later, Canadian canner Henry Doyle witnessed forty-three Fraser River Cannery boats selling thousands of sockeye salmon to the George and Barker cannery in Washington State. It was simply impossible, Doyle argued, that the American canners did not know the sockeye were from the Canadian side of the line.[14]

If caught buying fish illegally, American canneries could face serious financial penalties—mainly in the form of back customs duties. The Puget Sound collector of customs fined the Hillside Cannery at Port Townsend $400 for purchasing salmon from B.C. fishermen and failing to make entry in 1905, and the U.S. Customs Service had one of their luckiest years in 1912. Government agents discovered that three canning companies had illegally imported salmon for years and so owed duties ranging from $259 to $1,770. Also in 1912, the George and Barker Cannery on Puget Sound was forced to pay $15,000 in back customs charges on illegally imported B.C. salmon.[15] A fine that large may have made operators think twice about engaging in future illegal transactions.

That salmon tended to be first available on the U.S. side of the border also induced Canadians to fish in American waters and then sell their catch south of the forty-ninth parallel. This occurred repeatedly in the 1890s and early 1900s as both the high prices offered in Washington State and the presence of great numbers of fish lured Canadians into American waters. "There are no salmon as yet in the Fraser," a U.S. Customs agent reported in 1896, "but plenty of them here at the Point [on the American side], so these fishermen will take big chances where sockeyes are worth 22 & 25¢ a piece."[16] Though officials suspected he was trying to avoid paying his debt to a B.C. cannery, Canadian fisherman Phill Robertson insisted that he crossed the border in the early 1900s because fish were scarce and prices better on the U.S. side.[17] Yet other U.S. Customs agents reported frequently seeing "British Columbia Indians" traverse the border to net in American waters in the mid-1890s.[18]

Fishermen on both sides of the border took advantage of the higher prices offered by roving fish buyers as well.[19] By selling to these middlemen, fishers could both receive more money for their catch and pass on the risks involved in crossing the border. According to one group of Canadian canners, "buyers from the American side approach the fishermen, and tempting them with the offer of ready cash for their fish, induce them to sell their catch and defraud the cannery to which they are indebted. Heavy losses have been incurred by the Canners through this practice, and the Government was asked to assist in remedying the evil."[20] This is precisely what occurred at the height of the season in 1904. The Canadian Brunswick Cannery reported an American fish buyer over the line to purchase sockeye salmon for thirty cents apiece—a full ten cents more per fish than that offered by Canadian canners.[21]

Despite a "general understanding" between American and Canadian canners, American fish buyers breached the forty-ninth parallel again in the 1906 season. The Fraser River Canners' Association had agreed to pay twenty-five cents per fish for July and then just twenty cents until the end of the season, but the competition created by the infusion of American buyers quickly drove the price as high as forty cents per fish. "This action on the part of the American packers is much to be deplored," a local trade journal observed, for it could be "readily seen that the canners['] loss resulted in a corresponding gain on the part of the fishermen."[22] According to U.S. Customs agents, Canadian fish buyers also engaged in such practices and frequently dipped southward for fish depending on the timing of the runs and the demand for fish north of the border.[23] Interestingly, sometimes these transactions were planned well in advance. For instance, Washington's PP&N agreed to send employees to buy from some members of the B.C. Fishermen's Union in 1903. "There are all kinds of rumors here regards to opposition and interfering with you," the union representative warned the Americans, "but nothing definite."[24]

A number of issues influenced the direction of this transborder trade, and shifting conditions could redirect or even reverse the flow of fresh salmon over just one season. Import duties and export embargoes created particularly complex scenarios, especially when both were in place. When the U.S. government removed the duty on imported raw salmon in 1903, American cannery representatives immediately traveled up the Fraser River proclaiming their willingness to buy salmon at prices higher than those offered by the Canadians.[25] To prevent Americans from repeating that performance the following year, the Canadian government enacted an export embargo on fresh salmon in 1904.[26] The Americans then considered an export embargo of their own in an attempt to restrict American fishermen's sales to Canadian packers.[27] Annual changes in duties and embargoes affected the fines that attended illegal border buying as well as the going price for fish, and fishermen had to consider such economic concerns before deciding whether or not to cross the border.

Salmon behavior and the industry's supply needs further complicated these scenarios. The life cycles of the different Pacific salmon species also contributed to price shifts and the direction of worker movements. Sockeye runs are especially abundant every four years.[28] So prices for the fish were higher in the off-years when the fish were less numerous. The path of the salmon runs with respect to the border was also important, as it determined who had ready access to the bulk of the runs. In addition, the number of canneries and fish traps operated each season could likewise determine the directional flow of fish across the border. If more canneries were operating north of the border, then demand for fish might be higher in B.C. that year and the fishers likely to receive higher prices for their fish. Similarly, if a smaller number of traps were operated in Puget Sound, fish supplies overall could be lower and prices adjusted accordingly.

Still, both fishermen and fish dealers appear to have been able to manipulate the bifurcated fish market and the competition it generated to get a better price for salmon.[29] "You didn't have too much trouble getting rid of your fish," one retired fisherman recalled. "There were buyers out there and they were all after fish. . . . What you could do was look for the best market, the highest price. If one paid a penny more a day, you went to him."[30] According to a Canadian newspaper, B.C. fishermen were sorely tempted to sell their fish to American canners in the 1900 season, "and some of them did well at it."[31] In 1912, B.C. buyers purchased salmon from American fishers near Cape Flattery, and the competition between Canadian and American canners succeeded in driving up the prices then offered the U.S. fishermen.[32] Similar circumstances emerged in 1915, when American boats bought up salmon from B.C. fishers. According to the *Pacific Fisherman*, "in some instances these purchases were so heavy, and the price offered so high, that most of the Canadian canners were unable to compete and had to shut down."[33] U.S. fish buyers again undercut the Canadian canners a few years later by offering much better rates to Fraser River fishermen.[34]

WORKING THE LINE

Which workers engaged in such illicit border crossings changed over time as the burgeoning canned salmon industry attracted a wide variety of ethnic groups to the West Coast. By 1900, Washington boasted an extremely diverse population, with 22 percent of its residents listed as foreign-born; the average for the entire country at that time was just 14 percent. Whites and Asians constituted the bulk of these new immigrants, and these groups played increasingly important roles in the canning industry of the greater Salish Sea as the years passed.[35]

Although workers of all ethnicities took advantage of the opportunities the border created, the way that government officials and the larger public viewed their movements differed according to ethnicity. European, Euro-American, Euro-Canadian, and Native workers moved fairly freely across the forty-ninth parallel unless they were suspected of smuggling salmon or other contraband.[36] By the 1890s and early 1900s, whites generally understood the geography of Indian family and kinship ties and knew that although relatives would visit across the border, it was unlikely there would be a large-scale migration of Native peoples to either country. Some whites likewise still feared the local indigenous population and were hesitant to take firm steps to hinder their mobility.[37] Instead, whites referred to the dwindling Native population as a "dying race" that would, in time, simply cease to exist.[38] The same could not be said for the growing number of Asian immigrants arriving in these western borderlands. Whites thought of Asian workers as outsiders and a growing menace to white society and white worker success in the West. As both Canada and the United States passed increasingly strict immigration and head-tax laws after the 1880s, Asian workers faced far more risk in their border crossings than white or Native peoples did. In spite of these challenges, Japanese fishermen and Japanese and Chinese cannery workers also finessed the limited flexibility the border offered in pursuit of higher prices, more jobs, and higher wages.

Chinese immigrants began working in the salmon canneries on the Columbia River in the 1870s, but it was not until the 1880s and 1890s that they came to work in northwestern Washington, British Columbia, and Alaska.[39] Because of their relative mobility up and down the coast, precise or consistent numbers regarding the Chinese population are elusive. In two separate reports, the Canadian government estimated that more than ten thousand Chinese lived in British Columbia in 1884, and in 1885 the Department of Marine and Fisheries (DMF) reported 1,157 worked in the salmon canneries of the province. By 1901 the B.C. Chinese population had increased to sixteen thousand. A year later, government officials estimated that approximately six thousand Chinese labored in the salmon process-ing plants throughout B.C., but most worked on the Fraser.[40] Chinese can-nery workers migrated to Washington in significant numbers as well, but because Washington's canneries mechanized faster than B.C.'s, fewer Chi-nese worked there.[41] While the population of Chinese people in western Washington also grew, precise numbers—especially of those who toiled in the canneries—are also difficult to confirm. One source estimates that 550 Chinese lived in Seattle in 1876, but that 300 of them were itinerant labor-ers. In 1886, the year the white community engaged in anti-Chinese riots and forcibly removed many of them from the city, Seattle's Chinese resi-dent population had reached 500.[42] By 1902 the number of Chinese in the entire state was 3,629, and 1,725 Chinese and Japanese reportedly worked in regional salmon canneries.[43]

Hiring Chinese workers held special appeal for canners because of the Chinese labor contract system. Chinese-owned agencies had supplied workers on a contract basis for other industries since the 1850s, so extend-ing the same services to the salmon-packing plants made good business sense.[44] As the canners, contractors, and Chinese employees had negoti-ated various aspects of the contract system on the Columbia River, the pro-cedures were fairly well established by the time more workers were needed farther north. Canners paid contractors to hire Chinese crews and a Chi-nese "boss" responsible for managing the workers. The contractors trans-ported, fed, housed, and paid the workers, relieving the cannery owner from such day-to-day managerial problems and the communication dif-ficulties that might arise. By the 1880s the contracts included seasonal and daily pack guarantees, as well as provisions for hiring extra workers. If the pack fell short of the guaranteed quota, the company could refuse to pay the balance of the contract.[45]

Although packers came to rely heavily on skilled Chinese cannery workers, immigration restrictions on both sides of the border gradually limited their number by the early 1900s. The Chinese Exclusion Act of 1882, renewed in 1892 and made permanent in 1902, soon reduced the numbers of Chinese immigrants entering the United States. The Chinese laboring population in the country gradually declined as workers aged, died, or returned to China.[46] As Chee Foo, a Chinese merchant and labor contrac-tor in Portland, Oregon, observed in 1902, it "is hard to get twenty men now where I used to get 400, though I pay half more now. There are not half as many Chinese here now as ten years ago."[47] In 1906 another Chinese labor contractor reported that Chinese cannery workers "were so scarce that many of the plants would have to be content with Japanese."[48] The number of Chinese entering the United States was also reduced because of "the Canadian Agreement." Starting in the 1890s, the United States made arrangements for Canada to send all U.S.-bound Chinese in Canada to specific border points where they would be inspected according to standards of entry.[49] The strengthening of other laws further shored up the border for Chinese migrants. Rather than an outright ban, Canada instead imposed increasingly prohibitive head taxes on the Chinese coming into British Columbia. Although the head tax was just fifty dollars in 1885, B.C. successfully pressured the Dominion government to raise it to a hundred dollars in 1900 and then to five hundred dollars per person in 1904. Such high fees further deterred Chinese immigration into British Columbia.[50]

The gradual introduction of new canning technology in the early 1900s and 1910s also contributed to the decline of Chinese cannery workers. New inventions like automated washing machines, the Smith Butchering Machine (known as the "Iron Chink"), and can-filling and can-soldering machines gradually displaced the small numbers of remaining Chinese workers. This transition took several decades and varied according to region and establishment.[51] Skilled Chinese butchers were often still in demand in some canneries in B.C. and on the Columbia River because they packed high-quality, hand-packed canned salmon, but the total number of Chinese cannery workers in western Washington declined significantly by the 1910s.[52] As the *Anacortes American* observed in 1910, the remaining Chinese workers in Washington State were "like the soldiers of our civil war, gray and bent with the load of the passing year."[53]

Anti-Chinese immigration laws and growing government efforts to police the western borderlands meant that smuggling workers across the border soon became a profitable enterprise. Although Chinese labor contractors and merchants orchestrated some of these movements, Chinese individuals also moved across the border of their own initiative.[54] Due to the specific documentary requirements of the U.S. Exclusion Act and B.C.'s head-tax legislation, the business of smuggling and forging immigration papers became both lucrative and common in this region, especially for entry into the United States.[55] In the 1890s, for instance, Chinese elites colluded with government officials to run an extensive opium and labor smuggling system between British Columbia and Portland. This elaborate scheme not only involved a senior U.S. Customs official and a

U.S. Treasury Department agent, but the ringleaders also arranged to pay the Oregon notary public and a local attorney to print fake Chinese certificates.[56] Legally documented Chinese immigrants entering the United States likewise sent their papers back over the line so that their fellow countrymen could use them.[57]

Lured by higher wages or better work conditions, individual Chinese workers found creative ways to sneak across the line. In both 1901 and 1902 local newspapers reported "Canadian Chinese" crossing the border to take advantage of higher wages in Puget Sound.[58] Members of the Lummi tribe watched as two canoes ferried sixteen Chinese past their reservation on the way to B.C. late one night.[59] One Chinese man tried to capitalize on local authorities' ignorance and claimed he was Japanese.[60] Once across, some Chinese cleverly sought the legal sanctuary offered by Indian reservations and negotiated with local residents for canoe passage to a specific cannery or logging camp.[61] After catching twenty Chinese laborers attempting to come into the country illegally in 1890, James Swan, a local government employee, urged Congress to fine them each one hundred dollars. As it was, he believed, they were simply sent back to Canada at the government's expense and would undoubtedly try again. "The Marshall told me today," Swan wrote his superiors, "that he knows a Chinaman who has been sent to Victoria three times."[62] Well into the early 1900s, customs agents and immigration inspectors were catching groups of Chinese illegally crossing the border.[63] In its 1902 report the Immigration Bureau worried that the "Canadian border has become the most prolific field for the introduction into the United States of the Chinese coolie."[64]

Because they did not work as fishermen in the U.S.-Canada borderland region and so would have likely lacked extensive familiarity with boundary waters, many Chinese immigrants paid smugglers to sneak them across the border in fishing boats and canoes. "There is no doubt in my mind," the U.S. Customs agent at Port Angeles observed in the mid-1880s, "but there is a compleate [sic] organization in Victoria to sup[p]ly the demand for Cooly [sic] labour in this territory and Oregon."[65] Agent A. L. Blake echoed these sentiments. "This Chinese immigration is no fiction now," he reported in 1883, "I believe they are coming to our side every day, by water and by land, and by boats and canoes . . . it seems to me the Restriction Act, is almost worthless."[66] He was right. The Exclusion Act existed on paper in the 1880s, but until Canada and the United States devoted more resources to policing the border in the 1890s and early 1900s, people could fairly easily find ways across the forty-ninth parallel. In 1901, U.S. immigration inspector Charles Snyder reported that two "Chinese padrones" at the Alaska Packers Association cannery on Point Roberts were smuggling in Chinese workers at one hundred dollars per head, and local fishermen confirmed that smuggling Chinese was big business.[67]

One of the most notorious smugglers was Larry "Pig Iron" Kelly, whom Tacoma police caught bringing over six Chinese laborers in 1902. Local residents later recalled that when smugglers like Kelly were pursued, they dumped their Chinese customers overboard or abandoned them on one of the San Juan or Gulf islands. When interviewed by a reporter in 1911, Orcas Island resident John Gray insisted that the stories about Larry Kelly once dumping twelve Chinese overboard were true. "How could he handle so many . . . Kelly never let a Chinaman on b[oar]d without hog tieing [sic] him," Gray explained, "that was part of the bargain."[68] Kelly's nickname apparently resulted from a rumor that he once actually used pig iron to weigh down several of his customers before tossing them overboard. Elmer Vogt, a retired fisherman, remembered that the smugglers put the Chinese in sacks in the hold of a boat. If any patrols gave chase, "they just heaved the Chinamen overboard. There was enough weight, rocks in the sacks, and down they went," Vogt told his interviewer in the 1970s.[69] How many Chinese workers successfully crossed the border or met a watery end in the cold straits is hard to say, but the evidence suggests that such crossings grew less frequent as the numbers of Chinese in the region dwindled and as immigration and border policing efforts increased in intensity and overall effectiveness.[70]

The growing scarcity of Chinese labor in the early 1900s and the expansion of the canned salmon industry into Puget Sound, Alaska, and northern B.C. meant that the demand for additional sources of labor was on the rise by the late 1890s and early 1900s.[71] Although canners continued to hire Native people in some areas of British Columbia, Washington, and Alaska, their availability varied greatly according to location, timing, and season. The influx of whites into the region meant that western Washington canners with facilities close to coastal towns and growing cities were able to draw on this new population and hire increasing numbers of white women and girls to process the fish, but often there simply were not enough people to fill the available positions.[72] Because of their smaller population and the remote locations of many of their facilities, British Columbia canners did not hire white women for cannery work on the Fraser until 1905.[73] Labor scarcity on both sides of the border soon led to changes in the ethnic composition of what were still called the "Chinese labor crews," especially in canneries farther from towns and urban centers.

The arrival of larger numbers of Japanese in the United States from both Japan and Hawai'i and the need for labor meant that Japanese workers were soon employed in the canned salmon industry all along the Pacific Coast. Although a few Japanese immigrated to the Pacific Northwest in the early 1890s, the strict emigration policies of the Japanese government before 1885 limited the number of entrants. A small number of Japanese "school boys" came to study in the United States and Canada in the 1890s, but it was not until the late 1890s and early 1900s that large numbers of Japanese laborers arrived on the West Coast of the United States.[74] While more than 11,000 Japanese arrived at Canadian ports between July 1, 1899, and August 30, 1900, many did not remain; in fact, the Japanese population of B.C. in 1901 was estimated at only 4,544.[75] More than 27,000 Japanese people were admitted to the United States between 1891 and 1900, but few of them were laborers because of tightened restrictions on emigration companies in Japan. In 1890 there were just 125 Japanese in Seattle; by 1900 Seattle was home to 2,990 Japanese residents, and Washington State reported a Japanese population of 5,617—second only to that of California.[76]

As many Chinese contractors found themselves unable to fill their contracts with Chinese workers, they began hiring Japanese laborers, particularly in Alaska and Washington. Initially, since canners preferred the Chinese for their experience and skill, contractors could not completely supplant Chinese crews with Japanese. In 1909, for instance—a big year for sockeye—western Washington canners employed Japanese workers for nearly 50 percent of their cannery crews, but in off-years many of these facilities were able to rely on smaller Chinese crews. The more mechanized plants in Washington did not need the more expensive, skilled Chinese, so they hired greater numbers of unskilled Japanese laborers.[77] As E. B. Deming, the manager of the PAF noted in 1902, "It is realized now that Chinese are not cheap labour; they are skilled and don't have to work for little money."[78] The situation in B.C. differed in that many Japanese men worked as fishermen or boat pullers rather than in the canneries. Henry Bell-Irving, a prominent canner, reported that his company employed nearly 1,200 workers in six canneries on the Fraser River in the 1901 season: 180 whites, 300 Native women (also known as "Kloochmen"), and the balance

Chinese. According to Bell-Irving, "scarcely any Japanese and Indians are employed inside the canneries."[79] Although the Chinese in B.C. were also declining in number, they remained the primary cannery labor group for another decade immediately north of the border.[80] As a result, the Chinese also retained considerable power in negotiations with B.C. canners. In the late 1890s Chinese workers at one New Westminster cannery forced the cannery owner to fire fifteen to twenty white employees in favor of the Chinese.[81] Similarly, in 1909, Chinese workers in B.C. refused to work at the prices offered, and threatened to go on strike. As 1909 was a "big year" in the four-year cycle of the sockeye, these men were in an excellent bargaining position.[82]

While other ethnic groups began to work in the salmon industry, most newcomers headed north to the canneries in Alaska. Filipinos, Koreans, Hawaiians, Chileans, Portuguese, Puerto Ricans, Peruvians, Arabs, and some African Americans were working in Alaska canneries by the 1910s, but few of them seem to have stayed to work in northwestern Washington and southwestern B.C.[83] A few immigrants from Eastern India entered sawmill and cannery work in B.C. and Washington State in the early 1900s. Though small numbers arrived just after 1900, more than two thousand Eastern Indians came to B.C. in 1906. Labeled "Hindoos" by local whites, the newcomers consisted primarily of Sikhs from the Punjab region. Because of their origins, these immigrants could potentially take advantage of their legal status as British subjects and could vote. As a result, some B.C. residents feared their presence more than they did the Chinese and Japanese. "Is it true that the day of poor Lo as a cannery hand is passing?" a Vancouver newspaper quipped in 1900. "Must, indeed, the long-queued son of the Celestial Empire some day soon give way to the swarthy man from India for capability and desirability in the packing industry?"[84] Despite this journalist's fervor, the Eastern Indian populations in B.C. and Washington remained low, and the number of Eastern Indian Cannery workers appears to have been quite small. For example, the Imperial Cannery employed twenty "Hindoos" in 1910 as compared to ninety Chinese, fifty B.C. Natives, and twelve whites. In the same year the Currie & McWilliams Cannery hired fifteen Eastern Indians, sixty-five Chinese, twenty-eight B.C. Natives, and twelve whites.[85]

Many Japanese who arrived in British Columbia at the turn of the twentieth century managed to obtain work as fishermen north of the forty-ninth parallel. In 1896 Japanese fishers held 452 of the 3,533 fishing licenses available; by 1901, 1,985 of 4,722 provincial fishing licenses were given to Japanese boats. Since each boat held two men, nearly four thousand Japanese may have engaged in fishing on the river.[86] Most of the Japanese fishers initially worked on the Fraser River in the major cannery town of Steveston, which by the turn of the century had a resident Japanese population of more than two thousand.[87] At the beginning of the fishing season, canners negotiated with Japanese "bosses" who managed the Japanese fishers. The Japanese bosses sometimes owned portions of the fishing gear used by the fishers and earned a commission based on the catch of their men; in return, they took responsibility for the debts of their charges.[88] The canners would negotiate advances—either as cash or supplies—and, according to the president of United Canners Limited, the Japanese were then "morally bound to sell us their fish."[89]

How the Japanese in British Columbia came to outnumber white and Native fishermen by the early 1900s is likely explained by the demographic history of the province, the industry's need for labor in the 1890s, and the DMF's discriminatory approaches to Indian fishing. Compared with B.C., Washington experienced a higher rate of immigration in the late nineteenth century, but there were more canneries in British Columbia in the 1880s and 1890s. As a result, Canadian canners found themselves with a serious need for labor but fewer local residents. This situation, coupled with the fact that many of the Japanese immigrating into British Columbia in the 1890s and early 1900s were experienced fishermen from fishing villages in eastern Japan (especially a village called Mihama-mura, then known as Mio-mura), may explain how Japanese men were able to move into these positions with little reaction from the local white population.[90] In fact, it was only when whites realized that the Japanese dominated the fishing and boat-building industries that they started protesting Japanese involvement.[91]

The need for fishermen, fish trap builders, and trap operators in western Washington was likewise significant by the 1890s, but the burgeoning white population was more able to fill those positions. Washington canners' reliance on fish traps would also have meant less demand for fishermen. Although it is possible that some Asians attempted to work as fishermen south of the forty-ninth parallel, evidence from the Columbia River fishery suggests that white fishermen used intimidation and violence to dissuade Asians from fishing. It was "the unwritten law of the Columbia that any Chinaman daring to fish for salmon is to be killed on sight," one government official noted in the late 1880s. "So they do not fish."[92]

Like their Chinese predecessors, Japanese fishers and cannery workers also often crossed the border to pursue seasonal work opportunities and higher wages, and Japanese fishermen were known to engage in illegal border fish sales. Although there were no specific legal restrictions on Japanese border crossings before 1907, officials from various agencies and regional white residents with strong anti-Asian leanings were very concerned about the movements of Japanese laborers. The result was that the Japanese began to evolve clandestine ways to cross the border.[93] According to U.S. Customs inspector Samuel Walker in 1900, "The fisheries in British Columbia are now closing, and there are more than three thousand Japanese laborers at this time on the Frazer [sic] river fishing banks, awaiting favorable opportunity to enter our district by stealth." Although Walker's figures were probably exaggerated, he claimed to have caught more than thirty Japanese immigrants in just a few days' time and deported twenty-six.[94] A regional newspaper reported more than a hundred Japanese reentering the United States following the fishing season the following year.[95] "No one told me before I arrived that I could get work," Kutiro Akure admitted following his capture in 1901, "but I have been here three times and go back to British Columbia in the fishing season."[96] Unlike the Chinese, many Japanese who worked as fishermen in Canada either owned their own boats or had access to one, and it may have been easier for Japanese workers to cross the border or to hitch rides. In fact, when hundreds of Japanese fishers in the United States went to work on the Fraser for the 1903 season, immigration officials reported that a favorite method for entering Canada was by boat from Point Roberts.[97]

Similar accounts persisted for the next decade and suggest that many Japanese crossings were attempts to garner higher wages, fish prices, and greater numbers of salmon. Customs officials caught two Japanese over the line in 1907 and believed that a dozen more small boats carrying Japanese workers had landed near Bellingham, Washington. "It is an easy matter," the *Bellingham Herald* observed, "for a fishing boat to slip from the Canadian side take a cruise among the islands and when conditions are favorable land their cargoes of Japs on this side of the line."[98] In 1909 the *Vancouver World* nervously reported that because Japanese fishermen were dissatisfied with the salmon prices offered by B.C. packers, they were "swarming toward the boundary with the intention of worming their way to Seattle by the various 'underground' routes."[99] This reporter was only partly correct, however, since the newly invigorated U.S. Immigration Bureau refused to allow hundreds of Japanese laborers across the land border that year.[100] Still, the mobility and actions of Japanese fishermen out on the water were harder to control. Japanese fishermen contracted to B.C. facilities were caught selling salmon to roving American buyers who ventured northward for fish that same season.[101] Canadian canners responded by printing notices—in both Japanese and English—that warned their contract fishers to sell only to the canneries listed in their agreements.[102] A few years later, U.S. patrols caught a total of nine Japanese boats illegally fishing over the border and immediately fined two of them $250 each.[103]

Japanese fishermen who crossed the boundary for the fishing season also learned how to manipulate government documentation to qualify for the fishing papers needed in British Columbia. DMF regulations required that all fishers hold licenses, and one had to be a British subject to receive a license. After declaring their intention to reside in Canada, newcomers received naturalization papers, which allowed them to apply for a fishing license. Bribing government officials and swapping papers became common practices that enabled greater numbers of Japanese from both Japan and the United States to receive licenses.[104] It was also typical for Japanese residing in the United States—and, when fares were reasonably low, in Japan—to cross into British Columbia for the fishing season to work as boat pullers.[105]

As with the Chinese, restrictive legislation on both sides of the border gradually limited the number of Japanese and Eastern Indians allowed into both the United States and B.C. In response to white protests against continuing Asian immigration, the U.S. government passed a law prohibiting aliens from landing in the United States if their passports were issued for a different destination. This 1907 law, together with the Gentlemen's Agreement the United States secured with the Japanese government, quickly reduced the numbers of Japanese immigrants entering U.S. ports.[106] Canada also worked out an informal agreement with the Japanese government to restrict the immigration of Japanese laborers to Canada in 1899. Worried about continued Japanese arrivals, however, the provincial legislature passed several of its own immigration laws after 1900 that attempted to limit the entry of Japanese and Eastern Indians. As the Canadian federal government reserved the right to enact immigration laws, it disavowed most of the province's efforts to control Asian immigration. Still, the passage and implementation of B.C.'s Natal Act of 1900—which required immigrants to submit to an English language test—forced the

Japanese government to commit to greater emigration restrictions, and the number of Japanese entering B.C. decreased over the next decade. The Canadian government's commitment to their own Gentlemen's Agreement with the Japanese government in 1908 further limited the number of Japanese emigrants to four hundred per year. Due to both the Natal Act and their icy reception, Eastern Indian immigration declined in the early 1900s as well.[107]

Before World War I, the ethnic groups that lived, worked, and moved through the Canada-U.S. borderlands developed ways to use the economic competition created by the international boundary and the nature of the physical environment to their advantage. Although they were harassed and faced increasingly strict laws against their mobility, Asian workers also defied attempts by both states to shore up their borders. Using the economic and regulatory disjunctures created by the forty-ninth parallel to increase fish supplies, raise monetary returns, and expand available job opportunities became a common aspect of life in this western fishery. For a time, the nature of these Pacific borderlands seemingly offered something for everyone.

BUILDING HOUSES OF LABOR

The desire for economic gain definitely factored into workers' decisions to sell fish to other than their designated cannery. It also encouraged them to fish illegally and to clandestinely cross the border. Yet all of these acts could translate into more than just extra money. Because of the ethnic and racial diversity of the industrial workforce and the competitiveness that infused interethnic relations, the ability of fishery workers to cooperate with each other in their negotiations with the canners was severely limited. Although these workers tried to create viable labor organizations on both sides of the border, the divisions of ethnicity and gear type inhibited their ability to consistently and collectively band together against their employers. The canners' attempts to cooperate in lowering prices or to limit border sales further exacerbated the tensions between workers and their employers. As unionizing efforts faltered in the 1890s and early 1900s, the social borders already erected between ethnic groups and between classes solidified. Some labor leaders flirted with socialism and the International Workers of the World, while others sought to use the legislative arena to influence work conditions, but the workforce remained largely nonunionized. Fishermen and other fish workers were undoubtedly frustrated at their inability to control the terms of their employment, at their failure to form a lasting labor organization, and, especially for whites and the few Native peoples still working in the industry, at the ongoing presence of Chinese and Japanese workers.

Although workers had difficulty navigating the turbulent waters of labor relations, their knowledge of the marine environment facilitated their ability to impact the distribution of salmon supplies. Fishermen had to abide by the timing and routes of the annual migration cycles of the various salmon species, cope with changing weather conditions, learn to read and navigate the tides and passages throughout their fishing area, and catch the fish themselves. Their skills on the water and the physical environment itself offered many workers ways to transgress both the restrictive economic boundaries created by their cannery contracts and the national and regulatory boundaries created by the state. Cannery workers likewise chopped up fish, disposed of fish offal, and used other transformed natural resources to pack fish away in cans. All of these actions required laborers to engage with their physical environment and the salmon that were so central to their work; ignorance of both could mean a poor catch or even death. Traversing the border thus provided workers with a way to use their knowledge of place to take charge of their own labor in an industry that tried to both economically and physically circumscribe its workforce.

The ethnic and racial diversity that distinguished the Pacific slope by the turn of the twentieth century impeded the formation of a lasting and effective interethnic labor organization. In addition to the influx of Asian laborers, a variety of ethnic white immigrants arrived in the region. While those groups of whites were not always unified, Indians and whites saved their strongest feelings of animosity for Asians. Many white newcomers hailed from European countries and from the midwestern United States and Canada. Norwegians and Croatians in particular came to play important roles within the canned salmon industry south of the forty-ninth parallel. Although Scandinavians constituted 25 percent of Washington State's foreign-born population by 1910, Norwegians made up just a small percentage of that total. Still, canners and trap owners hired primarily male Norwegian immigrants to work their fish traps, as these men often had experience with traps in the Great Lakes region. Beginning in 1880, increasing numbers of ethnic Croatian immigrants from Austria, the Dalmatian Coast, and Croatia—then referred to as "Slavonians"—also arrived in Washington. Large numbers of Greeks and Italians began filtering into the area as well.[108]

In contrast, immigrants from Britain and eastern Canada predominated in British Columbia. In 1901, 20 percent of the provincial population hailed from Britain; Americans made up 10 percent, Asians 11, and other Europeans just 5 percent. Fifty-five percent of all B.C. residents were Canadian-born, a figure that included twenty-five thousand Native people.[109] Contemporary observers noted that Newfoundlanders, Norwegians, Finns, Greeks, some Basques, and Adriatic Islanders built communities along the lower Fraser River and worked in the fishing industry. Immigrant Swedes, and, from the 1870s on, a small number of people of African descent (almost all of whom came from the United States) also worked in the B.C. fishing industry.[110] Gradually, these groups built "scow houses"—floating homes on rafts—that filled the south arm of the Fraser River, from New Westminster to the coast. According to one visitor in the 1890s, "Europe, Asia, Africa and America here shake hands and live together in such a colourful mixture as cannot be found anywhere else."[111]

Because of the political beliefs and labor organizing experiences of many immigrants to the Northwest, the labor movement was complicated and robust, with much transborder organizing and interaction between local laborers. Still, unionizing efforts were stronger and more successful in the region's mining and timber industries. Many fishermen worked on a seasonal basis and tended to divide themselves according to ethnicity and gear type. These conditions did not foster many alliances. While fish workers did try to form labor unions and collectively negotiate with the canners throughout the 1890s and early 1900s, these remained periodic gestures wracked by interethnic conflict.[112]

Groups of B.C. fishermen began to form labor organizations beginning in the 1890s. Fearing that licensing changes would threaten their privileged position in the job hierarchy, white contract fishers organized a fishermen's union and then struck at the start of the 1893 season. The strong anti-Japanese stance of this early fishermen's organization and their inability to truly speak for fishermen working varying wage systems essentially limited their appeal to other than contract workers. Although negotiations with canners and efforts to promote licensing legislation brought different groups of fishermen together for a time during the 1890s and they were occasionally able to influence piece rates, a larger labor organization was not formed again until the turn of the twentieth century.[113]

NATIONALITY	NUMBER	NATIONALITY	NUMBER
Canadian	286	Austrian	42
English	139	American	11
Scotch	90	Hollander	1
Indian	295	Chilian [sic]	4
Greek	53	Italian	8
Norwegian	143	Russian	12
Swede	42	Dane	4
Jap [sic]	1,320	French	5
German	9	Turk	1
Finlander	47	Hawaian [sic]	1
French Canadian	17	Philippino	1
Icelander	3	Pole	1
Irish	15	Welsh	1
Spanish	25	Maltese	1

Whites 962, Indians 295, Japs 1,320

TABLE 4.1   Nationality of Fraser River Fishing License Holders, 1915
Source: Cited in Harris, *Landing Native Fisheries*, 136. Original source: F. H. Cunningham, chief inspector of fisheries, to D. N. McIntyre, provincial deputy commissioner of fisheries, August 26, 1915, file 157, box 18, GR-0435, B.C. Archives.

White fishermen built on their active participation in the B.C. legislative arena and formed the B.C. Fishermen's Union in response to the canners' creation of a cooperative organization in 1899. As the canners' new group—the Fraser River Canners' Association—proposed to both regulate production and fix fish prices, the fishermen believed that they too needed an organization to protect their interests. Starting in New Westminster and Vancouver, white fishermen gradually united into one fishermen's union under the leadership of Frank Rogers. Likely a result of Rogers's radical views and recognition that Japanese participation was crucial, union leaders and members from the original Vancouver organization fought for the inclusion of both Indians and Japanese. The small number of Native fishers still active on the Fraser generally joined the union, but persuading the Japanese to sign up was a different matter. Although Rogers personally tried to enlist the Japanese by arranging a meeting with the bosses at Steveston, the white labor movement's history of anti-Japanese sentiment and renewed public protests against the Japanese in B.C. made the Japanese fishermen understandably hesitant.[114] The language barrier may also have been a factor, as many of the Japanese fishermen did not speak English. In the end the Japanese refused the invitation and formed their own organization: the Japanese Fishermen's Benevolent Society—or, in Japanese, the Gyosha Dantai.[115]

In 1900 white, Native, and Japanese fishermen joined forces to strike for higher fish prices, but despite an initial unified front their ranks soon split along ethnic lines. As many of the Japanese were in debt to the canners and depended on fishing for their subsistence, their vulnerability forced them back to work sooner than the indigenous and white fishers.[116] Needless to say, when the Japanese gave in, already fragile interethnic cooperative efforts faltered. Tensions heightened further when the canners—using both exaggerated and fabricated descriptions of the strikers' behavior—persuaded local government officials to call in the militia. Risking loss of income for the season and resentful of Japanese competition, the Native fishermen remained on strike with their white counterparts. "There is no doubt that the imbittered [sic] feeling against the Japanese, stood largely in the way of settlement," the head of the DMF reported to the minister of justice, "and I am of the opinion their presence in such numbers, is the real if not the exciting cause for all or most of the dissatisfaction on the river."[117]

Similar instances of interethnic conflict persisted the following year when the non-Japanese fishermen tried to prevent the Japanese from fishing during the 1901 strike. According to local newspapers, confrontations devolved into fist, oar, and stick fights, as both sides organized their own patrols to protect their respective fleets. When interviewed by the provincial attorney general, one constable reported arresting two Chilean and one black man for trying to stop several Japanese from fishing.[118] Another white fisherman admitted to cutting a net because he thought it belonged to a Japanese-owned vessel. According to a witness in that case, the guilty fisherman asserted that "the Japanese were taking the bread from all the white men" and that he would cut their nets because "that was the only way to do with them."[119] Fishermen on both sides of the strike cut nets, bashed boats, and forcibly removed others from the river. At the height of tensions, twelve armed non-Japanese patrol boats marooned five Japanese boat crews on Bowen Island and, by the end of the strike, two Japanese fishermen had disappeared.[120]

Despite additional strike efforts in 1902 and 1903, ethnic tensions of the same shrill tenor continued and attempts at a unified movement failed.[121]

On the northern B.C. rivers, Japanese and Native fishers sometimes forced each other to cease fishing at gunpoint, and the courts convicted two Haida of murdering a Japanese fisherman in 1902.[122] "Even between Japanese who should help each other there are fights," old-time fisherman Rintaro Hayashi observed, "so you can imagine how it is with fishermen of different nationalities."[123]

Conflicts erupted throughout the early 1900s. Arson attacks devastated B.C.'s Chinatown and destroyed the Chinese and Japanese living quarters at a local cannery in 1907.[124] Although not directly related to the fishing business, a riot later that year further exacerbated race relations in the region.[125] "The best fishing grounds are crowded," fisherman Peter Smith warned Canada's Royal Commission on Chinese and Japanese Immigration in 1902. "If any more Japanese come in there will be bloodshed."[126] B.C. Indians were virulently anti-Japanese because the Japanese fishermen were helping to push Indians out of the industry, especially in the southern reaches of the province. "The Japanese kill us," Chief Harry James of the Skwxwú7mesh tribe complained to the commission. "They are killing Indians, killing whites. My people have no chance to make a living."[127] In 1913 yet another coordinated strike fizzled when an "impregnable organization" of Chinese, Japanese, and whites on the Fraser River fell apart overnight.[128] In 1914 a group of white and Indian fishermen successfully formed the Fraser River Fishermen's Protective Association, but their stated goal of eliminating Asians from the river did not exactly foster a broader sense of worker solidarity.[129] Cooperating across racial boundaries for any extended period of time was clearly a challenge.

The success of labor organizing among fishermen and fish workers in northwestern Washington is much harder to ascertain. Because of the prevalence of fish traps on the U.S. side, there were fewer fishermen overall, and while scattered evidence suggests that there were several organizations for both fishermen and cannery workers that sometimes worked together, none remained in the news for long. The *Seattle Union Record* included a fishermen's union in its union lists in the early 1900s and announced the creation of a separate Fairhaven fishermen's union in one 1902 paper, but by 1904 the fishermen's union office was based in San Francisco.[130] Although Columbia River fishers successfully organized a union in the 1890s, and the San Francisco office became the headquarters for a coast-wide umbrella union that boasted 6,725 members by 1908, it is not clear if this union then represented the men fishing in northwestern Washington for companies based in the Puget Sound region.[131] The United Fishermen of the Pacific approved a constitution in 1906 and had an agency in Seattle, but again details are elusive.[132] LaConner fishermen formed a union in 1907, and purse seiners had apparently tried to organize several times by 1914.[133] Still, when a reporter asked why the purse seiners did not create a union to "do a little dictating to the canners," the seiners replied that "it was impossible to get the seiners to stick together the way they should."[134] Other than these fleeting efforts, Washington fishermen do not appear to have had continuous union representation with the packers of the Salish Sea until the 1930s.[135]

The persistence of interethnic conflicts in western Washington and the repeated calls for canners to cease employing Asians suggest that frustrations similar to those in B.C. plagued the industry south of the border. The widespread anti-Chinese riots of the mid-1880s marked the beginning of decades of conflict between Asians and whites. The white residents of Aberdeen drove the Chinese out of the small town in the early 1890s and only allowed Chinese workers to return in 1906 because a local cannery was desperate for labor.[136] In the early 1900s a near riot occurred at one of the PAF canneries in Bellingham when someone ripped down a Japanese flag that Japanese cannery workers had hung beside the Stars and Stripes.[137] White encroachments on tribal reservation fisheries further contributed to already fraught interethnic relations. Following the B.C. strike of 1900, many Japanese crossed into the United States, but the residents of the border town of Blaine forced them back across the line at gunpoint.[138] A few years later, Japanese workers in Blaine chased a white worker out of a cannery for stabbing a fellow Japanese. Blaine's whites then gathered forces to protect the man, and four Japanese workers were injured in the ensuing scuffle.[139]

Such violent encounters did not dissipate with time. In 1909 a conflict between a white and a Japanese worker in an Anacortes cannery devolved into a "rough-and-tumble" fight involving others from both ethnic groups that eventually landed two Japanese workers in jail.[140] Although it is not clear to what degree white fishermen adhered to these ideals, a local central labor council drafted a resolution and legislative bill aimed at preventing intermarriage between whites and nonwhites; the rapid influx of Japanese into the region was cited as their primary motivation.[141] By 1915, due to a rise in overall unemployment, anti-Japanese sentiments peaked, and riots erupted in the cannery towns of Anacortes and Blaine.[142] Soon after, anti-

Japanese agitators blew up one of Blaine's water mains and posted a sign warning employers to cease hiring Japanese workers—or else.[143]

Though similarly discriminated against by the white population, Chinese and Japanese workers rarely saw eye to eye. Chinese laborers failed to support Japanese workers during strikes or incidents such as those described above. White strikers recognized this intra-Asian animosity and in the 1900 B.C. labor dispute actually tried to persuade the Chinese cannery workers to refuse Japanese-caught salmon once the Japanese broke ranks and commenced fishing.[144] Both groups frequently declined to share the same cannery bunkhouse and had significant disagreements over cannery food.[145] "Those who entered the Japanese camps were better off than those who went into a camp containing Chinese," former Japanese cannery worker Hideo Miyazaki recalled. "The Chinese blew their noses with their fingers, spit on the floor and smoked opium in the evening," he complained. "They smelled bad," Miyazaki insisted.[146] Both Miyazaki and Yahachi Suzuki had only negative memories of the food. "We ate dried foods from China which we softened and fried in lard. It was just terrible; probably even 'coolie' meals were better than ours," Suzuki recounted.[147]

The use of different fishing technologies and the fact that many fishermen on the Fraser fished only part of the year further divided fishermen. Fishers of the same ethnicity tended to work the same kinds of equipment; by the early 1900s animosities among purse seiners, gillnetters, and trollers—and thus different ethnic groups—had grown common. Italian, Croatian, and Japanese fishermen dominated the purse seine sector, while primarily English, Scandinavian, and Scottish fishers engaged in trolling and gillnet fishing. As each group tended to hire its own, they further entrenched the ethnic divisions in the industry. After 1900 the few fishermen unions that existed also tended to be grouped according to gear type in a manner similar to the craft union movement championed by the leader of the American Federation of Labor, Samuel Gompers. Although the extent of Gompers's influence on fishery workers is unclear, gillnetters, purse seiners, and trollers organized separately according to their specific "craft." Gillnetters and trollers deplored purse seines as particularly destructive, and all groups lobbied government officials for regulations that would benefit their own type of equipment, so alliances between these groups remained sporadic and tenuous at best.[148] Since many of the fishermen on the Fraser fished only during the sockeye season and worked in other industries for the rest of the year, their interests likewise diverged from those of the year-round, full-time fishermen who increasingly owned their own boats. "Us practical fishermen is killed by the drygoods clerks and counter-jumpers that goes fishing," full-time fisherman G. W. West complained in 1905. "They just does it for a holiday."[149]

These social boundaries were further strengthened by the canners' business practices and the way they treated their workers. The canners' insistence on employing Asian and "alien" workers as well as their efforts to consolidate the canner class into fewer, more powerful entities made their workers wary. Against the wishes of many resident whites and Indians, Canadian canners continued to hire Chinese and Japanese as well as laborers from Washington State.[150] According to Newfoundlander William Rhodes, "the consequence is that we have been sadly disappointed to find that we *cannot* make a *living* with the *existing monopoly* held by the *cannery-men*, and *especially Foreigners* who, invade the river during the fishing season."[151] B.C. fishermen of northern European descent complained about Canadian canners hiring the eastern and southern European fishers who came north from Washington during the sockeye season, but most distressing were the Japanese workers.

Professional, bona fide, white fishermen who were British subjects were not only hard to find, the B.C. canners argued, they were not nearly as efficient as the Japanese. "Were it not for the Japanese," canner Henry Doyle charged, "we could not develop the business as it can and should be developed."[152] One canner claimed that the Japanese fishermen he hired caught 50 percent more salmon than their white counterparts in the industry.[153] Cannery manager E. B. Welsh was more adamant. "Most of the whites we get are the scum of the earth," he asserted. "They steal our boats and nets and give us continual trouble. We did not bring the Japs here, but now that we have them here we'll use them."[154] Although the Japanese did not possess nearly as much influence among canners in Washington State, white and Native workers continued to view their presence and that of the Chinese as potentially threatening. As packers on both sides of the border consolidated their businesses and ignored the complaints of their white and Indian workers, they heightened already existing ethnic and class tensions among the region's workforce.

The various license and payment systems canners negotiated with fishermen from the 1890s on also strained relations between fishermen of different ethnicities and the canners to whom they were contracted. Fishermen negotiated a wide variety of arrangements for leasing gear and

boats, as well as for payment for their catch. Until 1897, B.C. canners generally paid Indian fishermen and boat pullers a set daily wage; they justified
this by claiming the Indians were less productive and unreliable.[155] In some
cases, the fishers "leased" boats and nets from the cannery and were paid
on a "share" basis—the cannery paid out per fish and deducted approximately one-third of that payment as the cannery's share for providing the
gear. Fishing on shares appears to have started because of the limits put on
licenses. If a fisher could not get his own license, then he was forced to take
a cannery boat and work on shares. Shares were usually made with whites
of various ethnic backgrounds. In the shares arrangement the company
remained responsible for the upkeep of the gear. Other fishermen leased
boats and nets from canning companies for the entire year and assumed
responsibility for their care. Some fishermen owned their own boats and
simply rented nets for the season from the canning companies. There were
also fishermen who owned their own nets, gear, and licenses—often called
"independent" fishers—who negotiated agreements with the packing companies at a set price per fish. Because some of these so-called independent
fishers relied on the canneries for credit, however, they were vulnerable as
one or two bad seasons could translate into significant debt. The credit-
granting canners then had the power to confiscate entire catches as well as
boats and nets.[156]

The workers' failure to organize lasting, consolidated labor unions
meant that the industry's workforce had few ways to negotiate or protest
the terms of their employment. There is some evidence to suggest that
fishermen on both sides of the border were able to influence their respective legislative bodies, but since the canners had significant political clout,
these efforts were not always successful.[157] Local fishermen and fish workers must have been disappointed at their inability to collectively challenge
the canners, particularly as they experienced a changing economic climate
that seemed to only strengthen the canners' position. Regional laborers
saw a decline in real wages between 1900 and 1920, and economic down-
turns in the 1910s may have spurred additional illegal fishing and related
sales.[158] In addition, the tenor of local politics undoubtedly encouraged
some of these illicit activities. The Pacific slope was a radical place rife with
public discussions of socialism, populism, the rights of labor, and other
progressive movements. The prevalence of such ideas and related debates
likely galvanized workers' discontent and their willingness to develop
alternative strategies to counter the power of the canner class.[159] Cross-

ing the international border in defiance of cannery contracts and deciding where to sell their salmon for the best return became a way for this polyglot workforce to assert some control over its own labor and benefit monetarily in the process. Still, watching workers abscond with "their fish" frustrated the big packers and spurred them to action.

BORDER BANDITRY AND BIG BUSINESS

Cannery owners, managers, and labor contractors all sought effective ways to curb worker mobility across the border. Because many Native and white fishermen used cannery-owned gear and boats and were party to cannery contracts that earmarked their catch for a specific establishment, canners deemed any fish sale a breach of contract and as potentially diminishing their pack. This problem was more pronounced on the Fraser River, as B.C. canners were generally more reliant on the fishers' catch than the canners in northwestern Washington. Labor contractors likewise sought to regulate the flow of Asian workers across the border.

Because both canners and labor contractors were simultaneously manipulating the border for their own purposes, however, their actions must be viewed with caution. The shifting nature of capital and ownership shares in the canneries around Washington and in the emerging centers of northern B.C. and Alaska suggest that the canners' ranks were split in complex ways that did not necessarily align with the divisions of nation or categories of citizenship.[160] In fact, the border granted packers an additional mechanism with which to try to regulate salmon supply levels for their own benefit and in accordance with market conditions. However, the structure of the industry meant that the canners often found themselves at the mercy of the fishermen and fish buyers who caught and delivered the catch. For their part, labor contractors found that a shifting labor market and increased competition between contractors challenged their ability to check the movements of Asian workers.[161] Although members of both groups took steps to limit the options available to the regional workforce, they simply could not control how the industry's workers manipulated both the border environment and the border economy.

The best way to dictate where and how salmon were sold was for canners on both sides of the border to simply agree not to buy from each other's contracted fishermen. Efforts to create such cooperative arrangements were sometimes successful, but the highly competitive nature of the business rendered transborder pacts sporadically made and easily broken.[162] For example, in 1903 several Canadian and American canners agreed not to buy fish across the border or from one another's contract fishermen; a mere forty-eight hours later, a rogue American cannery began frantically buying salmon from B.C. fishermen.[163] To prevent such purchases, these same players managed to persuade all of the Puget Sound packers to assent to a voluntary reliance on trap-caught fish in 1905. However, as the Puget Sound Canners' Association dissolved for a time following that season, this cooperative effort ground to a halt as well.[164] Cannery owners in all three northern Pacific fisheries—Alaska, B.C., and Puget Sound—established local umbrella organizations and occasionally tested the waters for larger coastal combines that would allow them to control the prices and sales of both fresh and canned salmon. As cannery owner Henry Bell-Irving enthusiastically observed to a business associate in the late 1890s, "Everywhere combination, combination seems to be the cry—on Fraser—Puget Sound & Columbia River & there will be a grand amalgamation one of these days." Despite Bell-Irving's predictions, such ambitious plans proved fleeting.[165]

Finding cooperative agreements unsustainable and unenforceable, packers in Washington and British Columbia tried to shape government fishing regulations and pushed for legal rulings that would grant them greater control over their workers. Washington canners successfully sponsored laws in the mid-1890s that required local fish buyers to be licensed and report on their transactions, while Canadian packers continually worked for more stringent regulations, particularly regarding trade parameters.[166] Presumably at the behest of local canners, the Dominion government forbade American sloops weighing less than fifteen tons to cross into British waters in the 1880s. This guaranteed British boats the border fish trade and instantly raised the penalties for U.S. fish dealers found illegally over the line.[167] B.C. canners persuaded the DMF to enact an embargo on the exportation of fresh sockeye salmon into the United States in the mid-1890s, but efforts to keep these laws in place or expand them to include other types of salmon required constant vigilance and frequently failed.[168] B.C. packers also used their political influence to limit import duties on fresh salmon so as to guarantee themselves the freedom to purchase additional supplies from American sellers when needed.[169] As Professor Edward Prince of the DMF noted in 1897, "Nearly 2,000,000 lbs of fresh salmon were brought from U.S. to B.C. canneries to be packed and the effect was no doubt *to give the canners* a certain amount of *independence* so that the *fishermen* could *not* dictate prices."[170] In 1912 a lawyer for the PAF went so far as to boast openly that he and the other large canners' legal counsel had essentially written the fishery statutes of Washington State.[171]

As illegal sales across the international border persisted in spite of the laws and duties imposed, Canadian companies in particular took other, more creative steps to protect their interests. Likely hoping to capitalize on local ethnic tensions during one of the few fishermen's strikes on the Fraser at the turn of the century, one B.C. canners' association initiated a rewards system wherein informants might receive up to one hundred dollars for reporting any illicit activities among the workforce.[172] In 1903 the Fraser River Canners' Association tried to blacklist fishermen and boat pullers known to sell their fish across the border.[173] Canadian packers also issued leaflets to buyers and neighboring canneries that identified their contract fishermen and warned outsiders not to buy their fish.[174] Although such sales were technically legal, at least one B.C. cannery had a watchman record the boat numbers of those fishermen selling salmon to outside fish dealers.[175] Several Canadian packers also continually called on the B.C. Provincial Police and the DMF patrol service to prevent sales of fish and direct where their contract fishers took their catch.[176] In 1913 at least one large B.C. packing company considered stopping all cash advances to its fishermen in retaliation for their border fish sales.[177] B.C. cannery owners also enlisted the help of local politicians to pressure the DMF, but this did not sit well with government authorities. "It was to be expected that the canners would attempt to get *every class* of the community to write to the Dept., *except* the *main class interested* viz: the *fishing population* whose livelihood depends upon fishing," one of the department's officers fumed. "The fishermen are poor, & the canners have all made wealth out of the fisheries."[178]

Although it rarely worked to their benefit, B.C. packers also looked to the courts for ways to restrict the outside sales of their contract fishermen. Canadian cannery owners had long argued that their contractual agreements with fishermen were legally binding, but the courts and the DMF did not agree. Despite a ruling in the early 1900s that declared contract fishermen free to sell their catch to whomever they chose, B.C. canners repeatedly challenged this decision both in the legal system and in their communications with government officials.[179] The Great Northern Cannery on the Fraser River tried to overturn this standing legal opinion again in 1915. They arrested one of their own fishermen for stealing five sockeye salmon. The company argued that the fish belonged to the cannery by virtue of the contract the fisherman signed at the beginning of the season. Although the magistrate agreed that such an act constituted theft, he dismissed the case based on the fisherman's testimony.[180]

Cannery operators on both sides of the border complained to their respective governing agencies about the injustices rained upon them by border bandits and wayward fishermen, but many of those same canners were simultaneously using the border to increase their own profits. In fact, canners illegally purchased supplies of fish from fishermen and fish dealers, and some canners began to invest in establishments on both sides of the line and in Alaska. As early as the 1890s, Henry Bell-Irving, the head of the ABC Packing Company in B.C., purchased the Fidalgo Island Packing Company in the San Juan Islands; by 1910 the ABC was the largest stockholder in five additional fishing companies in Washington State waters.[181]

According to Bell-Irving, several Fraser River canners followed his lead and invested south of the line as of 1897, and in 1899 he was already thinking of leaving the Fraser River entirely. "Looking at the situation in B.C. generally," Bell-Irving reported to one of his London contacts, "the conviction is forced upon us that United States waters, whether those of Puget Sound or of Alaska, offer at the present time greater advantages for making money than the Fraser River."[182] Other B.C. interests similarly invested across the forty-ninth parallel. For instance, James Goodfellow merely operated a trap at Point Roberts that was owned by Thomas Ladner of Ladner's Landing, B.C., and in 1905 a B.C. syndicate acquired control of a Bellingham cannery and several fish traps near Lopez Island.[183] Rumors also filtered throughout the region that when the U.S. Army finally opened Point Roberts to settlement in 1892, B.C. packers would promise financial support to "settlers" who would then file for dummy waterfront claims on that lucrative fishing peninsula.[184]

Fewer American canners invested across the border in southern B.C. canneries, but Washington trap owners quickly realized they could earn additional profits by leasing some of their trap sites to B.C. canners. The PAF and Bell-Irving made one such deal in 1904. Bell-Irving agreed to build the trap, buy the license, and pay the PAF seven cents for all sockeye caught after the first thirty thousand.[185] A DMF representative noted that the B.C. canners' attempts "for many years to oppress the B.C. fishermen is shown by their *large investments* in fishing stations in Washington territory & their determination to *buy fish* from the *United States* & not from the Fraser River fishermen."[186]

Labor contractors hired most of the Chinese and Japanese workers on both sides of the boundary during this period, but while they too were concerned about worker mobility, their capacity to regulate such movements appears to have fluctuated depending on border conditions and the availability of workers. Initially, Asian labor bosses likely had significant power over their charges because many were new immigrants with few language skills and their arrivals were concentrated at the major western ports. Labor contractors' power was greatest when entry points were limited, and such middlemen were then critical to workers' ability to navigate the immigration process. Labor bosses provided destination addresses, pocket money, and coaching on how to successfully maneuver through the system.[187]

Once Asian workers had labored in the West, gained knowledge of the region's landscapes and seascapes, and possibly learned a little English, they appear to have become less dependent on labor bosses. Relying on tactics strikingly similar to the big salmon packers, labor contractors strove to identify and blacklist workers who abandoned their positions, made off with cash advances, or sold fish that were never reported to either the canneries or the bosses. The intense competition between fishery contractors along the Pacific slope and the proximity of the porous border likewise presented significant obstacles for many labor contractors. Due to the scarcity of labor and boss rivalries, workers were likely able to get work even if blacklisted. As the number of competing bosses gradually declined and the border became more heavily policed over time, it must have become more difficult for Asian fishery workers to manipulate their labor bosses and international borders for higher wages and better jobs.[188]

Still, for a time, many Chinese and Japanese workers appear to have successfully crossed the international border to improve their work conditions and they used the labor boss system for their own purposes. In the early 1900s a group of Japanese labor bosses wrote to B.C. canners asking for a commission per fisherman hired (presumably in addition to that received for the fish their fishers caught) because they were losing money on workers who left and neglected to pay their debts. According to these bosses, their Japanese workers had promised to return to work and pay them back, but "a great many dishonest debtors went away and would not come back; the consequence was a great loss to us."[189]

Chinese labor contractors also experienced losses when their workers made off with cash advances. In 1901, Chinese bosses refused to hire contract workers for northern B.C. canneries and claimed they simply lost too much money "by the men smuggling themselves over the line without paying."[190] The following year, contractors operating in Canada again sustained losses as many of their Chinese workers slipped over the border for higher wages in Washington and took their cash advances with them.[191] In response to these problems, Chinese contractors tried organizing an association of contractors and canners for "mutual protection" in 1903 and fined members who tried to make secret deals, but the dwindling number of Chinese workers and persistent, fierce competition soon put many labor contractors out of business.[192] One such individual was Lo June. When confronted with high wage demands from Asian workers in 1906, this particular Chinese boss publicly announced his decision to change careers.[193]

That fish packers and labor contractors worried about workers' mobility and went to such lengths to influence where fishermen sold their salmon suggests that these ongoing worker movements represented contested issues of power. Even as they vied for control of the regional salmon supply, these groups also manipulated the nature of the international line for their own benefit.

Despite the financial opportunities offered by the proximity of the forty-ninth parallel in the western Canada-U.S. borderlands, these myriad border transgressions ultimately confounded efforts to regulate the fishery and control the total salmon catch. Still, while border bandits remained wage laborers, some fishermen pushed the limits further and raised the stakes for all involved in the Salish Sea salmon fishery. The locals called them "fish pirates."

5

Pirates of the Salish Sea

O N ANY GIVEN NIGHT IN THE FIRST DECADES OF THE TWEN-
tieth century, a man named Bert Jones might quietly set out from
one of the many small West Coast fishing towns or from one
of the islands scattered around the Salish Sea. Anacortes, Blaine, Friday
Harbor, Steveston, or perhaps Tsawassen—all played host to fish pirates
and smugglers like Jones. He would move his boat slowly around Point
Roberts, being careful to maneuver around the trap pilings that occupied
former Indian reef net locations. Sometimes Jones followed cormorants to
traps that were sure to be writhing with salmon. He would then shut down
his lights and engines, drift up to the structure, and softly paddle alongside
the spiller. Jones might then pause and peer into the fog to make sure he
was alone, especially eager to avoid the few government patrol vessels that
policed the area. If the coast were clear, Jones would quickly scoop thousands of live fish from the trap and load up his boat before silently pushing
off into the darkness. Jones used his knowledge of place to avoid capture
and to find full traps.

"I'd keep hid during the day and come out during the evening after the
patrol boats had all left," Jones remembered. "The nighttime was when I
done my work, and they done theirs in the daytime. . . . Oh, the fish traps
was thick. God, they were thick. Every night I used to get a load of fish."[1]
Fish piracy emerged in western boundary waters soon after whites commandeered Indian fishing locations at the turn of the twentieth century.[2]
Like other industry players, fish pirates wanted to make money, but their

actions, goals, and effects on the Salish Sea salmon fishery add another complex layer to the fishery's history.

Salish Sea fish piracy was at its height during the Progressive Era, a time of significant reform on both sides of the border. Progressives particularly valued the conservation of natural resources, and Progressive Era politicians, activists, and government officials had come to believe in the need for the scientific management of natural resources to ensure future supplies. As a result, authorities in both the United States and Canada passed regulations to restrict how and when their constituents harvested nature's bounty. The institution of limits on how people used natural resources, however, was not always a straightforward, fair, or uncontested process.[3] Throughout this period upper- and middle-class, native-born white, largely Protestant ideas about nature and the proper uses of the natural world prevailed, were enshrined in law, and superseded local knowledge and customs. State-backed conservation laws did not just eclipse local access to resources; they also allowed certain parties to appropriate valuable natural resources at the expense of others in the name of conservation and efficiency. In the salmon fishery of the Salish Sea, the wealthier fish trap owners successfully did just that.

Fish pirates understood that fish traps and the regulations governing them granted their privileged owners control over two precious commodities in this western waterscape: salmon and space. Although the original expense of building a trap was approximately five thousand dollars, some investors sold single lucrative traps for between twenty thousand to ninety thousand dollars in the late 1890s.[4] Because both building and operating traps required significant financial outlay, they were unquestionably, in the words of one government official, "beyond the financial means of the ordinary fisherman."[5] Traps likewise decreased demand for regular fishermen—especially in Washington State—because traps were incredibly productive and their maintenance required few hands. Just one of the twenty-one traps used by the Fidalgo Island Packing Company took nearly two hundred thousand fish in 1898, most of them the valuable sockeye.[6] In addition to monopolizing the fishery through the use of expensive, efficient gear, fish traps also took up huge expanses of coastal sea space. The traps were large, sprawling structures that clever owners strategically placed to maximize their access to migrating salmon.

Embracing the Euro-American and Euro-Canadian legal doctrine that defined fish as common property and adopting the rhetoric of conservation for their own purposes, fish pirates argued against fish traps and defended their own questionable activities. Regional fish poachers scorned the illegal actions of the trap owners and canners, claimed the larger packers wasted fish, and advocated reclaiming resources owned in common for the entire community, not just the privileged few. Fish pirates thus used the nature of the Anglo-American border to contest the corporate takeover of the Salish Sea salmon fishery, but in so doing, they contributed to its complexities and heightened the tensions that plagued U.S.-Canadian relations in this bifurcated western waterscape.

A DAY IN THE LIFE

Bert Jones, nicknamed "Spider," lived in the Puget Sound area at the height of the regional canned salmon boom. Surprisingly forthcoming about his fish-rustling days, Jones's later accounts offer a fascinating glimpse into the fish-pirate world of the early twentieth century.[7] Men like Jones, who had once worked as a cannery fisherman, used their knowledge of the intricate waterscape of the Salish Sea to find fish and elude regional patrol vessels. According to the *Bellingham Reveille*, "Revenue cutters have tried to catch them [pirates], but the men are familiar with local conditions and make it a point to keep 'tabs' on government vessels."[8] Years later, Jones confirmed these claims: "I run without lights altogether. I wouldn't run onto no rocks because I knew where to go. That was the easiest part. I'd look up in the sky. Or to get to a trap on a reef way out in the middle out there I used to follow the skags [cormorants]."[9] Trap rustlers were able to move filched fish throughout boundary waters because there was simply no way to identify the stolen merchandise. Owners knew on sight that their traps had been robbed, but as another newspaper reporter joked, "If they do not catch the thieves in the act [the trap owners] must conclude that the fish forgot to run the night before."[10] It rapidly became clear to both Americans and Canadians that fish poaching was financially rewarding, and salmon capers grew increasingly common after 1900. Some pirates branched out and began stealing nets, boats, and fish from cannery docks. All involved frequently relied on their knowledge of regional waters to slip across the international border, avoid capture, and receive the highest returns for their fish.

Because Washington State waters contained the most traps, fish rustling was more common south of the forty-ninth parallel, but fish pirates targeted Canadian traps when it made good business sense to do so.

"Canadian traps are not immune from injury," the *Pacific Fisherman* announced when fish pirates attacked the traps of Findlay, Durham & Brodie and made off with some thirty thousand fish in 1905. Though initially labeled an accident, company officials soon realized that a "serious criminal action" had occurred.[11] In 1909, B.C. packers were convinced that their traps in Boundary Bay, just east of the Point Roberts peninsula, had been robbed blind. That same season the secretary of the Fraser River Canners' Association recorded that he had asked the "police to scare pirates" and that "officers are notified of Depredation of Marauders on both sides of the line, and are requested by canners' association to take steps to capture thieves." When the police investigated, nearby American canners denied seeing anything amiss. As the Americans may well have purchased some of the stolen salmon, it could have been in their interest to feign ignorance when confronted by authorities.[12]

Like other fishery workers, fish pirates successfully exploited the jurisdictional and economic divisions created by the international border. That Canadian waters played host to a smaller number of fish traps meant that demand for fish was generally higher in B.C., although this fluctuated according to the total number of canneries operating each season. Illegal border crossings were reportedly quite common as pirates took advantage of shifting supply needs.[13] In 1909, for instance, Washington canners blamed Canadian culprits for a massive trap raid. According to an American canner, forty armed poachers attacked his traps near Boundary Bay, loaded up several scows with salmon, and crossed the border into Canadian waters to dispose of the fish and outmaneuver American patrols. In response, the American trap operators hired more armed trap watchmen. Newspaper headlines accusing Canadian pirates fanned the flames of international rivalry and competition until authorities discovered that American citizens were actually responsible for this particular act of piracy.[14] In 1911 and again in 1912 the owners of the few Canadian traps on the west coast of Vancouver Island reported thefts; witnesses identified several of the boats as American-owned and from Seattle.[15] Also in 1912, Canadian patrols chased another American vessel attempting to flee across the line to the jurisdictional safety of U.S. waters. When the Canadian patrols asked to be let aboard, one of the rustlers taunted: "You come to Neah Bay [in Washington State] and you can come aboard." Despite such bravado, the poachers' boat was too slow to make the border, and the Canadian patrols struck the vessel, rolled it, and took it into custody.[16]

Although some fish pirates remained undetected as they took live fish from the traps, most were able to bribe or otherwise garner assistance from the night watchmen hired by the trap owners. Sometimes trap watchmen cooperated with fish pirates for free, using signal lights to guide rustlers safely to the trap.[17] Most, however, earned a little money for their trouble. "That's one thing, I don't understand, how stupid those guys could get," former fish pirate Walter Scott remarked on the trap owners' reluctance to pay the watchmen higher wages. "All they could think of was so much a month there. They didn't want to pay 'em enough, so they would take care of the trap owners['] interests. They just didn't give a damn, that's all."[18] Seasoned fisherman Elmer Vogt confirmed that the watchmen's poor pay was one incentive for taking bribes and reminisced about a young trap watchman working for the Bellingham Canning Company in the 1910s. According to Vogt, American fish pirates approached the watchman one night and offered to pay the man five hundred dollars for the ten thousand fish in his trap. The watchman not only agreed, but he also helped the poachers load up their boat and hitched a ride to shore since the five hundred dollars was more than he would earn for the remainder of the season.[19] Bert Jones confirmed that he paid trap watchmen anywhere from one hundred to seven hundred dollars for a load of fish. "I used to take lots of money with me," he recalled.[20] "The watchmen figured the fish were made for everybody and they wanted their share. Everybody wanted to make money."[21] In fact, according to Scott, it was bad form for fish pirates to *not* pay the trap watchmen. "Sometimes we would ask the watchmen for a little dip, for gas and grub," Scott asserted, "and that was the only fish we took for free." Despite Scott's claims, this does not seem to have been a universal rule in the greater pirating community.[22]

Some pirates devised a system of coded phone calls that led them to traps ripe for rustling. According to Jones, he would occasionally receive a call from the west coast of Whidbey Island, an area frequented by pirates. The caller, who would later earn about a hundred dollars for her or his trouble, would use agreed-upon language to indicate that trap fish were available at that location. The callers would tell him: "'My engine's broke down and I wondered if you would come and help me tow it in.' I says, 'All right, I'll be right over.' That was coming to get a load of fish." Other messages were less subtle, and not really codes at all. Another caller simply said, "'Come up to Lummi. Come north to the high peak,'" and meant precisely that. "I had some great codes," Jones said. "I could stay home here and know right where to go for a load of fish."[23] Retired fisherman W. J. Beale suggested that poachers created such codes because the authorities were known to tap local phone lines to track suspected pirates, but the government record suggests that the rustlers had little to worry about since local authorities rarely employed such sophisticated tactics.[24]

Technological innovations that were beginning to transform the fishing industry also may have helped fish pirates elude authorities. Small internal combustion engines became widely available after 1900, and Fraser River gillnetters quickly began using these engines. By 1913 more than 80 percent of gillnetters operating on the Fraser were motorized. Cannery tenders and purse seiners also started using small gas engines in their boats. This new mobility allowed fishers to fish farther away from the canneries and exploit new fishing areas. For fish pirates, the engines might have helped them outrun the larger government and cannery patrol vessels. Though some fish pirates used small sailing sloops because of their affordability and their ability to move quietly, many soon replaced their sloops with engine-powered boats. By the early twentieth century, pirates needed vessels with just two features: adequate storage for a profitable number of fish and an engine powerful enough to evade government patrols.[25]

Trap owners were determined to protect their traps, and violent encounters between fish pirates and trap watchmen escalated over time. Jones avoided using force while engaged in his trade, but there were numerous less discerning pirates and trap employees. Jones claimed that he once hired an assistant who shot at a trap watchman. "I fired him as soon as I got home," he remembered. "I told him to get off, I don't want you around here. I ain't killed anybody for fish or anything else."[26] Still, as several canners armed their trap watchmen and ordered them to fire at pirates on sight, violence was inevitable. "This may seem rather harsh measures to adopt," the *Anacortes American* admitted of the "shoot-first" policy, "but it will no doubt prove effective."[27] Most fish pirates were not so easily intimidated, however. Pirates shot out the windows of one watchman's quarters on an Alaska Packers' Association (APA) trap near Point Roberts in 1903 and boarded another APA trap in 1908. In the 1908 incident the poachers ordered the watchman "to throw up his hands, and when he attempted to use his gun they wrenched it from his grasp, and in a twinkling had him gagged and bound," the *Vancouver World* reported.[28]

Confrontations during the next decade involved threats and shootings on both sides of the border. The secretary of the Fraser River Canners'

Association reported that American pirates, with guns blazing, raided Canadian traps in the Strait of Juan de Fuca in 1911. Fortunately, the only casualty was a lucky trap watchman's hat.[29] In 1912 a Canadian trap watchman "opened fire" on fish pirates who responded with shotguns and rifles.[30] In 1917 a dead body was discovered in the spill of a trap on Whidbey Island; when authorities identified the deceased as the trap watchman, they immediately suspected regional fish pirates.[31] Bert Jones also recalled a fatal shooting that likely occurred in the 1910s, when the son of a local cannery owner shot and killed a poacher making off with some chum or dog salmon. This incident is striking because chum were the least valued species on the market. Perhaps the rustler was desperate or perhaps chum were the only fish available for the taking. Whatever the reasons, the son's extreme response suggests that some canners and trap owners were exasperated—to the point of violence—by persistent acts of fish thievery.[32]

Despite the dangers, fish pirates on both sides of the border profited fairly easily from border fishing and fish rustling. In fact, fish pirating appears to have increased when prices for fish were high. "The fish thieves have always been sufficiently plentiful to cause great annoyance to the trap operators," the *Pacific Fisherman* reported in 1906, "but the price of fish this year proved too great a temptation, and the numbers were considerably increased."[33] Jones claimed he never had trouble selling his fish because the buyers knew he would have fish that had all been removed from the water at the same time. "They knew mine were fresh," he asserted. "But a purse seiner will catch a hundred fish and not bother to find a fish buyer right away. He'll keep the fish for a couple of days and them fish'll be rotten when they get to the cannery."[34] Thanks to the efficiency of the traps, Jones and other fish pirates were able to take thousands of fish at a time. Jones often took so many, he said, that his decks were nearly underwater.[35] Former fish rustler Walter Scott routinely sold his fish to a cannery tender whose sole purpose was to ply boundary waters and buy fish. The tender "was out there all the time to get fish when we had 'em; sometimes we had to unload and go back and get another load," Scott recalled.[36]

By the 1910s fish pirates likely earned more than legitimate fishermen. On average, Bert Jones could haul about twenty-five hundred fish at a time on his boat; depending on the type of fish and the market price each year and season, he might receive from between six hundred and eighteen hundred dollars per boatload—not bad for one night's work. While regular fishermen might be able to match this catch, they usually then had to pay the canners for use of their boat and gear and sometimes for food.[37] Jones used his fish-poaching income to build his family's house, to travel, and in 1978 he bragged that he still had more than twenty thousand dollars from his fish pirating days.[38] Accounts from other fish rustlers also suggest that pirating brought significant rewards to those involved. Walter Scott, for example, knew a Norwegian trap watchman who swore he sold no fish on the side, "but when he got fired," Scott noted, "he went and bought a farm and paid cash for it."[39] Elmer Vogt believed that one of the workers on his company's traps sold fish to pirates one year. Though he had no proof, Vogt became suspicious when the man spent two thousand dollars more that fall than he had earned during the season. Vogt also observed that Red Custer, one of the region's most notorious fish pirates, made a comfortable living from his poaching activities. According to Vogt, Custer "would pirate for three months out of the year and the rest of the time he had enough money to live real nice."[40]

It is difficult to know who decided to become fish pirates. The pirates who operated in southeastern Alaska from the 1910s on tended to be disgruntled purse seiners, but it is hard to say who pirated the Salish Sea.[41] A variety of records from the late nineteenth and early twentieth centuries contain tantalizing hints about other characters involved in pirating and smuggling but little other information about who these people were. While the pirates' nicknames are colorful enough—including Spider Jones, Red Custer, Cowboy Terry, and Speckled Harry, Terror of the Gulf—they tell us little about their ethnic or geographical origins.[42] One man arrested for fish pirating in the early 1900s was apparently "very intelligent and comes of a highly respected family that has resided in this county for a number of years."[43] Interviews with former fish pirates and other people living in Puget Sound suggest that most fish pirates fluctuated between wage work in the industry and more prosperous pirating work. There were some Native pirates, but the majority appear to have been of European, Euro-American, or Euro-Canadian descent. Asians—particularly the Japanese fishermen active in B.C. who had ready access to boats—may also have engaged in fish piracy. Many pirates operated locally, hiding their identity behind masks, or, at the other extreme, boasting openly about what they did for a living.[44]

Estimates of the number of people engaged in salmon piracy on a regular basis run the gamut from a few to several hundred at any one time.[45] Local resident W. J. Beale remembered at least four boats carrying from eight to sixteen people operating from the small town of Anacortes, and argued that the total number of pirates in the vicinity was much greater.[46] In the early 1900s the Pacific American Fisheries (PAF) reported that three boats containing from four to six men each robbed the company's Boundary Bay traps, which meant that twelve to eighteen men engaged in poaching that one small area on a single summer evening.[47] A 1909 trap attack involved as many as forty men working together to rob traps near the forty-ninth parallel.[48] Though likely an exaggeration (or perhaps an attempt to explain his department's poor arrest record), the Whatcom County sheriff insisted there were at least five hundred men engaged in fish pirating around northern Puget Sound in 1902.[49] Concrete numbers are impossible to determine, but the historical record is replete with references to fish pirates and the headaches they caused for regional trap owners.

Pirates created even more hassles for trap owners and canners by not limiting their take to fish. Some people also stole gear, nets, and boats from the larger canning companies. "Harbor pirates" struck Port Townsend in 1898, but the robbers escaped despite a "hot pursuit."[50] The members of the Fraser River Canners' Association were favored targets for this type of thievery. In the early 1900s W. D. Burdis, the secretary of the association, repeatedly wrote to local authorities about the depredations of American gear thieves and illegal fish smuggling. He pleaded with the B.C. Provincial Police to provide additional protections between Bowen Island and Point Roberts, "to prevent the stealing of boats, nets and gear by scoundrels from the American side."[51]

As with fish pirating, boat and gear thefts seem to have escalated over time, and it was common for canners to report several thefts a day during the fishing season. Some of Burdis's letters read like a laundry list of gear thefts: "On Monday night a boat and net were stolen from the Brunswick Cannery." On a typical day in 1909, he complained: "Last night, boats and nets disappeared from the Terra Nova Cannery, to say nothing of the nine nets stolen from the British America Cannery some time ago, none of which have been recovered."[52] Throughout the 1910s, as fishing gear and nets grew more expensive and owning one's own boat became increasingly difficult, B.C. canners in particular experienced frequent thefts of their boats, nets, and sails. Many of the robbers used the border to avoid discovery; if Canadian or American officials recovered the stolen merchandise, it was often found on the American side of the line. Possibly to avoid detection, some gear thieves from the United States went as far north as Rivers

Inlet and the Skeena River to steal nets and boats by the mid-1910s.[53]

Fish pirates and gear thieves developed highly effective methods for traversing the Anglo-American border to exploit fish traps, the marine environment, and different legal jurisdictions. They stole thousands of salmon and manipulated the border for the highest prices possible. But why risk being shot at or possibly arrested? What drove these men to live life on the edge of the law?

PIRACY ABOUNDS

Fish pirates saw the injustices that plagued the Salish Sea salmon fishery and set out to do something about it. The wealthier canners' monopoly of the fishery that fish traps made possible translated into unequal access to salmon. Although several small canning businesses continued to operate on both sides of the border, most canneries and the best trap sites came to be owned by big corporations or individuals with significant financial resources. Increasingly unable to get work or unable to afford expensive seining technology, former fishermen embraced the possibilities offered by pirating traps. The West was supposed to be a place of opportunity and free labor for white men in the late nineteenth and early twentieth centuries.[54] It was not supposed to be a place of corporate monopolies and exploitative wage work, particularly when it came to a resource that was theoretically owned in common. Fish piracy, many white men apparently decided, simply evened the odds.

In interviews conducted decades after the fact, former fish pirates and local residents recalled that salmon thieves specifically targeted only the traps owned by the large corporations. Elmer Vogt, a trap operator for twenty years, claimed to have had just one trap watchman who may have taken money from pirates. Vogt's experiences with poachers made him certain that they bypassed his company's traps because his was a small operation and his watchmen generally refused to take bribes. Instead, the fish pirates primarily struck the traps that belonged to big companies such as PAF, Fidalgo, or the Bellingham Canning Company. "Actually," Vogt mused, "they were like some radical people are today. There are some people say, 'That is government, I'll take all I can get. They are throwing the money away anyway.' They would talk like that about the big companies. 'The companies are making a killing.' . . . 'It won't hurt them. Be good to get some of their fish.' That was the attitude."[55]

Another former fish pirate claimed that he and some of his fellow rustlers preferred to sell their fish to smaller, independent canneries.[56] Of
course, those canneries would also likely be most in need of fish and willing to pay top dollar if they had it. Sometimes the robberies were more
personal. Bill Lowman, the head of one of the largest canning operations
on Puget Sound, was convinced that Spider Jones was out to get him. "I
guess Lowman thought they were picking on him," former fisherman
Albert Ginnett recalled in a 1970s interview. "You know, that they were
pirating his fish traps more than they were Sutter's, Sebastian Stewart's or
somebody else's. Course Lowman, I guess, had some pretty good locations
out there."[57]

Lowman did have some pretty good locations "out there," and he, like
other cannery operators of means, went to extreme measures to protect
his most lucrative sites. Fish pirates were well aware of the wealthy trap
owners' desire to dominate the best trap spots in the Salish Sea and appear
to have factored this into their target selection process. Local community
members watched as Lowman and the other canners repeatedly and ruth-
lessly responded to anyone attempting to usurp the locations that they had
just stolen from the Indians. The state of Washington issued 525 fish trap
licenses collectively valued at more than a million dollars by 1909, and
disputes between the corporations and others attempting to "jump" a trap
site were common.[58] At the same time the large companies were grappling
with the regional Native population over the Indians' traditional fishing
sites, they were also fighting with one another to secure the best sites first.
When the APA and a B.C.-based company tried to move in on the traps
of the Fidalgo Island Packing Company in 1896, the Fidalgo immediately
took the companies to court.[59] Roughly a decade later, Victoria's Capitol
City Canning and Packing Company filed suit against the ABC Packing
Company for operating a trap on a Canadian site to which it held lease.[60]
Issues surrounding disputed trap locations appear in several other court
cases from the same period and further attest to continual infighting
among the larger canning corporations.[61] Independent fishermen sometimes tried to contest the trap locations of the large corporations but were
rarely successful.[62]

In addition to establishing claim to the best fishing locations, the spatial reach of the traps interfered with the ability of fishermen to use other
types of gear nearby. Prior to government regulation of traps, trap owners commonly strung their traps together to blockade huge sections of

water. In 1895 government officials discovered three such structures linked together that extended a mile out into coastal waters from Point Roberts. In response to these practices and related protests by seiners and gillnetters, Washington State finally began to regulate traps in 1897. The state required trap mouths to be located at least six hundred feet apart and traps had to have at least twenty-four-hundred lateral feet between them. Leads, the walls of webbing that directed fish into the interior of the trap, could be no longer than twenty-five-hundred feet.[63] Theoretically, at least, some salmon would find ways to bypass all of these underwater obstructions on their journey to the spawning grounds.

Trap owners, however, used these laws—intended to conserve salmon by spacing out the traps and limiting the length of the leads—to strategically locate active, "experimental," and "dummy" traps. "Experimental" traps were attempts to find new and better trap locations that may or may not be fished from year to year, depending on their overall productivity.[64] "Dummy" traps might catch a few salmon, but their real purpose was to prevent competing fishermen or trap holders from interfering with other nearby active traps. By occupying so much fishing space in those areas where different types of gear might be effective, the real, "experimental," and "dummy" traps could prevent mobile fishermen from fishing an entire fishing area.[65] The big packers actually talked openly about maintaining some trap locations simply "to protect" others, and some went so far as to purchase set gill net licenses to lay claim to additional, potential trap locations they had no intention of actually using. Because the gill net licenses were significantly cheaper than trap licenses, this clever practice simultaneously saved the trap owners money.[66]

Regular fishermen and some fish pirates reacted to the spatial obstructions presented by the traps in various ways. The most effective response was to simply "cork" the traps—that is, to fish directly in front of the structures and intercept the inbound salmon. In 1905 several fishers employed this tactic and used a gill net to obstruct the flow of fish into a trap in Washington State.[67] The persistence of trap operator complaints about trap corking suggests that it was a common occurrence.[68] To garner assistance policing traps during the 1905 weekly closed periods, Washington State Fish Commissioner T. R. Kershaw capitalized on these animosities and deputized purse seiners, albeit without pay. Practices like these merely fueled the divisions between fishermen using different types of gear. According to one local newspaper, the seiners naturally "kept close watch on the traps, eager to report any violation."[69] Fish pirates likewise took action against the physical presence of the traps and were known to purposely ram traps with their boats. Such destructive behavior not only cost the trap owners money, it also suggests how fish pirates viewed both the traps and the people who owned them.[70]

In addition to their objection to the corporate monopoly of the fishery, stealing fish from traps could have offered some white men a way to assert their manhood in an industry that increasingly devalued their labor as fishermen. According to one government official writing at the height of the regional industrial fishery, using fish traps "reduces the number of persons employed in the fisheries, and the owners, who are usually the packers or others closely affiliated with them, can, if they so desire, render themselves largely independent of other fishermen."[71] Although pirates rarely spoke about such issues in later interviews and memoirs, the hundreds of fish traps in Washington State rendered many fishing jobs obsolete and presented a new method of fishing that white fishermen in particular may have deemed less masculine than gill nets or seines. If trap fishing was not "real fishing" and if men were denied jobs as fishermen, then they might well have to work inside the canneries alongside Asian men, Native women, and increasing numbers of white women. Such prospects may have rankled and given some men another rationale for illicit fish appropriations.

The intersections of age and pure economic need also appear to have influenced why some white men turned to fish piracy and why others may have been sympathetic to the pirates' cause. At least one of the big packers suspected that its older trap employees were more likely to make deals with fish pirates. To counter this, the PAF began pairing an older watchman with a younger, newly hired man. The PAF superintendent admitted that "these double watchmen will cost us something near $2,000.00 extra for the season," but, he countered, "there is no doubt but the old-time watchmen sell us out very often."[72] There are several possible explanations for why older men might have more readily engaged in piracy. Older men working as trap watchmen were more likely to have been forced out of fishing by trap competition. If they had lived in the region for any length of time, they may have been active in the local labor movement or possibly supported the union cause. Older employees also had more economic responsibilities than their younger counterparts, who may have still lived with their parents. Feeding a family, paying rent, and staying ahead of other debts could weigh heavily on a man deprived of his former livelihood.

While all of these issues may have factored into individuals' decisions to cross the line to piracy, the trap owners' own illegal fishing gave pirates an additional concrete reason to take salmon with a clear conscience. "Oh gosh, I used to be a crook," Bert Jones admitted, "but I wasn't any more crooked than they were. They fished their traps during the closed season and were just as bad as me."[73] According to William Propst, another former fish poacher, the fish trap owners were supposed to shut their traps during the closed time each week. However, the owners were known to offer an extra day's pay to watchmen who agreed to secretly fish the traps during the weekly closed time.[74] "It is all right for a fish trap to catch 60,000 fish on one tide," Jones complained, "but if I got two thousand I was a pirate."[75] Several fish pirates believed that since the corporate trap owners broke conservation laws, they deserved to be robbed. As long as they obeyed the law, Jones claimed, so would he. "But if they start to steal the fish out of season," he declared, "I'll have a little hand in it myself."[76]

The poachers' accusations were well founded; the large canning companies were just as guilty of clandestine trap dealings as the pirates who took "company fish." In 1905 the Washington State fish commissioner told a local newspaper that he knew the trap operators would ignore the new law that outlawed trap fishing a few hours a week.[77] He was right. That same year one B.C. trap owner wrote several letters complaining of illegal fishing by American traps. "We can *say positively that* a number of traps *and other* nets *are operating* and *have been* operating for some time *on the Sound*," J. H. Todd & Sons' manager asserted, "*and do not observe any close season whatever.*"[78] The B.C. Fishery Patrol investigated and found *both* American and Canadian traps breaking the law. Likely in response to complaints from the Canadian inspector of fisheries, Washington State authorities finally arrested and fined three American trap owners later that season.[79] Because the fines were fairly low, however, they did not deter many trap owners from continuing to break the law. In this case the trap owners had actually calculated that it was more profitable to fish illegally during the weekly closed period and pay the fine rather than to let the fish escape. "The injustice to other interests, of course, did not count with the men guilty of the depredations," the *Victoria Colonist* sourly reported.[80] In 1906 members of a newly invigorated (and apparently short-lived) Puget Sound fishermen's union likewise wrote letters to the state governor protesting the illegal fishing of the trap owners.[81]

Trap operators continued to illegally catch fish because there was little incentive to halt the practice until 1915. In 1911 an official studying Pacific salmon fisheries admitted that although the laws in Washington dictated the precise methods and times for closing the traps and on paper appeared to be effective, "in practice it is quite otherwise." Because one or two people were capable of opening or closing a trap in one or two minutes' time, a trap watchman could manipulate the trap as needed. According to the same agent, it was thus "practically impossible to detect any but the boldest or most careless violations of the law."[82] When Walter Scott worked as a trap watchman, he devised a system whereby he propped the trap apron open with wooden pins he then tied to strings that led to his bunkhouse. If someone approached the trap, Scott would simply give the strings a tug to pull the wooden pins loose and shut the apron. To outside observers, Scott was merely taking a nap in his quarters.[83] Beryl Troxell Mason further corroborates such activities among trap owners. Her father owned and operated several fish traps in Puget Sound in the 1910s and 1920s. When the runs were small or prices low, her father would often spend the weekend alone on one of his traps. If he saw fish approaching the trap during the legal closed time, he would sometimes surreptitiously open it up and let the fish swim right in. According to his daughter, a few such catches "just might tip the scales to profitability—so long as no one saw him do it."[84]

Because the larger white community also tended to think that every citizen (of Euro-American or Euro-Canadian descent, anyway) should have access to fish, neither the poachers themselves nor other local residents viewed trap thievery in a negative light.[85] "I'm not ashamed of it, you know," poacher William Propst insisted to an interviewer in the late 1970s. "I'm not ashamed of what they call me, 'Fish Pirate,' I don't care. Lot of people done that. They loved me."[86] In 1902 the *Anacortes American* reported that "the robbers of the fish traps do not consider themselves pirates at all, nor do they think there is the least thing criminal about their acts in invading the traps and fishing in the very center of them."[87] Many people living around northern Puget Sound regularly communicated with local fish rustlers and expressed no special outrage at or even disapproval of their activities. As a young man, fisherman Lee Bauter became acquainted with several local fish pirates. Bauter once visited Red Custer's home near Blaine with a fellow worker who had befriended Custer. Custer talked to Bauter "like a father" and advised him to avoid a particularly crooked and vengeful operator at Cherry Point. At the time Bauter thought "this was exceptional advice from a known and well-known fish pirate like Red Custer." Bauter followed Custer's counsel and averted trouble.[88] Pirate Bert Jones once took several curious local young women out on a cruise to demonstrate his poaching techniques.[89]

The strength of community solidarity is further suggested by the frequency with which local residents exchanged jokes and good-natured barbs with regional fish pirates. "I was fairly well acquainted with the pirates that were really getting fish," Elmer Vogt admitted. "You know, we'd banter back and forth and talk." The pirates would tease Vogt about robbing his trap, but only once did they actually follow through on their threats.[90] Edith and Ray Robinson, former trap owners, remembered Bert Jones fondly even though he stole fish from their traps. "Oh sure," Mrs. Robinson recalled of Jones, "he would go [o]ut and rob your fish trap and come in and sell you the fish. Think nothing of it."[91] Beryl Troxell Mason remembered that her father had some trouble with fish pirates on his traps, but he still socialized with suspected poachers. One friend the Troxells believed was a fish pirate spent an evening visiting with the family when Mason was a child. After saying goodnight, the man laughingly offered to leave a fish on the family's gate in the morning. "Wouldn't you know it?" Mason recounted. "There *was* a dressed Sockeye hanging on the back gate next morning."[92]

One of the consequences of this local support for fish pirates—or at least the lack of local condemnation—was that the few pirates and thieves apprehended by authorities were usually released. In the 1890s, when three men were caught stealing fishing gear on the Fraser, the fishery guardian moved the trial location upriver, "knowing the condition of public feeling there and believing that it was almost impossible to get a conviction." This change of venue did not work, however, as the jury still refused to convict the men.[93] Local residents were also clearly aware of the trap owners' tendency to illegally fish their own traps during the weekly close time. As one Canadian official noted in 1895, complaints had been made to his office that "while *poor fishermen* are *fined, large canners* are allowed to defy *the law* with *impunity*."[94] Perhaps law-abiding locals supported pirates based on a shared sense of injustice that outside corporate interests could move in, monopolize a common property resource, and deprive legitimate fishermen from making a living at their trade.

Fish pirates likewise tapped into Progressive Era concerns about scientific management, natural resource conservation, and wastefulness to justify their clandestine activities. They frequently aligned themselves with the cause of conservation in their complaints about the wealthy trap and cannery owners as wasteful villains; fish pirates, they implied, were supporters of conservation whose access to the fishing commons had been wrongfully curbed.[95] These injustices drove men to piracy. In making these charges, fish pirates raised important questions about which industrial player or gear type was the most wasteful and thus perhaps in need of greater regulation—a debate that persisted on the public stage for several decades and became a major sticking point in salmon conservation talks between the United States and Canada.

Despite fish pirates' claims, the question of trap wastefulness is not easily answered.[96] Trap supporters argued that traps were actually less wasteful than other gear types because they were fixed. Fishermen—especially the growing number of purse seiners who increasingly pursued salmon on the open ocean—could follow fish; traps could not. In addition, since fish were theoretically only removed from the traps when the canneries needed additional supplies for canning, traps could prevent the oversupply of processing facilities and thus fish spoilage. Moveable gear fishermen and fish pirates who opposed traps instead argued that traps, unlike fishermen, never slept. The only restriction on fish traps was the weekly closed time, which was impossible to fully enforce. Anti-trap proponents insisted that trap structures themselves posed other threats: if too many salmon entered the traps, the fish could suffocate. There are hints that this happened, but it is hard to know how often because neither trap watchmen nor trap owners themselves had any incentive to admit it.[97] Until the government more strictly regulated trap net mesh sizes, traps also had problems with bycatch that was often sacrificed to save canners time and money.[98]

Still, the debate over the wastefulness of fish traps masks the more important issue of wastefulness in general. For years many canners instructed their workers to use only the prime bellies of the fish and throw out the rest.[99] Between fish traps that could catch ten thousand to twenty thousand fish at a time and the growing number of purse seines and gill nets on both sides of the border, fishermen regularly delivered more fish than the local canneries could handle. "No man should have it in his power to say," the *Daily British Colonist* insisted as early as 1877, "that 'Fraser River is *alive* with dead fish from Harrison River to its mouth!'"[100] The situation only worsened as the industry expanded. In 1889 the *Victoria Daily Colonist* reported that hundreds of dead salmon filled the Fraser.[101]

A study a few years later, in 1892, found that fish offal in the Fraser River system amounted to almost nine million pounds each season, much of it flesh suitable for consumption. "It is apparent that, unless some protective measures are enforced to restrain the cupidity of the fishermen," the inspector of fisheries for B.C. reported in 1893, "the future of the salmon fishing industry of the Fraser River and the state of Washington as well, is menaced."[102] In 1901 the B.C. commissioner of fisheries found that canneries on both sides of the international boundary not only filled every can available, but they threw away more salmon than they used.[103] The canneries "would bring in scowload after scowload of salmon," a longtime cannery town resident remembered, but "they couldn't use them . . . in a heavy run season, [the canneries] would take several scowloads of fish back out and dump them because they were spoiled."[104]

Rampant waste did plague the Salish Sea fishery at the turn of the twentieth century, but everyone played a part. Fish trap operators had the potential to limit how many fish they removed from their traps and roughly balance trap removals with the cannery's capacity to process them. Fish pirating, however, potentially upset that balance and introduced additional salmon to the region's processing facilities that may well have added to the oversupply on the docks. Trap owners fished illegally, cannery operators wasted fish, and fishermen pursued salmon with ever-efficient gear farther from shore and out onto the high seas. Few in the industry had any incentive to abide by fishing regulations or conserve salmon, so few did. As Albert Ginnett recalled, "You know, they were so hoggish in the early days. Lowman's for one, would bring in scowload after scowload of salmon. They couldn't use them. They just didn't have manpower enough to handle them."[105] "I've seen eighty thousand fish on a scow and I've seen them shovel them all overboard," Bert Jones recalled. "Tons and tons of sockeye just went to the bottom. Dirty shame."[106]

Fish pirates stole fish to make money and capitalized on local solidarity to avoid capture and censure. Although they successfully manipulated community sentiments toward their questionable activities, their efforts to cast themselves as the antithesis of the trap owners were not borne out by their poaching activities. Fish pirates instead introduced new ways to fish salmon irresponsibly and, in the process, created additional hassles for fishery regulators. Fish pirating was yet another provocative challenge to the region's canners and trap owners, and these powerful industry players responded in kind.

THE CANNERS FIGHT BACK

Canners and trap owners on both sides of the forty-ninth parallel were clearly frustrated by fish rustlers and gear thieves. The PAF superintendent, Bert Huntoon, was irritated with the constant attacks on his company's traps. "Most of the watchmen told me last night that they had had visits every night from pirates," Huntoon reported to his business associates in 1903, "who upon looking into the traps and noting that there were no fish remarked that they would be around later and would be willing to divide with the watchmen, but that in any case when the fish came they proposed to have them one way or another."[107] Huntoon was far from alone in his concerns. In 1911 the *Bellingham Reveille* reported that although local cannery men "refused to discuss the situation, . . . [they] admitted that they had been hampered by fish pirates in former years and would certainly use their utmost efforts to prevent this leak in the company's financial assets this season."[108] According to one local resident, PAF President E. B. Deming purportedly even once confronted the recalcitrant Red Custer on the sidewalks of Bellingham. A chance meeting allowed Deming, his anger clear, to bawl Custer out for stealing his trap salmon. "I know you are stealing my fish," Deming barked, "but it wouldn't be so bad if you'd sell them to me and at least let me can them."[109]

Large cannery owners gradually took steps to prevent pirating and other thefts; in the process they ultimately spent a significant amount of time and money dealing with their piracy problems. When depredations against their traps were particularly frequent, B.C. canners tended to call on the Dominion Department of Marine and Fisheries (DMF) and the local police to increase the fishery patrols on the Fraser River and in boundary waters.[110] Because piracy was more common south of the forty-ninth parallel, northern Puget Sound packers were far more proactive in their campaigns. "If invention, courage, law, and guards can suppress the persistent fish pirate," the *Pacific Fisherman* noted, "his career is not to run forever."[111] In addition to hiring two watchmen per trap and pairing older and younger watchmen, the PAF also rotated their men to different traps every ten days to make it more difficult for pirates to know who would be working where. In 1902 trap owners hired patrol boats equipped with searchlights, heavily armed their watchmen, and instructed them to "capture or kill every man caught in the act of robbing a trap."[112]

Widespread piracy also induced canning companies to cooperate in their efforts to halt salmon thefts. In 1911 canners from Anacortes, Bellingham, and Blaine inaugurated a "big campaign" against fish pirates. The PAF built a special vessel, while other companies contributed their fastest boats to a new pirate patrol fleet. These efforts did little to limit poaching.[113] "For years salmon have been stolen from the trap nets of Puget Sound," the *Pacific Fisherman* lamented in 1910, "and the victims have been powerless to do more than partially check the evil."[114] American canners ultimately negotiated a joint policing effort between the cannery tenders and the newly established Coast Guard in the late 1910s, but according to Walter Scott, "some of the deals that they thought up to keep us out of the traps were pitiful."[115] In their zeal to control border sales by fish pirates, canners sometimes tried to set uniform prices across the border to discourage salmon thefts and related border crossings. This happened in 1903, when Washington State and B.C. canners negotiated prices for fresh salmon, but they could not come to terms. The main reason the American canners argued for lower prices was "to reduce the inducement to piracy from the traps." Because the B.C. canners insisted on paying a higher piece rate, however, the Washington canners found that they too had to follow suit and, in the process, risk higher rates of rustling from their traps.[116]

Canners on both sides of the line also periodically found themselves taking steps to limit fish thievery on their cannery docks by both workers and unknown individuals. On the Fraser River in 1900, for instance, four Japanese men stole cannery fish valued at $118.80 and quickly sold them.[117] Similarly, B.C. police arrested R. Roberts and Albert Mather in July 1908 for stealing fish from the warehouse of another B.C. packing company. "For weeks past there has been systematic thieving of fish from along the wharves," the *Victoria Colonist* reported, "so brazen have the thieves become that it was a common occurrence for the company to lose from forty to fifty fish a day." Authorities suspected cannery fishermen and other employees of stealing fish and selling them to local Chinese fish peddlers for a fair sum.[118] The PAF took serious steps to halt thefts of both fresh and canned salmon from inside their Bellingham plant in 1905. The company erected a tall fence around the premises, posted watchmen at the main gates, and limited visitor passes to prevent losses. Each afternoon they also searched employee lunch pails and baskets to ensure their workers were not pilfering fish.[119] Such actions may well have increased local workers' sympathy for pirates and other rogue fish workers.

Frustrated with the frequency of fish poaching, Washington State cannery owners tried to use the courts to prevent salmon and gear thefts, but this rarely worked to their advantage because the state laws against fish piracy were inexplicit for many years. In July 1902 the Wright Brothers and the PAF charged five men with stealing fish from their traps. Though the defendant was accused of grand larceny, the jury's verdict was simply "attempt to commit petit larceny" and it is not clear that the accused ever served any jail time.[120] Several fishermen and others involved in the Washington fisheries recalled another crucial court case that likely occurred in the early 1900s involving some fish pirates and the Carlisle Packing Company. The defendants argued that "as fish are of a roving nature[,] their being in the traps did not constitute possession." According to Walter Scott, this case proved that the fish were common property until removed from the water.[121] Subsequent court cases resulted in even fewer consequences for fish pirates. In one case the defense attorney laid three salmon on a courtroom table and asked the trap owner to identify his stolen property; when the plaintiff was understandably unable to do so, the case was dismissed.[122]

Washington canners were unable to induce the state legislature to pass a law explicitly prohibiting fish pirating even though precedents existed in several other states. Trap owners argued that trapped salmon were essentially private property and so removing them from the traps without permission was stealing. A 1902 ruling in Ohio on fish larceny and other earlier court cases agreed, but the State of Washington did not institute its own anti–fish piracy law until 1915.[123] Perhaps due to the rise of piracy in the early 1900s, the state fish commissioner finally took concrete steps to specifically outlaw pirating and discourage the practice. Not only was stealing fish from traps, wheels, seines, or nets made a gross misdemeanor that year, but the state also fined watchmen who failed to close their traps during the prescribed closed period. It is not clear whether the canners supported this legislation, as the fines for wayward watchmen ranged from $250 to $2,000 and significantly upped the stakes for all involved in piratical mischief.[124] Perhaps the canners reasoned that they could still play both sides of the fence by inducing their watchmen to fish illegally and then letting them take the blame for the fine if caught or paying the fine on the watchman's behalf.

Despite their claims of indignation, trap owners and canners also held some responsibility for the perpetuation of poaching. Knowingly or not, their companies bought salmon from fish pirates and thus helped keep the rustlers in business. Former fisher Bill Bessner remembered fish pirates bringing their loads directly to the canneries on Puget Sound. "The canneries are always glad to buy fish," he insisted, "and they didn't care where they got them and didn't ask questions." So, if the canneries needed additional salmon supplies, fishers or fish pirates "were always able to get rid of their fish."[125] In an interesting twist, trap owners and canners also sometimes hired fish pirates to steal from their competitors' traps, but it is hard to say how often this occurred, and occasionally attempts to broker such deals backfired. Bill Lowman, the Bellingham canner, once approached William Propst and asked him to take fish from a rival's trap. The men almost came to blows. "God damn," Propst remembered saying. "I should hit you as crooked as you are."[126] Stealing fish from one's competitors was one way to alleviate a small catch and to undercut other companies' supplies of fish. "The different companies, they pirated between themselves, too, a whole lot," fisherman Albert Ginnett asserted, "a lot more than a lot of people know. That was one of the big games."[127]

Fish piracy was yet another tactic local fishermen developed for maintaining control of the conditions of their own labor and profiting from their specific skills on the water in the face of an increasingly capital-intensive, monopolistic industrial fishery. Despite their rhetoric on trap wastefulness, however, regional poachers did not set out to save salmon and nothing indicates they supported stricter conservation measures. Instead, their defiant actions contributed to the regulatory nightmare that unfolded on the water and that confronted government officials in these turbulent decades.

6

Policing the Border

IKE HIS FELLOW CUSTOMS AGENT GEORGE WEBBER, PETER Cain firmly believed in enforcing the law. So when Cain watched the *Emma,* a steamer from Victoria, slink southward from the Fraser River in 1890, slip over the international border, and begin loading salmon in the vicinity of Point Roberts, he was determined to perform his duties as U.S. Customs inspector. Cain managed to board the vessel and ordered the captain to dock in the nearby border town of Blaine. The captain refused. Because Cain was unarmed, his only recourse was to repeat his entreaties and attempt to assert his authority. The *Emma's* crew remained unimpressed. The captain then turned his vessel northward and crossed back into British waters with both Cain and a full load of smuggled fish aboard. Cain somehow disembarked in B.C. and immediately wired a customs inspector named Buchanan for assistance. Because Buchanan had no men to spare, he telegraphed one of the U.S. Customs Revenue Cutters to go to Cain's aid. Cain waited patiently, but the revenue cutter never showed. After going without food for thirty-six hours, he finally gave up his pursuit. Back in his office in Blaine, fuming, he wrote a letter to his superiors about his ordeal. Fish smugglers not only taunted officials across the forty-ninth parallel, they were also brazen enough to ignore agents like Cain who dared carry out their duties with nothing more than a badge and some misplaced courage. Policing the western Canada-U.S. border, as many men quickly discovered, could be a dangerous and humbling pursuit.[1]

Ironically, some of the least powerful people roaming western boundary waters were those who drew the most ire from border agents like Peter Cain. The illegal fishing, trap thievery, and related border crossings engaged in by wayward contract fishermen and fish pirates all focused official attention on the porosity of the forty-ninth parallel. Canners and trap owners were worried about the mobility of their workforce and their inability to control where fishermen ultimately unloaded their salmon. Because these industry players tended to be wealthy, influential community members, government officials usually took their complaints seriously. When concerns about the future viability of the Salish Sea salmon fishery heightened in the early 1900s, implementing more comprehensive conservation measures and policing the international border took on new urgency. To protect and preserve each nation's fishing industry and respective salmon supplies, someone needed to secure the forty-ninth parallel, especially out on the water.

Government authorities on both sides of the line thus set out to guard the border and implement more comprehensive conservation laws. Over time, various agencies gradually dedicated more staff, energy, and money to regulating the aquatic borderland and its adjacent waterways. These efforts began in the 1890s, when representatives from both countries met to discuss joint regulations, but for many reasons these early talks did not get very far. Although neither government devoted adequate financial resources to solidifying the forty-ninth parallel or to effectively enforcing the few conservation laws that were on the books, policing efforts did lead to a stronger state presence in the region over time, particularly for Asian workers.

Despite the increasingly emphatic conservation rhetoric employed by some canners, fishermen, and government officials, the industry's need for fish ruled the day on both sides of the border. The great boom of the Salish Sea canned salmon industry that had begun in the mid-1890s went bust by 1918. Water pollution, urban development, riverine obstructions, shifting oceanic conditions, and overfishing and wastefulness all had negative impacts on regional salmon. Inaction on conservation regulations and a devastating 1913 rockslide on the Fraser River, however, were critical to the decline of both sockeye and pink salmon. Persistent animosities between American and Canadian industry players and ongoing competition for fish meant that international discussions waxed and waned, even as the number of returning salmon decreased each year. In 1918, Americans and

Canadians faced one another across the forty-ninth parallel and perhaps for the first time understood how the nature of their border both divided *and* united them.

ON PATROL

Although Canada's rules and policing efforts were more comprehensive from the outset, agencies on both sides of the border encountered significant challenges in their attempts to enforce the law. Even as the need to restrict widespread border fishing grew more acute, however, neither country was willing to commit the resources truly necessary to solidify the forty-ninth parallel. State-sponsored patrols became more numerous over time, but their inadequacies and the environment they sought to regulate hindered their effectiveness. While the risks attending fish smuggling and illegal border crossings gradually increased, manipulating the border for higher returns generally remained a viable way to make a living throughout the heyday of the industrial Salish Sea salmon fishery.

The Washington legislature did not appoint its first state fish commissioner until 1890, and he hired just three deputies: one to police the entire Columbia River, one to watch Grays Harbor on the coast, and one to patrol the then less valuable fishery of Puget Sound.[2] Early fishing regulations dictated periodic closed seasons or prohibitions on particular areas, gear and net mesh sizes, and the size, location, and reach of fixed appliances like fish traps. These laws also dealt with licenses and increasingly made distinctions between fishing with a hook and line versus other fishing appliances used in the commercial fishery.[3] Still, despite the rapid expansion of the canned salmon industry of Puget Sound in the 1890s, both the laws on the books and the number of fishery patrols remained quite limited. The situation was so dire that when Fish Commissioner T. R. Kershaw took office in 1902, he was shocked to find that the department employed no deputies at all. Because the state legislature had failed to appropriate enough funds to cover the fiscal year, Kershaw was on his own. "This led to a great deal of annoyance and inconvenience, as the closed season was then on," Kershaw reported, "and complaints from all over the state were continually coming in regarding the violation of the law. But with no funds at my command I was powerless to enforce the law, or to pacify those law-abiding citizens who had a right to complain."[4] The Department of Fish and Game had purchased a patrol boat for Puget Sound in 1901, but it remained tied up at the docks unless Kershaw himself captained the vessel.[5]

Ten years later, conditions were only slightly better. An official inquiry revealed that the Washington Department of Fish and Game still had but one patrol boat, the *Bessie*. This vessel was not "sufficiently seaworthy" to cover even the inland waters of the Sound, and its top speed was a mere ten miles an hour. Although the fish commissioner hired one additional boat to patrol during the 1911 season, it also was "too small and of insufficient speed to be of any real practical value."[6] The early patrol and later Coast Guard boats were also quite noisy. "Coast Guard boats couldn't sneak up on us," former fish pirate Walter Scott explained. "They made so much noise, and we knew every kind of boat there was; those Coast Guard boats were always after us going full speed, instead of sneaking along."[7] In response to these negative reports and persistent complaints from Canadian authorities and canners, the Washington fisheries department finally hired additional patrol boats in 1913. The department commissioned the *Elisha P. Ferry*—a sixty-five-foot launch—and retrofitted the ailing *Bessie*, rechristening it the more stately *Governor John R. Rogers*. Although such serious names suggested that the department meant business, names alone could not change the odds these patrols faced. These two vessels roamed the expansive waters of the Salish Sea searching for fish pirates and illicit border crossers in the nooks and crannies of the region's coastlines, but the state fish commissioner still admitted: "I find it is practically impossible for our own boats to discover violations of the law."[8]

The U.S. Customs Service also played an active border-policing role in Washington State before World War I, especially on the waters of the Salish Sea. The Immigration Bureau was increasing in size and significance, but its primary concern was the movement of people—primarily those of Asian descent—not fish.[9] Starting in the 1850s, however, the U.S. Customs Service had placed several employees in western Washington to track imports, exports, and duty payments; they confronted many of the same challenges as the fisheries department in their attempts to enforce customs laws. Though the collector of customs technically had charge of two small launches from the Revenue Cutter Service in the 1890s, the boat captains frequently ignored the collector, did as they pleased, and only occasionally boarded boats to cite them for trivial infractions of the law. "It seems to me that they have not been very industrious in their efforts to prevent smuggling judging by the results obtained," the new collector of customs, F. D. Huestis, complained to the secretary of the treasury in 1897, "which have been *nil.*"[10] The relationships between the collector of customs and the crews of the revenue cutters remained tenuous throughout the decade, but the two groups finally began working together more closely by the late 1890s, perhaps in response to the growing amount of fishery-related traffic across the border.[11]

Over the years each successive collector of customs struggled to get more funding from the federal government to finance their smuggling patrols, but they met with limited success. Attempts to hire a larger vessel in the 1890s failed, and as late as 1912 the customs officers in western Washington had access to just four vessels: the *Scout*, the *Arcata*, the *Snohomish*, and the *Guard*.[12] Yet all of these boats were too small and too slow to tow more than a few vessels at a time into custody.[13] Other agents stationed along the coast were even worse off, as they had no access to transportation at all.[14] Such unlucky officers had little choice but to hastily hire canoes and small boats from local residents only after spotting suspected smugglers. Needless to say, these transactions took precious time that fleeing suspects used to their advantage, and often such small craft were no match for the treacherous waters of the Sound.[15] With the advent of gas engines, it became even more difficult for local authorities to overcome the swift boats of the region's various border bandits since the federal government was so slow to upgrade its water patrols.[16]

In addition to the dearth of adequate equipment, other work conditions confronting U.S. Customs officials presented serious challenges to effective policing efforts. Customs agents complained constantly of being short-staffed, rife nepotism meant that many officers had few skills to apply to their position, and scandals were frequent.[17] As many of the men were also poorly trained, their inexperience sometimes delayed action on suspected infractions of the law. The officers remained in constant communication with their superiors, asking questions and clarifying the details of fishing and customs regulations. Puget Sound customs agents frequently wrote to the collector at Port Townsend, seeking answers to extremely basic questions regarding border crossings and seized vessels. One admirably thorough agent once requested an audience with the U.S. collector, because "there are so many small perplexing questions arising here that the Regulations are silent on."[18] Because of the evolving nature of the customs and Chinese exclusion laws, the collector of customs himself sometimes wrote the U.S. attorney general or customs officials in Washington, D.C., for assistance.[19] These queries could sometimes cause embarrassment or delay legal action on a case.[20] Working as a Puget Sound customs officer was also not the most lucrative job in the 1890s and early 1900s. In fact, Washington State customs agents were among the poorest paid in the continental United States, with the collector of customs earning several thousand dollars less per year than his counterparts in other border regions.[21]

In British Columbia the federal Department of Marine and Fisheries (DMF) was the main agency responsible for creating and enforcing fishing regulations, and it too worked with other provincial and federal agencies. The B.C. Provincial Police, the Canadian Customs and Excise Service, and the B.C. Department of Fish and Wildlife all periodically assisted in the DMF's attempts to halt border fishing and illegal fish smuggling.[22] Like its counterparts in the United States, the Canadian Immigration Service also came to play an increasingly important border-policing role in the early 1900s, but it is not clear how often it assisted with fish smuggling cases. Instead, it appears to have focused its attention on the land border and the mobility of Asian workers.[23] Because British Columbia inherited regulations already refined by the DMF in the eastern provinces, B.C.'s fishing laws were more comprehensive than those of Washington State from the outset. Starting in the 1870s, the DMF imposed a weekly closed period during which no one could fish, in addition to requiring fishing licenses. Canadian authorities also experimented with boat license limitations in the 1880s and 1890s.[24]

Although Canadian fishing laws were more sophisticated than those of the United States, the DMF's commitment to fishery patrols also remained minimal until the 1920s and 1930s. The agency employed just five fishery guardians for the entire province in the 1890s; two of them perused the Fraser River while the other three were assigned to one northern river each.[25] Recognizing the significance of the international water boundary, B.C. fishery guardians appointed one boat to patrol the waters between the mouth of the Fraser and the tip of Point Roberts.[26] Still, because B.C. officials witnessed large numbers of unlicensed Japanese and white American fishermen catching salmon "outside"—that is, in marine waters opposite the mouth of the Fraser—it was abundantly clear that more fishery guardian patrols were needed as early as the 1890s, especially closer to the border.[27] The number of government vessels and workers rose throughout the early 1900s, and by 1915 the B.C. patrol crews closest to the border used a total of twelve boats.[28] Local canners also urged the B.C. Provincial Police to provide additional guards on the Fraser and near Point Roberts. The police department somewhat grudgingly appointed one or two officers to patrol the river during the height of the salmon runs, but it too was short-staffed.[29] While B.C. police officers were hesitant to make arrests because they did not accept the canners' legal arguments about fishermen contracts, they still toyed with appointing a provincial constable on the water at the border in 1903.[30] Canadian authorities were thus at a slight advantage compared with their counterparts in Washington State, but they were likewise trying to accomplish much with little.

B.C.'s fishery patrols faced many of the same limitations and hardships as the agencies operating in Washington State. As in Washington, insufficient funding made it difficult for B.C. authorities to hire a boat fast enough to catch wrongdoers. "I would very much like to pick up some of these offenders," police officer W. T. Collenson lamented in 1908, but it was "not a very easy task as some of them have very fast launches and no doubt will resist capture if possible."[31] Canadian fishery patrols were also often unsure of the laws governing transborder fishing and passage across the international border, so they too regularly wrote to their superiors in Ottawa for assistance.[32] In addition, B.C. fishery guardians and Canadian customs officials were accused of taking bribes and participating in a coastal labor and opium smuggling ring.[33] One such case on the Fraser, if true, was particularly egregious. According to the DMF's special fishery overseer William Galbraith, C. F. Green, the customs officer stationed at Ladner's Landing on the Fraser River, regularly took bribes in the 1890s. "All I know is that hundreds of tons of salmon are brought from the American side to the canneries at Ladner's, and no notice is taken, and no duty paid," Galbraith reported in 1895. "Boats trade up and down the river on a customs receipt. They are American boats on one side, and Canadian boats on the other, all for a fee of $10. This is the class of man who is, and always will be, appointed by the members of Parliament," Galbraith charged.[34]

Patrols on both sides of the border employed innovative, and sometimes successful, tactics in their quest to overcome their weaknesses and apprehend more border bandits. The Canadian fisheries department, for example, experimented with hiring detectives during the salmon fishing season in the 1890s. Finding an extra pair of eyes helpful, they periodically repeated the practice.[35] Also in the 1890s, the DMF tried to control canner manipulations of the border by refusing canning licenses to B.C. packers who sold fish at Point Roberts or who moved any of their establishments to the American side of the line.[36] Two decades later, the DMF considered passing a law that would require all boats to show national colors while in Canadian waters so as to ease the identification of Canadian vessels.[37] Perhaps finding it less expensive than hiring detectives, the U.S. Customs Service simply paid local residents for intelligence regarding suspicious activities. If locals refused to cooperate, the agents considered hiring spies as well.[38] Washington State fishery officers likewise periodically disguised themselves as regular fishermen; in 1913 they borrowed some cannery boats, pretended to go out fishing, and managed to catch two purse seiners breaking the law.[39] The U.S. Customs Service also hired people unknown to local industry players because "it is hard for those who are known as Customs officers" to detect law violations.[40]

Mostly, however, government officials like Charles McLennan simply relied on patience and persistence to capture poachers. McLennan, a U.S. Customs agent, watched a Canadian steamer illegally collecting fish from several small sloops, and "concluded from day to day, to see if they would not get bolder and come a little closer so that it would be an utter impossibility for them to escape [us] in the chase." Although he could have simply arrested the small sloops as accessories, McLennan held off. "What I want," he declared, "is the Steamer, and I am going to lay low and get her." By stowing away on an unmarked boat and waiting for the right opportunity, McLennan eventually succeeded in catching the border buyers red-handed.[41]

The nature of the border environment that pirates, bandits, and regular fishermen knew and used so well tended instead to hamper authorities. Successfully navigating these waterscapes demanded knowledge of the tides and ocean, the intricate island geography of the Sound, and excellent boating skills. Because the majority of government positions in B.C. in particular were political appointments, however, many of the men had little experience on the water.[42] The vast area in need of coverage was a problem as well. "There is such a coastline to these islands," U.S. Customs agent James Izett observed, "that unless all Boats could be made to report to the Officer here there is little chance to intercept them no matter how diligent we are."[43] In 1897 the U.S. collector of customs pleaded for a larger patrol boat as "there are other portions of this Sound that cannot be guarded or watched by these Launches on account of the rough water or weather."[44] The B.C. patrols encountered similar circumstances. "We cover the entire coast," one B.C. patrol boat captain complained in 1906, "and while we are up north the Americans know that we cannot get south again for at least a week, and it gives them a good chance to get in their work."[45] Visibility was likewise often an issue. In addition to rain and fog, locals contended with dense smoke caused by the clearing fires that burned around the straits.[46] Though deemed signs of "progress" and "civilization" by most, this thick smoke impeded the successful imposition of state order and law on the water.

Peter Cain and the other men who tried to enforce state fishery laws in and around the Salish Sea also quickly learned that patrolling boundary waters could be dangerous. Because many U.S. Customs agents were unarmed, they could not force guilty parties to obey their orders. Some industry players responded with verbal or physical threats. Mr. Smith, the manager of the Alaska Packers' Association cannery at Point Roberts, swore revenge on the local U.S. Customs agent for fining one of his company scows. "It is very unpleasant to have a man of the stamp of Smith to sneak around like a 'coyote,'" agent George Webber complained to his superiors, "to have or at least try to have me removed simply to *get even* on me when you know I did what I swore to do and what I am paid for."[47] Two angry B.C. Natives gathered twelve of their friends to confront another U.S. official at gunpoint and demand the return of their seized vessel.[48] Although that encounter ended peacefully, others did not. Lawbreakers shot and seriously wounded U.S. Customs inspector Gillespie one night, and U.S. Customs officials killed a man and wounded another while trying to take them into custody in the 1890s.[49]

The B.C. Fishery Patrol experienced similar conflicts in the line of duty, as they too were sworn at, routinely ignored, and even attacked by both fishers and canners. According to one inspector, the American fishermen fishing outside the mouth of the Fraser River were all armed and "will shoot anyone interfering with them."[50] Because of the prevalence of violent acts of retribution against fishery guardians, the DMF stopped hiring local farmers as part-time officers in the early 1900s. In response to a 1901 farmer's application, the commissioner of fisheries explained, "poachers are often very malicious, and a farmer acting as a fishery officer has frequently had his buildings burned down or has had horses and cattle injured by persons whom he has detected violating the fishery laws and inflicting fines upon them."[51]

Even cannery owners were known to interfere with fishery officials. J. A. Kendall of the J. A. Kendall & Sons Packing Company chased down and physically assailed the fishery guardian who confiscated one of his cannery nets for illegal fishing in 1913. The patrolman filed suit for aggravated assault, but Kendall hired a lawyer and confronted the head of the fisheries department. The chief inspector of fisheries, F. H. Cunningham, warned Kendall of the illegality of his actions, and the men engaged in a heated exchange. "He told me then he intended to fish this area," Cunningham wrote to Ottawa, "and if I went there to seize his nets he would club me or anybody else."[52] Cannerymen were likewise known to use their political influence against fishery guardians they perceived to be "overly-vigilant." "Should he attempt to do his duty as a Fishery officer," special inspector Galbraith observed of fishery guardians working the Fraser, "he at once excites the malignity of the cannery men, who will not scruple to make use of any means to ruin him or cause his removal."[53]

Other industry players limited their abuse to verbal assaults and taunts, as fishery inspector Samuel North discovered. North attempted to give testimony against B.C. fishermen in 1908 but found a hostile audience in the courtroom. "The room was well filled with fishermen," he explained, "and during the time I gave evidence I was repeatedly laughed at and sneered at by them, and on one occasion a fisherman called out that my evidence was false."[54] Because of conditions like these, as early as the 1890s, agent Galbraith not only recommended employing faster, larger steam launches for patrol, he insisted that the pilot houses on these new vessels should be bullet proof and supplied with rifles. "The whole Department is completely demoralized, and requires to be altogether reorganized on a totally different basis," Galbraith admonished his superiors.[55]

Seeking to protect "their fishermen," some Canadian and American authorities found themselves drawn into the industry's web of international economic rivalry, and they began seizing their neighbors' boats for what were often minor infractions. In 1899, when the sockeye ran almost entirely on the American side of the border, B.C. fishermen illegally pursued them across the forty-ninth parallel. The U.S. Customs patrol captured twenty-six fishing boats that summer season, twenty-one of which were clearly from British Columbia.[56] Uncertainty among American officials about the laws applicable to border fishing and the complaints of wrongful seizure made by B.C. fishermen via the British Embassy all pressured the Puget Sound collector of customs to return several of the vessels.[57] Hoping to quickly defuse the situation and avoid violence on the water, American authorities then allowed B.C. boats to operate as far as one mile south of the forty-ninth parallel.[58] Similar seizures occurred repeatedly in the early

1900s. Canadian forces arrested one American vessel in 1904 and another "Yankee Poacher" fishing too close to shore the following year.[59] In 1911, B.C. patrols made several attempts to seize dozens of American salmon boats "preying" on the inward-bound salmon off of Vancouver Island but managed to take only one into custody.[60]

The events of 1912 further demonstrate how authorities became enmeshed in such escalating salmon strife between Canadian and American fishermen. The Canadian arrest of two American seine boats, the *Thelma* and the *Bonita*, sparked a flurry of letters to D.C. and Ottawa. According to the Puget Sound Canners' Association, the Canadian patrol was "entirely too anxious to make seizures" that summer and took advantage of fishermen who accidentally drifted inside of the three-mile coastal limit.[61] The Seattle Chamber of Commerce likewise called for new U.S. patrols to guard the waters between the west coast of Vancouver Island and the entrance of the Strait of Juan de Fuca.[62] Soon after the Canadian seizure, American forces captured six Canadian salmon boats for fishing in American waters. The Canadians deemed this last arrest strictly retaliatory. "It is a well known fact that the American fishermen are 'sore' against the Canadian authorities in seizing American vessels recently engaged in fishing off the British Columbia coast," the *Vancouver Province* observed.[63] American sources are silent on these accusations, but Washington State officials did unnecessarily—and somewhat suspiciously—retain custody of the Canadian boats for several weeks after the case was dismissed in court and, as they performed no maintenance on the nets, effectively ruined them for future fishing.[64]

A few weeks later, the cases involving the *Thelma* and the *Bonita* led to exchanges between the U.S. secretary of state and the Canadian Department of External Affairs. The DMF assured the undersecretary of state in Ottawa that the captains of the seized American vessels would be given every opportunity to prove their innocence in Canadian courts. The Canadian fisheries department had no desire to seize American vessels, the deputy minister of fisheries wrote, but he suggested that the Americans "should prevent the necessity for such, by refraining from fishing in Canadian waters."[65] Though the owner of the *Thelma* was convicted in the B.C. courts, an appeal to the Canadian Supreme Court reversed the decision, and the owner eventually received forty-five hundred dollars for what then became a wrongful seizure.[66] The charges against the *Bonita* apparently held, as the boat disappears from the historical record.[67]

International conflicts like these and the ongoing annual race for salmon understandably fostered wariness between Americans and Canadians, even those acting in an official capacity. Although U.S. and Canadian immigration agents appear to have worked well together during this period, the agencies shared the same goal with regard to illicit immigration: they were to prevent "undesirable" Asians from crossing the international border. Other government officials, in contrast, sometimes found themselves privileging their fellow countrymen's economic interests over joint governing efforts.[68] For example, concerns about illegal fishing south of the border prompted the B.C. Provincial Fisheries Department to secretly hire a yacht to check on American fish traps and seiners in 1909. B.C. officials posed as tourists out for a day's jaunt among the San Juans, but instead of taking in the surrounding scenery, the Canadians took notes on American violations of the weekly closed fishing laws.[69] In 1911, Washington trap owners denied Canadian patrols the right to tie up or land at their trap structures. The Americans claimed this was to prevent damage to their traps, but it was more likely a way to limit the Canadians' ability to track American illegal fishing practices.[70] In 1912 a Canadian fisheries department employee met with Pinkerton's National Detective Agency in Seattle to inquire about hiring someone to spy on several canneries, presumably on the U.S. side of the line.[71]

Despite such waves of mistrust, American and Canadian fishery authorities recognized the need for cooperation and begrudgingly began working together in the 1890s. The U.S. Customs Service and the Immigration Bureau occasionally collaborated with the B.C. Fishery Patrol and Provincial Police to monitor border fishing and fish sales.[72] While these agencies initially relied on the telegraph, the advent of the telephone in the late nineteenth century made it far easier for Salish Sea fishery officials to work in tandem to catch thieves. When in pursuit of a particular offender, agents would phone across the border with a description of the suspect, their boat, and the items stolen. If given sufficient lead-time, such tactics could be quite effective unless the accused managed to offload their booty onto one of the many islands in the Sound or to another boat.[73] Perhaps because of the success of their American network, U.S. agents also began to cultivate fresh informants on the B.C. side of the line. "This boundary country is difficult to guard," the American immigration inspector Charles Snyder explained to the collector, "and one can only do his work with any success by working in connection with parties in B.C. officers and citizens."[74]

A fair amount of time, energy, and resources were obviously put toward policing the transborder salmon fishery, but did these efforts bear any real fruit? The U.S. Customs Service made increasingly more seizures over the 1890s and early 1900s, but their total number remained small. The Washington State Department of Fish and Game recorded just a few arrests before 1913.[75] From that year on, Washington fishery patrols made between fifty to seventy-five arrests every year for offenses ranging from fishing without a license to illegal border fishing and fish pirating. Fines ranged from between one dollar for gaffing salmon to three hundred dollars for fishing traps and purse seines during the closed period.[76] Similarly, B.C. fishery guardians only started regularly reporting on their arrest record after 1908. From 1908 to 1911 the DMF published comparative statistics on the arrests made by the fishery patrols in all of the Canadian provinces. B.C. consistently recorded the highest number of violations and earned several thousand dollars in annual revenues from fines and related gear sales.[77]

When caught, regular fishermen and cannery managers sometimes claimed innocence on certain infractions, but the canners' tendency to test the limits of the law and their privileged position within the industry made authorities less prone to leniency.[78] J. Goodfellow, one of the trap owners at Point Roberts who took his fish across the border to be processed on the Fraser River, asked the U.S. Customs Service for relief when two of his fishing boats were seized. Goodfellow charged that the deputy collector abruptly changed the rules of reporting without properly notifying the public. Upon investigation, the agency found Goodfellow's arguments persuasive and they dropped the charges.[79] E. A. Wadhams, a cannery owner at Ladner, B.C., was not so fortunate. American revenue officials seized his steamer, the *Winifred*, in 1892. Wadhams claimed he had been allowed to buy fish and cross the border "without hindrance" for several years and that "he had no knowledge that any law of the United States was violated by such action." He insisted on his innocence and ignorance of the customs laws. These assertions did not hold up to scrutiny, however, as authorities quickly found that several of Wadhams's cannery boats had been warned and seized in the previous three years for similar infractions. Furthermore, investigators soon discovered that Wadhams owned the *Emma*, the same vessel that had absconded with stolen salmon and a flustered customs officer named Peter Cain just two years previous. Finally, the agents rightfully asked, if the captain of the *Winifred* was truly unfamiliar with the customs laws, why did he try to flee when confronted by the U.S. Customs Service in this most recent incident? The fourteen-hundred-dollar fine remained firm.[80]

The fluidity of the border environment created further headaches for authorities, because many of the accused insisted they had unknowingly and unintentionally drifted over the forty-ninth parallel, especially when out on the more open water of the northern Sound or the Strait of Juan de Fuca. H. O. Knudsen and his brother argued that heavy fog had caused them to lose sight of their position in 1898. Knudsen swore he knew crossing the border to fish was an infraction of the law, "but in this instance owing to the fog and the tide running out we were unable to know our exact position and it was only an accident, not intent, that the boat drifted into American waters." Since the B.C. cannery that employed them would require the fishermen to pay their own fine, the official in charge deemed this a significant hardship and released the two brothers.[81] Fishermen and patrolling officers constantly argued about where they were in relation to the international line because the border was not physically marked, and usually neither side could offer definitive physical proof either way. Such uncertainties made it even more difficult for patrolling officers to secure convictions in the courts.[82]

Although more government officials could be found policing boundary waters as the years passed, the Anglo-American water border remained quite permeable into the 1920s. Hundreds of boats regularly fished the Salish Sea during the height of the salmon runs, and many of them flitted back and forth across the border to sell or purchase fish, but arrest rates appear to have remained quite low.[83] Canners, trap owners, and government agents continued to complain about illegal border sales and fish pirates, and they spoke ever urgently about the need to solidify the border in the late 1910s and 1920s, but neither government wanted to expend the resources necessary to truly fortify the border and restrain fishing.[84] The Washington, D.C. offices of the Revenue Cutter Service and later Coast Guard reprimanded the Puget Sound patrols for their poor record in 1911 and again in 1915.[85] Contemporary observers likewise found the fishery police ineffective. Fish trap operator Elmer Vogt could not recall fish pirates ever being caught by local authorities. The pirates "just got away with it," he recalled. "It was just a case of trying to out fox them and not let them get away with too many fish."[86] Former poacher Walter Scott remembered: "Those guys never got us. We slipped through their fingers every time. Oh, they pinched us or cited us for different things, and we got out of every doggone one. I never paid a five cents fine."[87] Bill Bessner agreed: "Those days you never heard about the Fisheries Department much."[88]

TRANSBORDER DIPLOMACY

Even as Canadian and American patrols sought additional support to shore up the forty-ninth parallel and restrict border fish trafficking, government officials recognized early on that effective conservation of the Fraser River salmon runs could be achieved only through either uniform or complementary regulations spanning the forty-ninth parallel. Because of successes in negotiating treaties on seals and migratory birds, an international treaty seemed the logical solution to the thorny issue of transnational salmon conservation.[89] Members of both federal and local agencies took the first steps toward drafting such laws, but differences in government authority with regard to fish created significant problems. In Canada the Dominion government had jurisdiction over the fisheries of British Columbia as administered through the DMF. On the U.S. side the state of Washington managed its fisheries, and state officials were quite adamant about retaining that power. Because states do not have the authority to make agreements with foreign governments, however, both sides found themselves at an impasse with regard to a treaty. The resistance of politically powerful and well-connected cannery owners, strained relations and suspicions across the border due to ongoing conflicts and related boat seizures, and this important disjuncture in governmental powers all stymied progress on meaningful transnational conservation regulations.

The first attempt to cooperate in the management of the shared fisheries of Canada and the United States occurred in the 1890s. Persistent problems regarding their numerous shared boundary waters led both countries to form a joint international commission in 1892. Each nation appointed a representative to study the issues, but they were charged with investigating *all* of the shared fisheries along the Canada–U.S. border, including those on the East Coast and the Great Lakes. In addition, although the commission had the power to make recommendations, they had no power to do anything else. The commission's long-overdue 1896 report argued that more regulations should be applied to the West Coast sockeye salmon fishery if it were to remain a viable commercial enterprise. Despite these recommendations, the Joint High Commission meeting of 1898 failed to address the West Coast border fisheries issue, and neither government took further steps to deal with the problem for several more years.[90]

Anxiety regarding the wanton wastefulness of fish and a decline in the amount of sockeye salmon packed on both sides of the border rapidly led to increased animosities between residents of B.C. and Washington State. "If the decline in this fishery is due to excessive fishing," the provincial commissioner of fisheries in B.C. declared in 1903, "the censure for it rests principally, if not wholly, at the door of the state of Washington, as the unbridled fishing conducted in her waters is indefensible and unjustifiable, and, if continued, will wipe out the salmon fishery of the Fraser."[91] In addition to minimal regulations and their lax enforcement in Washington, Canadian government officials, canners, and fishermen all complained about the large number of fish traps used on the American side of the line. For their part Washington State officials acknowledged that their regulations were inadequate but insisted that the additional regulations B.C. had in place were also ineffective.[92] Transborder infighting quickly became more prevalent than transborder problem-solving.

Frustration with the inaction of the federal agencies in Washington, D.C. led the Canadian DMF to initiate their own negotiations with Washington State. The Canadian fisheries minister appointed another B.C. Fisheries Commission in 1905 and asked the governor of Washington to do the same. Washington governor Albert Meade complied and named the members of the state Fish and Game Commission as well as others familiar with the fishing industry—primarily the owners of large canneries—to the American committee. Those selected held local hearings regarding proposed fishing regulations and met to discuss potential changes to the regulations of B.C. and Washington. Both commissions submitted their recommendations to their respective regulatory bodies the following year. The laws they called for dealt with the length and size of nets, longer weekly closed times, effective methods for closing traps, more severe fines for trap violations, and additional appropriations for fishery patrols on both sides of the line.[93] The B.C. commission's John Brown disagreed with the proposed regulations; Brown's minority report objected to the proposal to close the Fraser River twenty-four hours longer than the waters outside the river's mouth. Brown's objections were for familiar reasons: such a long closed time would "subordinate the right of our fishermen to the profit and advantage of the Puget Sound fishing interests" and would also be "a most unjust discrimination in favor of the Japanese, as against the white fishermen."[94]

Nearly simultaneously, several Puget Sound and B.C. canners proposed even more drastic steps in the fishing regulations. Falsely claiming to speak for all processors with investments in southwestern B.C. and Puget Sound, a select group of cannery owners called for closing down the Fraser River to sockeye salmon fishing during the 1906 and 1908 seasons. In return, the Americans in this group agreed to draft a bill outlining regulations that matched B.C.'s for passage in the Washington State legislature.[95] Both American and Canadian fishermen of all gear types understandably protested.[96] The DMF, however, saw this agreement as a necessary first step toward concrete transborder cooperation on uniform fishing regulations, and they were eager to mollify opposition and at the very least persuade Washington State to commit to longer weekly closed periods. Moreover, because of the nature of law-making in Canada, it was generally a small matter for the DMF to make and revise fishing regulations. As the majority government in a parliamentary system almost never loses a vote on a bill, it was usually simple for the Canadian authorities to pass and amend fishing regulations.[97] In contrast, the Washington State legislature met biennially and each new regulation had to be approved by that eclectic, easily swayed body. Canadian authorities thus supported the proposed closures, despite the impact they would have on local fishermen and cannery workers. Because of the strong opposition of unidentified fishermen's unions, the smaller canners, and the general public, however, the Washington State legislature voted against the bill and most of the recommendations of the joint commission.[98]

In the meantime American and Canadian federal authorities were again attempting to revive their border fishery treaty negotiations. A new opportunity for such cooperation arose when President Theodore Roosevelt appointed Elihu Root secretary of state in 1905. Although disagreements between officials on both sides caused setbacks, Root and Canadian ambassador Sir James Bryce finally drafted a treaty in 1908. Instead of initiating fishing regulations, however, the document merely created yet another commission that would then draw up fishery regulations for the international waters shared by the two countries. Unfortunately, the treaty granted the new two-member commission just six months to fulfill their extensive duties. After much negotiation and numerous delays, the American representative, David Starr Jordan, and the Canadian scientist Edward Prince drafted a set of regulations in April 1909.[99]

Canada immediately passed the Inland Fishery Treaty and supported it for several years, but opponents on the American side successfully thwarted its congressional approval. In March 1910 the Canadian Parliament passed a bill that enabled the Privy Council to enact the new laws whenever it chose. Conditions south of the border were not nearly so favorable. Since Roosevelt had left office by the spring of 1909 and neither preservationists nor conservationists championed the cause of salmon conservation, there was no strong political figure or group to usher the treaty through Congress. As a result, the measure languished in the Senate Foreign Relations committee. Strong protests from several border state senators and fishery workers then compelled a Senator William Alden Smith from Michigan to radically alter the proposed regulations in 1911. The Canadians had conceded to a few minor alterations, but this new document was completely revamped without Canadian approval. The Senate passed the revised version of the bill, but Canada balked and set a March 1914 deadline for the United States to restore the original treaty parameters.[100]

The advent of the new Wilson administration initially engendered hope that the agreement might still succeed. The Senate passed the original bill in February, and for a brief period in late 1913 and early 1914 it seemed like it might finally happen.[101] Persistent complaints from local fishing interests and lack of familiarity with the issues in the House of Representatives soon slowed deliberations. Furthermore, Washington State industry players strongly opposed federal control of the state's fisheries, claiming that such a transmission of power was unconstitutional.[102] "Our proud boast that 'the people rule,'" the state fish commissioner protested, "is constantly met by the steady leakage of local administration to federal bureaus thousands of physical miles and millions of sympathetic miles from the real subject of concern—the people." Canada waited in vain through the summer, but the U.S. government took no further steps to pass the Inland Fisheries Treaty until after World War I.[103]

Simultaneous with the battles raging in Washington, D.C. and Ottawa, local authorities again tried to breach the issue of complementary transborder regulations. In response to Canadian complaints about lax Washington State fishery patrols, the state governor decided not to crack down on wayward American fishermen and fish trap owners but to instead appoint yet another committee to investigate the issues in 1911. Not surprisingly, that committee's assessment of the fishery echoed that of earlier such bodies: Washington State patrols needed proper funding and equipment. The commission also called for a firmer hand with fish trap owners. If owners were caught fishing during the weekly closed time, the commission suggested the fish trap be invalidated for one year; two such offenses should result in the appliance being sold at public auction. The committee likewise advocated licensing trap watchmen and permanently revoking the licenses of watchmen found guilty of illegal trap fishing. Despite several meetings with Canadian and Washington State representatives, however, stricter laws regarding fish traps did not pass until 1915.[104] Washington gradually appropriated more funding and equipment to the state patrols, but they remained woefully inadequate for the task at hand.

The transborder bickering that infused American-Canadian dialogue on their shared fishery and Washington State's unwillingness to match Canada's more comprehensive fishery laws prompted Canadian officials to repeatedly relax their own conservation regulations. In 1894, for instance, Canadian attempts to persuade their southern neighbors to commit to stricter pound net restrictions failed.[105] At the time the only commercial nets allowed in B.C. waters were gill nets, but the DMF decided to allow a few fish traps in Boundary Bay because of vociferous B.C. complaints and Washington's adamant refusals to rein in fish trap operators. The measure was designed to "place Canadian canners on a more even footing with their neighbours across the line."[106]

When Commissioner Edward Prince tried to eliminate these few B.C. traps in 1897 and again in 1900, the trap owners skillfully reiterated these arguments to retain their productive fishing structures.[107] Going even further, Henry Bell-Irving, the Canadian owner of the Boundary Bay traps, asked for exemption from the weekly closed time imposed in 1900.[108] When the local fishery guardian asked officials in Ottawa how to respond, Prince advised that "if in your judgment it may be best not to strictly enforce it [the closed period law] in Boundary Bay, in view of the United States nets being under less restrictions, you may for this season take no action."[109] These debates regarding fish traps in Canada persisted in the early 1900s, when the DMF appointed a small commission to investigate the viability and potential impact of increasing the number of traps in B.C. waters.[110] Still, Ottawa did not grant every request put forth by B.C. canners and fishermen. Some thirty-two individuals made application for fish traps in 1902, and a local fishermen's union asked for permission to use seines and longer nets, but the DMF denied them all.[111]

The 1902 pause was brief, however, as the practice of rescinding or watering down B.C. fishing regulations intensified the following decade. In 1904 the Canadian commissioner suggested lifting the weekly closed time entirely due to American competition, and though outlawed or severely restricted in every other province, he allowed purse seines to fish salmon in B.C. waters that same year.[112] Similarly, when the Washington State legislature failed to agree to the proposed 1906 and 1908 sockeye closures discussed earlier, the DMF let B.C. traps fish longer and for species other than sockeye. Tellingly, the fisheries commissioner specifically encouraged the trap owners to catch "American cohoes" as retribution. "It is *advantageous* to capture *all we can* of these inferior kinds [of fish] *belonging* to *U.S. waters*," the DMF's Edward Prince insisted in 1906, "in view of the toll taken of *B.C. Sockeyes* by the U.S. traps."[113] B.C. canners continued to pressure authorities for even more fish traps, but officials remained hesitant to grant too many additional licenses.

Canadian authorities may have been cautious about allowing more fish traps in B.C. waters, but they still continued to bend restrictions in response to American competition for salmon. In 1906 and again in 1907 officials in Ottawa agreed to extend the open season for the traps fishing coho on the west coast of Vancouver Island.[114] While urging the DMF to match Washington's law and reduce the closed period on fishing from forty-two to thirty-six hours in 1909 and 1910, one canner argued that "it was the general opinion that we, on this side, have done everything possible to preserve the industry, and it is now up to the United States to make reciprocal efforts."[115] The chief inspector of fisheries, F. H. Cunningham, advocated nonimposition of the closed period on the Fraser in 1912 because of American competition, and canners continued to push for additional fish traps in Canadian waters.[116] Other federal and provincial fishery authorities agreed with the decision to lift the closed period that year. "We are all of the opinion that as the American annual close season for the same period is a dead letter," the deputy commissioner wrote, "It is not advisable to observe ours as it only handicaps our fishermen."[117] In 1913, because the U.S. Senate continued to sit on the 1908 salmon conservation treaty pending in Congress, the DMF granted yet another fishing season extension.[118] The fault for weakening conservation regulations clearly lay on both sides of the border.

When the DMF extended the open season for salmon in the summer of 1913, Washington State Fish Commissioner L. H. Darwin wrote to the

Dominion commissioner of fisheries, obviously confused. New to his post and apparently not realizing the long history of attempts to create transborder fishing regulations, Darwin assumed that B.C. and Washington State had a "gentlemen's agreement" to set identical closed seasons for fishing sockeye salmon. "This annual close season on the Canadian side of the line was one of the suggested regulations," DMF Commissioner W. J. Bowser explained of the original and still pending 1908 treaty, "and the relaxation of it . . . merely presages the denunciation of the treaty which will take place if effect is not given by the Government of the United States." With regard to the gentlemen's agreement, Bowser sadly noted, "I regret that no such agreement has existed despite all that has been done on this side of the line looking either to gentlemen's agreement or to action by treaty."[119]

As each successive effort to pass an international sockeye salmon treaty stalled, Canadian authorities and B.C. fishing interests considered other possible—and increasingly desperate—strategies for limiting Washington fishers' access to "Canadian salmon." A recurring proposition was to dig a ditch from the Fraser River to Boundary Bay in the hopes that sockeye salmon would swim up this canal to the Fraser and bypass American traps. Some Canadians suggested building some kind of barrier in the Strait of Juan de Fuca that would divert the salmon northward into Canadian waters.[120] Canadian officials also tried to purchase Point Roberts outright, but the small peninsula had become so critical to the success of the Washington fishery that U.S. authorities politely declined the repeated offers.[121]

Many involved in the B.C. canning industry believed that if they lifted their regulations completely and allowed more seines and traps, the Americans would be frightened into enacting more stringent laws or supporting the international treaty. "Let us then commence to use traps and fight them with their own weapons," a local resident urged his government representative, "and if the fish begin to diminish they will be only too glad to diminish the traps or abolish the traps altogether."[122] Representatives of the B.C. Salmon Canners' Association also advocated this course of action. At a meeting in the fall of 1909 one member of that association stated that "the only way to bring the Puget Sound gentlemen to time, is to abandon all protective regulations on the Fraser, until such time as proper enforcement is made of adequate regulations by the American Authorities."[123]

Even as disagreements about salmon conservation and boat seizures roiled above the water's surface, ignorance about what was happening underwater was also critical to the dwindling health of the Salish Sea salmon fishery. Knowledge of salmon biology and salmon propagation in the late nineteenth and early twentieth centuries was still quite basic. From the 1890s to the late 1910s officials gradually learned more about the behavior of Pacific salmon, but significant gaps in their understanding of the species persisted well into the twentieth century.[124] Both U.S. and Canadian officials approached the issue of conservation by building hatcheries, nominally trying to limit overfishing, and allowing sufficient escapement of salmon to ensure their propagation. Before the 1890s some scientists and many North Americans generally believed that the oceanic fisheries were so vast that they were inexhaustible.[125] Around the turn of the twentieth century, however, declines in several fisheries and ongoing research led scientists to advocate more regulations to facilitate the sufficient escapement of spawning fish. Arriving at the number of fish that should be allowed to spawn was problematic, even when no other variables were factored into the equation.[126]

Fishery officials on both sides of the forty-ninth parallel likewise put far too much trust in the ability of hatcheries to cover the losses caused by overfishing and habitat destruction—particularly in Washington State.[127] Although Canada changed its policy on hatcheries in the 1930s, before World War I it too still had high hopes for the success of fish culture.[128] Opponents of conservation laws as well as some government officials assured politicians that hatcheries would revitalize the salmon runs. Canada built fifteen hatcheries on B.C. rivers between 1884 and 1933 (eight of them on the Fraser), and most attempted to raise sockeye salmon. Washington State officials also built hatcheries, but because the Skagit is the state's only sockeye-producing river, they made several attempts to negotiate a hatchery deal with B.C. processors and authorities.[129] The DMF held that the hatcheries already in place were sufficient, and yet again urged Washington State to both enact more stringent conservation regulations and actually enforce them. Despite dwindling numbers of sockeye salmon and no clear evidence that hatchery-produced fish were increasing the salmon population, Washington State officials continued to advocate for additional hatcheries as late as 1915.[130] "As against their proposition of the limiting of the number of fish taken," the state fish commissioner reported after meeting with B.C. fishery officials that year, "we hold to the idea that the proper solution is increased artificial propagation."[131]

When negotiations on the border fisheries treaty stalled in 1914, Washington officials developed a scheme to propagate sockeye salmon in the Samish River. Though sockeye did not run up the Samish naturally, the Washington fish commissioner maintained that they could tow sockeye salmon in boxes some fourteen miles up the Samish River to Samish Lake, where the fish would then spawn. There is no evidence that this plan—or the other artificial propagation projects then in progress—was effective, but it was not until 1925 that the state fisheries supervisor admitted that Washington's hatcheries may have been less successful than previously assumed.[132]

Building hatcheries that would theoretically increase the number of Salish Sea salmon was politically expedient and popular; preserving salmon habitat during this period of tremendous population growth and urban development was not. Developers and engineers on both sides of the border instigated a wide range of environmental changes that did salmon no favors. Mining companies and placer miners built dams on salmon-bearing tributaries and released debris into river waters. Seattle's engineers remade the waterways around the city, destroying prime salmon habitat in their efforts to "improve" on nature. Growing numbers and types of industries dumped sawdust, oil, gasoline, and other industrial byproducts into waterways with little consideration of the consequences, and the regional population used the same waterways to disperse its sewage.[133] These environmental changes seriously challenged salmon runs and contributed to far less favorable conditions for salmon throughout the region. The overfishing and wastefulness that typified this industry during its brief heyday were just part of a much larger, more complex picture of environmental change and declining habitat health.

By the end of World War I, both American and Canadian authorities recognized that Fraser River sockeye were endangered, but all efforts to devise transnational fishery regulations had failed. "We now know that for the past six or seven years we have over-fished our salmon," the state fish commissioner finally admitted in his annual report in 1918.[134] Transborder competition for fish, local infighting, a blind reliance on hatcheries, conflicts over jurisdiction, and the inability of United States treaty proponents to override regional protests against an international agreement all hindered the passage of a salmon conservation treaty. The Canadian tendency to relax their regulations in response to American inaction further exacerbated the rates and manner of fishing. Rock debris at Hell's Gate and ongoing regional urban development presented even more physical obstacles to the health of Salish Sea salmon. Finally, the signs were too obvious to ignore. This borderlands salmon fishery was in decline.

By 1918, Canada and the United States confronted the costs involved in drawing borders so disconnected from the natural world. It was not until well after World War I that both sides gradually committed to negotiating new types of borders with regard to sockeye salmon; in the process they unwittingly emulated the Native borders that once ordered the waters of the Salish Sea and its tributaries.

Conclusion

The Future of Salish Sea Salmon

H UMAN BORDERS HAVE ALWAYS MATTERED TO THE SALMON populations that spawn in the waterways of the Salish Sea. Northwest indigenous peoples demarcated space with attention to salmon availability, and, because their salmon fishing efforts largely remained in rivers or close to shore, Native borders successfully constrained excessive salmon harvesting. Regional Indians developed restrictive customs that limited access to the most productive fisheries at certain times while the common practice of sharing food made this conservation of fish and this border system of collective interest to the broader community.

In contrast, white newcomers drew borders that revealed the cultural and economic marginalization of salmon and created a new social geography that would remain permeable and contested for decades. Border banditry, fish piracy, and other illegal border crossings granted regional fishermen and fish workers opportunities for higher catches, additional income, and better wages. Fishermen of all ethnicities broadened the spatial reach of the fishery to reach the fish first. They took advantage of the jurisdictional outlet created by the border to protest both the terms of their employment and the corporate takeover of the fishery. As a result, the system's porosity fostered mistrust and sharpened competition across the forty-ninth parallel. These diverging geographies in the Salish Sea are fundamental to understanding both the sustainability and the decline of the Fraser River runs over time. Borders have both helped and hindered human attempts to manage this fishery for maximum benefit.

The realization that their shared sockeye salmon fishery was in trouble prompted Canada and the United States to return to the negotiating table after World War I, but persistent infighting and disagreements over how to jointly manage this resource continued to plague diplomatic discussions for the remainder of the twentieth century. Despite increasingly clear signs that conservation regulations were direly needed, it still took nearly twenty years for the two nations to agree to a system of joint management.[1] Although the 1937 Sockeye Salmon Convention constituted an important attempt to rethink the relationships between nations, borders, and salmon, it rested on a series of compromises that impeded its effectiveness from the outset. To garner support from purse seiners and ocean trollers who operated largely beyond the three-mile territorial limit, negotiators agreed not to regulate fishing on the high seas. By the time the treaty passed, the actual reach of the sockeye salmon fishery had already outstripped the range of treaty waters.[2] The United States also wanted eight years of additional scientific studies before conservation measures could be implemented, further delaying regulatory action. Still, the passage of this measure was a victory for conservation advocates at the time. Industry players and borderland residents had reason to look forward with hope for the future of their shared salmon fishery.[3]

The treaty created the six-member International Pacific Salmon Fisheries Commission (IPSFC) to study Pacific salmon and to regulate fishing on specified treaty waters between Washington and British Columbia. When the IPSFC finally introduced its rules in 1946, however, bickering between the United States and Canada over shared pink salmon runs began almost immediately. Because the Hell's Gate blockage and overfishing had also taken a significant toll on Fraser River pink salmon, both countries considered adding the run to the IPSFC's regulatory list in the 1950s.[4] When the United States hesitated, the Canadian minister of fisheries, James Sinclair, warned: "I hope our Canadian fishing fleet goes out and catches a much greater number of pinks off the West Coast." He added, "For once we get the bulk of this run, I think we will find, as with the sockeye, that our American friends will realize the value of an international commission to conserve the fisheries and divide the catch between the two nations."[5] More haggling resulted in the Pink Salmon Protocol of 1957 that gave the IPSFC authority to manage pink salmon in addition to sockeye.

Unfortunately, since the 1950s, many of the same problems that beset the Salish Sea fishery at the turn of the twentieth century have persisted, multiplied, and spread from Oregon to Alaska and farther out into the Pacific

Ocean. As scientists learned more about the vast territory traversed by salmon, both Canada and the United States set out to manage the geographic entirety of a salmon's life. In response to new understandings of salmon migration and to better protect other fisheries from predation by foreign fishermen, many countries, including the United States and Canada, began declaring two-hundred-mile "exclusive economic zones" in the 1970s. The 1982 United Nations Convention on the Law of the Sea confirmed this practice, and both the United States and Canada affirmed it again in the 1990s.[6]

New rounds of talks in the 1970s and 1980s led to a revamped 1985 treaty that replaced the IPSFC with the Pacific Salmon Commission (PSC) and extended treaty waters north to Alaska. Nevertheless, the complaints that began on the Salish Sea in the 1890s were quickly heard all along the Pacific Coast: Americans were catching too many "Canadian salmon" and Canadians were catching too many "American salmon." Even worse, because the treaty guaranteed each nation's fishermen an equal portion of the catch, fishermen were allowed to continue fishing severely depleted Columbia River runs that should have been off limits.[7]

Recognizing that fishing for salmon outside the relatively new two-hundred-mile territorial zone persisted and potentially threatened endangered stocks, Canada, Japan, Korea, Russia, and the United States initiated even more comprehensive joint conservation plans. Building on an informal agreement between Canada, Japan, and the United States from the 1950s, these countries formed the North Pacific Anadromous Fish Commission (NPAFC) in 1993. The purpose of the NPAFC was to prohibit high seas fishing for anadromous stocks in the North Pacific north of the thirty-third parallel, and member nations committed to enforcing this mandate with patrol ships and aircraft.[8]

Ongoing signs of decline in salmon numbers and growing evidence that Canadians and Americans were catching each other's fish undermined joint regulation of PSC waters by the mid-1990s. Disputes over international harvest allocations led Canada to try to charge American vessels a fee to pass through British Columbia waters en route to Alaska in 1994. American officials then threatened to raise duties on Canadian boats traversing the Strait of Juan de Fuca. Disagreements escalated and culminated in the United States lifting all restrictions on fishing Fraser River sockeye and Canadian boat captains blockading an American ferry in northern British Columbia. Known collectively as "the fish wars," these events surprised many onlookers, but they were simply new iterations of past conflicts.[9]

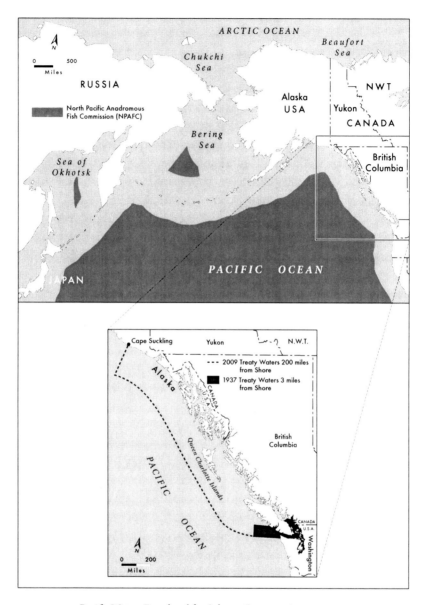

MAP 7.1 Pacific Waters Regulated for Salmon Conservation, 2011.

The United States and Canada managed to move past this impasse, and they agreed to yet another version of the Pacific Salmon Treaty in 1999 and again in 2009. The PSC works in conjunction with the Fish and Game Departments of Alaska and Washington, the Department of Fisheries and Oceans Canada, and various other industry players in their efforts to conserve Fraser River sockeye and pink salmon runs. Although the current Pacific Salmon Treaty is certainly a longer and more complicated version of the original, it continues to abide by many of the compromises made in the 1930s. The latest rendition still rests on catch parity between American and Canadian fishers, does little to restore vital salmon habitat, and despite a record run of Fraser River sockeye in 2010, does not seem to be reversing the overall decline of the runs under its purview.[10]

The geographically ambitious salmon conservation programs of the PSC and the NPAFC are attempts to align the scope of management with the spatial extent of actual fishing activity, but even with the technological advancements of recent years, policing the high seas is still a difficult proposition. Between 1993 and 2007, for instance, the NPAFC apprehended a total of just sixteen vessels engaged in illegal salmon fishing in the North Pacific. NPAFC reports suggest how hard it is to discover, track down, and apprehend fishing vessels on the open ocean.[11] Merely declaring the geographic scope of managed fishing space does not immediately translate into a tightly controlled fishery. As both harvesting and managing salmon have expanded out onto the high seas, it has become increasingly difficult to assess the impact of either one on the myriad runs that intermix in the North Pacific Ocean.

Fish farms off the coasts of Washington and especially British Columbia present yet another unsuccessful attempt to enclose marine space and control mobile organisms.[12] Salmon farming companies raise large numbers of anadromous Atlantic salmon in netted pens. Containing the fish allows fish farmers to control the growth and harvest rates of the fish while simultaneously protecting their private property. Despite recent efforts to limit such occurrences, Atlantic salmon have escaped through torn sections of net and predators in pursuit of a readymade snack have broken in. As a result, unknown numbers of Atlantic salmon have escaped in the past two decades. The ultimate impact of these escapes on the wild salmon population remains to be seen, but because researchers are finding Atlantic salmon scattered throughout coastal rivers, scientists are concerned that these escapees could jeopardize Pacific salmon habitat, compete with wild salmon for food, and potentially interbreed with wild Pacific salmon stocks.[13] Adult farm fish also regularly become infected with sea lice. Although sea lice are not a danger to those adults, they can infect outmigrating juvenile wild salmon who pass by the farms on their way out to sea. If not lethal for young wild salmon, sea lice can weaken the juveniles and make them easier prey for nearby predators. Because nets, like political boundaries on a map, do not create impermeable walls, these large pens release uneaten food pellets, antibiotics, feces, and toxic antifoulants into surrounding waters.[14] In addition, fish farms depend on tremendous numbers of small fish for feed.[15] The Environmental Protection Agency estimates that two to five kilograms of wild-caught small fish are required to produce just one kilogram of farmed fish.[16] Fish farms thus represent a new large-scale marine experiment, and the consequences for wild salmon remain contested and uncertain.

The history of the Salish Sea salmon fishery illustrates how international competition for a mobile aquatic resource has shaped the course of conservation politics and fishery management practices in both the United States and Canada. By the late twentieth century, this international competition for salmon expanded to include many other countries with interests in the fisheries of the Pacific Ocean. Canada, the United States, and now several other nations patrol the ocean portion of this fishery with ships and aircraft. These patrols, heavily dependent on fossil fuel, span the entire North Pacific in their quest to control who catches salmon where. Hoping to assist an ailing nature, the members of the NPAFC (and many other countries) have spent and continue to spend millions of dollars on salmon hatcheries with questionable results. In addition, many of these same countries are simultaneously pursuing the development of fish farming industries that could do even more harm to wild salmon and wild salmon habitat. Advances in technology, increased global demand for salmon, and delays in regulation drove this course of events, but we have reached a shaky and contradictory precipice.

The scale, intensity, and futility of these management tactics and related decisions are all the more surprising in light of the lessons embedded in the deeper reaches of this fishery's history on the Northwest Coast. As Native peoples realized by the pre- and early-contact periods, and as some fishery managers are learning of late, certain types of social, physical, and regulatory borders can lead to more sustainable fishing practices. Dividing fishing space into discrete management areas that are small enough to be policed effectively, more carefully limiting the number of fishermen allowed on those grounds, and more strictly regulating the total number of fish caught are all management approaches that are showing signs of success in both salmon and non-salmon fisheries.[17] Implementing such viable international salmon management practices will likely require emulating another aspect of time-honored Indian fishing practices: the cessation of high seas fishing and a return to riparian and coastal fishing. Such approaches will not benefit everyone equally, but perhaps, as Native peoples once discovered, that is the price of managing salmon sustainably.[18]

This history demonstrates the value of a transborder perspective on environmental change and the need, in the words of Lance van Sittert, for historians to "get their feet wet."[19] The transnational character of the Salish Sea salmon fishery has been crucial to how and why salmon were harvested and managed, and it continues to present challenges to fishery managers in many of the same ways today. In the western Canada–U.S. borderlands, these problems played out on an international, permeable water stage that thwarted easy regulation or containment. Each country claimed national sea territory and specific fish populations, but because fish are considered common property and people cannot control salmon migration routes, attempts by either country to lay claim to this mobile resource failed. Border banditry, fish pirating, and illegal border crossings exacerbated the conditions that led to the decline of Fraser River runs of salmon, and possibly harmed some of the Washington and Oregon runs as well. As fishing spread farther north and west, Canadian and American fishermen competed in an increasingly larger arena. The inability of managerial and territorial borders to hem in and control the spatial reach of commercial salmon fishing had and continues to have similar effects on runs all along the coast.

Fishing practices, management tactics, and salmon themselves have all changed over time, but these changes are difficult to appreciate while drifting on the seemingly timeless waters of the Salish Sea. Back on that deep green water weaving between the rocks and islands that still obstruct and guide the underwater routes of returning salmon, it is easy to imagine legitimate commercial fishermen and fish pirates navigating these currents more than a hundred years ago. Maneuvering in pursuit of salmon or to evade authorities, these men knew these waters and this archipelago intimately. Believing salmon were so abundant that they could never take them all, people fished with abandon and enhanced their earnings thanks to the proximity of the Canada–U.S. border. While the beauty of this amazing waterscape continues to dazzle, the implications of this legacy are ongoing and not yet fully understood. Still, the view from the Salish Sea on a sunny day is capable of seducing even the most skeptical observer into believing that these waters need wild Pacific salmon. The long, contested history of this fishery shows us that despite the many missteps there have been along the way, the lessons are there. Whether or not we will heed them remains to be seen.

Abbreviations

APAC: Alaska Packers Association Collection, Newspapers and Clippings, Center for Pacific Northwest Studies, Western Washington University, Bellingham, WA

Aiston Collection: Peggy Aiston Collection, Center for Pacific Northwest Studies, Western Washington University, Bellingham, WA

BIA, NAS: RG 75, Bureau of Indian Affairs Records, National Archives and Records Administration–Pacific Alaska Region, Seattle

CPNWS WWU: Center for Pacific Northwest Studies, Western Washington University, Bellingham, WA

DMMF: Deputy Minister of Marine and Fisheries

Doyle Papers: Henry Doyle Papers, University of British Columbia Special Collections, Vancouver

GR-0055, BCA: GR-0055, B.C. Police Force, Superintendent Correspondence Inward, 1891–1910, B.C. Archives, Victoria

GR-0061, BCA: GR-0061, B.C. Provincial Police Force, Correspondence Outward, 1864–1918, B.C. Archives, Victoria

GR-0063, BCA: GR-0063, Superintendent of Provincial Police, Correspondence Inward from Attorney General, 1898–1912, B.C. Archives, Victoria

GR-0397, BCA: GR-0397, B.C. Provincial Police Force, Vancouver-Westminster Police Records, 1899–1949, B.C. Archives, Victoria

GR-0419, BCA: GR-0419, B.C. Attorney General Records, B.C. Archives, Victoria

GR-0435, BCA: GR-0435, B.C. Department of Fisheries, B.C. Archives, Victoria

GR-1576, BCA: GR-1576, B.C. Provincial Police Force, Correspondence, 1890–1911, B.C. Archives, Victoria

IPSFC: International Pacific Salmon Fisheries Commission Collection, University of British Columbia Special Collections, Vancouver

MR: Microfilm Roll

MS-1, CVA: MS-1, Bell-Irving Family Fonds, City of Vancouver Archives, Vancouver

MS-870, CVA: MS-870, Anglo-British Packing Company Records, City of Vancouver Archives, Vancouver

MS-0105, BCA: MS-0105, James Murray Yale fonds, B.C. Archives, Victoria

PAFC: Pacific American Fisheries Collection, Center for Pacific Northwest Studies, Western Washington University

RG 10, LAC: Record Group 10, Department of Indian Affairs, B.C. Superintendency, Library and Archives Canada, Ottawa

RG 10, BS, LAC: Record Group 10, Black Series, Department of Indian Affairs, Library and Archives Canada, Ottawa

RG 13, LAC: Record Group 13, Department of Justice Records, Library and Archives Canada, Ottawa

RG 21, NAS: Record Group 21, Circuit Court Western District of Washington, Northern Division, Seattle, Civil and Criminal Case Files 1890–1911, National Archives and Records Administration–Pacific Alaska Region, Seattle

RG 23, LAC: Record Group 23, Department of Marine and Fisheries, Library and Archives Canada, Ottawa

RG 26, NADC: RG 26 United States Coast Guard, Revenue Cutter Service, National Archives and Records Administration, Washington, D.C.

RG 36, NAS: Record Group 36, U.S. Customs Service, Puget Sound District, National Archives and Records Administration–Pacific Alaska Region, Seattle

RG 36, NADC: Record Group 36, U.S. Customs Bureau, National Archives and Records Administration, Washington, D.C.

RG 75, WASIA: RG 75, Records of the Washington Superintendency of Indian Affairs, 1853–1874 (copies on microfilm at the University of Washington Library)

SCOHC: Skagit County Oral History Collection, Center for Pacific Northwest Studies, Western Washington University, Bellingham, WA

WDF, WSA: Washington State Department of Fish and Game, Washington State Archives, Olympia, WA

Notes

PACIFIC BORDERS

1   Kruckeberg, *Natural History of Puget Sound Country*, 82–84, 88–102, 112–15.

2   Taylor, *Making Salmon*, 5–6.

3   Bert Webber, a biologist, coined this term in the 1970s but only recently has it come into favor. Both the British Columbia Geographical Names Office and the Washington State Board on Geographic Names approved the use of "Salish Sea" to refer to the body of water that includes Puget Sound, the Strait of Juan de Fuca, and Georgia Strait. The former names are also still applicable. See "State Board on Geographic Names Approves 'Salish Sea,'" October 30, 2009, Washington State Department of Natural Resources, Science and Environment News, available online at http://www.dnr.wa.gov/ResearchScience/News/Pages/nr09_177.aspx.

4   Boyd, *Coming of the Spirit of Pestilence*, 3.

5   Alexandra Harmon, "Coast Salish History," in Miller, *Be of Good Mind*, 40. Historians have only recently started to move beyond modern political borders in their treatments of Native American history. See, for instance, John Lutz, "Work, Sex, and Death on the Great Thoroughfare: Annual Migrations of 'Canadian Indians' to the American Pacific Northwest," in Findlay and Coates, *Parallel Destinies*, 80–103; McManus, *Line Which Separates*; Raibmon, *Authentic Indians*; Thrush, *Native Seattle*; and Michel Hogue, "Between Race and Nation: The Creation of a Métis Borderland on the Northern Plains," in Johnson and Graybill, *Bridging National Borders in North America*, 59–87.

6   The geographic focus of this book is the western boundary waters of southwestern British Columbia and northwestern Washington. To draw a more complete picture of Native life prior to contact, I have drawn upon studies of all Northwest coastal groups in the pre- and early-contact eras.

7   Several Northwest Native groups engaged in similar practices. See, for example, Powell, "Coming Full Circle?"; and Montgomery, *King of Fish*, 46.

8   U.S. society has a long and troubled history of equating Native American peoples with environmentalism or granting them a heightened environmental ethic. See, for example, Krech, *Ecological Indian*; and Arnold, *Fishermen's Frontier*, chap. 1.

9   Montgomery, *King of Fish*, 25.

10   See, for instance, Arthur R. Kruckeberg, "A Natural History of the Puget Sound Basin," in Goble and Hirt, *Northwest Lands, Northwest Peoples*, 70–71; Broughton, "Late Holocene Resource Intensification in the Sacramento Valley, California"; and Butler, "Resource Depression on the Northwest Coast of North America."

11   On state-building, see, for example, Scott, *Seeing Like a State*.

12   White, *Organic Machine*; and Richard White, "Are You an Environmentalist or Do You Work for a Living?" in Cronon, *Uncommon Ground*, 171–86.

13   For compelling work on these topics in the Colorado coal mines, see Andrews, "'Made by Toile'?"; and Andrews, *Killing for Coal*.

14   There are hints that some similar border issues may have emerged later along the Alaska–British Columbia border in the north. Unfortunately, a comparison of the conditions in both borderlands is beyond the scope of this project.

15   For some of the early efforts in this direction, see Tyrrell, "American Exceptionalism in an Age of International History"; McGerr, "Price of the 'New Transnational History'"; and Thelen, "Rethinking History and the Nation-State."

16   On the broadening of borderlands history, see McKinsey and Konrad, *Borderland Reflections*; Lecker, *Borderlands*; Peter M. Slowe, "The Geography of Borderlands: The Case of the Quebec-U.S. Borderlands," in Girot, *The Americas*, 3–17; Alper, "Idea of Cascadia"; Hirt, *Terra Pacifica*; Kiy and Wirth, *Environmental Management on North America's Borders*; Ladow, *Medicine Line*; Ramirez, *Crossing the 49th Parallel*; and Findlay and Coates, *Parallel Destinies*. For work on comparative borderlands, see Baud and Van Schendel, "Toward a Comparative History of Borderlands"; Adelman and Aron, "From Borderlands to Borders"; Gabaccia, "Is Everywhere Nowhere?"; Peck, *Reinventing Free Labor*; Citino, "Global Frontier"; and Johnson and Graybill, *Bridging National Borders in North America*.

17   Studies of the "Atlantic World" are an early example of this, and that field is now quite substantial. In fact, "Atlantic World" research most likely prompted historians to think more broadly about the Pacific Rim. See, for example, Igler, "Diseased Goods"; Igler, "Re-Orienting Asian American History through Transnational and International Scales"; Chang, "Enforcing Transnational White Solidarity"; Chang, "Circulating Race and Empire"; and Igler, "On Coral Reefs, Volcanoes, Gods, and Patriotic Geology."

18   Alfred Crosby was one of the first historians to write a history about mobile nature, and Richard White and Ian Tyrrell have been calling for environmental historians to move beyond the nation-state since the 1990s. Crosby, *Columbian Exchange*; White, "Naturalization of Nature"; and Tyrrell, "American Exceptionalism in an Age of International History,"1048–50.

19   My thanks to Bob Wilson for interesting discussions on these issues. See, for

instance, Fiege, "Weedy West"; Marsh, *Drawing Lines in the Forest*; and Wilson, *Seeking Refuge*.

20 For an overview of these destructive practices, see Taylor, *Making Salmon*, 47–67.

21 This book builds on numerous excellent studies of the West Coast fishing industry. On Canadian fisheries, see Marchak, Guppy, and McMullan, *Uncommon Property*; Newell, *Development of the Pacific Salmon-Canning Industry*; Newell, *Tangled Webs of History*; Meggs, *Salmon*; Muszynski, *Cheap Wage Labour*; Harris, *Fish, Law, and Colonialism*; and Harris, *Landing Native Fisheries*. U.S. histories of the Pacific fisheries have historically neglected Puget Sound and focused more on the Columbia River, Alaska, or one ethnic group's experience along the entire Pacific coast. See, for example, Boxberger, *To Fish in Common*; Friday, *Organizing Asian American Labor*; Mighetto, *Saving the Salmon*; White, *Organic Machine*; Taylor, *Making Salmon*; and Arnold, *Fishermen's Frontier*. The two works that have been more transborder in nature have dealt with the diplomatic realm. See Joseph Taylor III, "The Historical Roots of the Canadian-American Salmon Wars," in Findlay and Coates, *Parallel Destinies*, 155–80; and Dorsey, *Dawn of Conservation Diplomacy*.

1. NATIVE BORDERS

1 Barnett, *Coast Salish of British Columbia*, 89.

2 Jenness, *Faith of a Coast Salish Indian*, 18–21.

3 Lichatowich, *Salmon without Rivers*, 11, 13.

4 Ibid., 15.

5 Kruckeberg, "A Natural History of the Puget Sound Basin," in Goble and Hirt, *Northwest Lands, Northwest Peoples*, 51–69; and Lichatowich, *Salmon without Rivers*, 9–23.

6 For different perspectives on when and how people first arrived on the west coast of North America, see Gibbons, "Geneticists Trace the DNA Trail of the First Americans"; Dillehay, "Great Debate on the First Americans"; Meltzer, "Clocking the First Americans"; Fladmark, *British Columbia Prehistory*, 13–15; and Ames and Maschner, *Peoples of the Northwest Coast*, 57–72, 81–86.

7 Ames and Maschner, *Peoples of the Northwest Coast*, 48–53, 67–72; and Fladmark, *British Columbia Prehistory*, 11–12.

8 Ames and Maschner, *Peoples of the Northwest Coast*, 113–28, 137–46; and Fladmark, *British Columbia Prehistory*, 36. When exactly salmon became a more important food source remains a major debate in the field of archaeology. See, for instance, Kusmer, "Changes in Subsistence Strategies at the Tsawwassen Site"; and Moss and Erlandson, "Reflecting on North American Pacific Coast Prehistory," 20–21.

9 See, for example, Drucker, *Indians of the Northwest Coast*, 6; and Ames and Maschner, *Peoples of the Northwest Coast*, 147–76.

10 For more on the language groups located south of the forty-ninth parallel, see Ruby and Brown, *Guide to the Indian Tribes of the Pacific Northwest*. On northern groups, see the studies cited in this chapter and in chapter 2. The Clatskanie, Tillamook, Alseans, Kalapuyans, Siuslawans, Coosans, Athapaskans, and Takelma occupied

the region between northern California and the Columbia River, but contact between these groups and those located farther north was less frequent. Because of this, I focus on the people who lived north of the Columbia River because they more commonly shared trade, intermarriage, and warfare networks.

11　Ames and Maschner, *Peoples of the Northwest Coast*, 113–5. According to Ames and Maschner, Wayne Suttles and Andrew Vayda initiated investigations into these assumptions in the 1960s and other scholars have followed suit since then. See, for example, Adams, *Gitksan Potlatch*, 86–92.

12　Donald and Mitchell, "Some Correlates of Local Group Rank among the Southern Kwakwaka'wakw."

13　Suttles, *Coast Salish Essays*, 47–51; Jewitt, *Narrative of the Adventures and Sufferings of John R. Jewitt*, 115; Sproat, *Scenes and Studies of Savage Life*, 53; Fraser, *Letters and Journal of Simon Fraser*, 125; and Maclachlan, *Fort Langley Journals*, 74, 106.

14　Jewitt, *Narrative of the Adventures and Sufferings of John R. Jewitt*, 68 (first quotation), 88 (second quotation).

15　Berringer, "Northwest Coast Traditional Salmon Fisheries," 39.

16　Jewitt, *Narrative of the Adventures and Sufferings of John R. Jewitt*, 88.

17　Ames and Maschner, *Peoples of the Northwest Coast*, 140–41; and R. G. Matson, "The Evolution of Northwest Coast Subsistence," in Croes, Hawkins, and Isaac, *Research in Economic Anthropology*, 386–87.

18　Berringer, "Northwest Coast Traditional Salmon Fisheries," 85–97, 101–11.

19　Jewitt, *Narrative of the Adventures and Sufferings of John R. Jewitt*, 87. See also Sapir and Swadesh, "Native Accounts of Nootka Ethnography," 42.

20　Fraser, *Journals and Letters of Simon Fraser*, 126 (quotation). See also Lamb, *Journals and Letters of Sir Alexander Mackenzie*, 361–62; Swan, *Northwest Coast*, 264; and Gunther, "Klallum Ethnography," 199–200.

21　Stewart, *Indian Fishing*, 79–92; Fraser, *Letters and Journals of Simon Fraser*, 114; Lamb, *Journals and Letters of Sir Alexander Mackenzie*, 371–72; and Berringer, "Northwest Coast Traditional Salmon Fisheries," 45–53.

22　Berringer, "Northwest Coast Traditional Salmon Fisheries," 28–36.

23　Ibid., 60–66.

24　Ames and Maschner, *Peoples of the Northwest Coast*, 145.

25　This is an extremely basic description of the complex reef net. For more details, see Suttles, "Economic Life of the Coast Salish of Haro and Rosario Straits," 152–61, and Stewart, *Indian Fishing*, 79, 93–94. According to Suttles's findings, reef net technology remained largely the same from the pre-Columbian period to 1900. Straits Salish were the only Northwest Coast people to use reef nets.

26　Maclachlan, *Fort Langley Journals*, 123 (quotation). "Joe" referred to a Cowichan man also known as Shashia. See ibid., 228–30.

27　Rathbun, "Review of the Fisheries in the Contiguous Waters of the State of Washington and British Columbia," 314.

28　Matson, "Evolution of Northwest Coast Subsistence," 385–89, 411–12, 417–19. As much of this interpretation rests on the presence or absence of salmon head bones in excavated Northwest Coast archaeological sites, other scholars warn that the fragility of salmon head bones could instead be the reason there are so few such remains. See Butler and Chatters, "Role of Bone Density in Structuring Prehistoric Bone Assemblages."

29   Gunther, "Klallam Ethnography," 202; and Elmendorf, "Structure of Twana Culture," 121.

30   Gunther, "Klallum Ethnography," 206-8; Jewitt, *Narrative of the Adventures and Sufferings of John R. Jewitt*, 87; Sproat, *Scenes and Studies of Savage Life*, 53-54; Stewart, *Indian Fishing*, 129-45; and de Laguna, *Under Mount Saint Elias*, vol. 7, part 1, 399-401.

31   Arnold, *Fishermen's Frontier*, 23-32; and Taylor, *Making Salmon*, 22-23.

32   Ames and Maschner, *Peoples of the Northwest Coast*, 93-96; and Fladmark, *British Columbia Prehistory*, 74-85.

33   Ames and Maschner, *Peoples of the Northwest Coast*, 177-94, 254-56; and Moss and Erlandson, "Reflections on North American Pacific Coast Prehistory," 24-25.

34   Suttles, *Coast Salish Essays*, 3-14; Gunther, "Klallum Ethnography," 260-65; and Rich, *Letters of John McLoughlin*, first series, 63.

35   Boas, *Kwakiutl Ethnography*, 51-53; and Codere, *Fighting with Property*, 5-7. For such practices among the Tlingit, see de Laguna, *Under Mount Saint Elias*, vol. 7, part 1, 461-69.

36   There are multiple compelling theories for why Northwest communities developed ranking practices. See, for instance, R. F. Schalk, "The Structure of an Anadromous Fish Resource," in Binford, *For Theory Building in Archeology*, 207-49; and Lepofsky et al., "Climate Change and Culture Change on the Southern Coast of British Columbia."

37   R. G. Matson, "Intensification and the Development of Cultural Complexity: The Northwest versus the Northeast Coast," in Nash, *Evolution of Maritime Cultures on the Northeast and the Northwest Coasts of America*, 138.

38   Kenneth M. Ames, "Toward a General Model of the Evolution of Ranking among Foragers," in Nash, *Evolution of Maritime Cultures on the Northeast and the Northwest Coasts of America*, 173.

39   Ames and Maschner, *Peoples of the Northwest Coast*, 145. The timing of the emergence of land tenure systems among Native groups is an ongoing debate. See, for instance, Ball, "Monopoly System of Wildlife Management," fn3, 37-41.

40   Drucker, *Northern and Central Nootkan Tribes*, 247-60; Cook and King, *Voyage to the Pacific Ocean*, 2:225-26; Boas, *Kwakiutl Ethnography*, 35-36; Ford, *Smoke from Their Fires*, 51-52; Oberg, *Social Economy of the Tlingit Indians*, 55-64; de Laguna, *Under Mount Saint Elias*, vol. 7, part 1, 361; and Seguin, *Tsimshian*, xii-xiii.

41   Ball, "Monopoly System of Wildlife Management," 40; and Arnold, *Fishermen's Frontier*, 36-37.

42   Sproat, *Scenes and Studies of Savage Life*, 79-81 (quotation on 81), 108-9.

43   Lamb, *Journals and Letters of Sir Alexander Mackenzie*, 393-94.

44   Suttles, "Economic Life of the Coast Salish of Haro and Rosario Straits,"152-63; and Berringer, "Northwest Coast Traditional Salmon Fisheries," 129-37. Female relatives collected the net materials and made the cordage from which each fisherman wove

his net section. To operate the nets, a crew of between ten to fourteen men worked from two anchored canoes beside the net, while the captain, or owner, stood in an offshore canoe to signal the men to close the net.

45   See, for instance, Elmendorf, "Structure of Twana Culture," 72–73, 269. The Quinault, Katzie, and Skagit were all known to build communal weirs but had different rules about communal access. See Olson, "Quinault Indians," 94; Suttles, "Katzie Ethnographic Notes," 22–23; and Collins, *Valley of the Spirits*, 113.

46   Suttles, *Coast Salish Essays*, 20.

47   Gunther, "Klallam Ethnography," 200. S'Klallam fish traps were not considered heritable property.

48   Suttles, "Katzie Ethnographic Notes," 22; Stewart, *Indian Fishing*, 79–80; and Berringer, "Northwest Coast Traditional Salmon Fisheries," 35, 64.

49   Sapir and Swadesh, "Native Accounts of Nootka Ethnography," 30.

50   Gunther, "Klallam Ethnography," 195; Collins, *Valley of the Spirits*, 80–81; and Suttles, "Katzie Ethnographic Notes," 23. These customs apparently persisted through the early twentieth century in some places. See Assu, *Assu of Cape Mudge*, 18.

51   Drucker, *Northern and Central Nootkan Tribes*, 251. No amount was specified, but each fisher gave what he could given his family's needs.

52   Elmendorf, "Structure of Twana Culture," 72.

53   Wayne Suttles, "The Ethnographic Significance of the Fort Langley Journals," in Maclachlan, *Fort Langley Journals*, 172–74; Ball, "Monopoly System of Wildlife Management," 41; and Stewart, *Indian Fishing*, 20.

54   Donald, *Aboriginal Slavery on the Northwest Coast*; Eells, *Indians of Puget Sound*, 349–50; and Sapir and Swadesh, "Native Accounts of Nootka Ethnography," 417. By the 1850s the average price for a single slave ranged from one hundred to five hundred dollars or twenty to one hundred blankets valued at five dollars each. See Swan, *Northwest Coast*, 166–67; Franchère, *Journal of a Voyage on the North West Coast*, 102; Sproat, *Scenes and Studies of Savage Life*, 89–92; and de Laguna, *Under Mount Saint Elias*, vol. 7, part 1, 469–75.

55   Among some groups, killing slaves was one means for displaying wealth. See Drucker, *Indians of the Northwest Coast*, 123; Drucker, *Northern and Central Nootkan Tribes*, 384; and Merk, *Fur Trade and Empire*, 100.

56   Maclachlan, *Fort Langley Journals*, 36, 57; and Suttles, "Ethnographic Significance of the Fort Langley Journals," in ibid., 203, 205–6.

57   Jewitt, *Narrative of the Adventures and Sufferings of John R. Jewitt*, 74. Jewitt clarified earlier visitors' confusion regarding the differences between wives and female slaves in Northwest Indian societies. Female slaves, not wives, were frequently offered to visiting men. See also Gunther, "Klallum Ethnography," 263–65; and Merk, *Fur Trade and Empire*, 101.

58   Similar practices prevailed along the Columbia River. See Taylor, *Making Salmon*, 25–26.

59   Boas, *Kwakiutl Ethnography*, 50; Collins, *Valley of the Spirits*, 97–107; Eugene Arima and John Dewhirst, "Nootkans of Vancouver Island," in Suttles, *Northwest Coast*, 394; Norton, "Patterns of Exogamy among Southern Coast Salish," 83–98; and

Suttles, "Ethnographic Significance of the Fort Langley Journals," in Maclachlan, *Fort Langley Journals*, 189–90. Note that due to the moiety and clan system of the Tlingit, Haida, and Tsimshian, marriages outside of that social system were far more rare. See de Laguna, *Under Mount Saint Elias*, vol. 7, part 1, 524–25.

60 Gunther, "Klallam Ethnography," 242–43. Despite these claims, Gunther found the reality of the situation in the 1920s did not support these statements. She believed depopulation by disease was the likely explanation.

61 See, for example, Maclachlan, *Fort Langley Journals*, 156, 202.

62 Eells, *Indians of Puget Sound*, 288–89 (quotation on 289).

63 See, for instance, Sapir and Swadesh, "Native Accounts of Nootka Ethnography," 209–10.

64 Boas, *Kwakiutl Ethnography*, 53–55.

65 Drucker, *Northern and Central Nootkan Tribes*, 344–53.

66 Suttles, "Economic Life of the Coast Salish of Haro and Rosario Straits," 212–13. Suttles suggests that while originally the Semiahmoo alone may have owned locations at Point Roberts, ownership of reef net sites diversified through intermarriage between the Semiahmoo and the Saanich (both Coast Salish) over time. See also Smith, "Nooksack, the Chilliwack, and the Middle Fraser," 337; and Croes and Blinman, *Hoko River*, 35.

67 Ames and Maschner, *Peoples of the Northwest Coast*, 165–71; Carlson and Bona, *Early Human Occupation in British Columbia*, 223; Lamb, *Journals and Letters of Sir Alexander Mackenzie*, 320; de Laguna, *Under Mount Saint Elias*, vol. 7, part 1, 346–48, 350–52; Sproat, *Scenes and Studies of Savage Life*, 78–79; and Jewitt, *Narrative of the Adventures and Sufferings of John R. Jewitt*, 36–40, 75–76.

68 Barman, *West Beyond the West*, 15.

69 Suttles, *Coast Salish Essays*, 22.

70 Taylor, *Making Salmon*, 24–25.

71 Sproat, *Scenes and Studies of Savage Life*, 19; and Lamb, *Journals and Letters of Sir Alexander Mackenzie*, 390.

72 The potlatch varied widely among the different Northwest Native groups. See, for example, Codere, *Fighting with Property*, 62–97; Boas, *Kwakiutl Ethnography*, 77–104; Elmendorf, "Structure of Twana Culture," 328–33, 337–43; Margaret Seguin, "Lest There Be No Salmon: Symbols in Traditional Tsimshian Potlatch," in Seguin, *Tsimshian*, 110–33; Suttles, *Coast Salish Essays*, 23–24; Gunther, "Klallam Ethnography," 306–10; and Sapir and Swadesh, "Native Accounts of Nootka Ethnography," 44.

73 Ames and Maschner, *Peoples of the Northwest Coast*, 199–200, 209, 217–18.

74 David M. Schaepe, "Rock Wall Fortifications," in Carlson, *Stò:lō Coast Salish Historical Atlas*, 52–53.

75 Ames and Maschner, *Peoples of the Northwest Coast*, 199–200, 209.

76 Assu, *Assu of Cape Mudge*, xiv–xv, 5 (quotation); Ames and Maschner, *Peoples of the Northwest Coast*, 200.

77 Drucker, *Northern and Central Nootkan Tribes*, 344–53.

78 Sapir and Swadesh, "Native Accounts of Nootka Ethnography," 362–67; 373–77.

For additional examples of such conflicts, see Ames and Maschner, *Peoples of the Northwest Coast*, 195–99; Suttles, "Ethnographic Significance of the Fort Langley Journals," 197–206; Suttles, "Economic Life of the Coast Salish of Haro and Rosario Straits," 35; Gunther, "Klallam Ethnography," 266–73; and Oberg, *Social Economy of the Tlingit Indians*, 55–56.

79   Boas, *Kwakiutl Ethnography*, 36.

80   Sapir and Swadesh, "Native Accounts of Nootka Ethnography," 427–33.

81   de Laguna, *Under Mount Saint Elias*, vol. 7, part 1, 233. According to de Laguna, going to war for territory was not one of the main causes for conflict among the Tlingit. See ibid., part 2, 580–81.

82   Gunther, "Klallum Ethnography," 267.

83   This is not to say that Native communities did not experience their share of conflict, but such events were usually a response to a poor chief or population pressures. There is little evidence to suggest that community members did not respect their own village's resource and territorial borders, or that they protested the social structures in place in their immediate community. See, for instance, Oberg, *Social Economy of the Tlingit Indians*, 56–59; Sproat, *Scenes and Studies of Savage Life*, 20, 188–96; Ford, *Smoke from Their Fires*, 57–61; Sapir and Swadesh, "Native Accounts of Nootka Ethnography," 114, 346–49, 373–77; Drucker, *Northern and Central Nootkan Tribes*, 318–19; and Taylor, *Making Salmon*, 37.

84   Sproat, *Scenes and Studies of Savage Life*, 89.

85   Eells, *Indians of Puget Sound*, 350.

86   Suttles, *Coast Salish Essays*, 18–20; and Jewitt, *Narrative of the Adventures and Sufferings of John R. Jewitt*, 134–35.

87   Anthropologist Steve Langdon found that the Tlingit salmon fishers on Prince of Wales Island in southeastern Alaska clearly understood the concept of "escapement." See Arnold, *Fishermen's Frontier*, 33–37.

88   Similar practices prevailed in the Columbia River region. See Taylor, *Making Salmon*, chap. 1.

89   Barnett, *Coast Salish of British Columbia*, 88–89.

90   Ford, *Smoke from Their Fires*, 75.

91   Sproat, *Scenes and Studies of Savage Life*, 79.

92   de Laguna, *Under Mount Saint Elias*, vol. 7, part 1, 361; and Drucker, *Northern and Central Nootkan Tribes*, 251–52. Note that the first scholars to study Northwest Indian fisheries did not attribute any awareness of the principles of sustainability to the Indians, but evidence now suggests otherwise. See, for example, Hewes, "Aboriginal Use of Fishery Resources in Northwestern North America."

93   Berringer, "Northwest Coast Traditional Salmon Fisheries," 74–77, 100; Elmendorf, "Structure of Twana Culture," 74; Gunther, "Klallam Ethnography," 199; and Ball, "Monopoly System of Wildlife Management," 41.

94   Drucker, *Northern and Central Nootkan Tribes*, 16.

95   Eells, *Indians of Puget Sound*, 158; Elmendorf, "Structure of Twana Culture," 65–67; and Newell, *Tangled Webs of History*, 42.

96   See, for example, Gunther, "Further Analysis of the First Salmon Ceremony,"

129–73; Sapir and Swadesh, "Native Accounts of Nootka Ethnography," 33; and Barnett, *Coast Salish of British Columbia*, 88–92.

97 Suttles, "Katzie Ethnographic Notes," 22. On other groups' salmon taboos, see Gunther, "Klallam Ethnography," 202–4, 237, 240; Elmendorf, "Structure of Twana Culture," 62–63, 66; Boas, *Kwakiutl Ethnography*, 157; Swan, *Northwest Coast*, 203–4; de Laguna, *Under Mount Saint Elias*, vol. 7, part 1, 383–84; part 2, 889–90; Sproat, *Scenes and Studies of Savage Life*, 211; and Franchère, *Journal of a Voyage on the North West Coast*, 96–97.

98 Joseph Taylor underscores this important point in his book. According to Taylor, "Aboriginal ceremonies and taboos nevertheless moderated harvest *effectively, if not intentionally.*" See Taylor, *Making Salmon*, 36 (emphasis in original).

2. FISH, FUR, AND FAITH

1 Vancouver, *Voyage of Discovery*, 2:524. Peter Puget writes of a similar event in his journal. See Anderson, "Vancouver Expedition," 199.

2 Jewitt, *Narrative of the Adventures and Sufferings of John R. Jewitt*, 24.

3 Ibid., 24–26. On this and other violent encounters, see Fisher, *Contact and Conflict*, 16–17.

4 Cook, *Flood Tide of Empire*, 9–17, 43–44. Although some people believe that Francis Drake reached the southern coast of Vancouver Island in his 1579 voyage, available evidence suggests he did not proceed further than the present Oregon-California border. See ibid., 7–9; Raymond H. Fisher, "Finding America," in Smith and Barnett, *Russian America*, 17–31; and Douglas W. Veltre, "Perspectives on Aleut Culture Change during the Russian Period," in ibid., 176–77.

5 Although the Spaniards traded for some local fish near Nootka in 1792, they were not concerned about obtaining outside provisions. See Caamaño, "Journal of Jacinto Caamaño." Spaniard Juan Jose Pérez Hernandez met the Haida and possibly the Nuu-chah-nulth in 1774, but as provisions aboard—poor as they were—apparently remained plentiful, he and his crew traded only for furs, blankets, and some sardines. See Beals, *Juan Pérez on the Northwest Coast*, 75, 77–79, 89; and Cook, *Flood Tide of Empire*, 59–65.

6 Cook, *Flood Tide of Empire*, 79–82.

7 Captain Cook traded with the Hawaiian islanders mostly for pigs, vegetables, potatoes, plantains, and taro root. See, for example, Cook and King, *Voyage to the Pacific Ocean*, 2:138, 144, 147, 150, and 152. For more on the emergence of Hawai'i as a supply port for visitors to the northwest coast, see Sturgis, *Journal of William Sturgis*, 15, 35; Koppel, *Kanaka*, 6–10; and Bradley, "Hawaiian Islands and the Pacific Fur Trade," 275–99.

8 Cook and King, *Voyage to the Pacific Ocean*, 2:220.

9 Ibid., 2:327–28, 334, 336–37 (quotation on 336); 3:87–88.

10 Fisher, "Northwest from the Beginning of Trade with Europeans to the 1880s," 125.

11 Vancouver, *Voyage of Discovery*, 2:516–17.

12 Ibid., 2:538. Vancouver and his men also reported seeing Natives bearing the scars

of the disease near Port Discovery, in Hood Canal, and near Whidbey Island. In the early 1800s other European explorers reported similar experiences up and down the coast: Meriwether Lewis and William Clark discovered the illness had raged near the mouth of the Willamette River some thirty years before their arrival; David Thompson noted the effects of the sickness among the Kootenay; and Simon Fraser saw evidence of the disease in 1808 along the Fraser River as well. See ibid, 2:528, 540, 559; Fraser, *Letters and Journals of Simon Fraser*, 94; and Harris, *Resettlement of British Columbia*, 14.

13 Harris, *Resettlement of British Columbia*, 4–10.

14 Jenness, "Faith of a Coast Salish Indian," 34.

15 Elmendorf, "Structure of Twana Culture," 272.

16 Suttles, "Post-Contact Culture Change among the Lummi Indians," 42.

17 Cook and King, *Voyage to the Pacific Ocean*, 3:127–28.

18 Dee, *Journal of John Work*, 81; and Maclachlan, *Fort Langley Journals*, 31, 36. Due to the HBC Fort Langley chief factor's later policy of not allowing Native women into the fort at night, venereal disease became less of a problem at Fort Langley than at other forts; see Maclachlan, *Fort Langley Journals*, 246fn32.

19 Some slave-owning women at Fort George prostituted out their female slaves to the male fur traders in the 1820s. See Merk, *Fur Trade and Empire*, 101. Though likely overstated, Gilbert Sproat observed an increase in prostitution as related to the slave trade in the 1860s; see Sproat, *Scenes and Studies of Savage Life*, 92. For more on these issues, see Cooper, "Native Women of the Northern Pacific Coast," 58–60.

20 Vancouver, *Voyage of Discovery*, 2:517fn1. On the instructions given to the *Daedalus* to go to New Zealand, see ibid., 1:120. Vancouver and the *Daedalus* finally met up a few days later than planned; see ibid., 1:146.

21 The ships commanded by both Alexander Walker and George Vancouver were forced to rely on locals for salmon and other foodstuffs in the 1780s and 1790s. See Fisher and Bumsted, *Account of a Voyage to the North West Coast of America in 1785 & 1786*, 40, 42, 43, 48; and Vancouver, *Voyage of Discovery*, 2:517, 528, 534–35.

22 Vancouver, *Voyage of Discovery*, 2:547.

23 Edward Bell, clerk of the *Chatham*, Personal Journal, January 1, 1791–February 26, 1794, May 1792, quoted in ibid., 2:517fn1.

24 Ibid., 2:624.

25 Ibid., 2:519, 631–32, 565, 652.

26 Fraser, *Letters and Journals of Simon Fraser*, 75.

27 On receiving salmon specifically, see ibid., 63, 65, 84, 87, 94, 98, 114, 125–26, 128; on receiving just "fish" but during the salmon season, see 81, 102, 117. On June 18, Fraser noted that they ate marmot, which was the first fresh meat—other than fish—they recorded eating since their departure from Fort George in May; see ibid., 86.

28 See, for instance, Lamb, *Journals and Letters of Sir Alexander Mackenzie*, 360–61, 365, 388–89.

29 The Nuu-chah-nulth, for instance, successfully maintained their maritime trade against the incursions of other Indians. See Cook and King, *Voyage to the Pacific Ocean*, 2:215–16, 219.

30   Fisher, *Contact and Conflict*, 29–34. Several different Native groups became what the HBC termed "home guards" for various forts along the coast. For a sampling, see Bowsfield, *Fort Victoria Letters*, 16; and Rich, *Letters of John McLoughlin*, first series, 53. Recognizing the control coastal Indians had on the routes to the interior, the HBC tried to circumvent Native middlemen on both the Nass and Stikine rivers, but they met with much resistance from the Indians and were not very successful. See Rich, *Letters of John McLoughlin*, first series, 311, 317–22; and Tolmie, *Journals of William Fraser Tolmie*, 283–86. The Tsimshian leader, Ligeex, held a monopoly on upriver trade near Fort Simpson and is an excellent example of how such powerful Native leaders secured and maintained lucrative trade routes. See Marsden and Galois, "The Tsimshian, the Hudson's Bay Company, and the Geopolitics of the Northwest Coast Fur Trade."

31   At the same time John Jacob Astor established Fort Astoria in 1811, the HBC, a serious rival in the fur trade, expanded into the Nor'westers' traditional territory and built a fort in the Peace River region in 1820. For HBC history, see Galbraith, *Hudson's Bay Company as an Imperial Factor*.

32   George Simpson wanted the forts to become as self-sufficient as possible. See Rich, *Letters of John McLoughlin*, first series, xxvi; and Merk, *Fur Trade and Empire*, 65, 87.

33   Tolmie, *Journals of William Fraser Tolmie*, 223.

34   Dee, *Journal of John Work*, 77.

35   Rich, *Letters of John McLoughlin*, first series, 205–6, 257–58, 281–82; Cullen, "History of Fort Langley," 34–35; and Dee, *Journal of John Work*, 74.

36   Rich, *Letters of John McLoughlin*, first series, 325; Tolmie, *Journals of William Fraser Tolmie*, 235, 254; and Dee, *Journal of John Work*, 86.

37   Merk, *Fur Trade and Empire*, 121.

38   Rich, *Letters of John McLoughlin*, first series, 37.

39   Ibid., first series, 37, 92.

40   Cole, *This Blessed Wilderness*, 74–75, 84, 87; and Cullen, "History of Fort Langley," 26.

41   Rich, *Letters of John McLoughlin*, first series, 155.

42   Cullen, "History of Fort Langley," 32.

43   Douglas quoted in ibid., 32. The HBC did have potential competition in the salmon trade in the mid-1830s from the American trader Captain Wyeth and from Captain John Couch in the early 1840s, but both were short-lived ventures. See Rich, *Letters of John McLoughlin*, first series, 128, 141; second series, 25.

44   Cullen, "History of Fort Langley," 26; Rich, *Letters of John McLoughlin*, first series, 124, and second series, 63, 82, 228, 274–75; and Cole, *This Blessed Wilderness*, 94.

45   Jones, *Annals of Astoria*, 72–82, 144, 158.

46   Dee, *Journal of John Work*, 69.

47   Ibid., 76 (quotation), 78. Fort McLoughlin in particular was known to be a dreary and remote location that undoubtedly exacerbated the men's problems with their salmon diet. See Tolmie, *Journals of William Fraser Tolmie*, 297, 307, 309, 315.

48   Tolmie, *Journals of William Fraser Tolmie*, 307; Maclachlan, *Fort Langley Journals*,

36. Fort Victoria and Fort Rupert also employed men who found the fish diet offensive; see Bowsfield, *Fort Victoria Letters*, 88–89, 113.

49   Cole, *This Blessed Wilderness*, 84.

50   Rich, *Letters of John McLoughlin*, second series, 7.

51   Ibid., second series, 265, 274, 305.

52   Bowsfield, *Fort Victoria Letters*, 6–7, 12, 24–25, 45, 101–2, 158.

53   See Williams, *London Correspondence Inward from Sir George Simpson*, 73–74, 108–9.

54   Bowsfield, *Fort Victoria Letters*, 6, 50, 189–90.

55   Ibid., 6.

56   Cullen, "History of Fort Langley," 35; and Bowsfield, *Fort Victoria Letters*, 193.

57   Maclachlan, *Fort Langley Journals*, 75, 124, 128.

58   Jones, *Annals of Astoria*, 148–49, 161.

59   Maclachlan, *Fort Langley Journals*, 32. For additional examples of large salmon purchases and Indians hesitating to sell fish, see ibid., 37, 59, 72, 74, 82, 123–24, 154–56. On high prices being related to scarcity, see also Dee, *Journal of John Work*, 58–60.

60   Maclachlan, *Fort Langley Journals*, 64.

61   Dee, *Journal of John Work*, 63.

62   Rich, *Letters of John McLoughlin*, first series, 265. On desertions, see, for example, Bowsfield, *Fort Victoria Letters*, 60, 66–67. Due to the shortage of labor, the HBC often hired Indians for various projects. See, for example, Tolmie, *Journals of William Fraser Tolmie*, 219.

63   Maclachlan, *Fort Langley Journals*, 36, 38; and Dee, *Journal of John Work*, 15. Some Indians at Fort Langley drove a hard bargain for sturgeon, but this could simply have been related to supply; see Maclachlan, *Fort Langley Journals*, 59.

64   Maclachlan, *Fort Langley Journals*, 123–24 (quotation, emphasis in original). See also Cullen, "History of Fort Langley," 49–50.

65   Boyd, *Coming of the Spirit of Pestilence*, 39–45.

66   Ibid., 49–52.

67   Ibid., 84–115. See also Rich, *Letters of John McLoughlin*, first series, 88, 96, 104; Tolmie, *Journals of William Fraser Tolmie*, 183; and Cook, "Epidemic of 1830–1833 in California and Oregon," 313–16.

68   Rich, *Letters of John McLoughlin*, first series, 271; and Boyd, *Coming of the Spirit of Pestilence*, 116–28, 135–36. The influx of whites into the U.S. and Canadian Wests from the 1840s on introduced wave after wave of disease that killed thousands of Northwest Natives over the course of the nineteenth century. See, for example, Boyd, *Coming of the Spirit of Pestilence*, 145–201; Swan, *Northwest Coast*, 55–59, 108, 110, 212; Bowsfield, *Fort Victoria Letters*, 21–23; and Smith, "Nooksack, the Chilliwack, and the Middle Fraser," 332.

69   Harris, *Resettlement of British Columbia*, 23.

70   Wayne Suttles, "The Ethnographic Significance of the Fort Langley Journals," in Maclachlan, *Fort Langley Journals*, 170–71.

71   Suttles, "Katzie Ethnographic Notes," 8–11.

72   Duff, *Upper Stalo Indians of the Fraser Valley*, 43–45.

73 Suttles, "Economic Life of the Coast Salish of Haro and Rosario Straits," 150.

74 Harris, *Resettlement of British Columbia*, 23; and Berringer, "Northwest Coast Traditional Salmon Fisheries," 136.

75 Lamb, *Journals and Letters of Sir Alexander Mackenzie*, 362. Later in his journey, Mackenzie manipulated these suspicions to stop Indian thievery by claiming that white men could prevent the salmon from running because they owned the seas; see ibid., 397.

76 Ibid., 366.

77 Ibid., 369–70.

78 Jones, *Annals of Astoria*, 55 (quotation), 56.

79 Tyrrell, *David Thompson's Narrative*, 511.

80 Cox, *Adventures on the Columbia River*, 152–53; and Jones, *Annals of Astoria*, 21, 24.

81 Jones, *Annals of Astoria*, 178.

82 Maclachlan, *Fort Langley Journals*, 123.

83 Tolmie, *Journals of William Fraser Tolmie*, 167.

84 Lamb, *Journals and Letters of Sir Alexander Mackenzie*, 361.

85 Jones, *Annals of Astoria*, 57.

86 Ibid., 165.

87 Maclachlan, *Fort Langley Journals*, 120.

88 Ibid., 64, 121.

89 Jones, *Annals of Astoria*, 53–54, 56.

90 Taylor, *Making Salmon*, 46, 61–62.

91 Dee, *Journal of John Work*, 60 (quotation), 63. For examples of HBC men fishing for salmon on their own, see ibid., 61, 67.

92 Maclachlan, *Fort Langley Journals*, 55, 64 (quotation), 65, 121, 123.

93 It is not clear how the HBC came by the Indian nets from the Columbia River; see ibid., 123.

94 Ibid., 106, 112; Bowsfield, *Fort Victoria Letters*, 170; and Tolmie, *Journals of William Fraser Tolmie*, 259–60. Clear, unambiguous references to any HBC employees or other whites fishing on their own are scarce. The American trader Captain John Couch seined for salmon briefly, but this was on the Columbia where the Indian population had suffered so significantly from disease by the 1840s. Rich, *Letters of John McLoughlin*, second series, 25.

95 Barman and Watson, *Leaving Paradise*.

96 Gibbs, "Tribes of Western Washington and Northwestern Oregon," 239.

97 de Laguna, *Under Mount Saint Elias*, vol. 7, part 2, 710; and Boyd, *Coming of the Spirit of Pestilence*, 53–54.

98 Rich, *Letters of John McLoughlin*, first series, 282.

99 Bowsfield, *Fort Victoria Letters*, 21–22 (quotation on 22).

100 Cox, *Adventures on the Columbia River*, 151; and Boyd, *Coming of the Spirit of Pestilence*, 45–46. "Two-spirit person" is a term recently coined by indigenous peoples to replace "berdache," as this term has several negative connotations. See Cameron, "Two-Spirited Aboriginal People."

101 Cook notes that the HBC may have spread this story among the Indians to discour-

age them from trading with anyone but the HBC. Still, it is most likely that the epidemic arrived on the coast by ship. See Cook, "Epidemic of 1830–1833 in California and Oregon," 308–9.

102   Tolmie, *Journals of William Fraser Tolmie*, 238.

103   Boyd, *Coming of the Spirit of Pestilence*, 110–15 (quotation on 112–13).

104   Gunther, "Further Analysis of the First Salmon Ceremony," 150–55. Gunther explains that many of the Northwest Coast Indians forbade ceremonially unclean individuals from either eating the first salmon or approaching the waters in which they are caught.

105   de Laguna, *Under Mount Saint Elias*, vol. 7, part 2, 889–90; and Gunther, "Klallam Ethnography," 203–4.

106   Quoted in Harris, *Resettlement of British Columbia*, 7–8.

107   Boyd, *Coming of the Spirit of Pestilence*, 55; Jenness, *Faith of a Coast Salish Indian*, 8; Elmendorf, "Structure of Twana Culture," 62–63; Lamb, *Journals and Letters of Sir Alexander Mackenzie*, 366, 370; Franchère, *Journal of a Voyage on the North West Coast of North America*, 96–97; and Wayne Suttles, "Coping with Abundance: Subsistence on the Northwest Coast," in Suttles, *Coast Salish Essays*, 46–51.

108   Maclachlan, *Fort Langley Journals*, 74–75.

109   Ibid., 125. The journals indicate that after the failed 1828 salmon run, the local Indians were starving. See ibid., 106.

110   There are numerous references to the very active and influential role Native women played in the maritime and land-based fur trade. See, for instance, Vancouver, *Voyage of Discovery*, 2:528, 567; Sturgis, *Journal of William Sturgis*, 34; Caamaño, "Journal of Jacinto Caamaño," part 1, 205; Fisher and Bumsted, *Account of a Voyage to the North West Coast of America in 1785 & 1786*, 47; Maclachlan, *Fort Langley Journals*, 31; and Tolmie, *Journals of William Fraser Tolmie*, 301. American fur trader William Sturgis and explorers Jacinto Caamaño and Alexander Walker were all offered Native women by Indian men. They all claimed they refused the offer, but some of Walker's crew appear to have paid for female Native prostitutes. Sturgis, *Journal of William Sturgis*, 60; Caamaño, "Journal of Jacinto Caamaño," part 1: 207, part 2: 273, 287; and Fisher and Bumsted, *Account of a Voyage to the North West Coast of America in 1785 & 1786*, 87.

111   Jewitt, *Narrative of the Adventures and Sufferings of John R. Jewitt*, 74.

112   Vancouver, *Voyage of Discovery*, 2:654. Captain Cook observed that the women at Nootka always behaved with the utmost propriety; see Cook and King, *Voyage to the Pacific Ocean*, 2:258. Unlike in Hawai'i and at some other Pacific islands, Cook makes no mention of Northwest Native women being offered to his men.

113   Cooper, "Native Women of the Northern Pacific Coast," 59–60; and Blackman, *During My Time*, 43–44. Both authors argue that obtaining goods for sex was an acceptable practice among the Haida, and as the Haida believed some women could impart special powers during intercourse, these women could have sexual relations with any number of men, even if married.

114   Jewitt, *Narrative of the Adventures and Sufferings of John R. Jewitt*, 125–31, 136–37. Since Jewitt was technically Maquinna's slave, his being allowed to marry and to

marry a high-status woman from another village would have been unusual. If his account is accurate, his status may have been heightened by his highly valued metalworking skills. It is also possible Jewitt embellished his story after the fact.

115   Blackman, *During My Time*, 69.

116   Tolmie, *Journals of William Fraser Tolmie*, 260; and Maclachlan, *Fort Langley Journals*, 21.

117   By the early nineteenth century, Native women were also becoming involved with a few Chinese men who had been shipwrecked or abandoned on the coast. See Koppel, *Kanaka*, 23–24; Barman and Watson, *Leaving Paradise*; and Sproat, *Scenes and Studies of Savage Life*, 27. Some encounters appear to have been homosexual in nature. See, for instance, Rich, *Letters of John McLoughlin*, first series, 185–86.

118   Jones, *Annals of Astoria*, 203; and Merk, *Fur Trade and Empire*, 87.

119   Tolmie, *Journals of William Fraser Tolmie*, 262.

120   Ibid., 260.

121   Maclachlan, *Fort Langley Journals*, 21.

122   Ibid., 99–100. On how resigned Archibald McDonald was to the practice, see ibid., 87.

123   Ibid., 85.

124   Ibid., 99–100, 114.

125   Jones, *Annals of Astoria*, 203.

126   Tolmie, *Journals of William Fraser Tolmie*, 219. Also at Nisqually, Tolmie met a striking Indian woman known as Princess Charlotte. Although she had apparently been a well-known partner to white men, her penchant for liquor and extravagance were deemed a problem, and the fort refused to allow her back; see ibid., 215.

127   Van Kirk contends that Indian women's labor was extremely important to fur trader forts throughout the region west of the Rockies; see Van Kirk, "*Many Tender Ties,*" 53–73. On Native women possibly being able to improve their status through intermarriage and residence at the forts, see Cooper, "Native Women of the Northern Pacific Coast," 54–56; and Van Kirk, "*Many Tender Ties,*" 75–94.

128   During the salmon season all the Native women and a few fort men were involved in processing salmon. Maclachlan, *Fort Langley Journals*, 82. Interestingly, the HBC reported having sent salted salmon with both their heads and backbones to London in 1839. Perhaps this shift meant that the local Natives could no longer compel the fort men to prepare the salmon in the Indian manner, or perhaps these were late-season salmon and so not subject to the same rules as early-season fish. In any case the bones were apparently being removed again by 1842. See, for example, Rich, *Letters of John McLoughlin*, second series, 228, 264–65.

3. REMAKING NATIVE SPACE

1   Suttles, "Economic Life of the Coast Salish of Haro and Rosario Straits," 8, 14, 22, 28, 34, 42.

2   Fish Trap Location Maps, Microfilm Reel (hereafter MR) 1–2, Washington State

Department of Fish and Game, Washington State Archives, Olympia, WA (hereafter WDF, WSA).

3   Harmon, *Indians in the Making*, 58, 67.

4   Stevens, *Life of Isaac Ingalls Stevens*, 1:448–77 and 2:1–9; Meeker, *Pioneer Reminiscences of Puget Sound*, 231–73; and Harmon, *Indians in the Making*, 82. Stevens negotiated the Medicine Creek Treaty in December 1854 with residents of southern Puget Sound, and the Point Elliot Treaty with northern Sound groups in January 1855. A week later he drafted the Point-No-Point Treaty with people from Hood Canal and the Strait of Juan de Fuca, in addition to the Neah Bay Treaty with the Makah on the Olympic Peninsula.

5   In February 1855, Stevens held the Chehalis Council to make a treaty with several of the Indian bands along the coast from the Columbia River to the Quinault. Only the Quinault and the Quileute agreed to sign. See Stevens, *Life of Isaac Ingalls Stevens*, 2:1–9.

6   American Friends Service Committee, *Uncommon Controversy*, 23.

7   The Yakima and Klickitat Indians on the east side of the Cascades wanted to expel whites, but very few Indians from the western side of the mountains participated. Wesley Gosnell to Isaac Stevens, December 31, 1856, MR 11, RG 75, Records of the Washington Superintendency of Indian Affairs, 1853–1874 (hereafter RG 75 WASIA), National Archives and Records Administration, Washington, D.C. (microfilm copies in the University of Washington Library); Meeker, *Pioneer Reminiscences of Puget Sound*, 245, 256–58; and Harmon, *Indians in the Making*, 86–95.

8   Thrush, *Native Seattle*, 50–56.

9   G. A. Paige to M. T. Simmons, September 26, 1856, MR 10, RG 75, WASIA.

10   W. B. Gosnell to J. W. Nesmith, December 31, 1857, MR 11, RG 75, WASIA.

11   S. D. Howe to C. H. Hale, October 13, 1862, MR 12, RG 75, WASIA; S. D. Howe to C. H. Hale, June 27, 1863, MR 12, RG 75, WASIA; and T. J. McKenny to N. G. Taylor, October 20, 1867, MR 5, RG 75, WASIA (quotation). After the Indian War of 1855–56, Stevens met with several rebel Indian representatives at Fox Island and promised to accede to Indian demands of additional reserve lands; Congress approved only this one revised treaty soon after. Harmon, *Indians in the Making*, 91.

12   M. T. Simmons to Edward Geary, September 9, 1860, MR 9, RG 75, WASIA.

13   R. G. Fay to Isaac Stevens, January 1, 1857, MR 10, RG 75, WASIA.

14   C. C. Finkbonner to T. J. McKenny, June 14, 1868, MR 12, RG 75, WASIA. The Tulalip Indian agents once went seven months without pay in 1879. See Harmon, *Indians in the Making*, 112. Many Indian groups did not receive any annuity goods from their 1850s treaties until the early 1860s. See George Paige to B. F. Kendall, October 4, 1861, and George Paige to B. F. Kendall, December 10, 1861, both from MR 13, RG 75, WASIA. There are too many examples of Indian complaints regarding nonfulfillment of their treaties to cite here. For a sampling, see Henry Webster to B. F. Kendall, September 24, 1861, MR 14; R. G. Fay to Isaac Stevens, April 13, 1857, MR 10; and E. S. Fowler to M. T. Simmons, September 23, 1856, MR 10, all in RG 75, WASIA.

15   George Paige to Isaac Stevens, December 24, 1856, MR 10, RG 75, WASIA.

16 George Paige to Isaac Stevens, February 28, 1857, MR 10, RG 75, WASIA.

17 R. G. Fay to Isaac Stevens, December 31, 1857, MR 10; M. T. Simmons to James Nesmith, November 27, 1857, MR 9; William Wells to W. B. Gosnell, January 1, 1858, MR 11; Warren Lowe to W. B. Gosnell, December 31, 1857, MR 11; and George Paige to C. H. Hale, March 31, 1864, MR 15, all in RG 75, WASIA. Although it is not clear what caused the run failures of 1857–58 or 1864, flooding was responsible for the 1862 failure on the Muckleshoot Reservation; see Daniel Manchester to C. H. Hale, June 2, 1862, MR 12, RG 75, WASIA.

18 Nathan Hill to Isaac Stevens, November 30, 1856, MR 10, RG 75, WASIA (quotation); and W. T. McKinny to N. G. Taylor, December 27, 1867, MR 5, RG 75, WASIA.

19 The federal government divided Washington Territory's Indian superintendency into separate agencies at Puyallup, Tulalip, Neah Bay, Skokomish, and Quinault in the 1860s to facilitate their administration. Grant's policy after the Civil War appointed religious personnel to Indian reservations, sought to draw more Indians to the reservations, and provided them with agricultural implements. See Harmon, *Indians in the Making*, 107–8. The Indian agent for the Makah was so frustrated with the prevailing federal policy, he suggested that in addition to the monies earmarked to promote agriculture, departmental funds be used to purchase schooners for the Indians. See Henry Webster to T. J. McKenny, April 10, 1867, MR 14, RG 75, WASIA; report of Oliver Wood, August 13, 1885, in United States, Department of Indian Affairs, *Annual Report of the Commissioner of Indian Affairs for the Year 1885*, 188.

20 Harmon, *Indians in the Making*, 104–5; and Thrush, *Native Seattle*, 79–104.

21 George Paige to W. W. Miller, August 20, 1861, MR 13; George Paige to W. W. Miller, August 26, 1861, MR 13; and H. C. Hale to T. J. McKenny, November 25, 1868, MR 12, all in RG 75, WASIA.

22 T. J. McKenny to N. G. Taylor, July 23, 1867, MR 5, RG 75, WASIA.

23 William Morrow to W. B. Gosnell, June 30, 1861, MR 9, RG 75, WASIA.

24 T. J. McKenny to Webster, November 17, 1867, MR 5, RG 75, WASIA.

25 T. J. McKenny to James Wilbur, March 26, 1867, MR 5, RG 75, WASIA.

26 Samuel Ross to E. S. Parker, September 1, 1870, MR 6, RG 75, WASIA.

27 T. J. McKenny to Lewis Bogg, February 11, 1867, MR 5, RG 75, WASIA.

28 Samuel Ross to E. S. Parker, May 2, 1870, MR 6, RG 75, WASIA.

29 Harmon, *Indians in the Making*, 113–14.

30 Accounts are usually filtered through Indian agents, but apparently some Northwest Indians who resided on the reservations supported allotment in the 1870s and 1880s. On the Lummi, see T. J. McKenny to Commissioner, October 1, 1871, MR 6, RG 75, WASIA. By 1884, 73 out of the 275 Lummi Indians on the reservation had received allotments; see Patrick Buckley to H. Price, August 22(?), 1884, p. 288, box 24, Tulalip Agency, RG 75, Bureau of Indian Affairs Records, National Archives and Records Administration–Pacific Alaska Region, Seattle (hereafter BIA, NAS); Byron Barlow to R. H. Milroy, September 15, 1872, in United States, Department of Indian Affairs, *Annual Report of the Commissioner of Indian Affairs for the Year 1872*, 357; and Boxberger, *To Fish in Common*, 32–34. On Puyallup, see Byron Barlow

to R. H. Milroy, October 1, 1873, MR 11; Daniel Beaty to R. H. Milroy, April 30, 1874, MR 11, both in RG 75, WASIA; report of Edwin Eells, August 16, 1886, in United States, Department of Indian Affairs, *Annual Report of the Commissioner of Indian Affairs for the Year 1886*, 242–44. On the Skokomish, see Edwin Eells to unidentified Supt., March 2, 1874; Edwin Eells to R. H. Milroy, May 26, 1874, both in MR 13, RG 75, WASIA. On Port Madison and the Muckleshoot, see Patrick Buckley to H. Price, June 13, 1884, p. 234, box 24, Tulalip Agency, RG 75, BIA, NAS; report of Patrick Buckley, August 18, 1886, in United States, Department of Indian Affairs, *Annual Report of the Commissioner of Indian Affairs for the Year 1886*, 245–46. Indian agents at Neah Bay did not recommend allotment as arable land was so scarce on that reserve; see C. A. Huntington to R. H. Milroy, April 14, 1874, MR 14, RG 75, WASIA.

31 Report of Edwin Eells, August 20, 1885, in United States, Department of Indian Affairs, *Annual Report of the Commissioner of Indian Affairs for the Year 1885*, 192–94; report of R. H. Milroy, August 31, 1880 and report of Edwin Eells, August 27, 1880, both in United States, Department of Indian Affairs, *Annual Report of the Commissioner of Indian Affairs for the Year 1880*, 157–59, 163–65.

32 Deposition of Susie Kanim, February 29, 1927, U.S. Court of Claims, *Duwamish, et al. v. United States*, Evidence for Plaintiff and Defendant, No. F-275, 1:207, copy in University of Washington, Special Collections. See also deposition of William Kanim, 1:186–95, in ibid.

33 Harmon, *Indians in the Making*, 111–24; and Thrush, *Native Seattle*, 69–78, 87–93.

34 Report of Edwin Eells, August 18, 1879, in United States, Department of Indian Affairs, *Annual Report of the Commissioner of Indian Affairs for the Year 1879*, 154–55; Edwin Eells to Marshall Blinn, January 20, 1874; Edwin Eells to R. H. Milroy, May 13, 1874, both in MR 13, RG 75, WASIA; and petition to Marshall Blinn from residents of New Dungeness, Clallum County, n.d. (c. December 1873), MR 25, RG 75, WASIA.

35 John O'Keane to R. E. Towbridge, August 20, 1880, p. 589, box 24, Tulalip Agency, RG 75, BIA, NAS; M. T. Simmons to Isaac Stevens, December 29, 1856, MR 9; C. C. Finkbonner to F. D.(?) McKinney, March 26, 1867, MR 12, both in RG 75, WASIA. The Skagit later contacted the Indian Affairs office pleading for their own reservation lands in response to significant encroachments by white settlers. See Charles Buchanan to the Commissioner of Indian Affairs, April 25, 1911, box 111, Tulalip Agency, RG 75, BIA, NAS.

36 Report of Eells, August 20, 1878, in United States, Department of Indian Affairs, *Annual Report of the Commissioner of Indian Affairs for the Year 1878*, 137.

37 See, for instance, Charles Willoughby, August 10, 1886, in United States, Department of Indian Affairs, *Annual Report of the Commissioner of Indian Affairs for the Year 1886*, 238–39; Samuel Ross to E. S. Parker, January 2, 1870, MR 6, RG 75, WASIA; report of John O'Keane, August 1, 1879, in *Annual Report of the Commissioner of Indian Affairs for the Year 1879*, 156–57; and W. H. Talbott to Commissioner, August 15, 1887, p. 73, box 25, Tulalip Agency, RG 75, BIA, NAS.

38 Douglas quoted in Fisher, "Indian Warfare and Two Frontiers," 43. See also Fisher,

Contact and Conflict, 60–61; and Bagley, "Attitude of the Hudson's Bay Company during the Indian War."

39   Vancouver Island was leased to the HBC in 1849, but because the British government felt that the company's interests ran counter to colonization, it appointed a non-HBC man, Richard Blanshard, as governor. Blanshard's term was short-lived, however, and he was replaced by the HBC's own James Douglas in 1851 on the condition that Douglas disassociate from the company, which he soon did. The HBC's lease on the island was up in 1859.

40   Harris, *Making Native Space*, 17–44.

41   Ibid., 18–19. The government report on aboriginal title argued that aboriginal peoples in New Zealand had only "qualified dominion" over their country consisting of a right to occupancy but not title to land. Until they cultivated their lands or formed a settled form of government, they could not be said to have individual property.

42   James Douglas to James Yale, May 7, 1850, James Murray Yale fonds, MS-0105, B.C. Archives, Victoria (hereafter MS-0105, BCA).

43   Archives of British Columbia, *House of Assembly Correspondence Book, August 12th, 1856 to July 6th, 1859*, Memoir 4, February 5, 1859, session, 46–47; and Archives of British Columbia, *Minutes of the Council of Vancouver Island, Commencing August 30th, 1851, and Terminating with the Prorogation of the House of Assembly, February 6th, 1861*, March 25, 1859, session, 36.

44   Harris, *Making Native Space*, 35–36; and Bowsfield, *Fort Victoria Letters*, 95–96.

45   Harris, *Resettlement of British Columbia*, 80; and Barman, *West beyond the West*, 65–66. Barman suggests more than thirty thousand men and women passed through B.C. in 1858 alone.

46   Harris, *Making Native Space*, 44.

47   Ibid., 56–69; and Fisher, *Contact and Conflict*, 160–67.

48   For more on confederation, see Sage, "Critical Period of British Columbia History," 424–43. Note that Vancouver Island and the B.C. mainland colonies joined together in 1866, and they began considering merging with the Dominion in 1867. Despite some clamoring to join the United States, most B.C. residents supported confederation with Canada, especially once promised a transcontinental railroad terminus. British Columbia joined the Dominion on July 20, 1871.

49   Harris, *Landing Native Fisheries*, 36–59.

50   Ibid., 8.

51   Ibid., 78–105.

52   Harris, *Making Native Space*, 81–86. See also, for example, J. M. McGackon to James Lenihan, April 15, 1878, vol. 1021, MR T-1459, Record Group 10, Department of Indian Affairs, B.C. Superintendency, Library and Archives Canada, Ottawa (hereafter RG 10, LAC); I. W. Powell to Lieut. Governor, June 21, 1873, vol. 1001, MR T-1455, RG 10, LAC; and September 25, 1891, entry, vol. 1022, MR T-1459, RG 10, LAC.

53   Quoted in Harris, *Resettlement of British Columbia*, 91–92. See also, for example, Malcolm Sproat to Supt. General of Indian Affairs, October 26, 1878, file 3756–18; Sproat to L. Vankoughnet, November 26, 1879, file 3756–21, both in vol. 3612, MR

C-10106, Record Group 10, Black Series, Department of Indian Affairs, Library and Archives Canada, Ottawa (hereafter RG 10, BS, LAC).

54   Petition enclosed in letter of Peter Ayesik to I. W. Powell, July 14, 1874, copy in vol. 1001, MR T-1455, RG 10, LAC (quotation); and Harris, "Nlha7kápmx Meeting at Lytton."

55   Aleais to Lenihan, May 18, 1875, vol. 1001, MR T-1455, RG 10, LAC (quotation); and Harris, *Making Native Space*, 85–86.

56   Quoted in Harris, *Resettlement of British Columbia*, 91.

57   Britain and the United States jointly occupied the Oregon country from the end of the War of 1812 until the 1846 Oregon Treaty. After extensive negotiations both sides agreed to make the forty-ninth parallel the new international border. However, the west coast's complicated island geography and disagreements over the contested San Juan Islands created problems and almost led to what is now known as the "Pig War." Both nations submitted the border question to the emperor of Germany for arbitration; he determined the United States should have authority over the San Juans. See, for instance, Cain and Hopkins, *British Imperialism*, 258–68; Stacey, "Britain's Withdrawal from North America"; Dawson, *War That Was Never Fought*; McDermott, "San Juan Island's Pig War"; and Milton, *History of the San Juan Boundary Question*.

58   Edwin Eells to E. A. Hoyt, December 13, 1878, file 5, box 9, vols. 17–18, Record Group 36, U.S. Customs Service, Puget Sound District, National Archives and Records Administration–Pacific Alaska Region, Seattle (hereafter RG 36, NAS).

59   For example, Washington settlers killed a Tsimshian Indian in 1854. See C. H. Mason to M. T. Simmons, May 7, 1854; C. H. Mason to George Manypenny, July 1, 1854; unsigned (most likely Isaac Stevens) to Manypenny, July 13, 1854; Isaac Stevens to Manypenny, August 15, 1854, all in MR 1, RG 75, WASIA. For additional conflicts, see Isaac Stevens to E. C. Fitzhugh, July 15, 1856, MR 2; Stevens to unknown, November 19, 1856, MR 2; Stevens to Commissioner, December 5, 1856, MR 3; M. T. Simmons to Isaac Stevens, April 4, 1857, MR 9; M. T. Simmons to Edward Geary, August 20, 1859, MR 9; John Knox to Mr. Huntington, December 6, 1865, MR 13; and E. M. Gibson to T. J. McKenny, August 5, 1872, MR 14, all in RG 75, WASIA. See also Lutz, "Inventing an Indian War." Lutz maintains that whites complained in an effort to convince the government to permanently station troops in the area and thus stimulate the regional economy.

60   This border trade regulation was included in all of the treaties negotiated with western Washington Indians. See Stevens, *Life of Isaac Ingalls Stevens*, 1:460. For copies of all western Washington Indian treaties, see Kapplar, "Indian Affairs." The treaties can be accessed according to each tribal name.

61   E. C. Fitzhugh to Isaac Stevens, February 8, 1856, MR 10, RG 75, WASIA.

62   For a sampling of northern Indian visits, see E. S. Fowler to Isaac Stevens, March 29, 1856; E. S. Fowler to Isaac Stevens, April 26, 1856; and E. S. Fowler to Isaac Stevens, July 15, 1856, all on MR 10, RG 75, WASIA. On settlers denying landings, see M. T. Simmons to Stevens, May 1, 1857, MR 9, RG 75, WASIA; Fisher, *Contact and Conflict*, 63; and Lutz, "Inventing an Indian War," 11–12.

63 Douglas even agreed to help American settlers in the Indian war of 1855–56; see Bagley, "Attitude of the Hudson's Bay Company during the Indian War," 298. On Douglas trying to control northern Indians in 1860s, see James Swan to Henry Webster, March 31, 1863, MR 14, RG 75, WASIA; and Fisher, *Contact and Conflict*, 63–66. Due to his long tenure in the region with the Hudson's Bay Company, Douglas was often able to successfully arbitrate disputes between northern Indians, other Indians, and non-Indians. However, as white settlement increased in the 1860s and 1870s, the white settlers around Victoria grew more uneasy about the large numbers of northern Indians that came to trade at Victoria every year, and began calling for their removal.

64 On whiskey smuggling, see Samuel Ross to E. S. Parker, November 27, 1869, MR 6; J. H. Hays to Samuel Ross, July 18, 1870, MR 14; C. C. Finkbonner to Mr. Waterman, September 16, 1865, MR 12 all in RG 75, WASIA; Charles Todd to I. W. Powell, March 20, 1882, vol. 2, B.C. Provincial Police Force, Correspondence Outward, 1864–1918, GR-0061, B.C. Archives, Victoria (hereafter GR-0061, BCA); and Charles Todd to Attorney General, July 31, 1876, vol. 2, GR-0061, BCA. On dogfish oil, see T. J. McKenny to N. G. Taylor, May 2, 1869, MR 5, RG 75, WASIA; and Raibmon, *Authentic Indians*, 101–2.

65 A. W. Bash to Folger, September 24, 1882, vol. 1, 255–57, box 37, RG 36, NAS.

66 J. H. Price to A. W. Bash, July 23, 1882, file 1, box 111, RG 36, NAS.

67 On crossing the border to escape punishment, see T. J. McKenny to F. A. Walker, May 15, 1872, MR 6, RG 75, WASIA; and report of W. L. Powell to Commissioner, August 17, 1886, in United States, Department of Indian Affairs, *Annual Report of the Commissioner of Indian Affairs for the Year 1886*, 236. On hop-picking, see Raibmon, *Authentic Indians*, 74–134; W. H. Talbott to Commissioner, September 12, 1887, p. 93; and W. H. Talbott to Commissioner, October 5, 1887, p. 105, both in box 25, Tulalip Agency, RG 75, BIA, NAS. For an extensive treatment of Native labor history, see Lutz, *Makúk*.

68 James Douglas began to receive negative reports on the quality of salmon shipped further than Hawai'i as of 1853. The company tried to improve the quality of their exports, but because of changes in their monopoly privileges, their overall economic activities in the region began to decline in the late 1850s. See James Douglas to James Yale, April 6, 1854, MS-0105, BCA; Robert Chuston(?) to Douglas, November 2, 1855; unidentified to Douglas, December 3, 1855; Douglas to James Yale, October 12, 1855, all in James Murray Yale fonds, MS-0537, B.C. Archives, Victoria. See also Cullen, "History of Fort Langley," 49–51, 96–97.

69 Heckman, *Island in the Sound*, 75; Meeker, *Pioneer Reminiscences of Puget Sound*, 58; Leighton, *West Coast Journeys*, 13, 16, 19–20; June M. Collins, ed., "John Fornsby: The Personal Document of a Coast Salish Indian," in Smith, *Indians of the Urban Northwest*, 307; Bowsfield, *Fort Victoria Letters*, 38–39; Hendrickson, "Two Letters from Walter Colquhoun Grant," 12; and Macfie, *Vancouver Island and British Columbia*, 166.

70 Vernon Carstensen, "The Fisherman's Frontier on the Pacific Coast: The Rise of the Salmon Canning Industry," in Clark, *Frontier Challenge*, 61–65; and Boxberger, *To Fish in Common*, 36.

71 Canada, Department of Marine and Fisheries, *Annual Report of the Department of Marine and Fisheries, 1892*, 193; and Meggs, *Salmon*, 19–22.

72 Lutz, *Makúk*, 186; and Rounsefell and Kelez, *Salmon and Salmon Fisheries of Swiftsure Bank, Puget Sound, and the Fraser River*, 706. It is not clear where exactly these authors obtained their figures, so their accuracy may be questionable. Still, the overall trend is confirmed by multiple sources: Native fishermen were gradually replaced by Japanese and white fishermen. See Harris, *Landing Native Fisheries*, 132, 230fn17.

73 Pittendrigh to Minister of Marine and Fisheries, January 24, 1886, Canada, Department of Marine and Fisheries, *Annual Report of the Department of Marine and Fisheries, 1885*, 277.

74 Boxberger, *To Fish in Common*, 46.

75 Report of Edwin Eells to R. H. Milroy, August 31, 1872, in United States, Department of Indian Affairs, *Annual Report of the Commissioner of Indian Affairs for the Year 1872*, 352; Patrick Buckley to H. Price, September 1883 (n.d.); and John O'Keane to E. A. Hoyt, September 1, 1879, both in box 24, Tulalip Agency, RG 75, BIA, NAS.

76 Report of Chas. Willoughby, August 26, 1882, in United States, Department of Indian Affairs, *Annual Report of the Commissioner of Indian Affairs for the Year 1882*, 154–59; report of Oliver Wood to Commissioner, August 11, 1884, in United States, Department of Indian Affairs, *Annual Report of the Commissioner of Indian Affairs for the Year 1884*, 163; and report of W. L. Powell, August 17, 1886, in United States, Department of Indian Affairs, *Annual Report of the Commissioner of Indian Affairs for the Year 1886*, 235–36.

77 A. L. Blake to A. W. Bash, July 19, 1883, file 4, box 109, RG 36, NAS (quotation); and Wilcox, "Fisheries of the Pacific Coast," 294.

78 Ira B. Myers to A. W. Bash, August 9, 1883, file 4, box 109, RG 36, NAS; A. M. White to H. F. Beecher, December 4, 1885, file 4, box 169, RG 36, NAS (quotation). On the Lummi, see John O'Keane to Commissioner, June 14, 1882, p. 263, box 24, Tulalip Agency, RG 75, BIA, NAS.

79 A. C. Anderson to Minister of Marine and Fisheries, September 19, 1883, file 1883-1618, vol. 58, Series A-2, Record Group 13, Department of Justice Records, Library and Archives Canada, Ottawa. Anderson did not go into detail about the ethnicity of the fishermen in question, but given the time period, it is quite likely that the fishermen were Indians.

80 A. L. Blake to Collector, July 19, 1883, file 4, box 109, RG 36, NAS; emphasis in original.

81 Ira Myers to A. W. Bash, August 9, 1883, file 4, box 109, RG 36, NAS.

82 Knight, *Indians at Work*, 180, 193–94.

83 Lutz, "After the Fur Trade," 83–91. Some groups actually potlatched more often after white settlement due to the enhanced wealth opportunities that accompanied trade with newcomers. See Codere, *Fighting with Property*.

84 Knight, *Indians at Work*, 180; Charles Todd to Mayor of Victoria, July 23, 1879, vol. 2, GR-0061, BCA; Newell, *Tangled Webs of History*, 54; and Meggs, *Salmon*, 26–27.

85 P. McTiernan to Supt. General of Indian Affairs, August 17, 1886, vol. 1022, MR T-1459, RG 10, LAC.

86   Many Washington Indians were regularly heading to the Fraser for the salmon fishing season by the 1890s. See, for example, W. L. Powell to Commissioner, August 9, 1894, in United States, Department of Indian Affairs, *Annual Report of the Commissioner of Indian Affairs for the Year 1894*, 317. Others went even further north; see D. C. Govan to Commissioner, August 28, 1896, in United States, Department of Indian Affairs, *Annual Report of the Commissioner of Indian Affairs for the Year 1897*, 316.

87   Knight, *Indians at Work*, 179–80.

88   Ibid., 190–94. See also Newell, *Tangled Webs of History*, 53; and Ford, *Smoke from Their Fires*, 192.

89   Columbia River packers actually enlisted the help of federal officials to replenish Columbia River salmon by building a hatchery. See, for example, Allard, *Spencer Fullerton Baird and the U.S. Fish Commission*, 145.

90   Canada, Department of Marine and Fisheries, *Annual Report of the Department of Marine and Fisheries, 1900*, 159; Washington State, Department of Fish and Game, *Thirteenth Annual Report of the State Fish Commissioner* (1902), 79; this number includes only those canneries operated that season—there were an additional five canneries that were not operated.

91   There are some discrepancies in the available figures for the canned salmon pack, and it is hard to know how government authorities compiled these statistics. Those used here are from Cobb, *Pacific Salmon Fisheries* (1921),152. George Rounsefell and George Kelez found that Americans consistently packed more salmon than their Canadian counterparts between 1898 and 1934. See Rounsefell and Kelez, *Salmon and Salmon Fisheries of Swiftsure Bank, Puget Sound, and the Fraser River*, 758.

92   Lutz, *Makúk*, 53, 64–66.

93   Suttles, "Economic Life of the Coast Salish of Haro and Rosario Straits," 152–53, 191–212; Rounsefell and Kelez, *Salmon and Salmon Fisheries of Swiftsure Bank, Puget Sound, and the Fraser River*, 714; Felix Solomon, Dora Solomon, Angeline Alexander, Aurelia Celestine, interviewed by K. Lee and Judy Thompson, April 13, 1973, transcribed tape recording #25–26, North West Tribal Indians Oral History Collection, Center for Pacific Northwest Studies, Western Washington University, Bellingham, WA (hereafter CPNWS WWU).

94   Cobb, *Pacific Salmon Fisheries*, 81–82.

95   Ibid., 85. See also Rathbun, "Review of the Fisheries in the Contiguous Waters of the State of Washington and British Columbia," 301.

96   Boxberger, *To Fish in Common*, 42.

97   Harris, *Landing Native Fisheries*, 150–53.

98   Wilson Duff Papers, Straits Field Notes, Summer 1950, file 27, STR-W-001, roll 2, Royal British Columbia Museum, copies in Dr. Keith Carlson's possession, University of Saskatchewan, Saskatoon, Canada. Although the Canadian Anglo-British Packing Company held a few fish trap locations in Boundary Bay, this was an anomaly in the 1890s. Canadian authorities allowed some additional fish traps in the early 1900s—mostly on the southern end of Vancouver Island. There were fifteen fish traps located near Victoria in 1908 that were valued at fifteen thousand

dollars. See Canada, Department of Marine and Fisheries, *Annual Report of the Department of Marine and Fisheries, 1908-1909*, 261, 263.

99   "Traps in British Columbia," *Pacific Fisherman* 2:7 (July 1904): 9.

100 Harris, *Landing Native Fisheries*, 150–62.

101 Wilcox, "Fisheries of the Pacific Coast," 294; Rathbun, "Review of the Fisheries in the Contiguous Waters of the State of Washington and British Columbia," 293, 314 (for maps, see insert between 302 and 303); and Fish Trap Locations, MR 1–2, WDF, WSA.

102 Rounsefell and Kelez, *Salmon and Salmon Fisheries of Swiftsure Bank, Puget Sound, and the Fraser River*, 723–24, 763.

103 Deposition of Sarsfield Kavanaugh, March 5, 1927, U.S. Court of Claims, *Duwamish, et al. v. United States*, Evidence for Plaintiff and Defendant, No. F-275, 1:304.

104 James Roe to E. Mills, n.d. (c. March 1900); Roe to Mills, March 24, 1900; Roe to Mills, May 21, 1901; Roe to C. M. Buchanan, July 22, 1901 all in box 104, Tulalip Agency, RG 75, BIA, NAS; and Buchanan to Lowman, White Crest Canning Co., August 8, 1901, p. 266, box 123, Tulalip Agency, RG 75, BIA, NAS.

105 Buchanan to Postal Telegraph Cable Co. Everett, July 25, 1901, p. 100; and Buchanan to Edward E. Cushman, July 31, 1901, pp. 182–83, both in box 123, Tulalip Agency, RG 75, BIA, NAS.

106 C. M. Buchanan to Pacific American Fisheries, July 25, 1901, file 4, box 115, Tulalip Agency, RG 75, BIA, NAS. J. C. Foster and the Seattle Fish Company were both far more responsive. See J. C. Foster to Edward Mills, May 10, 1901; Seattle Fish Co. to Edward Mills, May 9, 1901, both in file 4, box 115, Tulalip Agency, RG 75, BIA, NAS. The PAF responded to Buchanan in July and requested a meeting to discuss the issue. See Robert A. Smith to Buchanan, July 22, 1901, file 4, box 115, Tulalip Agency, RG 75, BIA, NAS.

107 Kerr and McCord to Mills, June 6, 1901, file 4, box 115, Tulalip Agency, RG 75, BIA, NAS.

108 Buchanan to James Roe, August 1, 1901, p. 193, box 123, Tulalip Agency, RG 75, BIA, NAS. Buchanan tried to get the injunction lifted, to no avail. See Buchanan to E. E. Cushman, August 10, 1901, pp. 286–90, box 123, Tulalip Agency, RG 75, BIA, NAS.

109 Buchanan to Attorney General, September 11, 1903, p. 262, box 125, Tulalip Agency, RG 75, BIA, NAS. The legal status of Indian reservation tidelands has been brought to court repeatedly since the dispute described here—with varied results. See Boxberger, *To Fish in Common*, 87–94.

110 Buchanan to Jesse A. Frye, December 5, 1903, p. 216, box 125, Tulalip Agency, RG 75, BIA, NAS; Buchanan to Pacific American Fisheries, July 31, 1913, p. 267, vol. Misc., box 136, Tulalip Agency, RG 75, BIA, NAS. For additional examples, see William McCluskey to Buchanan, September 20, 1911, p. 81, vol. Misc., box 133; Raymond Walker to McCluskey, October 24, 1911, p. 264, vol. Misc., box 133; Buchanan to Elmer Todd, April 17, 1912, p. 2, vol. Misc., box 134; Buchanan to Commissioner of Indian Affairs, August 5, 1913, file 4f, box 57; Buchanan to Hedham, May 10, 1915, p. 52, box 141; and Shell to Buchanan, July 21, 1915, file 5T, box 74, all in Tulalip Agency, RG 75, BIA, NAS.

111 The PAF offered to pay rent and Bill Lowman successfully arranged to build a trap off Indian lands in Tulalip Bay. See Buchanan to Farmer Swinomish, July 31, 1913, p. 291, vol. Misc., box 136; and Buchanan to District Engineer's Office, August 21, 1917, box 227, both in Tulalip Agency, RG 75, BIA, NAS.

112 McCluskey to Buchanan, March 9, 1914, file 4f, box 57, Tulalip Agency, RG 75, BIA, NAS.

113 State of Washington, Department of Fish and Game, *Thirteenth Annual Report of the State Fish Commissioner* (1902), 79.

114 Rathbun, "Review of the Fisheries in the Contiguous Waters of the State of Washington and British Columbia," 308; and Canada, *Report of the Royal Commission on Chinese Immigration*, 340. The Dominion Department of Marine and Fisheries kept statistics based on the number of fathoms for gill nets and seines. In 1899 there were 408,284 fathoms of gill nets and just 1,400 fathoms of seine nets in use in the province. "Lines" were also used, but no exact numbers are listed. Assuming the quoted average number of fathoms is correct (150), this figure would translate into approximately 2,700 gill nets in that year. For net fathoms, see Canada, Department of Marine and Fisheries, *Annual Report of the Department of Marine and Fisheries, 1900*, 162; and Rathbun, "Review of the Fisheries in the Contiguous Waters of the State of Washington and British Columbia," 307.

115 Berringer, "Northwest Coast Traditional Salmon Fisheries," 28–36.

116 The onset of the gas motor in the early 1900s transformed most fishing methods. The first power seine boat was built in 1902 and living quarters added in 1910. See John McMullan, "The Organization of the Fisheries: An Introduction," in Marchak, Guppy, and McMullan, *Uncommon Property*, 35–36; and Rounsefell and Kelez, *Salmon and Salmon Fisheries of Swiftsure Bank, Puget Sound, and the Fraser River*, 728–29.

117 See, for example, C. M. Buchanan to "the person occupying this boat," n.d. [c. September 1903], p. 234, box 125; Buchanan to Capt. James Thomas, October 19, 1903, p. 279, box 125; Buchanan to George Bremner, August 11, 1904, p. 387, box 126; and Buchanan to Bremner, August 19, 1904, p. 456, box 126 all in Tulalip Agency, RG 75, BIA, NAS.

118 Allen Bartow to C. M. Buchanan, November 20, 1901, box 102, Tulalip Agency, RG 75, BIA, NAS.

119 Allen Bartow to Jesse Frye, January 31, 1905; and Bartow to Buchanan, January 31, 1905 (quotation), both in box 102, Tulalip Agency, RG 75, BIA, NAS.

120 Acting Commissioner of Indian Affairs to Buchanan, June 8, 1904, pp. 143–49 (quotation); and Buchanan to George Bremner, June 13, 1904, pp. 149–50, both in box 133, Tulalip Agency, RG 75, BIA, NAS.

121 McCluskey to Buchanan, March 19, 1914, file 4f, box 57, Tulalip Agency, RG 75, BIA, NAS.

122 Harris, *Fish, Law, and Colonialism*, 62–63, 70–71; M. K. Morrison to Thomas Mowat, August 21, 1890, file 60, 926, vol. 3828, MR C-10145, RG 10, BS, LAC. The Gitksan and Nisga'a demanded payments and refused to purchase fishing licenses from officials in the late 1880s. The Kitkatla's Chief Shukes threatened to cut nets

if the Lowe Inlet Cannery did not cease fishing the tribe's sites and recognize the Natives' exclusive ownership of several specific locales. Banks Island Natives told a white boat captain they would shoot him if he lowered nets into their fishing waters. Ultimately, fighting between Indians and non-Indians in the north led to the creation of a three-person government commission in 1887. See Newell, *Tangled Webs of History*, 59–62; and Harris, *Landing Native Fisheries*, 98.

123 Chief Sekalim to P. McTiernan, August 13, 1888, file 50, 341, vol. 3802, MR C-10140, RG 10, LAC.

124 P. O'Reilly to Deputy Supt. of Indian Affairs, November 12, 1896, and December 23, 1896; and A. W. Vowell to Deputy Supt. of Indian Affairs, February 11, 1897, all in file 147, 194, vol. 3961, MR C-10167, RG 10, LAC.

125 Although the second reserve commissioner (and Trutch's brother-in-law), Peter O'Reilly, generally adhered to Trutch's philosophy on the question of land and B.C. Indians, he did set aside some Indian fishing sites in the Nass and Skeena river areas and on the Queen Charlotte Islands to prevent conflicts between the growing number of canneries and the local Indians. See Harris, *Landing Native Fisheries*, 153–62, 165–86.

126 Ibid., 116–26, 165–86.

127 Harmon, *Indians in the Making*, 157–59; and Boxberger, *To Fish in Common*, 51–53.

128 Affidavit of Kate Waller, June 14, 1895, p. 2; affidavit of D. Drysdale, June 15, 1895, pp. 5, 8; and affidavit of Horace Brewster, pp. 1–2, all in *U.S. et al. v. The Alaska Packers Association, et al.*, June 21, 1895, case 482, file 6, box 82, Record Group 21, Circuit Court Western District of Washington, Northern Division, Seattle, Civil and Criminal Case Files 1890–1911, National Archives and Records Administration–Pacific Alaska Region, Seattle (hereafter RG 21, NAS).

129 Affidavit of A. B. Estabrook, June 14, 1895, p. 2; and affidavit of C. W. Van Horn, June 14, 1895, p. 2, both in case 482, file 6, box 82, RG 21, NAS.

130 Affidavit of H. B. Kirby, June 15, 1895, pp. 7–8, case 482, file 6, box 82, RG 21, NAS.

131 Affidavit of E. A. Wadhams, June 15, 1895, p. 4, case 482, file 6, box 82, RG 21, NAS.

132 Affidavit of E. A. Wadhams, June 15, 1895, pp. 3–4; and affidavit of D. Drysdale, June 15, 1895, both in p. 2, case 482, file 6, box 82, RG 21, NAS.

133 Hanford's decision, case 482, file 6, box 82, RG 21, NAS; and Boxberger, *To Fish in Common*, 52.

134 Austin, *State of Washington Legislative Laws*, 1.

135 Charles Buchanan to Edward Bristow, May 31, 1902, box 112, Tulalip Agency, RG 75, BIA, NAS; "Indian Fishing Rights: References Found in Session Laws of Washington," Indian Affairs, Administrative Correspondence 1920–1962, box 1, WDF, WSA.

136 Austin, *State of Washington Legislative Laws*, 3–4.

137 Boxberger, *To Fish in Common*, 91–94.

138 Washington State, *Report and Opinions of the Attorney General of the State of Washington*, 89–90.

139 Boxberger, *To Fish in Common*, 90.

140 Buchanan to Commissioner of Indian Affairs, April 29, 1914, enclosed in C. R. Maybury to Roland Hartley, May 28, 1929, vol. L-33, box 6, WDF, WSA; Buchanan to

Darwin, August 14, 1914, p. 10, box 139, Tulalip Agency, RG 75, BIA, NAS. All but two of those arrested were let go. See Buchanan to Governor of Washington, October 23, 1914, pp. 204–5, box 139, Tulalip Agency, RG 75, BIA, NAS. Darwin continued to challenge Indian fishing rights in various capacities through these years. See, for example, Buchanan to Commissioner, July 8, 1915, file 3F(2), box 70, Tulalip Agency, RG 75, BIA, NAS; Buchanan to Commissioner, April 24, 1916, and Buchanan to Attorney General, May 9, 1916, both in file 1F-3F, box 70, Tulalip Agency, RG 75, BIA, NAS.

141 "To Make Indians Keep Salmon Laws," *Seattle Post-Intelligencer*, August 3, 1915, enclosed in Buchanan to Commissioner of Indian Affairs, August 10, 1915, file 3F(2), box 70, Tulalip Agency, RG 75, BIA, NAS.

142 "Lummi Indians Sue Darwin," *Pacific Fisherman* 12:2 (February 1915): 16, in box 120, Pacific American Fisheries Collection, Center for Pacific Northwest Studies, Western Washington University (hereafter PAFC); and "Indians Protest against Fish Trap," *Pacific Fisherman* 12:5 (May 1914): 17.

143 "Indians Must Conform to Fishery Regulations," *Pacific Fisherman* 13:9 (September 1915): 15, box 120, PAFC; E. B. Merritt to Buchanan, August 26, 1916, file 3F, box 77, Tulalip Agency, RG 75, BIA, NAS; Al Charles, interviewed by Jeff Wilner, April 26, 1973, tape #23, transcribed tape recording, North West Tribal Indians Oral History Collection, CPNWS WWU; and Boxberger, *To Fish in Common*, 92.

144 New York, ex. rel., *Kennedy v. Becker* No. 666, 241 U.S. 556. 36 S. Ct. 705; 60 L. Ed. 1166; 1916 U.S. LEXIS 1678.

145 Harris, *Fish, Law, and Colonialism*, 44–49, 57; and Harris, *Landing Native Fisheries*, 106–9.

146 Harris, *Landing Native Fisheries*, 132–35.

147 Harris, *Fish, Law, and Colonialism*, 66–69; Harris, *Landing Native Fisheries*, 106–11; and Newell, *Tangled Webs of History*, 88–97.

148 Harris, *Landing Native Fisheries*, 133–35, 138–47, and 153–62.

149 For a small sampling of such conflicts, see Royal Commission of Indian Affairs for the Province of B.C., miscellaneous Native testimonies, 1913–1915, boxes 1–2, MS-1056, Union of B.C. Indian Chiefs, B.C. Archives, Victoria; "Babine Indians in Open Revolt," *Vancouver Province*, August 29, 1906; "Babine Braves are Heavily Fined," *Vancouver Province*, September 29, 1906, both in box 53, International Pacific Salmon Fisheries Commission Collection, University of British Columbia Special Collections, Vancouver (hereafter IPSFC); Harry Guillod to A. W. Vowell, October 24, 1896, and John McNab to E. E. Prince, September 22, 1896, both in file 1469, part 1, vol. 239, MR T-3159, Record Group 23, Department of Marine and Fisheries, Library and Archives Canada, Ottawa (hereafter RG 23, LAC); Thomas Palmer to Mayor C. Hayward, March 31, 1902; J. H. Sutherland to Charles Hayward, April 1, 1902; Charles Hayward to J. H. Sutherland, April 10, 1902; Memorandum, E. E. Prince, April 11, 1902; Memorandum, E. E. Prince, October 8, 1902, all in file 1469, part 2, vol. 239, RG 23, LAC. On Indians selling fish and the limitations on Indian licenses, see Royal Commission of Indian Affairs meeting with Provincial Commission on Indian Affairs, December 23, 1915, file 107, 297-2, vol. 3908, MR C-10160, RG 10, BS, LAC.

150 "Indians Wiping Out Sockeyes," *Vancouver Province*, November 19, 1904, box 53, IPSFC.

151 The DMF had the most trouble with the Cowichan and Babine Lake tribes. See Harris, *Fish, Law, and Colonialism*, chapters 2 and 3.

152 "Chief's Protest," *Columbian* (unidentified location), July 31, 1914, and "Indians Resent Fish Embargo," *Columbian*, July 25, 1914, both in box 55, IPSFC; Royal Commission on Indian Affairs to Duncan Scott, November 26, 1914, file 517, vol. 11020, MR T-3957, RG 10, LAC; and Evenden, *Fish versus Power*, 36–38.

153 "Indian Chiefs Voice Objection," *Vancouver Province*, May 18, 1918, box 55, IPSFC.

154 Harris, *Landing Native Fisheries*, 114.

155 Edward Taylor et al. to Secretary, Royal Commission on Indian Affairs, July 2, 1914, 1914 #32 Cowichan Indian Inquiry file 9, box 183, GR-0435, B.C. Department of Fisheries, B.C. Archives, Victoria (quotation). For additional Indian complaints, see Frank Pedley to Deputy Supt. of Indian Affairs, February 10, 1909, file 6, part 4, vol. 79, MR T-2664, RG 23, LAC; Theodore Davie to Minister of Marine and Fisheries, June 15, 1894, file 6, part 1, vol. 78, MR T-2662; and Members of the KitaMaat Council to G. W. Maxwell, November 14, 1898, file 6, part 1, vol. 78, MR T-2663, both in RG 23, LAC.

156 Rounsefell and Kelez, *Salmon and Salmon Fisheries of Swiftsure Bank, Puget Sound, and the Fraser River*, 728–34; Montgomery, *King of Fish*, 51–52.

157 McCluskey to Charles Buchanan, March 9, 1914, file 4F, box 57, Tulalip Agency, RG 75, BIA, NAS. Lawyers for the Lummi Indians estimated that four-fifths of the Indians ceased fishing as a result of fish trap blockages. See Craven and Greene to Buchanan, August 10, 1914, p. 8, box 139, Tulalip Agency, RG 75, BIA, NAS.

158 Unaddressed letter (obviously written by Buchanan) pp. 378–92 (quotation on 380), box 140, Tulalip Agency, RG 75, BIA, NAS.

159 Deposition of Sarsfield Kavanaugh, March 5, 1927, *Duwamish et al. v. United States*, 1: 305.

160 A. W. Vowell, September 30, 1902, Canada, Department of Indian Affairs, *Annual Report for the Department of Indian Affairs for the Year 1902*, 334.

161 Newell, *Tangled Webs of History*, 85; 1915 statistics cited in Harris, *Landing Native Fisheries*, 136. The numbers listed by Rounsefell and Kelez are slightly different, but the overall trend is the same. See Rounsefell and Kelez, *Salmon and Salmon Fisheries of Swiftsure Bank, Puget Sound, and the Fraser River*, 706.

162 Newell, *Tangled Webs of History*, 85. While the general trend of job loss also characterized the Lekwungen (Songhee) experience at the turn of the past century, John Lutz found that J. H. Todd and Sons' Empire Cannery offered the Lekwungen seasonal employment for many years and thus helped to reverse this particular community's economic fortunes. Unfortunately, many groups were not as lucky. See Lutz, *Makúk*, 98–101.

163 Quoted in Evenden, *Fish versus Power*, 40.

164 Elliot, *Saltwater People*, 59.

4. FISHING THE LINE

1   George Webber to J. C. Saunders, August 27, 1895, file 3, box 103, Record Group 36, U.S. Customs Service, Puget Sound Collection District, National Archives and Records Administration–Pacific Alaska Region, Seattle (hereafter RG 36, NAS).

2   Unsigned (likely from either Minister or Deputy Minister of Marine and Fisheries Department, Ottawa) to James Gaudin, August 17, 1895, Microfilm Reel (hereafter MR) T-3122; Acting Deputy Minister of Marine and Fisheries to James Gaudin, May 23, 1900, MR T-3123, both in file 1075 part 1, box 207, Record Group 23, Department of Marine and Fisheries, Library and Archives Canada, Ottawa (hereafter RG 23, LAC); and Rathbun, "Review of the Fisheries in the Contiguous Waters of the State of Washington and British Columbia," 331.

3   For an overview of cannery payment systems, see Ralston, "1900 Strike of Fraser River Sockeye Salmon Fishermen," 32–33, 43–47, and 66–72.

4   Charles McLennan to A. Wasson, May 5, 1892, file 2, box 62, and George Ellsperman to Collector Saunders, April 6, 1896, file 1, box 63, both in RG 36, NAS; July 19, 1895, pp. 12 (quotation), 14, vol. 1, box 28, Records of the Joint Committee Relative to the Preservation of the Fisheries in Waters Contiguous to Canada and the U.S., 1893–95, Fraser River and Puget Sound Interview Notes, Record Group 22, United States Fish and Wildlife Service, National Archives, College Park, MD.

5   George Webber to J. C. Saunders, July 21, 1895, file 3, box 103, RG 36, NAS; and George Ellsperman to F. D. Huestis, May 28, 1898, file 3, box 64, RG 36, NAS. On special reporting procedures, see Ellsperman to Saunders, July 4, 1896, file 5, box 63; and Ellsperman to Huestis, September 9, 1895, file 1, box 64, both in RG 36, NAS.

6   (?) McGovern to B. Huntoon, July 29, 1903, file II, box 151, Pacific American Fisheries Collection, Center for Pacific Northwest Studies, Western Washington University, Bellingham, WA (hereafter PAFC). The PP&N was a short-lived umbrella company based in Bellingham that technically owned the PAF for a short period in the early 1900s. See Radke, *Pacific American Fisheries, Inc.*, 33–47.

7   "Poaching Fishermen," *Anacortes American*, August 10, 1899.

8   C. McLennan to A. Wasson, May 5, 1892, file 2, box 62, RG 36, NAS.

9   Theodore Spencer to Charles Bradshaw, July 31, 1891, file 2, box 62, RG 36, NAS.

10   James Elwood to A. W. Bash, July 17, 1883, file 4, box 109, RG 36, NAS; and James Elwood to A. W. Bash, July 15, 1883, file 3, box 165, RG 36, NAS (quotation).

11   George Ellsperman to J. C. Saunders, June 17, 1895, file 2, box 63, RG 36, NAS (quotation). On U.S. fish being taken into B.C., see John Hardie to E. L. Newcombe, November 21, 1894, file 1894-1105, vol. 1885, Series A-2, Record Group 13, Department of Justice Records, Library and Archives Canada, Ottawa (hereafter RG 13, LAC). On B.C. buyers coming into American waters, see *Pacific Fisherman* 3:11 (November 1905): 13–14. Though too numerous to cite in full, for a sampling of illegal border fishing in the U.S. Customs records, see Charles McLennan to Charles Bradshaw, July 29, 1891, file 2, box 62; George Webber to J. C. Saunders, July 10, 1896, file 2, box 104; George Webber to J. C. Saunders, April 24, 1895, file 4, box 103; George Webber to J. C. Saunders, August 31, 1896, file 5, box 63; Meriden Hill

to F. D. Huestis, June 28, 1899, file 5, box 64; and E. D. Warbass to J. C. Saunders, September 3, 1896, file 3, box 68, all in RG 36, NAS.

12   On the cannery contract system, see Henry Doyle to Aemilius Jarvis, May 17, 1904, file 2–3, box 2, Henry Doyle Papers, University of British Columbia Special Collections, Vancouver (hereafter Doyle Papers); W. D. Burdis to D. M. McIntyre, July 12, 1911, file 1911 #2, box 194, GR-0435, B.C. Department of Fisheries, B.C. Archives, Victoria (hereafter GR-0435, BCA). On export embargos, see W. D. Burdis to W. J. Bowser, February 7, 1912, file 1912 #1, box 194, GR-0435, BCA; and Rounsefell and Kelez, *Salmon and Salmon Fisheries of Swiftsure Bank, Puget Sound, and the Fraser River*, 761.

13   August 4, 1903 entry, vol. 1, GR-0397, B.C. Provincial Police Force, Vancouver-Westminster Police Records, 1899–1949, B.C. Archives, Victoria (hereafter GR-0397, BCA) (quotation); August 4, 1903 entry, file 11–4, box 11, Doyle Papers.

14   Henry Doyle to D. W. McIntyre, April 29, 1912, file 1912 #4, box 183, GR-0435, BCA; F. M. Halstead to Supervisory Agent, December 22, 1911, file 52795, box 779, Record Group 36, U.S. Customs Bureau, National Archives and Records Administration, Washington, D.C. (hereafter RG 36, NADC).

15   On first fine, see *Pacific Fisherman* 3:10 (October 1905): 13. For some reason, a number of records from 1912 have survived. The three canning companies caught in 1912 were the J. L. Smiley & Co. of Port Townsend, the Manhattan Canning Company of Port Angeles, and the West Coast Packing Company of Blaine. See J. F. Curtis to Collector of Customs, May 14, 1912; Everett Tawney to Harper, February 17, 1912; and Everett Tawney to Collector, March 2, 1912, all in file 52795, box 779, RG 36, NADC. On George and Barker Company, see F. M. Halstead to Supervisory Agent, December 22, 1911, file 52795, box 779, RG 36, NADC.

16   George Webber to J. C. Saunders, July 10, 1896, file 2, box 104, RG 36, NAS.

17   July 30, 1904 entry, p. 160, vol. 1, GR-0397, BCA.

18   George Ellsperman to J. C. Saunders, June 17, 1895, file 2, box 63, RG 36, NAS.

19   Rounsefell and Kelez, *Salmon and Salmon Fisheries of Swiftsure Bank, Puget Sound, and the Fraser River*, 733.

20   W. D. Burdis to Richard McBride, June 1, 1904, file 10–2, box 10, Doyle Papers.

21   July 25, 1904 entry, p. 158, vol. 1, GR-0397, BCA; Colin Campbell to Wm. Bullock-Webster, July 26, 1904, and W. D. Burdis to Colin Campbell, July 25, 1904, both in file 3, box 43, GR-0055, B.C. Police Force, Superintendent Correspondence Inward, 1891–1910, B.C. Archives, Victoria (hereafter GR-0055, BCA).

22   *Pacific Fisherman* 4:9 (September 1906): 8.

23   George Ellsperman to J. C. Saunders, June 17, 1895, file 2, box 63, RG 36, NAS. For more on fish buyers, see "Pirate Sloop off Fraser River," *Vancouver Province*, August 8, 1903, box 53, International Pacific Salmon Fisheries Commission Collection, University of British Columbia Special Collections, Vancouver (hereafter IPSFC). Note that this collection contains a series of newspaper article clippings; most articles are identified by newspaper and date, but occasionally an article is only partially identified.

24   H. J. Butterfield to D. C. McMillan, August 1, 1903, file II, box 151, PAFC.

25 "Will Raise the Price of Fish," *Vancouver Province*, August 3, 1903, box 53, IPSFC.

26 "Salmon," *San Francisco Trade Journal*, April 2, 1904, box 53, IPSFC; and Conley, "Relations of Production and Collective Action," 91, 103.

27 "The Americans Will Retaliate," unidentified newspaper, c. April 15, 1904, box 53, IPSFC.

28 Taylor, *Making Salmon*, 5–6.

29 James Conley has argued that because the canning companies diversified their forms of processing and competed with other buyers, regional fishermen had little recourse but to accept the canners' proposed prices for their fish. However, oral history testimonies and newspaper accounts suggest that the fishermen had more options at their disposal. Conley, "Relations of Production and Collective Action," 92.

30 W. J. Beale, oral history interview by Barbara Heacock (February 8, 1978), 12, transcribed tape recording, Skagit County Oral History Collection, Center for Pacific Northwest Studies, Western Washington University, Bellingham, WA (hereafter SCOHC).

31 "Stealing Sockeyes," *Victoria Colonist*, August 1, 1901, box 52, IPSFC.

32 *Pacific Fisherman* 10:9 (September 1912): 12.

33 *Pacific Fisherman* 8:10 (October 1915): 21, box 120, PAFC.

34 B.C. Salmon Canners' Association to H. B. Thomson, August 21, 1918, file 10–8, box 10, Doyle Papers.

35 Schwantes, *Pacific Northwest*, 186.

36 Chang, "Enforcing Transnational White Solidarity," 690–92.

37 A. W. Bash to Folger, September 24, 1882, pp. 255–58, vol. 1, box 37, RG 36, NAS.

38 Dippie, *Vanishing American*.

39 Friday, *Organizing Asian American Labor*, 26; and Newell, "Rationality of Mechanization," 635–36.

40 Canada, *Report of the Royal Commission on Chinese Immigration*, 8; and Canada, *Report of the Royal Commission on Chinese and Japanese Immigration*, 135, 271.

41 Canada, *Report of the Royal Commission on Chinese and Japanese Immigration*, 165; and Newell, "Rationality of Mechanization," 638.

42 Douglas W. Lee, "Sojourners, Immigrants, and Ethnics: The Saga of the Chinese in Seattle," in Lee, *Annals of the Chinese Historical Society of the Pacific Northwest*, 53. For more on the development of Vancouver's Chinatown, see Anderson, *Vancouver's Chinatown*.

43 Canada, *Report of the Royal Commission on Chinese and Japanese Immigration*, 271 (the total population of Washington State at that time was 518,000); and Washington State, Department of Fish and Game, *Thirteenth Annual Report of the State Fish Commissioner* (1902), 79.

44 Robert A. Nash, "The 'China Gangs' in the Alaska Packers Association Canneries, 1892–1935," in [Chinese Historical Society of America], *Life, Influence, and Role of the Chinese in the United States*, 263–65; and Muszynski, *Cheap Wage Labour*, 150–69.

45 Friday, *Organizing Asian American Labor*, 37–41. The canners agreed to pay a

specified amount for each case of packed salmon, which by the early 1900s grew extremely complicated as can sizes and the types of fish being canned expanded in number and variety. Canners also distinguished between the skill and time required for producing oval cans, hand-soldered and machine-soldered cans; ovals and hand-soldering required additional time and skill, and they fetched ten cents more per can than those treated by machine. See, ibid., 41–45; Cobb, *Salmon Fisheries of the Pacific Coast*, 35–36; testimony of Everell B. Deming, manager of Pacific American Fisheries, in Canada, *Report of the Royal Commission on Chinese and Japanese Immigration*, 163; Willard G. Jue and Silas G. Jue, "Goon Dip: Entrepreneur, Diplomat, and Community Leader," in Lee, *Annals of the Chinese Historical Society of the Pacific Northwest*, 45–46.

46 As is discussed at more length in chapter 6 of this book, the Immigration Service added employees in the early 1900s specifically to help curb Asian migrations across the Canada-U.S. border. See Chang, "Enforcing Transnational White Solidarity," 671–96; and Smith, "Immigration and Naturalization Service (INS) at the U.S.-Canadian Border," 127–47.

47 Testimony of Chee Foo, Chinese merchant, in Canada, *Report of the Royal Commission on Chinese and Japanese Immigration*, 164.

48 *Pacific Fisherman* 4:6 (June 1906): 16.

49 Chang, "Enforcing Transnational White Solidarity," 675–76; and Smith, "Immigration and Naturalization Service (INS) at the U.S.-Canadian Border," 128–32.

50 Roy, *White Man's Province*, 61, 107, 155–57. The law raising the tax to five hundred dollars was actually passed in 1903 but did not go into effect until January 1, 1904, because of questions raised by the Canadian Pacific Railway. See also Griffith, "Border Crossings"; and Lee, *At America's Gates*.

51 Newell, "Rationality of Mechanization," 626–55; O'Bannon, "Waves of Change." The *Pacific Fisherman* reported that canners extensively used the "Iron Chink" on Puget Sound for the first time in 1905; see *Pacific Fisherman* 4:4 (April 1906): 12. Note that Chinese workers did not take kindly to being replaced by machines and were known to protest the introduction of new machinery. See *Pacific Fisherman* 3:9 (September 1905): 23.

52 Friday, *Organizing Asian American Labor*, 95–96; William and Clara Propst, oral history interview by Peter Heffelfinger and Barbara Heacock (July 21, 1977), 5, transcribed tape recording, SCOHC.

53 "Immigration Inspector Bounds Up Chinamen," *Anacortes American*, August 18, 1910.

54 On Chinese labor bosses bringing Chinese cannery workers across the border, see Charles Snyder to F. D. Huestis, May 19, 1901, file 5, box 107, RG 36, NAS; and Chang, "Enforcing Transnational White Solidarity," 676–78. On Chinese crossing on their own, see "Chinese again Breaking the Laws," *Vancouver Province*, September 6, 1901, box 52; and "Wanted to Get under Stars and Stripes," *Vancouver Ledger*, June 10, 1903, box 53, both in IPSFC. On the persistence of illegal border crossings, see also Ettinger, "'We Sometimes Wonder What They Will Spring on Us Next.'"

55 For a sampling of evidence on false immigration documents, see J. A. van Bok-

kilm(?) to J. C. Saunders, October 3, 1893, file 3, box 101; Thomas Fisher to F. D. Huestis, August 6, 1900, file 1, box 107; and J. R. Miller to F. D. Huestis, September 21, 1897, file 5, box 95, all in RG 36, NAS.

56 Griffith, "Border Crossings," 480.

57 Thomas Fisher to F. D. Huestis, July 18, 1899, file 5, box 106, RG 36, NAS.

58 N-8, WB Wed. April 10, 1901, box 1, Peggy Aiston Collection, Center for Pacific Northwest Studies, Western Washington University, Bellingham, WA (hereafter Aiston Collection); and "Sockeye Plentiful," *Victoria Colonist*, August 6, 1902, box 52, IPSFC. The Aiston Collection presents some citation problems. Aiston was doing research on several Bellingham/Puget Sound newspapers that covered more than a century, and she developed a code to cross-reference her notes, some of which is difficult for subsequent researchers to decipher.

59 Ira Myers to A. W. Bash, August 9, 1883, file 4, box 109, RG 36, NAS.

60 C. J. Mulkey to Andrew Wasson, January 11, 1892, file 1, box 100, RG 36, NAS. Ettinger and Chang both also found that illegal border crossers manipulated their looks and their supposed nationalities to fool border patrols on the U.S.-Mexico border. See Chang, "Enforcing Transnational White Solidarity," 687; and Ettinger, "'We Sometimes Wonder What They Will Spring on Us Next,'" 175–78.

61 A. L. Blake to A. W. Bash, July 11, 1883, file 4, box 109; G. W. Million to C. M. Bradshaw, August 3, 1891, file 6, box 178; and W. Bolcum to A. Wasson, May 9, 1892, file 6, box 179, all in RG 36, NAS.

62 Swan to R. M. Hopkins, September 25, 1890, Outgoing Letters, Letterbook 1889–1891, box 1, James Swan Papers, University of British Columbia Special Collections, Vancouver.

63 Statement of O. H. Culver, August 12, 1904, file 281, box 480, RG 36, NADC. See also Chang, "Enforcing Transnational White Solidarity," 673–78; and Liestman, "'Various Celestials among Our Town,'" 101–3.

64 "Digest of, and Comment Upon, Report of Immigrant Inspector Marcus Braun," September 20, 1907, entry 9, file 51360, folder 44-D, RG 85, National Archives, Washington D.C., quoted in Chang, "Enforcing Transnational White Solidarity," 677.

65 H. Stratton(?) to Collector, November 13, 1883, file 1, box 166, RG 36, NAS.

66 A. L. Blake to A. W. Bash, September 9, 1884, file 2, box 110, RG 36, NAS.

67 Charles Snyder to F. D. Huestis, May 19, 1901, file 5, box 107; O. L. Spaulding to Collector, April 10, 1899, file 4, box 22; and O. L. Snyder to F. D. Huestis, January 2, 1902, file 3, box 107, all in RG 36, NAS. The ringleaders of the complex Portland-B.C. smuggling ring charged a similar amount ($120) to move illegal immigrants across the border. See Griffith, "Border Crossings," 480; and Chang, "Enforcing Transnational White Solidarity," 677–78.

68 N12, BH Sun July 2, 1911, box 1, Aiston Collection.

69 Elmer Vogt, oral history interview by Barbara Heacock (January 30, 1978), 25–26 (quotation), transcribed tape recording, SCOHC. See also "Smuggler Kelly in Trouble," *Seattle Post-Intelligencer*, July 16, 1898; "Kelly in the Lock-Up," *Anacortes American*, July 21, 1896; and A. L. Blake to A. W. Bash, September 9, 1884, file 2,

box 110, RG 36, NAS. There are numerous other examples of Chinese being illegally smuggled across the border in the U.S. Customs records.

70   Chang and Ettinger found the same in their research. See Chang, "Enforcing Transnational White Solidarity," 678; and Ettinger, "'We Sometimes Wonder What They Will Spring on Us Next,'" 170.

71   See, for example, testimony of Charles F. Todd in Canada, *Report of the Royal Commission on Chinese and Japanese Immigration*, 153.

72   "Biggest Run on Record," *Anacortes American*, August 1, 1901; Friday, *Organizing Asian American Labor*, 91; and Lutz, *Makúk*, 204–10.

73   *Pacific Fisherman* 3:8 (August 1905): 24.

74   Friday, *Organizing Asian American Labor*, 94; Ichioka, *The Issei*, 7–19; and Canada, *Report of the Royal Commission on Chinese and Japanese Immigration*, 327–29.

75   Roy, *White Man's Province*, 92. Canada, *Report of the Royal Commission on Chinese and Japanese Immigration*, 327–28, lists population of Japanese in B.C. at 4,578.

76   Ichioka, *The Issei*, 55–56; Canada, *Report of the Royal Commission on Chinese and Japanese Immigration*, 328–29; and Friday, *Organizing Asian American Labor*, 94.

77   Friday, *Organizing Asian American Labor*, 95–99; *Pacific Fisherman* 3:10 (October 1905): 8; and Cobb, *Salmon Fisheries of the Pacific Coast* (1911), 75.

78   Testimony of E. B. Deming in Canada, *Report of the Royal Commission on Chinese and Japanese Immigration*, 162.

79   Testimony of Henry O. Bell-Irving, in ibid., 143. See also testimony of Frank Burnett and "Summary," in ibid., 148, 166.

80   Testimony of Mar Chan, Chinese contractor of Victoria, and testimony of Thomas Robinson, Assistant to the Inspector of Fisheries, in ibid., 141–42, 156.

81   Roy, *White Man's Province*, 142.

82   "Chinks Form Union, May Strike," *Vancouver World*, June 9, 1909, box 54, IPSFC.

83   Friday, *Organizing Asian American Labor*, 100–1.

84   Roy, *White Man's Province*, 164; and "Preparing for Big Salmon Season," *Vancouver World*, June 19, 1900, box 54, IPSFC (quotation).

85   "Report of Inspection of Salmon Canneries," 1910, file 3515, part 1, vol. 387, MR T-3378, RG 23, LAC. One estimate based on the census of 1910 indicates there were 1,414 Eastern Indians in Washington and approximately 5,000 in B.C. See Das, *Hindustani Workers on the Pacific Coast*, 17, 20–21; and Misrow, "East Indian Immigration on the Pacific Coast."

86   Canada, *Report of the Royal Commission on Chinese and Japanese Immigration*, 340; and Adachi, *Enemy That Never Was*, 47.

87   Marlatt, *Steveston Recollected*, 11; and Adachi, *Enemy That Never Was*, 30–32.

88   Testimonies of Frank Burnett and David Douglas in Canada, *Report of the Royal Commission on Chinese and Japanese Immigration*, 341, 342.

89   Testimony of Frank Burnett, in ibid., 340–41.

90   Marlatt, *Steveston Recollected*, Appendix A, 96.

91   Roy, *White Man's Province*, 81–88.

92   Goode, *Fisheries and Fishery Industries of the United States*, 748. Such behavior is further confirmed by sources cited in Vernon Carstensen, "The Fisherman's

Frontier on the Pacific Coast: The Rise of the Salmon-Canning Industry," in Clark, *Frontier Challenge*, 77.

93 Despite the lack of laws on the books prior to 1907, U.S. Customs officials regularly pursued, caught, and deported Japanese border crossers before 1907. Chang found that U.S. immigration officials used the Foran Act of 1885 to justify deporting Japanese workers. See Chang, "Enforcing Transnational White Solidarity," 679.

94 Samuel Walker to F. D. Huestis, September 7, 1900, file 1, box 107, RG 36, NAS.

95 "Japanese Are Going South," unidentified newspaper, c. September 10, 1901, box 52, IPSFC.

96 Statement of Kutiro Akure, December 23, 1901, file 4, box 107, RG 36, NAS.

97 "Busy, Are Immigration Officers in Keeping Out Japanese," *Vancouver World*, July 10, 1903, box 53, IPSFC. On using water routes, see also Meriden Hill to F. D. Huestis, July 12, 1899, file 5, box 64, RG 36, NAS. For a small sampling of illegal Japanese crossings in the Canadian archives, see C. B. Sword to Department of Marine and Fisheries, December 21, 1909; John Williams to Department of Marine and Fisheries, December 19, 1909; and L. P. Brodeur to Mackenzie King, December 29, 1909, all in file 6, part 5, vol. 80, MR T-2664, RG 23, LAC. On the same topic in U.S. archives, see Charles Snyder to F. D. Huestis, February 28, 1900, file 3; and *U.S. v. Koma Skahara*, sworn statement of T. Yamasaki, May 1899, file 1, both in box 106, RG 36, NAS.

98 N12, BH Fri. November 29, 1907 (quotation); and N12, BH Mon. December 9, 1907, both in box 1, Aiston Collection.

99 "Japs Desert Big Canneries," *Vancouver World*, July 5, 1909, box 54, IPSFC.

100 Chang, "Enforcing Transnational White Solidarity," 671.

101 "Salmon Bought by Americans," *Vancouver World*, September 22, 1909, box 54, IPSFC.

102 July 2, 1909 entry, p. 213, box 52, Minutes of Meetings, Fraser River Canners' Association, IPSFC.

103 "Japs Asking Information of Arrest," *Vancouver Sun*, September 10, 1917, box 55, IPSFC.

104 Canada, *Report of the Royal Commission on Chinese and Japanese Immigration*, 347–54. Chang also found evidence that Japanese laborers sold U.S. passports across the border. On this and other common tactics discovered by the Immigration Bureau, see Chang, "Enforcing Transnational White Solidarity," 687–89.

105 Boat pullers were required to have permits as of 1899, but because of the protests of both canners and fishermen, it is not clear how strictly this law was enforced in the early 1900s. See Minister of Marine and Fisheries to His Excellency in Council, March 29, 1899, file 6, part 2, vol. 79, MR T-2663, RG 23, LAC; W. D. Burdis to J. P. Babcock, July 2, 1909, file 1908 #1, box 194, GR-0435, BCA; "Officers Stopped Fishing on the Skeena," unknown newspaper, May 30, 1908; "Will Bar Aliens from the Fraser," *Vancouver Province*, June 10, 1908; and "Japs Threaten Appeal to Consul If Kept off River," *Vancouver Province*, June 12, 1908, all in box 53, IPSFC.

106 Ichioka, *The Issei*, 69–71; and Chang, "Enforcing Transnational White Solidarity," 681, 684.

107 Roy, *White Man's Province*, 103–9, 164, 168–69. On Canada's 1908 Gentlemen's

Agreement, see Kobayashi and Jackson, "Japanese Canadians and the Racialization of Labor in the B.C. Sawmill Industry," 41, 51.

108 Jorgen Dahlie, "Old World Paths in the New: Scandinavians Find Familiar Home in Washington," in Halseth and Glasrud, *Northwest Mosaic*, 45; Schwantes, *Pacific Northwest*, 188; Arestad, "Norwegians in the Pacific Coast Fisheries," 8; W. H. Bessner, oral history interview by Barbara Heacock (October 4, 1977), 16, transcribed tape recording, SCOHC; Boxberger, "Ethnicity and Labor in the Puget Sound Fishing Industry," 184–86; and Petrich and Roje, *Yugoslav in Washington State*. For a breakdown of the ethnicity of workers in the Washington State fishery, see Wilcox, "Fisheries of the Pacific Coast," 258. On Italian fishermen, see, for example, James Izett to A. W. Bash, July 10, 1883, file 4, box 165, RG 36, NAS.

109 Roy, *White Man's Province*, 92.

110 On Newfoundlanders, see testimony of Hezekiah Stead, testimony of Rev. John Perry Bowell, and testimony of Capt. JL Anderson, all in Canada, *Report of the Royal Commission on Chinese and Japanese Immigration*, 156,157–58, 159. On Norwegians and Swedes, see testimony of Alexander Ewen in ibid., 138. On African Americans, see R. F. Greer to Charles Wilson, July 16, 1904, file 5, box 2, GR-0063, Superintendent of Provincial Police, Correspondence Inward from Attorney General, 1898–1912, B.C. Archives, Victoria (hereafter GR-0063, BCA); and Rathbun, "Review of the Fisheries in the Contiguous Waters of the State of Washington and British Columbia," 295, 308. An African American man named John Sullivan Deas owned and managed a salmon cannery on what later became Deas Island in the 1870s. See Ralston, "John Sullivan Deas." Prior to the Civil War, a number of African Americans moved to B.C. from California, but many of them returned to the United States following that conflict.

111 Von Hesse-Wartegg, "Visit to Anglo-Saxon Antipodes," 34 (quotation); and Barman, *West beyond the West*, 138–43.

112 Schwantes, *Radical Heritage*. Kornel Chang has argued that white ethnic workers in both the United States and B.C.—and indeed around the Pacific Rim—banded together and embraced their whiteness against Asians in this period. While there is certainly evidence to support this in the salmon fishing industry of the Salish Sea, the added distinction of gear type may have made European ethnic differences on the water more pronounced. See Chang, "Circulating Race and Empire," 678–701; and Chang, "Enforcing Transnational White Solidarity," 687–93. For more on the trans-Pacific debates on race and white supremacy, see Lee, "'Yellow Peril' and Asian Exclusion in the Americas," 550–56.

113 Meggs, *Salmon*, 40–42; and Ralston, "1900 Strike of Fraser River Sockeye Salmon Fishermen," 39–92.

114 Ralston, "1900 Strike of Fraser River Sockeye Salmon Fishermen," 93–104; and Meggs, *Salmon*, 60–73. For more on the anti-Asian sentiments pervading the B.C. labor movement and how labor militancy influenced worker solidarity prior to World War II, see Creese, "Exclusion or Solidarity?"

115 Marlatt, *Steveston Recollected*, 29–30; and Adachi, *Enemy That Never Was*, 58.

116 Adachi, *Enemy That Never Was*, 59; and Marlatt, *Steveston Recollected*, 31–34.

117 E. P. Bremner(?) to David Mills, August 11, 1900, file 1968, part 1, vol. 272, MR T-3195, RG 23, LAC (quotation); and Conley, "Relations of Production and Collective Action," 101–2.

118 The King v. Opeaga et al., July 13, 1901, file 419, 1901/120, box 90, GR-0419, B.C. Attorney General Records, B.C. Archives, Victoria (hereafter GR-0419, BCA).

119 The King v. Anderson, July 30, 1901, file 419, 1901/113, box 90, GR-0419, BCA.

120 Adachi, *Enemy That Never Was*, 59–60; "Fishermen's Demonstration: A Big Parade of the Strikers in Vancouver," *Victoria Daily Colonist*, July 15, 1900; "The Canneries Will Be Closed: Result of Fishermen Refusing to Accept Twenty Cents a Fish," *Victoria Daily Colonist*, July 20, 1900; "Striking Fishermen: Frank Rogers One of the Leaders Charged with Intimidation," *Victoria Daily Colonist*, July 24, 1900; July 10, 1900 entry, p. 56, box 52, Minutes of Meetings, Fraser River Canners' Association, IPSFC; "White Men and Brown in Battle: Union Fishermen on the Fraser Attack the Japanese," *San Francisco Examiner*, July 9, 1901, copy in Alaska Packers Association Collection, Newspapers and Clippings, Center for Pacific Northwest Studies, Western Washington University, Bellingham, WA (hereafter APAC). On negotiations between the white and Japanese unions see June 14, 1902 entry, pp. 173–88, and May 20 and May 30, 1903 entries, no page number, box 52, Minutes of Meetings, Fraser River Canners' Association, IPSFC; F. S. Hussey to Sgt. Murray, July 8, 1901, file 4, box 1, GR-1576, B.C. Provincial Police Force, Correspondence, 1890–1911, B.C. Archives, Victoria (hereafter GR-1576, BCA); and J. A. Russell to F. S. Hussey, July 21, 1902, file 5, box 1, GR-1576, BCA. Chinese cannery workers also took advantage of the high value placed on their labor in 1901 and made several demands at various canneries in British Columbia. See Meggs, *Salmon*, 69.

121 Conley notes that as the northern B.C. fisheries grew in importance, most strike efforts took place in the north and not on the Fraser. Despite this, northern fishermen still had a difficult time maintaining a union from season to season. See Conley, "Relations of Production and Collective Action," 88, 102, 107–8.

122 Charles Harrison to C. B. Sword, March 11, 1902, file 2916, vol. 335, MR T-3020, RG 23, LAC.

123 Marlatt, *Steveston Recollected*, 30.

124 "Steveston's Chinatown Is Reduced to Smoking Ashes," *Daily Columbian* (possibly from New Westminster), April 6, 1907; and "Visited by Another Fire: Sixty Cabins Owned by Lighthouse Cannery Destroyed by Fire Yesterday Morning," *Vancouver World*, April 9, 1907, both in box 53, IPSFC.

125 Chang, "Circulating Race and Empire," 687–93; Lee, "'Yellow Peril' and Asian Exclusion in the Americas," 550–53; and Adachi, *Enemy That Never Was*, 63–85. For additional conflicts between Indians and Japanese, see S. Drake to W. H. Bullock-Webster, July 5, 1904, file 1, box 44, GR-0055, BCA.

126 Quoted in Canada, *Report of the Royal Commission on Chinese and Japanese Immigration*, 344.

127 Quoted in ibid., 346.

128 "Salmon Strike a Fizzle," *Seattle Union Record*, August 9, 1913 (quotation); and Conley, "Relations of Production and Collective Action," 102.

129 Conley, "Relations of Production and Collective Action," 104.

130 On *Seattle Union Record* references, see issues dated February 16, 1901, April 20, 1901, October 25, 1902, May 7, 1904. For other evidence of early fishermen unions in Puget Sound, see *Pacific Fisherman* 4:3 (March 1906): 18; and *Pacific Fisherman* 4:8 (August 1906): 23.

131 Dahlie, "Social History of Scandinavian Immigration," 60. There is more information regarding unions on the Columbia River than is available for Puget Sound. For instance, striking Columbia River fishers were believed to have set fire to an Astoria cannery in 1896, and the local paper discussed the possibility that the militia might be called in to protect nonunion strikers; see "A Cannery Is Burned," *Anacortes American*, June 11, 1896. For more on early history of the Columbia River fishermen's union, see Wilcox, "Fisheries of the Pacific Coast," 241–42; and Schwantes, *Radical Heritage*, 99.

132 The United Fishermen of the Pacific formulated a constitution that was then ratified by the Fishermen's Protective Union of the Pacific Coast and Alaska and the Columbia River Fishermen's Protective Union in 1906. See United Fishermen of the Pacific, "Constitution of the United Fishermen of the Pacific: Organized March 16, 1906."

133 "Fish Buyers and Cannerymen Attention," *Anacortes American*, September 5, 1907. The Salmon Purse Seiners Union apparently started publishing a trade magazine in 1937, but there is little indication as to their activities or origins before the 1930s.

134 "March Answers the Purse Seiners," *Seattle Union Record*, June 6, 1914.

135 J. Conrad Graham, "Memories of Pacific American Fisheries and the Fish Trap Industry in Puget Sound," oral history interview by Michael A. Runestrand (June 20, 1976), Accession WTC 75-29mr, tape 1 side 2, p. 1, transcribed tape recording, Washington State Oral/Aural History Program, Washington State Archives, Olympia, WA (microfiche copy in Wilson Library, Western Washington University, Bellingham, WA). For more on the later incarnations of the Pacific Coast fishermen's union from the 1930s to the 1950s, see Mann, "Class Consciousness and Common Property."

136 *Pacific Fisherman* 4:10 (October 1906): 17.

137 *Pacific Fisherman* 4:8 (August 1906): 22–23.

138 Samuel Walker to F. D. Huestis, September 7, 1900, box 107, file 1, RG 36, NAS.

139 Friday, *Organizing Asian American Labor*, 99.

140 "More Trouble with the Japs," *Anacortes American*, August 26, 1909.

141 "Laws Proposed to Protect White Race," *Anacortes American*, July 29, 1909. For more on white workers' anti-Asian sentiments, see Chang, "Circulating Race and Empire," 678–701.

142 "Anacortes Race 'Riot' Has Peaceful Ending," *Anacortes American*, July 22, 1915; Boxberger, "Ethnicity and Labor in the Puget Sound Fishing Industry," 187–88; and Friday, *Organizing Asian American Labor*, 99.

143 Friday, *Organizing Asian American Labor*, 99–100. For more on the Chinese in Washington, see Liestman, "'Various Celestials among Our Town.'"

144 Ralston, "1900 Strike of Fraser River Sockeye Salmon Fishermen," 145.

145 Cobb, *Salmon Fisheries of the Pacific Coast* (1911), 35; and Helen Comfort Pike Loop, oral history interview by Peter Heffelfinger and Barbara Heacock (August 8, 1977), 6, transcribed tape recording, SCOHC.

146 Quoted in Ito, *Issei*, 357.

147 Quoted in ibid., 356.

148 Casaday, "Labor Unrest and the Labor Movement in the Salmon Industry," 517–18; and Boxberger, "Ethnicity and Labor in the Puget Sound Fishing Industry," 183–86. Divisions according to gear type have a long history in the U.S. fishing industry. In fact, debates over fish traps versus line fishing contributed to the formation of the first U.S. Fish Commission in 1871. See Allard, *Spencer Fullerton Baird and the U.S. Fish Commission*, 76–85.

149 Quoted in Conley, "Relations of Production and Collective Action," 100, see also 95–97 and 103.

150 D. Bell-Irving and R. J. Ker to Premier and Council of the Provincial Government of B.C., January 30, 1902, file 876 1902–1903, box 90; F. H. Cunningham to D. N. McIntyre, June 10, 1912, file 342: 1912, box 39, both in GR-0435, BCA. On hiring eastern and southern Europeans from Washington, see John McNab to E. E. Prince, February 13, 1895; Memorandum from E. E. Prince, February 21, 1895, both in file 1075 part 1, vol. 207, MR T-3122, RG 23, LAC. On hiring "Americans," see copy of article from the *Daily Colonist*, July 26, 1897, file 6, part 1, vol. 78, MR T-2662; Memorandum of E. E. Prince, n.d. [c. 1899], file 6, part 2, vol. 79, MR T-2663; and B.C. Fishermen's Union to W. Templeman, February 26, 1909, file 6, part 4, vol. 79, MR T-2664, all in RG 23, LAC.

151 William Rhodes to John Costigan, March 20, 1895, file 6, vol. 78, MR T-2662, RG 23, LAC, emphases in original. While American fishermen were known to travel to work in the B.C. canneries, how they then navigated their nationality out on the water is hard to tell from available evidence. It appears that when American fishermen were fishing for establishments north of the border and flying a Canadian boat flag, they were essentially pretending to be Canadian for the duration of their employment.

152 Henry Doyle to D. N. McIntyre, October 25, 1912, file 1912 #2, box 195, GR-0435, BCA.

153 "Deputation of B.C. Canners' Association Interview with Hon. W. J. Bowser, Parliament Buildings," October 13, 1913, p. 35, file 10–4, box 10, Doyle Papers.

154 Testimony of E. B. Welsh, Proceedings, January 28, 1902, Sixth Session, "Fishery Commission, B.C., 1902," file 2918, vol. 335, MR T-4020, RG 23, LAC.

155 Ralston, "1900 Strike of Fraser River Sockeye Salmon Fishermen," 41, 45. Indian fishermen in the 1880s made $2.25 per day; boat pullers earned $2.

156 Casaday, "Labor Unrest and the Labor Movement in the Salmon Industry," 25–27. See also Ralston, "1900 Strike of Fraser River Sockeye Salmon Fishermen," 33; and Conley, "Relations of Production and Collective Action," 93.

157 On B.C., see Conley, "Relations of Production and Collective Action," 105–6; and Ralston, "1900 Strike of Fraser River Sockeye Salmon Fishermen," 174–75. On Washington, see Lissa Wadewitz, "The Scales of Salmon: Diplomacy and Conserva-

tion in the Western Canada-U.S. Borderlands," in Johnson and Graybill, *Bridging National Borders*, 141–64.

158   Allen Seager and David Roth, "British Columbia and the Mining West: A Ghost of a Chance," in Heron, *Workers' Revolt in Canada*, 238–39, 243; and McCormack, *Reformers, Rebels, and Revolutionaries*, 11–12.

159   Schwantes, *Radical Heritage*, 22–114.

160   Keith Ralston, "Patterns of Trade and Investment on the Pacific Coast, 1867–1892: The Case of the British Columbia Salmon Canning Industry," in Ward and McDonald, *British Columbia*, 296–305; and Alicja Muszynski, "Major Processors to 1940 and Early Labour Force: Historical Notes," in Marchak, Guppy, and McMullan, *Uncommon Property*, 46–57. Note that both studies demonstrate that Americans did not own large parts of the B.C. cannery system by the end of the nineteenth century, but the U.S. Customs Service letters indicate that several of the traps at Point Roberts were at least partially owned by Canadian interests, and many others were often leased to B.C. companies.

161   Paul Yee, "Sam Kee: A Chinese Business in Early Vancouver," in McDonald and Barman, *Vancouver Past*, 86–87.

162   Conley, "Relations of Production and Collective Action," 91.

163   "Agreement between Canadian and American Salmon Canners re Territorial Rights," *Vancouver World*, August 6, 1903, and "Pirate Sloop Off Fraser River," *Vancouver Province*, August 8, 1903, both in box 53, IPSFC. For other examples of transborder cooperation among canners, see August 3, 1903 entry, p. 272, box 52, Minutes of Meetings, Fraser River Canners' Association, IPSFC; H. Bell-Irving to "John," May 21, 1902, file/vol. 84, box 500-A-7, MS-1 Bell-Irving Family Fonds, City of Vancouver Archives, Vancouver (hereafter MS-1, CVA); and Henry Doyle to Amelius Jarvis and Co., March 28, 1902, file 2–1, box 2, Doyle Papers.

164   *Pacific Fisherman* 3:8 (August 1905): 18.

165   Bell-Irving to "John," June 1, 1899, p. 616, file 83 (1897–1899), box 500-A-6, MS-1, CVA (quotation). One such combination failure was initiated by men named Kelley-Clarke and Onffrey; see "The Proposed Combine of Salmon Canneries," New York *Chamber of Commerce*, March 19, 1901; "Alaska Packers Ask Too Much," *Astoria Daily News*, May 19, 1901, both in Newspapers and Clippings, APAC. See also unsigned to Lowman, July 17, 1906, Mansfield Lovell Co. 1905–07, box 12, PAFC; W. D. Burdis to Skeena River Commercial Co., April 18, 1904, box 1; Henry Doyle to Ernest Evans, January 31, 1902, file 2–1, box 2, both in Doyle Papers; August 13, 1900 entries, pp. 72, 75, box 52, in Minutes of Meetings, Fraser River Canners' Association, IPSFC. On such combines on Puget Sound, see H. Bell-Irving to "John," May 17, 1899, p. 598, file 83, box 500-A-6, MS-1, CVA; and Dominion Fishery Regulations 1894, file 2 1911–1912, box 155, GR-0435, BCA.

166   W. D. Burdis to Brewster, March 7, 1917, B.C. Canners Assn. 1917, file 10–7, box 10, Doyle Papers.

167   Ira Myers to A. W. Bash, August 9, 1883, file 4, box 109, RG 36, NAS.

168   W. D. Burdis to W. J. Bowser, February 7, 1912, file 1912 #1, box 194, GR-0435, BCA.

169   Charles Stanley to L. H. Davies, April 30, 1898; Memorandum of E. E. Prince,

September 29, 1898, both in file 222, vol. 131, MR T-2819, RG 23, LAC; unsigned to Corbould, June 20, 1895, file 2265, box 293, MR T-3218, RG 23, LAC; and Frank Winslow to H. Beecher, July 18, 1885, file 3, box 168, RG 36, NAS.

170   Memorandum from E. E. Prince, March 16? 1897? (unclear date), file 2265, box 293, MR T-3218, RG 23, LAC, emphasis in original.

171   Radke, *Pacific American Fisheries, Inc.*, 36.

172   July 10, 1900 entry, p. 56, box 52, Minutes of Meetings, Fraser River Canners' Association, IPSFC.

173   "Canners Have a Blacklist," *Vancouver Province*, August 7, 1903, box 53, IPSFC.

174   July 10, 1900 entry, p. 56, box 52, Minutes of Meetings, Fraser River Canners' Association, IPSFC.

175   July 15, 1904 entry, p. 150, vol. 1, GR-0397, BCA.

176   W. D. Burdis to F. S. Hussey, July 2, 1907, file 8, box 38; and Colin Campbell to F. S. Hussey, July 11, 1905, file 1, box 43, both in GR-0055, BCA.

177   Advisory Board Meeting Minutes, October 8, 1913, vol. 4, box 590-G-4, MS-870, Anglo-British Packing Company Records, City of Vancouver Archives, Vancouver (hereafter MS-870, CVA).

178   Memorandum from E. E. Prince, n.d. [c. February 1899], file 6, part 1, vol. 78, MR T-2663, RG23, LAC, emphasis in original.

179   Deputy Attorney General Maclean to Wm. Bullock-Webster, July 28, 1904, file 4, box 2; and Maclean to Wm. Bullock-Webster, August 11, 1904, file 5, box 2, both in GR-0063, BCA.

180   *Pacific Fisherman*, 13:9 (September 1915): 21, box 120, PAFC.

181   "Finding Aid Description," 2; Annual Stockholder Meeting, May 8, 1900, Fidalgo Island Packing Co. Minutes, 1895–1901, vol. 9, both in MS-870, CVA; H. Bell-Irving to "John," April 12, 1899, p. 558; and H. Bell-Irving to "John," August 3, 1899, p. 655, both in file 83 (1897–1899), box 500-A-6, MS-1, CVA.

182   Bell-Irving to J. Whitall & Co., August 9, 1899, p. 663, file 83, box 500-A-6, MS-1, CVA (quotation). See also Robert Ward & Co. to James Gaudin, October 21, 1895, file 1469, vol. 239, MR T-3159, RG 23, LAC; and H. Bell-Irving to "John," December 17, 1897, file 83, box 500-A-6, MS-1, CVA.

183   Charles McLennan to C. Bradshaw, August 13, 1892, file 1, box 62, RG 36, NAS. On B.C. syndicate, see *Pacific Fisherman* 3:6 (June 1905): 17.

184   Charles McLennan to A. Wasson, May 5, 1892, file 2, box 62, RG 36, NAS.

185   J. A. Kerr to B. W. Huntoon, February 11, 1904, file II, box 151; unsigned to B. W. Huntoon, April 3, 1903, file II, box 150, both in PAFC. On American investments in B.C., see *Pacific Fisherman* 14:9 (September 1916): 15, box 120, PAFC. Bill Lowman, a prominent Puget Sound packer, was one American canner to cross the border and buy a controlling interest in the B.C.-based C. L. Packing Company in the fall of 1916.

186   Memorandum from E. E. Prince, n.d. [c. February 1899], file 6, part 1, vol. 78, MR T-2663, RG 23, LAC; emphasis in original.

187   Peck, *Reinventing Free Labor*, 15–48. Note that people in the Northwest occasionally called labor bosses "padrones" or "tyees," but the most common term used in this region was "labor boss." For an overview of one Canadian Chinese labor contrac-

tor's activities, see Paul Yee, "Sam Kee: A Chinese Business in Early Vancouver," in McDonald and Barman, *Vancouver Past*, 70–96.

188   Friday, *Organizing Asian American Labor*, 85–87; and "Cannery Workers Very Scarce," *Vancouver Province*, June 9, 1906, box 53, IPSFC. Chinese labor contractors were also known to abscond with the wages of the Chinese crews. To prevent this, Chinese cannery workers formed the Chinese Cannery Employees' Union in 1904. See Muszynski, *Cheap Wage Labour*, 181.

189   Japanese labor contractors to Fraser River Canners' Association, May 14, 1904, enclosure, W. D. Burdis to the Fraser River Canners' Association, June 3, 1904, file: Letters Incoming, F-H, box 1, Doyle Papers.

190   "Canning Machines; Chinese Object to New Patent and Refuse to Work with It" (unidentified newspaper) October 8, 1901, box 52, IPSFC.

191   "Sockeye Plentiful," *Victoria Colonist*, August 6, 1902, box 52, IPSFC.

192   Untitled, *Daily News-Advertiser* (Vancouver), November 25, 1903 and "Chinese Paid $1000 Fine," *Vancouver Province*, April 14, 1904, both in box 53, IPSFC.

193   "Cannery Workers Are Very Scarce," *Vancouver Province*, June 9, 1906, box 53, IPSFC.

5. PIRATES OF THE SALISH SEA

1   "Bert Jones: Fish Pirate," in Strickland, *River Pigs and Cayuses*, 12.

2   Historians have found various instances of "piracy" in different water resource contexts, particularly those that have more readily lent themselves to claims of private ownership. See, for instance, Booker, "Oyster Growers and Oyster Pirates in San Francisco Bay"; and McCay, "Pirates of Piscary."

3   For a brief sampling of work on this and related topics in the European context, see Hobsbawm, *Bandits*; Hobsbawm, *Social Bandits and Primitive Rebels*; Thompson, *Whigs and Hunters*; and Sahlins, *Forest Rites*. In the U.S. context, see Jacoby, *Crimes against Nature*; Warren, *Hunter's Game*; and McCay, *Oyster Wars and the Public Trust*.

4   Cobb, *Pacific Salmon Fisheries* (1921), 85; and Fidalgo Island Packing Company Minutes,1895–1901, Stockholders' Meeting, May 9, 1899, file 1, vol. 9, MS-870, Anglo-British Packing Company Records, City of Vancouver Archives, Vancouver (hereafter MS-870, CVA). For a list of fish trap locations around Puget Sound in 1905 that identifies which large companies owned which locations, see *Pacific Fisherman* 3:4 (April 1905): 25–26. The largest canning companies in the region clearly owned and operated 159 of the 213 listed traps.

5   Cobb, *Salmon Fisheries of the Pacific Coast* (1911), 37.

6   Fidalgo Island Packing Company Minutes,1895–1901, Stockholders' Meeting, May 9, 1899, file 1, vol. 9, MS-870, CVA.

7   Based on his age, Jones most likely began fish pirating in the 1910s and continued in these activities until fish traps were abolished by Washington State in 1934. See Bert Jones, oral history interview by Peter Heffelfinger and Barbara Heacock (February 7, 1978), transcribed tape recording, Skagit County Oral History Collection, Center

for Pacific Northwest Studies, Western Washington University, Bellingham, WA (hereafter SCOHC).

8   "Salmon Men Fear the Work of Fish Pirates," *Bellingham Reveille*, April 29, 1911, file 12.3, box 107, Pacific American Fisheries Collection, Center for Pacific Northwest Studies, Western Washington University, Bellingham, WA (hereafter PAFC).

9   Quoted in Strickland, *River Pigs and Cayuses*, 12.

10 "Salmon Department," *Trade Register* (unknown location), May 6, 1911, box 54, International Pacific Salmon Fisheries Commission Collection, University of British Columbia Special Collections, Vancouver (hereafter IPSFC).

11 "Malicious Injury to Traps," *Pacific Fisherman* 3:8 (August 1905): 25.

12 Daily Report of Fraser River Canners' Association, no date (c. August 1909), box 54, IPSFC (quotation); July 31, 1909 entry, file 11–9, box 11, Henry Doyle Papers, University of British Columbia Special Collections, Vancouver (hereafter Doyle Papers); W. D. Burdis to F. S. Hussey, July 30, 1909, file 4, box 40, GR-0055, B.C. Provincial Police Force, Superintendent Correspondence Inward, 1891–1910, B.C. Archives, Victoria (hereafter GR-0055, BCA); and Otway Wilkie to Colin Campbell, August 7, 1909, file 5, box 47, GR-0055, BCA.

13 Everett Tawney to the Secretary of Treasury, July 9, 1915, file 1919, box 692, Special Agents' Reports and Correspondence, U.S. Customs Bureau, Record Group 36, National Archives and Records Administration, Washington, D.C.

14 "Say Fish Pirates Came from Fraser," *Vancouver Province*, August 19, 1909, box 54, IPSFC.

15 "Salmon Poachers Busy on the West Coast," *Daily News* (unknown location), August 26, 1911, and "Poachers Fire on Guard," unidentified newspaper, c. August 2, 1912, both in box 54, IPSFC; and "Pirates Raid Todd Traps," *Pacific Fisherman* 10:8 (August 1912): 18.

16 "Exciting Chase after Poachers," *Daily News-Advertiser* (Vancouver), July 18, 1912, box 54, IPSFC. That the Canadian Department of Marine and Fisheries managed to roll this vessel was unusual and suggests they hired a more powerful boat that season or the fleeing suspect lacked good boating skills.

17 Strickland, *River Pigs and Cayuses*, 11.

18 Walter Scott, "Early Fishing Days/Working the Fish Traps and Remembrances," oral history interview by Michael A. Runestrand (April 15, 1975), tape 1 side 1, p. 9, transcribed tape recording, Washington State Oral/Aural History Program, Washington State Archives, Olympia, WA (microfiche copy in Wilson Library, Western Washington University, Bellingham, WA).

19 Elmer Vogt, oral history interview by Barbara Heacock (January 30, 1978), p. 33, transcribed tape recording, SCOHC.

20 Quoted in Strickland, *River Pigs and Cayuses*, 11.

21 Ibid., 11.

22 Scott interview, tape 1, side 1, pp. 8–9; tape 2, side 2, pp. 2–3 (quotation on 3), Washington State Oral/Aural History Program, Washington State Archives; W. J. Beale, oral history interview by Barbara Heacock (February 8, 1978), tape 1, side 1, p. 25, transcribed tape recording, SCOHC; "Fish Piracy Story Doubted," *Bellingham Rev-*

eille, August 2, 1908, Newspapers and Clippings, 1908, Alaska Packers Association Collection, Center for Pacific Northwest Studies, Western Washington University, Bellingham, WA; B. Huntoon to James Kerr, August 6, 1903, file II, box 150, PAFC. On not paying watchmen, see Bert Jones, oral history interview by Peter Heffelfinger and Barbara Heacock (February 7, 1978), pp. 19–20, transcribed tape recording, SCOHC.

23 Jones interview, pp. 14–15, SCOHC.

24 Beale interview, tape 1, side 1, p. 26, SCOHC.

25 Millerd, "Windjammers to Eighteen Wheelers," 32, 34; "Increasing Use of Gasoline Engines in Fishing Industry," *Pacific Fisherman* 4:6 (June 1906): 9; "Salmon Men Fear Work of Fish Pirates," *Bellingham Reveille*, April 29, 1911, file 12.3, box 107, PAFC; and Rounsefell and Kelez, *Salmon and Salmon Fisheries of Swiftsure Bank, Puget Sound, and the Fraser River*, 708, 728–34.

26 Jones interview, p. 44, SCOHC.

27 "Cannerymen and Trapmen Are Experiencing Trouble with Thieves," *Anacortes American*, September 29, 1898.

28 B. Huntoon to James Kerr, August 6, 1903, file II, box 150, PAFC; "Salmon Pirates at Bellingham," *Vancouver World*, August 1, 1908 (quotation); and "Fish Pirates Take Scowloads of Salmon," *Vancouver Province*, August 1, 1908, both in box 53, IPSFC.

29 W. D. Burdis to D. N. McIntyre, July 12, 1911, file 1911 #2, box 194, GR-0435 B.C. Department of Fisheries, B.C. Archives, Victoria (hereafter GR-0435, BCA); and "Robbers in Launch Fusilade Watchmen," *Daily News-Advertiser* (Vancouver), July 12, 1911, box 54, IPSFC.

30 "Pirates Raid Todd Traps," *Pacific Fisherman* 10:8 (August 1912): 18.

31 "Port Townsend," *The Columbian* (Olympia), October 12, 1917, box 55, IPSFC.

32 Jones interview, p. 37, SCOHC.

33 "Fish Pirates on the Sound," *Pacific Fisherman* 4:9 (September 1906): 14.

34 Quoted in Strickland, *River Pigs and Cayuses*, 11–12.

35 Ibid., 9, 11; and July 25, 1907 entry, file 11–8, box 11, Doyle Papers.

36 Scott interview, tape 1, side 2, p. 7, Washington State Oral/Aural History Program, Washington State Archives.

37 Regional newspapers noted that the five thousand salmon stolen in one 1908 robbery would bring in more than two thousand dollars. See "Salmon Pirates at Bellingham," *Vancouver World*, August 1, 1908; and "Fish Pirates Take Scowloads of Salmon," *Vancouver Province*, August 1, 1908, both in box 53, IPSFC. Some fishermen estimated they caught between fifteen hundred and three thousand fish per day. Prices for fish varied widely each season and according to species, but sockeye generally fetched from ten to twenty-five cents apiece. If just ten cents, regular fishermen might catch between $150 and $300 worth of fish in one day. However, because of what they owed the canners, they were often happy to walk away with just $150 by the end of the season. See, for example, Knight and Koizumi, *Man of Our Times*, 10; and Rathbun, "Review of the Fisheries in the Contiguous Waters of the State of Washington and British Columbia," 321.

38   Jones interview, pp. 15, 24, 38, SCOHC.

39   Scott interview, tape 2, side 2, p. 4, Washington State Oral/Aural History Program, Washington State Archives.

40   Vogt interview, pp. 31 and 34 (quotation), SCOHC.

41   Arnold, *Fishermen's Frontier*, 108–12.

42   "There Was a War in Haro Strait," *The Daily Colonist* (Victoria), April 8, 1962; Edith Robinson, oral history interview by Barbara Heacock (March 8, 1978), p. 24, transcribed tape recording, SCOHC; W. H. Bessner, oral history interview by Barbara Heacock (October 4, 1977), p. 41, transcribed tape recording, SCOHC; J. A. von Bokkilm to J. C. Saunders, October 3, 1893, file 3, box 101, Record Group 36, U.S. Customs Service, Puget Sound Collection District, National Archives and Records Administration, Seattle; and Jones interview, p. 47, SCOHC.

43   "Pirates vs. Fish Traps," *Anacortes American*, July 24, 1902.

44   John McNab to Deputy Minister of Marine and Fisheries, February 27, 1895, file 1469, part 1, vol. 239, Microfilm Reel (hereafter MR) MR T-3159, Department of Marine and Fisheries, Record Group 23, Library and Archives Canada, Ottawa (hereafter RG 23, LAC); and B. Huntoon to James Kerr, August 6, 1903, file II, box 150, PAFC.

45   On recalling just a few pirates, see Vogt interview, p. 27, SCOHC. Perhaps due to difficulties remembering details, Bert Jones claimed that he was the only local fish pirate and also that many people engaged in the practice; see Jones interview, pp. 45, 47, SCOHC.

46   Beale interview, p. 26, SCOHC.

47   B. Huntoon to James Kerr, August 6, 1903, file II, box 150, PAFC.

48   "Say Fish Pirates Came from Fraser," *Vancouver Province*, August 19, 1909, box 54, IPSFC.

49   "Pirates vs. Fish Traps," *Anacortes American*, July 24, 1902.

50   "Harbor Pirates at Port Townsend," *Seattle Post-Intelligencer*, August 23, 1898.

51   W. D. Burdis to Colin Campbell, July 10, 1905, file 1, box 43, GR-0055, BCA (quotation). See also W. D. Burdis to F. S. Hussey, July 20, 1903; W. D. Burdis to F. S. Hussey, July 22, 1903; W. D. Burdis to F. S. Hussey, July 27, 1903, all in file 4, box 37, GR-0055, BCA; Colin Campbell to F. S. Hussey, May 3, 1905, file 1, box 43; Colin Campbell to Provincial Police Office, July 18, 1904, file 3, box 43; Colin Campbell to F. S. Hussey, October 7, 1906, file 2, box 44, all in GR-0055, BCA; and "Boat Thief at Work," *Vancouver World*, August 20, 1906, box 53, IPSFC.

52   W. D. Burdis to F. S. Hussey, July 30, 1909, file 4, vol. 40, GR-0055, BCA.

53   June 17, 1916 entry, p. 73, vol. 3, Minutes of Meetings, Fraser River Canners' Association, IPSFC. On B.C. gear recovered in the United States, see, for example, May 26, 1903 entry, p. 106; July 3, 1903 entry, p. 108; July 27, 1903 entry, p. 112; June 16, 1904 entry, p. 148; July 18, 1904 entry, p. 156; John Deaville to W. D. Burdis, August 16, 1905, p. 258, all in vol. 1, GR-0397, B.C. Provincial Police Force, Vancouver-Westminster Police Records, 1899–1949, B.C. Archives, Victoria (hereafter GR-0397, BCA) and August 6, 1904 entry, p. 38; and August 24, 1904 entry, p. 56, both in GR-0399, B.C. Provincial Police, Steveston District, B.C. Archives, Victoria. On

Americans going north, see Scott interview, tape 2, side 2, p. 2, Washington State Oral/Aural History Program, Washington State Archives; and W. D. Burdis to Bowser, June 8, 1916, file 1916 #4, box 193, GR-0435, BCA.

54 On these types of assumptions among white workers, see, for example, Chang, "Enforcing Transnational White Solidarity," 682–83.

55 Vogt interview, pp. 28, 32 (quotation), SCOHC.

56 William and Clara Propst, oral history interview by Peter Heffelfinger and Barbara Heacock (July 21, 1977), p. 3, transcribed tape recording, SCOHC. William Propst also notes that fish pirates sold to some independents who had traps, but their traps caught few fish and were not highly valued.

57 Albert V. Ginnett, oral history interview by Peter Heffelfinger (March 1, 1978), p. 20, transcribed tape recording, SCOHC.

58 Cobb, *Salmon Fisheries of the Pacific Coast* (1911), 77.

59 "The Canning Season Opens," *Anacortes American*, June 25, 1896; and "More Trap Litigation," *Anacortes American*, May 28, 1896.

60 "Sue for Trespass," *Pacific Fisherman* 3:8 (August 1905): 25.

61 For a sampling of additional suits, see "Fish Trap Litigation," *Anacortes American*, May 30, 1901; "Fisheries Suit Up Again," *Pacific Fisherman* 2:12 (December 1904): 9; "Packers Settle," *Vancouver Province*, July 12, 1906, box 53, IPFSC; *J. A. Gould v. Matison Fredenburg, et al.*, No. 2300, Supreme Court of Washington, 16 Wash. 699, 47, p. 736, 1897 Wash., LEXIS 379; *William Legoe v. Chicago Fishing Company*, No. 3463, Supreme Court of Washington, 24 Wash. 175, 64, p. 141, 1901 Wash., LEXIS 512; *A. Demers v. Sandy Spit Fish Company et al.*, No. 3777, Supreme Court of Washington, 24 Wash. 582, 64, p. 799, 1901 Wash. LEXIS 574; and *Fall and Sockeye Fish Company v. Point Roberts Fishing and Canning Company*, No. 3698, Supreme Court of Washington, 24 Wash. 630, 64, p. 792, 1901 Wash., LEXIS 583.

62 "Fishermen to Appeal," *Pacific Fisherman* 3:3 (March 1905): 17.

63 Rounsefell and Kelez, *Salmon and Salmon Fisheries of Swiftsure Bank, Puget Sound, and the Fraser River*, 716.

64 Ibid., 716–17.

65 Austin, *State of Washington Legislature Laws Pertaining to Puget Sound Fisheries*, 1.

66 J. A. Kerr to B. W. Huntoon, February 11, 1904, file II, box 151, PAFC; and Rounsefell and Kelez, *Salmon and Salmon Fisheries of Swiftsure Bank, Puget Sound, and the Fraser River*, 713.

67 "Stealing Fish from Traps," unidentified newspaper, c. January 14, 1905, box 53, IPSFC.

68 See, for example, Joseph Goodfellow, interviewed by Wm. Wakeham and R. Rathbun, p. 45, vol. II, box 28, Records of the Joint Committee Relative to the Preservation of the Fisheries in Waters Contiguous to Canada and the U.S., 1893–95, Fraser River and Puget Sound Interview Notes, United States Fish and Wildlife Service, Record Group 22, National Archives and Records Administration, College Park, MD.

69 "To Guard Fish Traps," *Vancouver Province*, July 28, 1905, box 53, IPSFC; "Warrants for Trap Owners," *Vancouver World*, July 25, 1905, box 53, IPSFC (quotation).

70 "Pirates Infest Victoria Waters," *Victoria Colonist*, August 11, 1909, box 54, IPSFC.

71   Cobb, *Salmon Fisheries of the Pacific Coast* (1911), 37.

72   B. W. Huntoon to James Kerr, June 18, 1903, file II, box 151, PAFC.

73   Quoted in Strickland, *River Pigs and Cayuses*, 8.

74   Propst interview, p. 3, SCOHC.

75   Jones interview, p. 45, SCOHC.

76   Quoted in Strickland, *River Pigs and Cayuses*, p. 13.

77   "May Break the Law," *Pacific Fisherman* 3:7 (July 1905): 31.

78   J. H. Todd & Sons to Ralph Smith, May 5, 1905 (quotation, emphasis in original); and Ralph Smith to R. Prefontaine, May 11, 1905, file 6, part 3, vol. 79, MR T-2663, RG 23, LAC.

79   Inspector of Fisheries to L. Kershaw, July 24, 1905, file 6, part 3, vol. 79, MR T-2663, RG 23, LAC; and July 24, 25, 26, and 31, 1905 entries, file 11-6, box 11, Doyle Papers. The fines were for either fifty or five hundred dollars; the document is unclear.

80   "Traps Took Large Numbers of Fish," *Victoria Colonist*, July 26, 1905, box 53, IPSFC.

81   "Fishermen's Union Active Again," *Pacific Fisherman* 4:8 (August 1906): 23.

82   Cobb, *Salmon Fisheries of the Pacific Coast* (1911), 38.

83   Scott interview, side 1, p. 8, Washington State Oral/Aural History Program, Washington State Archives.

84   Mason, *John Franklin Troxell, Fish Trap Man*, 84.

85   David Arnold found similar sentiments existed in the southeastern Alaskan fishery. See Arnold, *Fishermen's Frontier*, 111-12.

86   Propst interview, p. 28, SCOHC.

87   "Pirates vs. Fish Traps," *Anacortes American*, July 24, 1902.

88   Lee Bauter, oral history interview by Galen Biery (December 6, 1988), tape 22, transcribed tape recording, box 17, Galen Biery Collection, Center for Pacific Northwest Studies, Western Washington University, Bellingham, WA.

89   Jones interview, p. 48, SCOHC.

90   Vogt interview, pp. 31-32 (quotation on 31), SCOHC.

91   Robinson interview, pp. 18-19 (quotation on 19), SCOHC.

92   Mason, *John Franklin Troxell, Fish Trap Man*, 27. See also Bessner interview, p. 5, SCOHC.

93   Charles Wilson to E. L. Newcombe, May 23, 1895, file 1469, part 1, vol. 239, MR T-3159, RG 23, LAC.

94   Memorandum, E. E. Prince, March 1895, file 1469, part 1, vol. 239, MR T-3159, RG 23, LAC; emphasis in original.

95   See, for instance, Cobb, *Salmon Fisheries of the Pacific Coast* (1911), 37-38.

96   Arnold, *Fishermen's Frontier*, 93-105.

97   "Decidedly Too Many Fish," *Puget Sound American*, July 17, 1905, box 53, IPSFC.

98   Cobb, *Salmon Fisheries of the Pacific Coast* (1911), 38.

99   Rathbun, "Review of the Fisheries in the Contiguous Waters of the State of Washington and British Columbia," 304.

100   *Daily British Colonist*, December 21, 1877, quoted in Canada, Department of Marine and Fisheries, *Annual Report of the Department of Marine and Fisheries, 1893*, cxii.

101   "Salmon on the Fraser," *Victoria Daily Colonist*, July 28, 1889.

102 Quoted in Carrothers, *British Columbia Fisheries*, 66. On fish offal, see ibid., 15–16.

103 Report cited in Singleton, *Constructing Cooperation*, 57.

104 Ginnett interview, pp. 38–39 (quotation), SCOHC. See also Meggs, *Salmon*, 28–29; Robinson interview, pp. 15–16, SCOHC; J. A. Kendall to Raymond Prefontaine, October 14, 1904, file 1469, part 2, vol. 239, MR T-3159, RG 23, LAC; and Propst interview, pp. 8–9, SCOHC.

105 Ginnett interview, p. 38, SCOHC.

106 Jones interview, pp. 10–11, SCOHC. There is some evidence that the PAF cannery sometimes allowed the local community to take fish that was at risk of spoiling, but it is difficult to know how frequently this occurred. See, for example, the photograph with caption "Free Salmon at Pacific American Fisheries," by J. Wayland Clark, photograph 1996.0010.001526, Whatcom Museum Collections, Bellingham, WA.

107 B. Huntoon to James Kerr, August 6, 1903, file II, box 150, PAFC.

108 "Salmon Men Fear Work of Fish Pirates," *Bellingham Reveille*, April 29, 1911, file 12.3, box 107, PAFC.

109 Quoted in Vogt interview, p. 28, SCOHC.

110 See, for example, W. D. Burdis to F. S. Hussey, July 30, 1909, file 4, box 40, GR-0055, BCA.

111 News section, *Pacific Fisherman* 8:7 (July 1910): 19.

112 "Pirates vs. Fish Trap," *Anacortes American*, July 24, 1902.

113 "Salmon Men Fear Work of Fish Pirates," *Bellingham Reveille*, April 29, 1911, file 12.3, box 107, PAFC; and *Pacific Fisherman* 9:5 (May 1911): 17.

114 News section, *Pacific Fisherman* 8:7 (July 1910): 19.

115 Scott interview, tape 1, side 1, p. 10, Washington State Oral/Aural History Program, Washington State Archives.

116 August 3, 1903 meeting minutes, p. 272, box 52, Minutes of Meetings, Fraser River Canners' Association, IPSFC.

117 May 26, 1900 entry, p. 17, vol. 1, GR-0397, BCA.

118 "Theft of Fish," *Victoria Colonist*, July 22, 1908, box 53, IPSFC.

119 "Decidedly Too Many Fish," *Puget Sound American*, July 17, 1905, box 53, IPSFC.

120 N-8 WB Wed. January 28, 1903, Peggy Aiston Collection, Center for Pacific Northwest Studies, Western Washington University, Bellingham, WA (hereafter Aiston Collection). The Aiston Collection presents some citation problems. Aiston was doing research on several Bellingham/Puget Sound newspapers that covered more than a century, and she developed a code to cross-reference her notes, some of which is difficult for subsequent researchers to decipher.

121 Scott interview, tape 1, side 2, p. 7, Washington State Oral/Aural History Program, Washington State Archives. For other accounts of this trial, see Vogt interview, pp. 33–34, SCOHC; N-8 WB Wed. January 21, 1903, box 1, Aiston Collection (quotation); and "Pirates vs. Fish Trap," *Anacortes American*, July 24, 1902.

122 Propst interview, p. 2, SCOHC.

123 *The State of Ohio v. Shaw et al.*, no case number in original, Supreme Court of Ohio, 67 Ohio St. 157, 65 N.E. 875, 1902 Ohio LEXIS 126. An earlier court case on hunting

took place in New York in 1805 and ruled that property in wild animals could be achieved by possession. See *Pierson v. Post*, Supreme Court of New York, 3 Cai. R. 175, and 1805 N.Y. LEXIS 311, p.1. The illegality of fish larceny from traps was upheld by the federal courts in 1917 and again in 1927. See *Miller et al. v. United States*, Case No. 2231, Third Circuit Court of Appeals, 242 F. 907, 1917 U.S. App. LEXIS 1963 and *Klemm v. United States*, Case No. 5039, Ninth Circuit Court of Appeals, 22 F.2d, and 1927 U.S. App. LEXIS 3528.

124 Washington State, *State Session Laws* (1915), chap. 31, sec. 63 and 64, pp. 97–98.

125 Bessner interview, p. 5, SCOHC.

126 Propst interview, pp. 52–53 (quotation on 53), SCOHC.

127 Ginnett interview, p. 16, SCOHC.

6. POLICING THE BORDER

1 Peter Cain to Charles Bradshaw, July 28 1890, file 1, box 97, Record Group 36, U.S. Customs Service, Puget Sound Collection District, National Archives and Records Administration–Pacific Alaska Region, Seattle (hereafter RG 36, NAS).

2 Washington State, Department of Fish and Game, *First Annual Report of the State Fish Commissioner* (1891), 5–6.

3 Austin, *State of Washington Legislative Laws Pertaining to Puget Sound Salmon Fisheries*, 1, 12. On requiring fishing licenses and restricting them to state citizens, see Washington State, *Biennial Report of the Attorney General* (1893), 213–14. On additional regulations in the 1890s and early 1900s, see Austin, *State of Washington Legislative Laws*, 2. See also copy of *Fish and Game Laws of the State of Washington and Decisions of the Supreme Court*, compiled by A. C. Little (1899), in file 1075, part 2, vol. 207, Microfilm Reel (hereafter MR) T-3123, Record Group 23, Department of Marine and Fisheries, Library and Archives Canada, Ottawa (hereafter RG 23, LAC).

4 As quoted in Washington State, Department of Fish and Game, *Thirteenth Annual Report of the State Fish Commissioner* (1902), 6.

5 Ibid, 20. Kershaw requested enough funds from the legislature to run these boats for the following season.

6 "Washington State Fisheries Report, 1913," enclosed in M. E. Hay to Richard McBride, December 26, 1912, file 912 1913, box 93, GR-0435, B.C. Department of Fisheries, B.C. Archives, Victoria (hereafter GR-0435, BCA).

7 Walter Scott, "Early Fishing Days/Working the Fish Traps and Remembrances," oral history interview by Michael A. Runestrand (April 15, 1975), tape 1 side 2, p. 4, transcribed tape recording, Washington State Oral/Aural History Program, Washington State Archives, Olympia (microfiche copy in Wilson Library, Western Washington University, Bellingham, WA).

8 L. H. Darwin to J. P. Babcock, August 13, 1913, file 912 1913, box 93, GR-0435, BCA (quotation); and Washington State, Department of Fish and Game, *Twenty-Fourth and Twenty-Fifth Annual Report of the State Fish Commissioner* (1915–17), 15–16.

9 Kornel Chang has found that the U.S. and Canadian Immigration Bureaus were

extremely concerned about restricting Asian immigration and they added personnel after the race riots of 1907. See Chang, "Enforcing Transnational White Solidarity," 675, 680, 683–85, 690. Chang also notes that before 1907, Japanese migrants in
particular passed easily across the international border. The U.S. Customs records
and fishery documents from both sides of the border suggest that fishery patrols
tried to regulate Asian fishery workers and restrict their mobility when it came to
controlling the destination of the salmon catch even before 1907. Both countries
wanted to repel Asians and keep salmon.

10   F. D. Huestis to Secretary of the Treasury, November 23, 1897, pp. 273–74, vol. 2, box
     42, RG 36 NAS; emphasis in original.

11   F. D. Huestis to Secretary of the Treasury, September 23, 1897, pp. 79–81, box 42;
     Thomas Stratton to A. W. Bash, July 8, 1883, file 4, box 165; and O. L. Spaulding to
     Collector of Customs, December 18, 1899, file 2, box 24, all in RG 36, NAS.

12   "Ordered to Anacortes," *Anacortes American*, October 3, 1901; C. S. Hamlin to J. C.
     Saunders, September 2, 1896, file 2, box 20; F. D. Huestis to Secretary of the Trea-
     sury, January 29, 1898, p. 476, vol. 2, box 42; and F. D. Huestis to Secretary of the
     Treasury, April 19, 1898, p. 191, vol. 3, box 42, all in RG 36, NAS. See also O. H. Cul-
     ver to F. C. Harper, October 17, 1912; F. M. Dunwoody to F. C. Harper, November 14,
     1912, both in file 621 General, 1902–1922, box 1401, 621 Enforcement of Navigation
     Laws, RG 26 United States Coast Guard, Revenue Cutter Service, National Archives
     and Records Administration, Washington, D.C. (hereafter RG 26, NADC); and F.
     M. Dunwoody to Commanding Officer, Coast Guard Cutter Arcata, October 11,
     1915, file 621 Arcata, box 1401, RG 26, NADC. The U.S. Customs Service also had the
     steamer *Grant* by 1904, but it disappears from the record by the 1910s. See statement
     of Lieut. H. G. Hamlet, August 15, 1904, file 281, box 480, Special Agents Reports
     and Correspondence, Record Group 36, National Archives and Records Adminis-
     tration, Washington, D.C. (hereafter RG 36, NADC).

13   L. D. Stenger to J. C. Saunders, August 4, 1896, file 5, box 63, RG 36, NAS.

14   R. K. Brown to Collector Saunders, July 2–? (date illegible), 1895, file 3, box 103; and
     L. H. Coon to F. D. Huestis, November 27, 1900, file 2, box 66, both in RG 36, NAS.

15   George Webber to J. C. Saunders, July 10, 1896, file 2, box 104, RG 36, NAS.

16   "Salmon Men Fear Work of Fish Pirates," *Bellingham Reveille*, April 29, 1911, file
     12.3, box 107, Pacific American Fisheries Collection, Center for Pacific Northwest
     Studies, Western Washington University, Bellingham, WA (hereafter PAFC).

17   George Ellsperman to F. D. Huestis, June 4, 1898, file 2, box 64, RG 36, NAS; O. L.
     Spaulding to Collector, September 25, 1899, file 4, box 24, RG 36, NAS; De Lorme,
     "The United States Bureau of Customs and Smuggling on Puget Sound," 80; and F.
     D. Huestis to George Webber, June 14, 1899, 119, box 124, RG 36, NAS. Webber was
     accused of excessive absences from his office and of engaging in smuggling between
     Puget Sound and Victoria, B.C., but his guilt remains unclear. See John H. Boyce to
     C. Bradshaw, March 7, 1909, file 3, box 96, RG 36, NAS. Collector J. C. Saunders was
     suspected of allowing Chinese immigrants into the United States illegally; see J. C.
     Saunders to Secretary of the Treasury, August 31, 1897, pp. 10–14, vol. 2, box 42, RG
     36, NAS. For an additional example, see A. J. Hinckley to Secretary of the Treasury,

November 12, 1893, file 1, box 29, RG 36, NAS. The secretary of the treasury actually warned the collector of customs to be more careful about who he hired in the early 1890s to avoid scandals; see D. G. Carlisle to Collector, June 23, 1893, file 2, box 18, RG 36, NAS.

18 George Ellsperman to J. C. Saunders, June 17, 1895, file 2, box 63, RG 36, NAS. See also O. L. Spaulding to Collector, November 7, 1899, file 3, box 24; and L. D. Stenger to F. D. Huestis, September 10, 1897, file 3, box 69, both in RG 36, NAS.

19 A. L. Blake to W. M. Harned, April 22, 1884, file 1, box 110; U.S. Attorney William Brinker to J. C. Saunders, August 13, 1893, file 1, box 101; and F. D. Huestis to Secretary of the Treasury, August 4, 1899, pp. 377–79, vol. 2, box 43, all in RG 36, NAS.

20 Washington State, *Report and Opinions of the Attorney General of the State of Washington* (1903), 61–62, 84–85, 212–13.

21 F. D. Huestis to Lyman J. Gage, Secretary of the Treasury, January 7, 1898, pp. 417–18, vol. 2, box 42, RG 36, NAS.

22 Deputy Minister of Marine and Fisheries (hereafter DMMF) to N. Clarke Wallace, January 4, 1894, file 107, part 1, box 111, MR T-2724; and R. N. Venning to Assistant Commissioner of Customs, October 10, 1908, file 6, part 4, box 79, MR T-2664, both in RG 23, LAC.

23 Chang "Enforcing Transnational White Solidarity," 671–97.

24 Canada, Department of Marine and Fisheries, *Annual Report of the Department of Marine and Fisheries, 1889*, 255; Ralston, "1900 Strike of Fraser River Sockeye Salmon Fishermen," 42–43; Canada, Department of Marine and Fisheries, *Annual Report of the Department of Marine and Fisheries, 1894*, cxi–cxii, cxxvii–cxxviii.

25 Canada, Department of Marine and Fisheries, *Annual Report of the Department of Marine and Fisheries, 1893*, 370.

26 James Gaudin to William Smith, May 14, 1894, file 785, part 1, vol. 185, MR T-2852, RG 23, LAC.

27 William Galbraith to DMMF, September 1894, file 1815, part 1, vol. 266, MR-T-3189, RG 23, LAC; Canada, Department of Marine and Fisheries, *Annual Report of the Department of Marine and Fisheries, 1900*, 158; W. D. Burdis to A. Johnston, July 8, 1910, file 6, part 5-A, vol. 80, MR T-2664, RG 23, LAC; and "Patrol Launches Fisheries," *Vancouver Province*, April 18, 1908, International Pacific Salmon Fisheries Commission Collection, University of British Columbia Special Collections, Vancouver (hereafter IPSFC). Note that this collection contains a series of newspaper article clippings; most articles are identified by newspaper and date, but occasionally an article is left unidentified.

28 See, for example, Canada, Department of Marine and Fisheries, *Annual Report of the Fisheries Branch, Department of Marine and Fisheries, 1915-16*, 353–58, 360–61.

29 W. D. Burdis to W. J. Bowser, July 29, 1912, file 1912 4, box 183, GR-0435, BCA; W. D. Burdis to F. S. Hussey, July 30, 1909, file 4, box 40, GR-0055, B.C. Provincial Police Force, Superintendent Correspondence Inward, 1891-1910, B.C. Archives, Victoria (hereafter GR-0055, BCA); Colin Campbell to F. S. Hussey, June 16, 1905, and Colin Campbell to F. S. Hussey, August 8, 1905, both in file 1, box 43, GR-0055, BCA.

30 Attorney General to F. S. Hussey, July 9, 1903, file 3, box 2, GR-0063, Superin-

tendent of Provincial Police, Correspondence Inward from Attorney General, 1898–1912, B.C. Archives, Victoria (hereafter GR-0063, BCA); and Memorandum, Colin Campbell to F. S. Hussey, July 11, 1905, file 1, box 43, GR-0055, BCA. Note that the Provincial Fish Commission established in 1901 also hired fishery overseers starting in 1907, but there is little indication they worked with federal agents in border waters.

31   W. T. Collenson to F. S. Hussey, August 3, 1908, file 4, box 47, GR-0055, BCA.

32   Name illegible (Ottawa office) to James Gaudin, August 17, 1895, file 1075, part 1, vol. 207, MR T-3122; and Acting Deputy Minister to James Gaudin, May 23, 1900, file 1075, part 1, vol. 207, MR T-3123, both in RG 23, LAC.

33   Griffith, "Border Crossings"; and "Smuggling Conspiracy," *Victoria Daily Colonist*, July 23, 1895. For additional complaints, see N. Coccolo to L. P. Brodeur, December 18, 1906; John Williams to R. N. Venning, January 19, 1907; and Memorandum, William Found, September 8, 1910, all in file 23 part 1, vol. 85, MR T-2669; H. C. Brewster to William Templeman, December 29, 1910, file 3264, vol. 372, MR T-4063; James Courbould to John Costigan, January 29, 1896, file 785, box 185, MR T-2952; and C. F. Green to Minister of Marine and Fisheries, November 15, 1894, file 1968, vol. 272, MR T-3195, all in RG 23, LAC.

34   W. M. Galbraith to Charles Tupper, March 30, 1895, file 785, part 1, vol. 185 (quotation); and John J. McGee(?), Clerk of the Privy Council, to the Minister of Marine and Fisheries, April 5, 1891, both in file 785, part 1, vol. 185, RG 23, LAC. For additional examples of such accusations, see John Williams to R. N. Venning, August 25, 1909; John Williams to R. N. Venning, September 22, 1909; and John Williams to R. N. Venning, May 27, 1910, all in file 3053, part 1, box 351, MR T-4034, RG 23, LAC.

35   DMMF to James Gaudin, May 2, 1894; and James Gaudin to William Smith, May 14, 1894, both in file 185, part 1, vol. 185, MR T-2952, RG 23, LAC.

36   James Gaudin to William Smith, December 15, 1893; and William Smith to James Gaudin, January 5, 1894, both in file 222, vol. 131, MR T-2819, RG 23, LAC.

37   A. Johnston to G. J. Desbarats, June 17, 1913, file 4468, vol. 407, MR T-3395, RG 23, LAC.

38   See, for example, William Reilly to A. Wasson, January 13, 1893, file 3, box 68; C. Ward to Collector of Customs, December 19, 1888, file 3, box 171; Frank Zent to F. D. Huestis, July 15, 1898, file 5, box 105, all in RG 36, NAS. Paying locals for information began in the 1880s. See A. L. Blake to A. W. Bash, December 8, 1883, file 5, box 109, RG 36, NAS. On locals refusing to cooperate, see F. C. Swayzee to Beecher, October 15, 1885, file 14, box 168, RG 36, NAS.

39   L. H. Darwin to J. P. Babcock, August 13, 1913, file 912 1913, box 93, GR-0435, BCA.

40   George Ellsperman to J. C. Saunders, March 31, 1895, file 2, box 63, RG 36, NAS.

41   Charles McLennan to A. Wasson, August 7, 1892 (first quotation), and Charles McLennan to A. Wasson, August 4, 1892 (second quotation) both in file 1, box 62, RG 36, NAS.

42   W. M. Galbraith to Charles Tupper, March 30, 1895, file 785, part 1, vol. 185, RG 23, LAC.

43   James Izett to A. W. Bash, January 7, 1882, file Misc. Jan.–Feb. 1882, box 164, RG 36,

NAS (quotation); and Peter Cain to C. M. Bradshaw, June 9 1890, file 2, box 97, RG 36, NAS.

44   F. D. Huestis to Secretary of the Treasury, September 23, 1897, pp. 79–81, vol. 2, box 42, RG 36, NAS.

45   "Prince Wants More Boats," *Vancouver World*, August 2, 1906, box 53, IPSFC.

46   "Preliminary Examination of Clallam Bay, WA," Letter from the Secretary of War, 53rd Congress, 3d. Session, House of Representatives, Ex. Doc. No. 226, January 19, 1895, 5, file 2, box 55, RG 36, NAS.

47   George Webber to J. C. Saunders, July 23, 1897 (quotation; emphasis in original); see also George Webber to Collector, September 4, 1897, both in file 3, box 63, RG 36, NAS.

48   L. D. Stenger to J. C. Saunders, August 4, 1896, file 5, box 63, RG 36, NAS.

49   W. R. Stockbridge to J. C. Saunders, June 6, 1897, file 5, box 65; and J. C. Baird to Deputy Collector of Customs, July 27, 1891, file 2, box 99, both in RG 36, NAS.

50   William Galbraith to DMMF, September 1894, file 1815, part 1, vol. 266, MR-T-3189, RG 23 LAC.

51   Commissioner of Fisheries to Mr. Dolan, March 28, 1901, file 785, part 1, vol. 185, MR T-2452, RG 23, LAC.

52   F. H. Cunningham to William Found, July 18, 1913 (quotation); G. J. Desbarats to Joseph Martin, August 11, 1914; Victor Harrison to Minister of Marine and Fisheries, August 18, 1914, all in file 3672, vol. 392, MR T-3382, RG 23, LAC. For other examples, see John McNab to DMMF, August 15, 1895; Memorandum for the Minister, J. S. Webster, August 23, 1895; DMMF to John McNab, September 26, 1895; L. C. York and Co. to Premier of Canada Tupper, May 23, 1896; Charles Wilson to E. L. Newcombe, March 25, 1895; Memorandum for Minister, E. E. Prince, April 6, 1895; Acting DMMF to E. L. Newcombe, April 8, 1895, all in file 1469, part 1, box 239, MR T-3159, RG 23, LAC.

53   William Galbraith to DMMF, September 1894, file 1815, part 1, vol. 266, MR-T-3189, RG 23 LAC.

54   Samuel North to W. J. Bowser, August 16, 1908, file 2, box 4, GR-0063, BCA. Note that John Kendall was also a member of this sneering crowd.

55   William Galbraith to DMMF, September 1894, file 1815, part 1, vol. 266, MR-T-3189, RG 23 LAC.

56   A. G. Collier to F. D. Huestis, July 20, 1899; Meriden Hill to F. D. Huestis, July 18, 1899; and A. G. Collier to F. D. Huestis, July 16, 1899, all in file 5, box 64, RG 36, NAS.

57   F. D. Huestis to Secretary of Treasury, August 4, 1899, pp. 377–79; F. D. Huestis to Secretary of Treasury, August 14, 1899, p. 410, both in vol. 2, box 43, RG 36, NAS. See also F. A. Vanderlip to F. D. Huestis, August 22, 1899, file 5, box 24; F. D. Huestis to Secretary of Treasury, September 8, 1899, p. 479, vol. 2, box 43; and A. E. Smith to Thomas Cridler, September 19, 1899, file 2, box 30, all in RG 36, NAS.

58   A. G. Collier to F. D. Huestis, August 8, 1899; and A. G. Collier to F. D. Huestis, July 27, 1899, both in file 5, box 64, RG 36, NAS.

59   "Ottawa Sustains Seizure," *Vancouver Province*, December 22, 1904; "Seized

Steamer Sold," *Vancouver Province*, February 2, 1905; and "Yankee Poacher Captured," unidentified newspaper, c. July 12, 1905, all in box 53, IPSFC.

60   "Pirating Sloop Is Seized," *Vancouver Province*, August 28, 1911, box 54, IPSFC.

61   W. I. Crawford, Puget Sound Canners' Association, to Senator Wesley Jones, August 3, 1912, file 4119, vol. 401, MR T-3390, RG 23, LAC. It is not clear why this particular seizure prompted such a response from the Washington interests.

62   Secretary, New Seattle Chamber of Commerce to Capt. B. P. Bertholf, June 5, 1912, file 4119, vol. 401, MR T-3390, RG 23, LAC.

63   "Fraser River Fishing Boats Are Seized," *Vancouver Province*, August 1, 1912, box 54, IPSFC (quotation). See also "Seized Fishing Boat Released," *Vancouver Province*, August 2, 1912, box 54, IPSFC.

64   W. D. Burdis to D. N. McIntyre, August 13, 1912, file 1912 4, box 183, GR-0435, BCA; and "Still Hold Fishing Boats," *Vancouver Province*, August 29, 1912, box 54, IPSFC. The boats were finally released in October. "Four B.C. Fishing Schooners Released," *Vancouver Province*, October 1, 1912, box 54, IPSFC.

65   A. Johnston, DMMF, to Under Secretary of State, September 26, 1912, file 4119, vol. 401, MR T-3390, RG 23, LAC.

66   Memorandum, William Found, February 16, 1914; and G. J. Desbarats to Macneill Bird, MacDonald and Darling Barristers, August 17, 1914, both in file 4119, vol. 401, MR T-3390, RG 23, LAC.

67   See also "Threaten Trouble Because Launch Is Seized by Canada: American Boat Held under Charge of Violating Fish Laws," unidentified newspaper, July 18, 1912, file/case no. 52795, box 778, RG 36, NADC.

68   United States, *Annual Report of the Commissioner General of Immigration, 1911*, 159; and Chang "Enforcing Transnational White Solidarity," 689.

69   Log of the Homespun, enclosed in Frank S. DeGrey to Bowser, August 26, 1909, file 718 1909, box 76, GR-0435, BCA.

70   S. North to McIntyre, September 22, 1911, file 723 1911, box 76, GR-0435, BCA.

71   P. K. Ahern to Bowser, May 31, 1912, file 1912 #4, box 183, GR-0435, BCA.

72   On transborder cooperation, see July 18, 1904 entry, p. 157; and July 28, 1905 entry, p. 246, both in vol. 1, GR-0397, B.C. Provincial Police Force, Vancouver-Westminster Police Records, 1899–1949, B.C. Archives, Victoria. See also August 6, 1904 entry, p. 38; August 7, 1904 entry, p. 39; August 5, 1904 entry, p. 37; July 27, 1905 entry, p. 66, all in GR-0399, B.C. Provincial Police, Steveston, B.C. Archives, Victoria; and L. Stenger to J. C. Saunders, December 1, 1894, file 1, box 103, and A. G. Collier to F. D. Huestis, July 27, 1899, file 5, box 64, both in RG 36, NAS. B.C. canners urged even more transborder policing cooperation; see July 20, 1903 entry, Minutes of Meetings, Fraser River Canners' Association, box 52, IPSFC.

73   "Telephone Outwits Japs," *Vancouver World*, April 15, 1908, box 53, IPSFC.

74   Charles Snyder to F. D. Huestis, April 3, 1902, file 3, box 108 (quotation); Frank Fisher to F. D. Huestis, April 19, 1902, file 3, box 108; Thomas Berry to J. C. Saunders, April 14(?), 1894, file 1, box 102; and J. R. Miller to J. C. Saunders, March 30, 1894, file 1, box 102, all in RG 36, NAS.

75   Very few Puget Sound records for the post-1900 period have survived. See, for

instance, miscellaneous statements of U.S. Customs officers, August 1904; C. W. Ide to Secretary of the Treasury, February 3, 1906, both in file 281, box 480, Special Agents Reports and Correspondence, RG 36, NADC; William(?) Ross to F. A. Lewis, Commanding USRCS, June 30, 1910, *Snohomish*, October 11, 1909–September 30, 1910, box 30, Correspondence of Cutters' Officers and Stations, RG 26, NADC; O. H. Culver to F. C. Harper, October 17, 1912, file 621, box 1401, General Correspondence, RG 26, NADC; and Washington State, Department of Fish and Game, *First Annual Report of the State Fish Commissioner* (1890), 18–21. Also, because most records did not indicate where the arrests took place, it is nearly impossible to isolate border offenses.

76 The statistics on arrests in Washington begin in 1913 but were not published until 1916. See Washington State, Department of Fish and Game, *Twenty-Fourth and Twenty-Fifth Annual Report of the State Fish Commissioner* (1913–15), 93–95, 168–71.

77 For early Canadian arrest record, see "Numbers of people convicted under the Fisheries Act," n.d. (c. October 1894), file 100, vol. 111, MR T-2724, RG 23, LAC; Canada, Department of Marine and Fisheries, *Annual Report of the Department of Marine and Fisheries, 1895*, 193. For B.C. arrest record as compared to other provinces, see Canada, Department of Marine and Fisheries, *Annual Report of the Department of Marine and Fisheries, 1908–09*, 363–64; Canada, Department of Marine and Fisheries, *Annual Report of the Department of Marine and Fisheries, 1909–10*, 367; and Canada, Department of Marine and Fisheries, *Annual Report of the Department of Marine and Fisheries, 1910–11*, 329.

78 See, for example, Assistant Secretary, Treasury Department to J. C. Saunders, September 30, 1893, file 2, box 18; J. C. Saunders to Secretary of the Treasury, September 20, 1893, pp. 264–65, vol. 3, box 40, both in RG 36, NAS. See also John McNab to DMMF, September 5, 1894; John McNab to E. E. Prince, January 18, 1896, both in file 1469, part 1, vol. 239, MR T-3159, RG 23, LAC.

79 Assistant Secretary of the Treasury to J. C. Saunders, September 29, 1893, file 2, box 18, RG 36, NAS.

80 O. L. Spaulding to Andrew Wasson, October 10, 1892, file 7, box 17, RG 36, NAS.

81 O. L. Spaulding to F. D. Huestis, September 3, 1898, file 2, box 22 (quotation); and F. D. Huestis to Secretary of Treasury, August 27, 1898, p. 45, vol. 1, box 43, both in RG 36, NAS.

82 There was talk of an effort to mark the international line with buoys in 1909, but it is not clear what happened with this project. See "Boundary Being Fixed: The Line along the Fuca Strait Being Marked," [New Westminster?] *News-Advertiser*, June 29, 1909, box 54, IPSFC. See also statement of John Roan, June 11, 1896; John McNab to E. E. Prince, June 12, 1896; and John McNab, June 22, 1896, all in file 1469, part 1, vol. 239, MR T-3159, RG 23, LAC.

83 See photo in the *Pacific Fisherman* 3:8 (August 1905): 9; and George Webber to J. C. Saunders, August 31, 1896, file 5, box 63, RG 36, NAS.

84 For later complaints in B.C., see W. D. Burdis to F. S. Hussey, July 30, 1909, file 4, box 40, GR-0055, BCA. On B.C. patrols being unable to prevent border sales, see William Found to C. B. Sword, July 16, 1910, file 6, part 5-A, vol. 80, MR T-2664, RG

23, LAC. For continued reports about poaching on the U.S. side, see, for example, F. M. Dunwoody to Captain Commandant, Coast Guard, July 23, 1915, file 621 Northwest Division, box 1406, General Correspondence, RG 26, NADC.

85 E. P. Bertholf to Commanding Officer, Northwest Division, December 9, 1911, file 621 Northwest Division, box 1406; F. M. Dunwoody to Commanding Officer, Coast Guard Cutter *Arcata*, October 11, 1915, file 621 Arcata, box 1401, both in RG 26, NADC.

86 Elmer Vogt, oral history interview by Barbara Heacock (January 30, 1978), p. 34, transcribed tape recording, Skagit County Oral History Collection, Center for Pacific Northwest Studies, Western Washington University (hereafter SCOHC).

87 Scott interview, tape 1, side 2, p. 2, Washington State Oral/Aural History Program, Washington State Archives, Olympia.

88 W. H. Bessner, oral history interview by Barbara Heacock (October 4, 1977), pp. 5, 22–23 (quotation on p. 23), transcribed tape recording, SCOHC. See also Lee Bauter, oral history interview by Galen Biery (December 6, 1988), tape 22, side 1, box 17, Galen Biery Collection, Center for Pacific Northwest Studies, Western Washington University, Bellingham, WA.

89 Dorsey, *Dawn of Conservation Diplomacy*, 19–104. A successful halibut conservation treaty that the United States and Canada passed in 1923 was also an important precedent for the Sockeye Salmon Treaty that was finally passed in 1937. See Thistle, "'As Free of Fish As a Billiard Ball Is of Hair.'"

90 Dorsey, *Dawn of Conservation Diplomacy*, 22–23, 40–41; Canada, Department of Marine and Fisheries, *Annual Report of the Department of Marine and Fisheries, 1892*, 81–86. On the 1896 report and lack of action, see Carrothers, *British Columbia Fisheries*, 65–66; Dorsey, *Dawn of Conservation Diplomacy*, 40–46, 52–55. On the Joint High Commission, see "Protocol of the Conference at Washington in May, 1898, preliminary to the appointment of a Joint Commission for the adjustment of questions at issue between the United States and Great Britain in respect to the relations of the former with the Dominion of Canada," file 2772, part 1, vol. 326, MR T-4011, RG 23, LAC. For excerpts of the 1896 report, see Washington State, Department of Fish and Game, *Fourteenth and Fifteenth Annual Report of the State Fish Commissioner* (1903–04), 29–30.

91 Quoted in Washington State, Department of Fish and Game, *Fourteenth and Fifteenth Annual Report of the State Fish Commissioner* (1903–04), 15–16.

92 See, for instance, "Jail for Men Who Break Fish Laws," *Vancouver World*, October 8, 1906, box 53, IPSFC; and W. W. Stumbles to L. Davies, July 12, 1899, file 6, part 2, vol. 79, MR T-2663, RG 23, LAC.

93 Washington State, Department of Fish and Game, *Sixteenth and Seventeenth Annual Reports of the State Fish Commissioner* (1905–06), 46–48; unsigned (likely E. B. Deming) to T. J. Gorman, September 16, 1906, file Gorman & Co. 1905-06, box 11, PAFC.

94 "Minority Interim Report," John C. Brown to L. P. Brodeur, October 2, 1906, 13 (quotation); and "Interim Report of the B.C. Fishery Commission," E. E. Prince to L. P. Brodeur, October 2, 1906, both in file 2918, vol. 336, MR T-4022, RG 23, LAC.

95 There are numerous documents regarding the negotiations for a closed season in
    1906 and 1908. For example, see A. E. Woolard to W. D. Burdis, January 18, 1905,
    file 6, part 3, vol. 79, MR T-2663, RG 23, LAC; September 18, 1907 entry, p. 157,
    Minutes of Meetings, Fraser River Canners' Association, box 52, IPSFC. There
    was also some talk of closing in the 1910 and 1912 seasons. See November 6, 1908
    entry, p. 186, Minutes of Meetings, Fraser River Canners' Association, box 52,
    IPSFC.

96 "Fishermen Protest Any Closed Season," unknown newspaper, c. February 13, 1905,
    box 53, IPSFC. The owner of J. H. Todd & Sons may have backed American oppo-
    nents of the measure as he deemed it a threat to his newly installed fish traps near
    Victoria. See D. Bell-Irving to R. Prefontaine, March 6, 1905, file 6, part 3, vol. 79,
    MR T-2663, RG 23, LAC.

97 On the Canadian department supporting the bill, see R. Prefontaine to W. Temple-
    man, et al., February 9, 1905; and Memorandum, "Points in Favor of Closing Down
    Salmon Fishing Operations in 1906 and 1908," E. E. Prince, n.d. (c. January 1905),
    file 6, part 3, vol. 79, MR T-2663, RG 23, LAC.

98 On white and Indian fishermen's complaints, see Chief Johnny, Coquitlam, and
    Chief Charley to R. Prefontaine, February 4, 1905; Mayor W. H. Keary to R.
    Prefontaine, January 30, 1905; and H. J. Butterfield, B.C. Fishermen's Union to R.
    Prefontaine, January 7, 1905, all in file 6, part 3, vol. 79, MR T-2663, RG 23, LAC. On
    fishermen's union objections, see J. P. Babcock to William Templeman, March 21,
    1905, file 6, part 3, vol. 79, MR T-2663, RG 23, LAC.

99 Dorsey, *Dawn of Conservation Diplomacy*, 55–75; and "Notes on fishery conditions
    in Contiguous international waters, with a draft of suggested Uniform Fishery
    regulations in the Canadian and U.S. Boundary," April 11, 1908, file 3728, vol. 394,
    MR T-3385, RG 23, LAC.

100 Dorsey, *Dawn of Conservation Diplomacy*, 81–97.

101 Ibid., 96–99. Although this treaty did not pass in the United States, as Dorsey notes,
    it did set important precedents for several conservation treaties that followed.

102 *Pacific Fisherman* 8:3 (March 1910): 16; Hazen to Bowser, April 18, 1912, and Bowser
    to Hazen, April 30, 1912, both in file 1912 #3, box 183, GR-0435, BCA; and United
    States, *Annual Report of the United States Commissioner of Fisheries for the Fiscal
    Year 1914*, 80.

103 Washington State, Department of Fish and Game, *Eighteenth and Nineteenth
    Annual Reports of State Fish Commissioner* (1907–08), 26 (quotation). On the failure
    of the bill, see United States, *Annual Report of the United States Commissioner of
    Fisheries for the Fiscal Year 1915*, 78. For a more thorough treatment of the role of
    Washington State in these negotiations, see Lissa Wadewitz, "The Scales of Salmon:
    Diplomacy and Conservation in the Western Canada-U.S. Borderlands," in John-
    son and Graybill, *Bridging National Borders in North America*, 141–64.

104 "Report on Fishing Industries, Majority Report," 1911, copy in Reports—Congres-
    sional Reports, box 18, Accession 1595-6, John N. Cobb Papers, University of Wash-
    ington Special Collections, Seattle.

105 Julian Pauncefort to Earl of Kimberly, July 19, 1894; and Julian Pauncefort to Earl of

Aberdeen, August 17, 1894, both in file 222, vol. 131, MR T-2819, RG 23, LAC.

106 Unknown to James Gaudin, September 18, 1894, file 222, vol. 131, MR T-2819, RG 23, LAC (quotation). For complaints from B.C. interests, see, for example, J. G. Maclure to Minister of Marine and Fisheries, August 2, 1894; and H. Bell-Irving to G. E. Corbould, April 10, 1894, all in file 222, vol. 131, MR T-2819, RG 23, LAC. A desire to enable B.C. canners to remain competitive with American canners also influenced the passage of import duties on fish. See, for example, unsigned to G. E. Corbould, June 20, 1895, file 2265, vol. 293, MR T-3218, RG 23, LAC.

107 H. Bell-Irving to L. H. Davies, March 20, 1897; E. E. Prince to John McNab, March 26, 1897; H. Bell-Irving to Aulay Morrison, April 5, 1900; L. H. Davies to Aulay Morrison, M.P., April 14, 1900; and L. H. Davies to Aulay Morrison, M.P., May 8, 1900, all in file 222, vol. 131, MR T-2819, RG 23, LAC.

108 H. Bell-Irving to C. B. Sword, July 10, 1900; C. B. Sword to E. E. Prince, July 12, 1900; and C.B. Sword to E.E. Prince, July 25, 1900, all in file 222, vol. 131, MR T-2819, RG 23, LAC.

109 E. E. Prince to C. B. Sword, July 20, 1900, file 222, vol. 131, MR T-2819, RG 23, LAC.

110 Unknown to E. E. Prince, August 19, 1901, in file 222, vol. 131, MR T-2819, RG 23, LAC; and "Fishery Commission British Columbia 1902," file 2918, vol. 335, MR T-4020 to T-4022, RG 23, LAC.

111 DMMF to misc. trap applicants, June 13, 1902; B.C. Fishermen's Union to Dr. Borden(?), October 10, 1901; F. Gourdeau to Charles Durham, B.C. Fishermen's Union, October 10, 1901; and B.C. Fishermen's Union to F. Gordeau, October 16, 1901, all in file 222, vol. 131, MR T-2918, RG 23, LAC.

112 R. Prefontaine to W. Templeman, February 2, 1904; Memorandum of E. E. Prince, February 3, 1904, both in file 6, part 2, vol. 79, MR T-2663, RG 23, LAC; Templeman to Prefontaine, April 4, 1904, file 6, part 3, vol. 79, MR T-2663, RG 23, LAC; Memorandum of William Found, April 13, 1909, file 6, part 5, vol. 80, MR T-2664, RG 23, LAC; "Conference on British Columbia Fishery Matters," June 26, 1903, file 6, part 2, vol. 79, MR T-2663, RG 23, LAC; and Governor General in Council Order, May 2, 1904, file 6, part 3, vol. 79, MR T-2663, RG 23, LAC. Federal officials did limit traps to the west coast of Vancouver Island. See "Fisheries Report for Last Season," *Victoria Times*, n.d. (c. 1903), copy in scrapbook, accession 860–1, John Pease Babcock Papers, University of Washington Special Collections, Seattle. B.C. canners apparently continued to push for more traps. See A. E. White to Prefontaine, March 18, 1904; and Howard J. Duncan to Prefontaine, February 27, 1904, file 6, part 3, vol. 79, MR T-2663, RG 23, LAC.

113 The "cohoes" referred to spawned in rivers on the U.S. side of the border. Memorandum of E. E. Prince, n.d. (c. August 1907) (quotation; emphasis in original), file 6, part 4, vol. 79, MR T-2663, RG 23, LAC.

114 E. E. Prince to DMMF, August 16, 1906; Memorandum of E. E. Prince, August 30, 1906; and Governor General in Council Order, September 4, 1906, all in file 6, part 4, vol. 79, MR T-2663, RG 23, LAC.

115 "Minutes taken at a conference between B.C. canners and E. E. Prince for International Commission," April 8, 1909, file 6, part 5, vol. 80, MR T-2664, RG 23, LAC.

116 F. H. Cunningham to D. N. McIntyre, August 7, 1912, file 343 1912, vol. 39, GR-0435, BCA.

117 Deputy Commissioner to F. H. Cunningham, August 10, 1912, file 343 1912, vol. 39, GR-0435, BCA.

118 W. J. Bowser to L. H. Darwin, August 25, 1913, file 912 1913, box 93, GR-0435, BCA.

119 W. J. Bowser to L. H. Darwin, August, 25, 1913, file 912 1913, box 93, GR-0435, BCA.

120 "Point Roberts Canal Scheme," *Vancouver Province*, September 3, 1903, box 53, IPSFC; and Thomas Connor to Minister of Fisheries, May 27, 1932, file B.C. Commercial Fisheries Branch, 1931–32, box 1, GR-1378, B.C. Provincial Fisheries Department, B.C. Archives, Victoria.

121 "Point Roberts Is Gage of Peace," *News-Advertiser*, November 12, 1913, box 55, IPSFC; and "Why Not Buy Point Roberts? Asks Maiden," *Vancouver Sun*, September 25, 1925, enclosed in Spence, Report of Conditions on the Fraser, September 1925, vol. L-8, box 7, Washington Department of Fish and Game, Washington State Archives, Olympia (hereafter WDF, WSA).

122 H. Hegelson to George Riley, February 26, 1902, file 6, part 2, vol. 79, MR T-2663, RG 23, LAC.

123 W. D. Burdis to L. P. Brodeur, September 14, 1909, file 6, part 5, vol. 80, MR T-2664, RG 23, LAC.

124 Evenden, *Fish versus Power*, 27–36, 48–51, 84–117.

125 Allard, *Spencer Fullerton Baird and the U.S. Fish Commission*, 71.

126 This theory about fishery management came to be known as the maximum-sustained yield theory (MSY) by the 1930s. See Smith, *Scaling Fisheries*, especially 237–66; McEvoy, *Fisherman's Problem*, 6–7; and Rathbun, "Review of the Fisheries in the Contiguous Waters of the State of Washington and British Columbia," 333–34, 336.

127 Taylor, *Making Salmon*.

128 Canada, Department of Marine and Fisheries, *Annual Report of the Department of Marine and Fisheries, 1895*, 193. See also Taylor, *Making Salmon*, 217–19. Some B.C. processors built hatcheries of their own, sometimes as a condition of holding an exclusive fishing license. See Newell, *Development of the Pacific Salmon-Canning Industry*, 10.

129 September 9, 1903 entry, p. 280, Minutes of Meetings, Fraser River Canners' Association, box 52, IPSFC; Washington State, Department of Fish and Game, *Thirteenth Annual Report of the State Fish Commissioner* (1902), 8–9; and Washington State, Department of Fish and Game, *Fourteenth and Fifteenth Annual Report of the State Fish Commissioner* (1903–04), 18–32. These negotiations continued into the 1920s, when Washington State fisheries officials secretly paid Henry Doyle one thousand dollars to explore the possibility of building a new hatchery on the upper Fraser River. See State Fisheries Board to Doyle, June 11, 1921, vol. L-2, box 7, WDF WSA; and Wadewitz, "Scales of Salmon."

130 Washington State, Department of Fish and Game, *Fourteenth and Fifteenth Annual Report of the State Fish Commissioner* (1903–04), 18–32.

131 For the quotation, see Washington State, Department of Fish and Game,

Twenty-Sixth and Twenty-Seventh Annual Reports of the State Fish Commissioner (1915–17), 20.

132   On the Samish propagation scheme, see Washington State, Department of Fish and Game, *Twenty-Sixth and Twenty-Seventh Annual Reports of the State Fish Commissioner* (1915–17), 18–20. For 1925 admission, see Washington State, Department of Fish and Game, *Thirty-Fourth and Thirty-Fifth Annual Report of the State Supervisor of Fisheries* (1923–25), 4.

133   Klingle, *Emerald City*, 170–78; Roos, *Restoring Fraser River Salmon*, 14–17; and Thrush, *Native Seattle*, 94–97.

134   As quoted in Washington State, Department of Fish and Game, *Twenty-Eighth and Twenty-Ninth Annual Reports of the State Fish Commissioner* (1917–19), 3.

CONCLUSION

1   Both countries signed the convention in 1930, but the U.S. Congress did not approve it until 1937. See Lissa Wadewitz, "The Scales of Salmon: Diplomacy and Conservation in the Western Canada-U.S. Borderlands," in Johnson and Graybill, *Bridging National Borders in North America*, 141–64.

2   Joseph Taylor III, "The Historical Roots of the Canadian-American Salmon Wars," in Findlay and Coates, *Parallel Destinies*, 171.

3   United States, Department of Fish and Game, *Annual Report of the United States Commissioner of Fisheries* (1936), 83.

4   Roos, *Restoring Fraser River Salmon*, 132–35.

5   Quoted in ibid., 132.

6   "Canada's Ocean Act," Canadian Department of Justice, available online at http://laws.justice.gc.ca/en/O-2.4/. In the United States the Magnuson–Stevens Fishery Conservation and Management Act was originally passed by Congress in 1976 but was substantially revised with the passage of the Sustainable Fisheries Act of 1996. See "Sustainable Fisheries Act," National Oceanic and Atmospheric Administration, available online at http://www.nmfs.noaa.gov/sfa/.

7   Taylor, "Historical Roots of the Canadian-American Salmon Wars," 172.

8   North Pacific Anadromous Fish Commission, news release, Eighteenth Annual Meeting, November 2010, available online at http://www.npafc.org/new/publications/Annual%20Report/2010/appendix3/NewsRelease10.pdf. Note that the NPAFC was preceded by the International North Pacific Fisheries Commission (INPFC) of 1952. The INPFC was an agreement between Canada, Japan, and the United States that restricted Japanese fishermen from fishing west of the 175th meridian. The INPFC also initiated research on high seas salmon behavior. The NPAFC replaced this agreement in 1993 and is far more proactive in its attempts to regulate high seas fishing. See "International North Pacific Fisheries Commission (1952–1992)," online at http://www.npafc.org/new/ipnfc.html.

9   Taylor, "Historical Roots of the Canadian-American Salmon Wars," 155, 173–74; Williams, "Pacific Salmon Treaty"; and Roos, *Restoring Fraser River Salmon*, 146–60.

10   For a critique of the equity principle, see Williams, "Pacific Salmon Treaty," 174–82.

11   "Evaluation of Results of Enforcement Activities in 2007," in *NPAFC Annual Report 2008*, available online at http://www.npafc.org/new/publications/Annual%20 Report/2008/EECM/Evaluation.htm.

12   Although the Department of Ocean Fisheries instituted a moratorium on fish farming in B.C. in 1996, they lifted that ban in 2002, much to the dismay of Alaskan fishermen. See Arnold, *Fishermen's Frontier*, 181–89. For information on Washington State fish farms, see the Washington Fish Growers Association, online at http://www.wfga.net/index.php.

13   Volpe, Anholt, and Glickman, "Competition among Juvenile Atlantic Salmon (*Salmo Salar*) and Steelhead (*Oncorhynchus mykiss*)"; Naylor et al., "Fugitive Salmon"; and Volpe et al., "Evidence of Natural Reproduction of Aquaculture-Escaped Atlantic Salmon in Coastal British Columbia."

14   Krkosek, Lewis, and Volpe, "Transmission Dynamics of Parasitic Sea Lice from Farm to Wild Salmon"; and Krkosek et al., "Epizootics of Wild Fish Induced by Farm Fish."

15   Naylor, Eagle, and Smith, "Salmon Aquaculture in the Pacific Northwest," 27–32.

16   Naylor et al., "Effects of Aquaculture on World Fish Supplies," available online via the Environmental Protection Agency, http://www.epa.gov/owow/watershed/wacademy/acad2000/pdf/issue8.pdf.

17   See, for example, Pala, "Victory at Sea"; National Marine Protected Areas Center, online at http://www.mpa.gov/; and the Food and Agriculture Organization of the United Nations, "Marine Protected Areas," online at http://www.fao.org/fishery/mpas/en.

18   Arnold, *Fishermen's Frontier*, 156–81.

19   van Sittert, "Other Seven Tenths," 108.

Bibliography

MANUSCRIPT COLLECTIONS

ANACORTES HISTORY MUSEUM, ANACORTES, WA
Fidalgo Island Packing Company Records.

BRITISH COLUMBIA ARCHIVES, VICTORIA, B.C.
Anderson, Alexander. Papers, 1834–1884.
British Columbia. Department of Fisheries Records (GR-0435).
———. Provincial Fisheries Department Records (GR-1378).
———. Attorney General Records (GR-0419).
———. Provincial Game Warden Records (GR-0446).
———. Provincial Police Force, Correspondence, 1890–1911 (GR-1576).
———. Provincial Police Force, Correspondence Outward, 1864–1918 (GR-0061).
———. Provincial Police Force, Daily Reports, 1913–1921 (GR-0445).
———. Provincial Police Force, Superintendent Correspondence Inward, 1891–1910; 1912–1922 (GR-0055 and GR-0057).
———. Provincial Police Force, Steveston (GR-0399).
———. Provincial Police Force, Vancouver-Westminster Police Records, 1899–1949 (GR-0397).
———. Superintendent of Provincial Police, Correspondence Inward from Attorney General, 1898–1912 (GR-0063).
———. Supreme Court, 1894–1912 (GR-2663).
Canada. Commission on the Salmon Fishing Industry in B.C., 1902 (GR-0213).
MacKay, Joseph William Papers, 1865–1899 (MS-1917).
Simpson, George McTavish. "Fifty Years Ago in the Canning Industry" (MS-0865).
Union of British Columbia Chiefs, Vancouver, 1914–1915 (MS-1056).
Yale, James Murray. Correspondence Inward and Other Papers, 1845–1871 (MS-0105).
———. Fort Langley HBC Trader, 1851–1858 (MS-0537).

CENTER FOR PACIFIC NORTHWEST STUDIES,
WESTERN WASHINGTON UNIVERSITY, BELLINGHAM, WA
Alaska Packers' Association Records and Newspaper Clippings.
Galen Biery Collection.
Northwest Tribal Indians Oral History Collection.
Pacific American Fisheries Collection.
Peggy Aiston Collection.
Skagit County Oral History Collection.

CITY OF VANCOUVER ARCHIVES, VANCOUVER, B.C., CANADA
Anglo-British Packing Company Records.
Bell-Irving Family Fonds.

HUNTINGTON LIBRARY, SAN MARINO, CA
Fort Nisqually Records.

LIBRARY AND ARCHIVES CANADA, OTTAWA
Canada. Department of Indian Affairs Records. British Columbia Superintendency Cor-
    respondence (Select Files, Record Group 10).
———. Department of Justice Records (Select Files, Record Group 13).
———. Department of Marine and Fisheries Records, 1880–1920 (Record Group 23).
———. Immigration Department (Select Files, Record Group 76).
———. Marine Branch Records (Select Files, Record Group 42).
———. Secretary of State Records (Select Files, Record Group 6).

NATIONAL ARCHIVES AND RECORDS ADMINISTRATION, WASHINGTON, D.C.
United States. Coast Guard, Revenue Cutter Service. Correspondence, 1865-1937 (Record
    Group 26).
———. Customs Service. Puget Sound Collection District Correspondence, Enforcement
    of Navigation Laws, 1900–1920s (Record Group 36).

NATIONAL ARCHIVES AND RECORDS ADMINISTRATION, COLLEGE PARK, MD
United States. United States Fish and Wildlife Service. Records of the Joint Committee
    Relative to the Preservation of the Fisheries in Waters Contiguous to Canada and the
    U.S., 1893–95 (Record Group 22).

NATIONAL ARCHIVES AND RECORDS ADMINISTRATION–PACIFIC ALASKA
REGION, SEATTLE, WA
United States. Bureau of Indian Affairs. Records for the Puyallup Agency (Record Group
    75).
———. Bureau of Indian Affairs. Records for the Taholah Agency (Record Group 75).
———. Bureau of Indian Affairs. Records for the Tulalip Agency (Record Group 75).
———. Circuit Court Western District of Washington, Northern Division, Seattle. Civil
    and Criminal Case Files 1890-1911 (Record Group 21).

———. Customs Service. Puget Sound Collection District Correspondence, 1860s–1900 (Record Group 36).

Washington State. Indian Affairs. Records of the Washington Superintendency of Indian Affairs, 1853–1874. Microfilm Copies of Records in the National Archives. No. 5. The National Archives and Records Administration, Washington, 1945. Copy located in University of Washington Library, MA171, Microfilm Rolls 1–25.

ROYAL BRITISH MUSEUM, VICTORIA, B.C.

Duff, Wilson. Papers. Straits Field Notes, Summer 1950, file 27, STR-W-001, roll 2 (viewed copies in Dr. Keith Carlson's possession, University of Saskatchewan, Saskatoon, Canada).

STÒ:LŌ NATION ARCHIVES, CHILLIWACK, B.C.

Orchard, Imbert. Oral History Interviews.

Wells, Oliver N. Oral History Interviews, 1961–1968.

Stò:lō Nation. Oral History Interviews.

UNIVERSITY OF BRITISH COLUMBIA SPECIAL COLLECTIONS, VANCOUVER, B.C.

Anglo-British Packing Company Records, 1891–1968.

Barnett, Homer. Papers.

Bell-Irving, Henry Ogle. Papers, 1882–1930.

Doyle, Henry. Papers.

Hill-Tout, Charles. Papers.

International Pacific Salmon Fisheries Commission Collection.

Japanese Canadian Collection.

Ladner, Thomas Ellis. Fonds.

Lee Family. Papers.

Swan, James. Papers.

Vancouver and District Labor Council. Fonds.

UNIVERSITY OF WASHINGTON, MANUSCRIPTS AND SPECIAL COLLECTIONS, SEATTLE, WA

Babcock, John Pease. Papers, 1901–1936.

Central Labor Council, Pierce and King Counties.

Cobb, John N. Papers.

Freeman, Miller. Papers, 1875–1955.

International Longshoremen's and Warehousemen's Union, Fisheries and Allied Workers Division, Local #3.

International Woodworkers of America, Local 3-101, 1935–79.

Meany, Edmond. Papers.

Nichols, Ralph D. Papers.

WASHINGTON STATE ARCHIVES, OLYMPIA, WA

Washington State. Department of Fish and Game Records.

Washington State. Governor Papers, Subject Files, Fisheries, 1901–1940.

INTERVIEWS

Bauter, Lee. Interviewed by Galen Biery, July 1988, Tape 21; December 1988, Tape 22. Galen Biery Collection. Transcript available at the Center for Pacific Northwest Studies, Western Washington University, Bellingham, WA.

Beale, W. J. Interviewed by Barbara Heacock, February 8, 1978. Skagit County Oral History Collection. Microfilm transcript available at the Center for Pacific Northwest Studies, Western Washington University, Bellingham, WA.

Bessner, W. H. Interviewed by Barbara Heacock, October 4, 1977. Skagit County Oral History Collection. Microfilm transcript available at the Center for Pacific Northwest Studies, Western Washington University, Bellingham, WA.

Charles, Al. Interviewed by Jeff Wilner, April 26, 1973. Northwest Tribal Indians Oral History Collection. Transcript available at the Center for Pacific Northwest Studies, Western Washington University, Bellingham, WA.

Cooper, Mrs. Albert. Interviewed by Imbert Orchard, n.d. Transcribed copy in Stò:lō Nation Archives, Chilliwack, B.C.

———. Interviewed by Oliver Wells, February 8, 1962. Transcribed copy in Stò:lō Nation Archives, Chilliwack, B.C.

Douglas, Amelia. Interviewed by Sonnie McHalsie, Randel Paul, Richard Daly, and Peter John, August 16–17, 1988. Transcribed copy in Stò:lō Nation Archives, Chilliwack, B.C.

Douglas, Edna. Interviewed by Sonnie McHalsie, January 16, 1985. Transcribed copy in Stò:lō Nation Archives, Chilliwack, B.C.

Elich, Tony. "History of Fishing in Puget Sound and Alaska, and Information of Slavic Community in Bellingham." Interviewed by Michael A. Runestrand, January 24, 1976. Washington State Oral/Aural History Program, Washington State Archives, Olympia, WA. Microfiche copy available in Wilson Library, Western Washington University, Bellingham, WA.

Emory, Steven. Interviewed by Sonnie McHalsie, August 10, 1988. Transcribed copy in Stò:lō Nation Archives, Chilliwack, B.C.

George, John. Interviewed by two unnamed Simon Fraser University students, October 3, 1997. Transcribed copy in Stò:lō Nation Archives, Chilliwack, B.C.

Ginnett, Albert V. Interviewed by Peter Heffelfinger, March 1, 1978. Skagit County Oral History Collection. Microfilm transcript available at the Center for Pacific Northwest Studies, Western Washington University, Bellingham, WA.

Graham, J. Conrad. "Memories of Pacific American Fisheries and the Fish Trap Industry in Puget Sound." Interviewed by Michael A. Runestrand, June 20, 1976. Washington State Oral/Aural History Program, Washington State Archives, Olympia, WA. Microfiche copy available in Wilson Library, Western Washington University, Bellingham, WA.

Gutierrez, Alan. Interviewed by Sonnie McHalsie and Randel Paul, October 13, 1989. Transcribed copy in Stò:lō Nation Archives, Chilliwack, B.C.

Gutierrez, Tillie. Interviewed by Sonnie McHalsie and Randel Paul, October 13, 1989. Transcribed copy in Stò:lō Nation Archives, Chilliwack, B.C.

Hope, Lawrence. Interviewed by Sonnie McHalsie, Randel Paul, and Richard Daly, November 25, 1988. Transcribed copy in Stò:lō Nation Archives, Chilliwack, B.C.

Jones, Bert. Interviewed by Peter Heffelfinger and Barbara Heacock, February 7, 1978. Skagit County Oral History Collection. Microfilm transcript available at the Center for Pacific Northwest Studies, Western Washington University, Bellingham, WA.

Loop, Helen Comfort Pike. Interviewed by Peter Heffelfinger and Barbara Heacock, February 7, 1978. Skagit County Oral History Collection. Microfilm transcript available at the Center for Pacific Northwest Studies, Western Washington University, Bellingham, WA.

Louie, Joe. Interviewed by K. Lee and Judy Thompson, May 24, 1973, Tape 11; May 1, 1973, Tape 35. Northwest Tribal Indians Oral History Collection. Transcript available at the Center for Pacific Northwest Studies, Western Washington University, Bellingham, WA.

Propst, William, and Clara Propst. Interviewed by Peter Heffelfinger and Barbara Heacock, July 21, 1977. Skagit County Oral History Collection. Microfilm transcript available at the Center for Pacific Northwest Studies, Western Washington University, Bellingham, WA.

Robinson, Edith. Interviewed by Barbara Heacock, March 8, 1978. Skagit County Oral History Collection. Microfilm transcript available at the Center for Pacific Northwest Studies, Western Washington University, Bellingham, WA.

Scott, Walter. "Early Fishing Days/Working the Fish Traps and Remembrances." Interviewed by Michael A. Runestrand, April 15, 1975. Washington State Oral/Aural History Program, Washington State Archives, Olympia, WA. Microfiche copy available in Wilson Library, Western Washington University, Bellingham, WA.

———. "Information on the Fish Traps and the Salmon Industry in Puget Sound." Interviewed by Michael A. Runestrand, February 17, 1976. Washington State Oral/ Aural History Program, Washington State Archives, Olympia, WA. Microfiche copy available in Wilson Library, Western Washington University, Bellingham, WA.

Solomon, Felix, Dora Solomon, Angeline Alexander, and Aurelia Celestine. Interviewed April 13, 1983. Northwest Tribal Indians Oral History Collection. Transcript available at the Center for Pacific Northwest Studies, Western Washington University, Bellingham, WA.

Vogt, Elmer. Interviewed by Barbara Heacock, January 30, 1978. Skagit County Oral History Collection. Microfilm transcript available at the Center for Pacific Northwest Studies, Western Washington University, Bellingham, WA.

SOURCES

Adachi, Ken. *The Enemy That Never Was: A History of the Japanese Canadians.* 1976. Reprint, McClelland & Stewart Inc. in association with the Multiculturalism Program, Department of the Secretary of State of Canada and the Publishing Centre, Supply and Services Canada, 1991.

Adams, John W. *The Gitksan Potlatch: Population, Flux, Resource Ownership, and Reciprocity.* Toronto: Holt, Rinehart and Winston of Canada, Ltd., 1973.

Adelman, Jeremy, and Stephen Aron. "From Borderlands to Borders: Empires, Nation-States, and the Peoples in Between in North American History." *American Historical Review* 104 (June 1999): 814–41.

Allard, Dean Conrad, Jr. *Spencer Fullerton Baird and the U.S. Fish Commission*. New York: Arno Press, 1978.

Alper, Donald K. "The Idea of Cascadia: Emergent Transborder Regionalisms in the Pacific Northwest–Western Canada." *Journal of Borderlands Studies* 11:2 (Fall 1996): 1–22.

American Friends Service Committee. *Uncommon Controversy: Fishing Rights of the Muckleshoot, Puyallup, and Nisqually Indians*. Seattle: University of Washington Press, 1970.

Ames, Kenneth M., and Herbert D. G. Maschner. *Peoples of the Northwest Coast: Their Archaeology and Prehistory*. London: Thames and Hudson, Ltd., 1999.

Anderson, Kay J. *Vancouver's Chinatown: Racial Discourse in Canada, 1875–1980*. Montreal: McGill-Queen's University Press, 1991.

Andrews, Thomas G. *Killing for Coal: America's Deadliest Labor War*. Cambridge: Harvard University Press, 2008.

———. "'Made by Toile'? Tourism, Labor, and the Construction of the Colorado Landscape, 1858–1917." *Journal of American History* 92:3 (December 2005): 837–63.

Anderson, Bern, ed. "The Vancouver Expedition: Peter Puget's Journal of the Exploration of Puget Sound, May 7–June 11, 1792." *Pacific Historical Quarterly* 30:2 (April 1939): 177–217.

Archives of British Columbia. *Minutes of the Council of Vancouver Island, Commencing August 30th, 1851, and Terminating with the Prorogation of the House of Assembly, February 6th, 1861*. Victoria, B.C.: Printed by William H. Cullin, 1918.

———. *House of Assembly Correspondence Book, August 12th, 1856 to July 6th, 1859*. Memoir 4. Victoria, B.C.: Printed by William H. Cullin, 1918.

Arestad, Sverre. "The Norwegians in the Pacific Coast Fisheries." *Pacific Northwest Quarterly* 34:1 (January 1943): 3–17.

Arnold, David. *The Fishermen's Frontier: People and Salmon in Southeast Alaska*. Seattle: University of Washington Press, 2008.

———. "Putting Up Fish: Environment, Work, and Culture in Tlingit Society, 1780s–1940s." Ph.D. dissertation, University of California, Los Angeles, 1997.

Assu, Harry, with Joy Inglis. *Assu of Cape Mudge: Recollections of a Coastal Indian Chief*. Vancouver: University of British Columbia Press, 1989.

Austin, A. Dennis. *State of Washington Legislative Laws Pertaining to Puget Sound Salmon Fisheries, 1889 through 1920*. State of Washington, Department of Fisheries, Management and Research Division, January 1972.

Bagley, Clarence B., ed. "Attitude of the Hudson's Bay Company during the Indian War of 1855-1856." *Washington Historical Quarterly* 8:4 (October 1917): 291–307.

Ball, Georgiana. "The Monopoly System of Wildlife Management of the Indians and the Hudson's Bay Company in the Early History of British Columbia." *B.C. Studies* 66 (Summer 1985): 37–55.

Barman, Jean. *The West beyond the West: A History of British Columbia*. Toronto: University of Toronto Press, 1991.

————, and Bruce McIntyre Watson. *Leaving Paradise: Indigenous Hawaiians in the Pacific Northwest, 1787-1898.* Honolulu: University of Hawai'i Press, 2006.

Barnett, Homer G. *The Coast Salish of British Columbia.* University of Oregon Monographs, Studies in Anthropology, no. 4. Eugene: The University Press, University of Oregon, 1955.

Baud, Michiel, and William Van Schendel. "Toward a Comparative History of Borderlands."*Journal of World History* 8:2 (1997): 211-42.

Beals, Herbert K., trans. and annotation. *Juan Pérez on the Northwest Coast: Six Documents of His Expedition.* Portland: Oregon Historical Society Press, 1989.

Berringer, Patricia. "Northwest Coast Traditional Salmon Fisheries: Systems of Resource Utilization." M.A. thesis, University of British Columbia, 1982.

Binford, Lewis R., ed. *For Theory Building in Archaeology: Essays on Faunal Remains, Aquatic Resources, Spatial Analysis, and Systemic Modeling.* New York: Academic Press, 1977.

Blackman, Margaret B. *During My Time: Florence Edenshaw Davidson, a Haida Woman.* Seattle: University of Washington Press, 1982.

Boas, Franz. *Contributions to the Ethnology of the Kwakiutl.* Columbia University Contributions to Anthropology, 3. New York: Columbia University Press, 1925.

————. *Kwakiutl Ethnography.* Edited by Helen Codere. Chicago: University of Chicago Press, 1966.

Booker, Matthew Morse. "Oyster Growers and Oyster Pirates in San Francisco Bay." *Pacific Historical Review* 75:1 (February 2006): 63-88.

Bouchard, Randy, and Dorothy Kennedy, eds. *Indian Myths and Legends from the North Pacific Coast of America.* A translation of Franz Boas's 1895 edition of *Indianische Sagen von der Nord-Pacifischen Küste Amerikas.* Translated by Dietrich Bertz. Vancouver: Talonbooks, 2002.

Bowsfield, Hartwell, ed. *Fort Victoria Letters, 1846-1851.* Publications of the Hudson's Bay Record Society. Vol. 32. Winnipeg: Hudson's Bay Company, 1979.

Boxberger, Daniel L. "Ethnicity and Labor in the Puget Sound Fishing Industry, 1880-1935." *Ethnology* 33:2 (Spring 1994): 179-91.

————. "In and Out of the Labor Force: The Lummi Indians and the Development of the Commercial Salmon Fishery of North Puget Sound, 1880-1900." *Ethnohistory* 35:2 (Spring 1988): 161-90.

————. *To Fish in Common: The Ethnohistory of Lummi Indian Salmon Fishing.* 1989. Reprint, with a foreword by Chris Friday. Seattle: University of Washington Press, 2000.

Boyd, Robert. *The Coming of the Spirit of Pestilence: Introduced Infectious Diseases and Population Decline among Northwest Coast Indians, 1774-1874.* Vancouver: University of British Columbia Press; Seattle: University of Washington Press, 1999.

Bradley, Harold Whitman. "The Hawaiian Islands and the Pacific Fur Trade, 1785-1813." *Pacific Northwest Quarterly* 30:3 (July 1939): 275-99.

Broughton, Jack M. "Late Holocene Resource Intensification in the Sacramento Valley, California: The Vertebrate Evidence." *Journal of Archaeological Science* 21:4 (July 1994): 501-14.

Butler, Virginia L. "Resource Depression on the Northwest Coast of North America." *Antiquity* 74:285 (September 2000): 649–61.

———, and James C. Chatters. "The Role of Bone Density in Structuring Prehistoric Bone Assemblages." *Journal of Archaeological Science* 21 (1994): 413–24.

Caamaño, Jacinto. "The Journal of Jacinto Caamaño." Edited by Henry R. Wagner and W. A. Newcombe. Translated by Captain Harold Grenfell, R.N. Parts 1 and 2. *British Columbia Historical Quarterly* 2:3 (July 1938): 189-222; and 2:4 (October 1938): 265-301.

Cain, P. J., and A. G. Hopkins. *British Imperialism: Innovation and Expansion.* London: Longman Group, 1993.

Cameron, Michelle. "Two-Spirited Aboriginal People: Continuing Cultural Appropriation by Non-Aboriginal Society." *Canadian Women's Studies* 24 (2005): 123–27.

Canada. Department of Marine and Fisheries. *Annual Report of the Department of Marine and Fisheries,* 1877–1929. Canada, Sessional Papers.

———. *Report of the Royal Commission on Chinese and Japanese Immigration: The Asian Experience in North America.* Advisory editor Roger Daniels. 1902. Reprint, New York: Arno Press, 1978.

———. *Report of the Royal Commission on Chinese Immigration: The Asian Experience in North America.* Advisory editor Roger Daniels. 1885. Reprint, New York: Arno Press, 1978.

Carlson, Keith Thor, ed. *A Stò:lō Coast Salish Historical Atlas.* Vancouver: Douglas & McIntyre, 2001.

Carlson, Roy L., and Luke Dalla Bona, eds. *Early Human Occupation in British Columbia.* Vancouver: University of British Columbia, 1996.

Carrothers, W. A. *The British Columbia Fisheries.* Toronto: The University of Toronto Press, 1941.

Casaday, Lauren Wilde. "Labor Unrest and the Labor Movement in the Salmon Industry of the Pacific Coast." Ph.D. dissertation, University of California, Los Angeles, 1938.

Chang, Kornel. "Circulating Race and Empire: Transnational Labor Activism and the Politics of Anti-Asian Agitation in the Anglo-American Pacific World, 1880–1910." *Journal of American History* 96:4 (December 2009): 678–701.

———. "Enforcing Transnational White Solidarity: Asian Migration and the Formation of the U.S.-Canadian Boundary." *American Quarterly* 60:3 (September 2008): 671–96.

[Chinese Historical Society of America]. *The Life, Influence, and Role of the Chinese in the United States, 1776-1960.* Proceedings/papers of the national conference held at the University of San Francisco, July 10–12, 1975. San Francisco: Chinese Historical Society of America, 1976.

Citino, Nathan. "The Global Frontier: Comparative History and the Frontier-Borderlands Approach in American Foreign Relations." *Diplomatic History* 25:4 (2001): 677–93.

Clark, John G., ed. *The Frontier Challenge: Responses to the Trans-Mississippi West.* Lawrence: University Press of Kansas, 1971.

Cobb, John N. *Pacific Salmon Fisheries: Report of the United States Commissioner of Fisheries for 1921.* Bureau of Fisheries. Washington, D.C.: U.S. Government Printing Office, 1921.

————. *Salmon Fisheries of the Pacific Coast.* Bureau of Fisheries. Washington, D.C.: U.S. Government Printing Office, 1911.

Codere, Helen. *Fighting with Property: A Study of Kwakiutl Potlatching and Warfare 1792–1930.* Monograph of the American Ethnological Society 18. Edited by Marian W. Smith. 1950. Reprint, Seattle: University of Washington Press, 1966.

Cole, Jean Murray, ed. *This Blessed Wilderness: Archibald McDonald's Letters from the Columbia, 1822–44.* Vancouver: University of British Columbia Press, 2001.

Collins, June McCormick. *Valley of the Spirits: The Upper Skagit of Western Washington.* Seattle: University of Washington Press, 1974.

Conley, James. "Relations of Production and Collective Action in the Salmon Fishery, 1900–1925." In *Workers, Capital, and the State in British Columbia: Selected Papers.* Edited by Rennie Warburton and David Coburn, 86–116. Vancouver: University of British Columbia Press, 1988.

Cook, Captain James, F.R.S.; and Captain James King, LL.D. and F.R.S. *A Voyage to the Pacific Ocean; Undertaken by Command of His Majesty for Making Discoveries in the Northern Hemisphere: Performed under the Direction of Captains Cook, Clerke, and Gore, in the Years 1776, 1777, 1778, 1779, 1780.* 4 vols. London: Printed for John Stockdale, Scatchered and Whitaker, John Fielding, and John Hardy, 1784.

Cook, Sherburne F. "The Epidemic of 1830–1833 in California and Oregon." *University of California Publications in American Archaeology and Ethnology* 43:3, 303–25. Berkeley: University of California Press, 1955.

Cook, Warren L. *Flood Tide of Empire: Spain and the Pacific Northwest.* New Haven: Yale University Press, 1973.

Cooper, Carol. "Native Women of the Northern Pacific Coast: An Historical Perspective, 1830–1900." *Journal of Canadian Studies* 27:4 (Winter 1992-93): 44–75.

Cox, Ross. *Adventures on the Columbia River, Including the Narrative of a Residence of Six Years on the Western Side of the Rocky Mountains, among Various Tribes of Indians Hitherto Unknown, Together with A Journey Across the American Continent.* New York: J & J Harper, 1832.

Creese, Gillian. "Exclusion or Solidarity? Vancouver Workers Confront the 'Oriental Problem.'" *B.C. Studies* 80 (Winter 1988): 24–51.

Croes, Dale R., and Eric Blinman. *Hoko River: A 2500 Year Old Fishing Camp on the Northwest Coast of North America.* Washington State University–Pullman, Laboratory of Anthropology, Report of Investigations, no. 58. Hoko River Archaeological Project Contribution, no. 1 (June 1980).

Croes, Dale R., Rebecca A. Hawkins, and Barry L. Isaac, eds. *Research in Economic Anthropology: Long-Term Subsistence Change in Prehistoric North America.* Supplement 6. Greenwich, CT: JAI Press, 1992.

Cronon, William. *Uncommon Ground: Toward Reinventing Nature.* New York: W. W. Norton, 1995.

Crosby, Alfred W. *The Columbian Exchange: Biological and Cultural Consequences of 1492.* Greenwood, CT: Greenwood Press, 1972.

Crutchfield, James A., and Giulio Pontecorvo. *The Pacific Salmon Fisheries: A Study of Irrational Conservation.* Baltimore: Johns Hopkins University Press, 1969.

Cullen, Mary K. "The History of Fort Langley, 1827–96." In *Canadian Historic Sites: Occasional Papers in Archeology and History*. No. 20. Prepared by the National Historic Parks and Sites Branch. Edited by Jean Brathwaite, 5–122. Hull, Quebec: Minister of Supply and Services Canada, 1979.

Dahlie, Jorgen. "A Social History of Scandinavian Immigration, Washington State, 1895–1910." Ph.D. dissertation, Washington State University, 1967.

Das, Rajani Kanta. *Hindustani Workers on the Pacific Coast*. Berlin: Walter de Gruyter & Co., 1923.

Dawson, Will. *The War That Was Never Fought*. Princeton: Auerbach Publishers, 1971.

Dee, Henry Drummond, ed. *The Journal of John Work, January–October, 1835*. Archives of British Columbia. Memoir No. 10. Victoria, B.C.: Charles F. Banfield, 1945.

de Laguna, Frederica. *Under Mount Saint Elias: The History and Culture of the Yakutat Tlingit. Smithsonian Contributions to Anthropology*. Vol. 7 (in three parts). Washington, D.C.: Smithsonian Institution Press, 1972.

De Lorme, Roland L. "The United States Bureau of Customs and Smuggling on Puget Sound, 1851 to 1913." *Prologue: The Journal of the National Archives* 5:2 (Summer 1973): 76–88.

Dillehay, Tom D. "The Great Debate on the First Americans." *Anthropology Today* 7:4 (August 1991): 12–13.

Dippie, Brian W. *The Vanishing American: White Attitudes and U.S. Indian Policy*. Middletown, CT: Wesleyan University Press, 1982.

Donald, Leland. *Aboriginal Slavery on the Northwest Coast of North America*. Berkeley: University of California Press, 1997.

———, and Donald H. Mitchell. "Some Correlates of Local Group Rank among the Southern Kwakwaka'wakw." *Ethnology* 14:4 (October 1975): 325–46.

Dorsey, Kurkpatrick. *The Dawn of Conservation Diplomacy: U.S.-Canadian Wildlife Protection Treaties in the Progressive Era*. Seattle: University of Washington Press, 1998.

Drucker, Philip. *Indians of the Northwest Coast*. Anthropological Handbook No. 10. Published for the American Museum of Natural History. New York: McGraw-Hill Book Company, 1955.

———. *The Northern and Central Nootkan Tribes*. Smithsonian Institution, Bureau of American Ethnology, Bulletin 144. Washington, D.C.: U.S. Government Printing Office, 1951.

Duff, Wilson. *The Upper Stalo Indians of the Fraser Valley, British Columbia*. Anthropology in British Columbia. Edited by Wilson Duff. Memoir No. 1. Victoria: B.C. Provincial Museum, 1952.

Eells, Myron. *The Indians of Puget Sound: The Notebooks of Myron Eells*. Edited by George Pierre Castile. Seattle: University of Washington Press, 1985.

Elliot, Dave. *Saltwater People: A Resource Book for the Saanich Native Studies Program*. Edited by Janet Poth. Saanich, B.C.: School District 63 (Saanich), 1983.

Elmendorf, William W. "Skokomish and Other Coast Salish Tales." *Research Studies* 29:1 (March 1961): 1–37; 29:2 (June 1961): 84–117; and 29:3 (September 1961): 119–50.

———. "The Structure of Twana Culture." Monographic Supplement No. 2. *Research Studies* 28:3 (September 1960): 1–576.

———. *Twana Narratives: Native Historical Accounts of a Coast Salish Culture.* Seattle: University of Washington Press, 1993.

Ettinger, Patrick. "'We Sometimes Wonder What They Will Spring on Us Next': Immigrants and Border Enforcement in the American West, 1882–1930." *Western Historical Quarterly* 37:2 (Summer 2006): 159–81.

Evenden, Matthew D. *Fish versus Power: An Environmental History of the Fraser River.* Cambridge: Cambridge University Press, 2004.

Farrar, Victor J., ed. "Diary of Colonel and Mrs. I. N. Ebey." *Washington Historical Quarterly* 8:1 (January 1917): 40-62; and 8:2 (April 1917): 124–52.

———, ed. "The Nisqually Journal." *Washington Historical Quarterly* 11:1 (January 1920): 59–65; 11:2 (April 1920): 136-49; 11:3 (July 1920): 294-302; 12:4 (October 1921): 300-3; and 13:3 (July 1921): 219-28.

Fiege, Mark. "The Weedy West: Mobile Nature, Boundaries, and Common Space in the Montana Landscape." *Western Historical Quarterly* 36:1 (Spring 2005): 22–47.

Findlay, John M., and Ken S. Coates, eds. *Parallel Destinies: Canadian-American Relations West of the Rockies.* Seattle: University of Washington Press, 2002.

Fisher, Robin. *Contact and Conflict: Indian-European Relations in British Columbia, 1774-1890.* Vancouver: University of British Columbia Press, 1977.

———. "Indian Warfare and Two Frontiers: A Comparison of British Columbia and Washington Territory during the Early Years of Settlement." *Pacific Historical Review* 50:1 (February 1981): 31–51.

———. "The Northwest from the Beginning of Trade with Europeans to the 1880s." In *North America.* Vol. 1, Part 2 of *The Cambridge History of Native Peoples of the Americas.* Edited by Bruce G. Trigger and Wilcomb E. Washburn, 117–82. Cambridge: Cambridge University Press, 1996.

———, and J. M. Bumsted, eds. *An Account of a Voyage to the North West Coast of America in 1785 and 1786.* Vancouver: Douglas & McIntyre, 1982.

Fladmark, Knut R. *British Columbia Prehistory.* Ottawa: Archeological Survey of Canada; National Museum of Man; National Museums of Canada, 1986.

Flores, Dan. "Place: An Argument for Bioregional History." *Environmental History Review* 18 (Winter 1994): 1-18.

Ford, Clellan S. *Smoke from Their Fires: The Life of a Kwakiutl Chief.* New Haven, CT: Yale University Press, 1941.

Franchère, Gabriel. *Journal of a Voyage on the North West Coast of North America during the Years 1811, 1812, 1813, and 1814.* Transcribed and translated by Wessie Tipping Lamb. Edited by W. Kaye Lamb. Series Publications of the Champlain Society. Vol. 45. Toronto: Champlain Society, 1969.

Fraser, Simon. *The Letters and Journal of Simon Fraser, 1806-1808.* Edited by W. Kaye Lamb. Toronto: Macmillan Company of Canada, 1960.

Friday, Chris. *Organizing Asian American Labor: The Pacific Coast Canned-Salmon Industry, 1870-1942.* Philadelphia: Temple University Press, 1994.

Fujita-Rony, Dorothy. "Water and Land: Asian Americans and the U.S. West." *Pacific Historical Review* 76:4 (November 2007): 563–74.

Gabaccia, Donna R. "Is Everywhere Nowhere? Nomads, Nations, and the Immigrant

Paradigm of United States History." *Journal of American History* 86:3 (December 1999): 1115–34.

Galbraith, John S. *The Hudson's Bay Company as an Imperial Factor, 1821–1869*. Berkeley: University of California Press, 1957.

Gibbons, Ann. "Geneticists Trace the DNA Trail of the First Americans." *Science*, new series, 259, no. 5093 (January 15, 1993): 312–13.

Gibbs, George. "The Tribes of Western Washington and Northwestern Oregon." *Contributions to North American Ethnology* 1 (1877): 157–361.

Girot, Pascal O. *The Americas: World Boundaries*. Vol. 4. London: Routledge Press, 1994.

Goble, Dale D., and Paul W. Hirt, eds. *Northwest Lands, Northwest Peoples: Readings in Environmental History*. Seattle: University of Washington Press, 1999.

Goode, George Brown. *The Fisheries and Fishery Industries of the United States*. Washington, D.C.: Government Printing Office, 1887.

Griffith, Sarah M. "Border Crossings: Race, Class, and Smuggling in Pacific Coast Chinese Immigrant Society." *Western Historical Quarterly* 35:4 (Winter 2004): 473–92.

Gunther, Erna. "A Further Analysis of the First Salmon Ceremony." *University of Washington Publications in Anthropology* 2:5 (June 1928): 129–73.

———. *Indian Life on the Northwest Coast of North America as Seen by the Early Explorers and Fur Traders during the Last Decades of the Eighteenth Century*. Chicago: University of Chicago Press, 1972.

———. "Klallum Ethnography." *University of Washington Publications in Anthropology* 1:5 (January 1927): 171–314.

Haeberlin, Hermann, and Erna Gunther. *The Indians of Puget Sound*. Seattle: University of Washington Press, 1980. Originally published in *University of Washington Publications in Anthropology* 4:1 (1930).

Hallett, Mary E. "A Governor-General's Views on Oriental Immigration to British Columbia, 1904–1911." *B.C. Studies* 14 (Summer 1972): 51–72.

Halseth, James A., and Bruce R. Glasrud, eds. *The Northwest Mosaic: Minority Conflicts in Pacific Northwest History*. N.p.: Pruett Publishing Company, 1977.

Hardin, Garrett. "The Tragedy of the Commons." *Science* 162 (December 1968): 1243–48.

Harmon, Alexandra. *Indians in the Making: Ethnic Relations and Indian Identities around Puget Sound*. Berkeley: University of California Press, 1998.

Harris, Cole. *Making Native Space: Colonialism, Resistance, and Reserves in British Columbia*. Vancouver: University of British Columbia Press, 2002.

———. *The Resettlement of British Columbia: Essays on Colonialism and Geographical Change*. Vancouver: University of British Columbia Press, 1997.

Harris, Douglas C. *Fish, Law, and Colonialism: The Legal Capture of Salmon in British Columbia*. Toronto: University of Toronto Press, 2001.

———. *Landing Native Fisheries: Indian Reserves and Fishing Rights in British Columbia, 1849–1925*. Vancouver: University of British Columbia Press, 2008.

———. "The Nlha7kápmx Meeting at Lytton, 1879, and the Rule of Law." *B.C. Studies* 108 (1995–96): 5–25.

Hay, Douglas, Peter Linebaugh, John G. Rule, E. P. Thompson, and Cal Winslow. *Albion's*

Fatal Tree: Crime and Society in Eighteenth-Century England. New York: Pantheon Books, 1975.

Heckman, Hazel. *Island in the Sound*. Seattle: University of Washington, 1967.

Hendrickson, James E., ed. "Two Letters from Walter Colquohoun Grant." *B.C. Studies* 26 (Summer 1975): 3–15.

Heron, Craig, ed. *The Workers' Revolt in Canada, 1917–1925*. Toronto: University of Toronto Press, 1998.

Hewes, Gordon W. "Aboriginal Use of Fishery Resources in Northwestern North America." Ph.D. dissertation, University of California, Berkeley, 1947.

Hirt, Paul W., ed. *Terra Pacifica: People and Place in the Northwest States and Western Canada*. Pullman: Washington State University Press, 1998.

Hobsbawm, Eric. *Bandits*. Revised edition with a new introduction by the author. New York: The New Press, 2000.

———. *Social Bandits and Primitive Rebels: Studies in the Archaic Forms of Social Movement in the Nineteenth and Twentieth Centuries*. Glencoe, IL: The Free Press, 1959.

Howay, Frederic William, et al. *British Columbia and the United States: The North Pacific Slope from Fur Trade to Aviation*. Toronto: The Ryerson Press, 1942.

Hunter, George. *Reminiscences of an Old Timer*. 4th edition. Battle Creek, MI: Review and Herald, 1889.

Ichioka, Yuji. *The Issei: The World of First Generation Japanese Immigrants, 1885–1924*. New York: The Free Press, 1988.

Igler, David. "Diseased Goods: Global Exchanges in the Eastern Pacific Basin, 1770–1850." *American Historical Review* 109:3 (June 2004): 693–719.

———. "On Coral Reefs, Volcanoes, Gods, and Patriotic Geology; Or, James Dwight Dana Assembles the Pacific Basin." *Pacific Historical Review* 79:1 (February 2010): 23–49.

———. "Re-Orienting Asian American History through Transnational and International Scales." *Pacific Historical Review* 76:4 (November 2007): 611–14.

Ito, Kazuo. *Issei: A History of Japanese Immigrants in North America*. Translated by Shinichiro Nakamura and Jean S. Gerard. Seattle: Executive Committee for Publication, Japanese Community Service, 1973.

Jacoby, Karl. *Crimes against Nature: Squatters, Poachers, Thieves, and the Hidden History of American Conservation*. Berkeley: University of California Press, 2001.

Jenness, Diamond. *The Faith of a Coast Salish Indian*. Anthropology in British Columbia. Edited by Wilson Duff. Memoir No.3. Victoria: British Columbia Provincial Museum, Department of Education, 1955.

Jewitt, John. *Narrative of the Adventures and Sufferings of John R. Jewitt, Only Survivor of the Crew of the Ship BOSTON during a Captivity of Nearly Three Years among the Savages of Nootka Sound*. Fairfield, WA: Ye Galleon Press, 1967.

Johnson, Benjamin H., and Andrew R. Graybill, eds. *Bridging National Borders in North America*. Durham, NC: Duke University Press, 2010.

Jones, Robert F., ed. *Annals of Astoria: The Headquarters Log of the Pacific Fur Company on the Columbia River, 1811–1813*. New York: Fordham University Press, 1999.

Kapplar, Charles J., comp. and ed. "Indian Affairs: Laws and Treaties." 1904. Available online at http://digital.library.okstate.edu/KAPPLER/Vol2/Toc.htm.

Kiy, Richard, and John D. Wirth, eds. *Environmental Management on North America's Borders*. College Station: Texas A&M University Press, 1998.

Klingle, Matthew. *Emerald City: An Environmental History of Seattle*. New Haven, CT: Yale University Press, 2007.

Knight, Rolf. *Indians at Work: An Informal History of Native Labour in British Columbia, 1858–1930*. 1978. Reprint, Vancouver: New Star Books, 1996.

————, and Maya Koizumi, eds. *A Man of Our Times: The Life-History of a Japanese-Canadian Fisherman*. Vancouver: New Star Books, 1976.

Kobayashi, Audrey, and Peter Jackson. "Japanese Canadians and the Racialization of Labor in the B.C. Sawmill Industry." *B.C. Studies* 103 (Autumn 1994): 59–81.

Koppel, Tom. *Kanaka: The Untold Story of Hawaiian Pioneers in British Columbia and the Pacific Northwest*. Vancouver: Whitecap Books, 1995.

Krech, Shepard III. *The Ecological Indian: Myth and History*. New York: W.W. Norton & Company, 1999.

Krkosek, Martin, Mark A. Lewis, Alexandra Morton, L. Neil Frazer, and John P. Volpe. "Epizootics of Wild Fish Induced by Farm Fish." *Proceedings of the National Academy of Sciences of the United States of America* 103:42 (October 17, 2006): 15,506–10.

Krkosek, Martin, Mark A. Lewis, and John P. Volpe. "Transmission Dynamics of Parasitic Sea Lice from Farm to Wild Salmon." *Proceedings of the Royal Society* 272:1564 (April 2005): 689–96.

Kruckeberg, Arthur R. *The Natural History of Puget Sound Country*. Seattle: University of Washington Press, 1991.

Kusmer, Karla D. "Changes in Subsistence Strategies at the Tsawwassen Site, a Southwestern British Columbia Shell Midden." *Northwest Anthropological Research Notes* 28:2 (Fall 1994): 189–210.

Ladner, T. Ellis. *Above the Sand Heads: A Vivid Account of Life on the Delta of the Fraser River, 1868–1900*. Cloverdale, B.C.: D. W. Friesen & Sons, Ltd., 1979.

Ladow, Beth. *The Medicine Line: Life and Death on a North American Borderland*. New York: Routledge, 2001.

Lai, Chuen-Yan. "Chinese Attempts to Discourage Emigration to Canada: Some Findings from the Chinese Archives in Victoria." *B.C. Studies* 18 (Summer 1973): 33–49.

Lamb, William Kaye, ed. *The Journals and Letters of Sir Alexander Mackenzie*. Published for the Hakluyt Society. London: Cambridge University Press, 1970.

Lecker, Robert, ed. *Borderlands: Essays in Canadian-American Relations*. Selected by the Borderlands Project. Toronto: ECW Press, 1991.

Leighton, Caroline C. *West Coast Journeys, 1865–1879: The Travelogue of a Remarkable Woman*. Seattle: Sasquatch Books, 1995.

Lee, Douglas W., ed. *The Annals of the Chinese Historical Society of the Pacific Northwest*. Chinese Historical Society of the Pacific Northwest and the Center for East Asian Studies. Bellingham, WA: Western Washington University, 1984.

Lee, Erika. *At America's Gates: Chinese Immigration during the Exclusion Era, 1882–1943*. Chapel Hill: University of North Carolina Press, 2005.

————. "The 'Yellow Peril' and Asian Exclusion in the Americas." *Pacific Historical Review* 76:4 (November 2007): 550–56.

Lepofsky, Dana, Ken Lertzman, Douglas Hallett, and Rolf Mathewes. "Climate Change and Culture Change on the Southern Coast of British Columbia, 2400–1200 CAL B.P.: An Hypothesis." *American Antiquity* 70:2 (April 2005): 267–93.

Lichatowich, Jim. *Salmon without Rivers: A History of the Pacific Salmon Crisis.* Washington, D.C.: Island Press, 1999.

Liestman, Daniel. "'The Various Celestials among Our Town': Euro-American Response to Port Townsend's Chinese Colony." *Pacific Northwest Quarterly* 85 (July 1994): 93–104.

Lutz, John Sutton. "After the Fur Trade: The Aboriginal Labouring Class of British Columbia, 1849–1890." *Journal of the Canadian Historical Association* n.s. 3 (1992): 69–93.

———. "Inventing an Indian War: Canadian Indians and American Settlers in the Pacific West, 1854–1864." *Journal of the West* 38:3 (July 1999): 7–13.

———. *Makúk: A New History of Aboriginal-White Relations.* Vancouver: University of British Columbia Press, 2008.

Macfie, Matthew. *Vancouver Island and British Columbia: Their History, Resources, and Prospects.* London: Longman, Green, Longman, Roberts & Green, 1865.

Maclachlan, Morag, ed. *The Fort Langley Journals, 1827–1830.* Vancouver: University of British Columbia Press, 1998.

Mann, Geoff. "Class Consciousness and Common Property: The International Fishermen and Allied Workers of America." *International Labor and Working-Class History* 61 (Spring 2002): 141–60.

Marchak, Patricia, Neil Guppy, and John McMullan, eds. *Uncommon Property: The Fishing and Fish-Processing Industries in British Columbia.* Toronto: Methuen Publications, 1987.

Marlatt, Daphne. *Steveston Recollected: A Japanese-Canadian History.* Victoria: Provincial Archives of Canada, 1975.

Marsden, Susan, and Robert Galois. "The Tsimshian, the Hudson's Bay Company, and the Geopolitics of the Northwest Coast Fur Trade, 1787–1840." *Canadian Geographer* 39:2 (Summer 1995): 169–83.

Marsh, Kevin R. *Drawing Lines in the Forest: Creating Wilderness Areas in the Pacific Northwest.* Seattle: University of Washington Press, 2007.

Mason, Beryl Troxell. *John Franklin Troxell, Fish Trap Man: Puget Sound and San Juan Islands, Washington.* Oak Harbor, WA: Watmough Publishers, 1991.

McCay, Bonnie J. *Oyster Wars and the Public Trust: Property, Law, and Ecology in New Jersey History.* Tucson: University of Arizona Press, 1998.

———. "The Pirates of Piscary: Ethnohistory of Illegal Fishing in New Jersey." *Ethnohistory* 31:1 (1984): 17–37.

McCormack, A. R. *Reformers, Rebels, and Revolutionaries: The Western Canadian Radical Movement, 1899–1919.* Toronto: University of Toronto Press, 1977.

McDermott, John Dishon. "San Juan Island's Pig War." *Journal of the West* 7:2 (April 1968): 236–45.

McDonald, Robert A. J., and Jean Barman, eds. *Vancouver Past: Essays in Social History.* Vancouver Centennial Issue of B.C. Studies. Vancouver: University of British Columbia Press, 1986.

McEvoy, Arthur. *The Fisherman's Problem: Ecology and Law in the California Fisheries.* New York: Cambridge University Press, 1986.

McGerr, Michael. "The Price of the 'New Transnational History.'" *American Historical Review* 96:4 (October 1991): 1056–67.

McIntosh, Dave. *The Collectors: A History of Canadian Customs and Excise.* Toronto: NC Press Limited in association with Revenue Canada, Customs and Excise and the Canadian Government Publishing Centre, Supply and Services, Canada, 1984.

McKinsey, Lauren, and Victor Konrad. *Borderland Reflections: The United States and Canada.* Borderlands Monograph Series no. 1. Orono, ME: The Borderlands Project, 1989.

McManus, Sheila. *The Line Which Separates: Race, Gender, and the Making of the Alberta-Montana Borderlands.* Lincoln: University of Nebraska Press, 2005.

Meany, Edmond S. "First American Settlement on Puget Sound." *Washington Historical Quarterly* 7:2 (April 1916): 136-43.

Meeker, Ezra. *Pioneer Reminiscences of Puget Sound; The Tragedy of Leschi.* Seattle: Lowman & Hanford, 1905.

Meggs, Geoff, and Duncan Stacey. *Cork Lines and Canning Lines: The Glory Years of Fishing on the West Coast.* Vancouver: Douglas & McIntyre, 1992.

———. *Salmon: The Decline of the B.C. Fishery.* Vancouver: Douglas & McIntyre, 1995.

Meltzer, David J. "Clocking the First Americans." *Annual Review of Anthropology* 24 (1995): 21–45.

Merk, Frederick. *Fur Trade and Empire: George Simpson's Journal.* Cambridge: Harvard University Press, 1931.

Mighetto, Lisa. *Saving the Salmon: A History of the U.S. Army Corps of Engineers Efforts to Protect Anadromous Fish on the Columbia and Snake Rivers.* Seattle: Historical Research Associates, 1994.

Miller, Bruce G. "The 'Really Real' Border and the Divided Salish Community." *B.C. Studies* 112 (Winter 1996-97): 63–79.

———, ed. *Be of Good Mind: Essays on the Coast Salish.* Vancouver: University of British Columbia Press, 2007.

Miller, Jay, and Carol M. Eastman, eds. *The Tsimshian and Their Neighbors of the North Pacific Coast.* Seattle: University of Washington Press, 1984.

Millerd, Frank W. "Windjammers to Eighteen Wheelers: The Impact of Changes in Transportation Technology on the Development of British Columbia's Fishing Industry." *B.C. Studies* 78 (Summer 1988): 28–52.

Milton, Viscount. *A History of the San Juan Boundary Question.* London: Cassell, Petter, and Galpin, 1869.

Misrow, Jogesh C. "East Indian Immigration on the Pacific Coast." M.A. thesis, Stanford Junior University, 1915.

Montgomery, David R. *King of Fish: The Thousand-Year Run of Salmon.* Cambridge: Westview Press, 2003.

Moss, Madonna L., and Jon M. Erlandson. "Reflections on North American Pacific Coast Prehistory." *Journal of World Prehistory* 9:1 (March 1995): 1–45.

Muszynski, Alicja. *Cheap Wage Labour: Race and Gender in the Fisheries of British*

Columbia. Montreal: McGill-Queen's University Press, 1996.

Nash, Ronald J., ed. *The Evolution of Maritime Cultures on the Northeast and the Northwest Coasts of America.* Publication 11, Department of Archaeology. Burnaby, B.C.: Simon Fraser University, 1983.

Naylor, Rosamond L., Josh Eagle, and Whitney L. Smith. "Salmon Aquaculture in the Pacific Northwest: A Global Industry with Local Impacts." *Environment: Science and Policy for Sustainable Development* 45:8 (October 2003): 18–39.

Naylor, Rosamond L., Rebecca J. Goldburg, Jurgenne Primavera, Nils Kautsky, Malcolm C. M. Beveridge, Jason Clay, Carol Folke, Jane Lubchenco, Harold Mooney, and Max Troell. "Effects of Aquaculture on World Fish Supplies." *Issues in Ecology* 8 (Winter 2001): 2.

Naylor, Rosamond L., Kjetil Hindar, Ian A. Fleming, Rebecca Goldberg, Susan Williams, John Volpe, Fred Whoriskey, Josh Eagle, Dennis Kelso, and Marc Mangel. "Fugitive Salmon: Assessing the Risks of Escaped Fish from Net-Pen Aquaculture." *BioScience* 55:5 (May 2005): 427–37.

Newell, Diane. *The Development of the Pacific Salmon-Canning Industry: A Grown Man's Game.* Montreal: McGill-Queen's University Press, 1989.

———. "The Rationality of Mechanization in the Pacific Salmon-Canning Industry before the Second World War." *Business History Review* 62 (Winter 1988): 626–55.

———. *Tangled Webs of History: Indians and the Law in Canada's Pacific Coast Fishery.* Toronto: University of Toronto Press, 1993.

Norton, Helen H. "Patterns of Exogamy among Southern Coast Salish." *Northwest Anthropological Research Notes* 28:1 (Spring 1994): 83–98.

O'Bannon, Patrick. "Waves of Change: Mechanization in the Pacific Coast Canned Salmon Industry, 1864–1914." *Technology and Culture* 28:3 (July 1987): 558–77.

Oberg, Kalervo. *The Social Economy of the Tlingit Indians.* Edited by Robert F. Spencer. The American Ethnological Society, Monograph 55. Seattle: University of Washington Press, 1973.

Olson, Ronald L. "The Quinault Indians." *University of Washington Publications in Anthropology* 6:2 (November 1936): 1–190.

Pala, Christopher. "Victory at Sea." *Smithsonian* (September 2008): 46–55.

Peck, Gunther. "The Nature of Labor: Fault Lines and Common Ground in Environmental and Labor History." *Environmental History* 11:2 (April 2006): 212–38.

———. *Reinventing Free Labor: Padrones and Immigrant Workers in the North American West, 1885–1930.* Cambridge: Cambridge University Press, 2000.

Petrich, Mary Ann, and Barbara Roje. *The Yugoslav in Washington State: Among the Early Settlers.* Tacoma: Washington State Historical Society, 1984.

Powell, Miles A. "Coming Full Circle? An Environmental History of Herring Spawn Harvest among the Heiltsuk." M.A. thesis, Simon Fraser University, 2005.

Radke, August C. *Pacific American Fisheries Inc.: History of a Washington State Salmon Packing Company, 1890–1966.* Edited by Barbara S. Radke. Jefferson, NC: McFarland & Company, Inc., 2002.

Raibmon, Paige. *Authentic Indians: Episodes of Encounter from the Late Nineteenth Century Northwest Coast.* Durham, NC: Duke University Press, 2005.

Ralston, Keith. "John Sullivan Deas: A Black Entrepreneur in British Columbia Salmon Canning." *B.C. Studies* 32 (Winter 1976–77): 64–78.

———. "The 1900 Strike of Fraser River Sockeye Salmon Fishermen." M.A. thesis, University of British Columbia, 1965.

Ramirez, Bruno. *Crossing the 49th Parallel: Migration from Canada to the United States, 1900- 1930*. Ithaca, NY: Cornell University Press, 2001.

Rathbun, Richard. "A Review of the Fisheries in the Contiguous Waters of the State of Washington and British Columbia." In *Report of the Commissioner for the Year Ending June 30, 1899*. Washington, D.C.: Government Printing Office, 1900.

Rediker, Marcus. *Between the Devil and the Deep Blue Sea: Merchant Seamen, Pirates, and the Anglo-American Maritime World*. Cambridge: Cambridge University Press, 1987.

———. "'Under the Banner of King Death': The Social World of Anglo American Pirates, 1716 to 1726." *William and Mary Quarterly*, 3rd. series, 38 (April 1981): 203–27.

Rich, E. E., ed. *The Letters of John McLoughlin: From Fort Vancouver to the Governor and Committee*. 3 vols. Publications of the Hudson's Bay Record Society. Toronto: The Champlain Society, 1941–44.

Roos, John F. *Restoring Fraser River Salmon: A History of the International Pacific Salmon Commission, 1937–1985*. Vancouver: Pacific Salmon Commission, 1991.

Rounsefell, George A., and George B. Kelez. *The Salmon and Salmon Fisheries of Swiftsure Bank, Puget Sound, and the Fraser River*. Bulletin of the Bureau of Fisheries 49. Washington, D.C.: U.S. Government Printing Office, 1938.

Roy, Patricia. *A White Man's Province: British Columbia Politicians and Chinese and Japanese Immigrants, 1858–1914*. Vancouver: University of British Columbia Press, 1989.

Ruby, Robert H., and John A. Brown. *A Guide to the Indian Tribes of the Pacific Northwest*. Norman: University of Oklahoma Press, 1986.

———. *John Slocum and the Indian Shaker Church*. Norman: University of Oklahoma Press, 1996.

Sage, Walter. "The Critical Period of British Columbia History, 1866–1871." *Pacific Historical Review* 1:4 (December 1933): 424–43.

Sahlins, Peter. *Forest Rites: The War of the Demoiselles in Nineteenth-Century France*. Cambridge: Harvard University Press, 1994.

Sapir, Edward, and Morris Swadesh. "Native Accounts of Nootka Ethnography." Publication 1 of the Indiana University Research Center in Anthropology, Folklore, and Linguistics. *International Journal of American Linguistics* 21:4 (October 1955): 1–457.

Schwantes, Carlos A. "From Anti-Chinese Agitation to Reform Politics: The Legacy of the Knights of Labor in Washington and the Pacific Northwest." *Pacific Northwest Quarterly* 88:4 (Fall 1997): 174–84.

———. *The Pacific Northwest: An Interpretive History*. Lincoln: University of Nebraska Press, 1989.

———. *Radical Heritage: Labor, Socialism, and Reform in Washington and British Columbia, 1885–1917*. Seattle: University of Washington Press, 1979.

Scott, James C. *Seeing Like a State: How Certain Schemes to Improve the Human Condition Have Failed*. New Haven, CT: Yale University Press, 1998.

Seguin, Margaret, ed. *The Tsimshian: Images of the Past: Views for the Present*. Vancouver: University of British Columbia Press, 1984.

Sharp, Paul F. "Three Frontiers: Some Comparative Studies of Canadian, American, and Australian Settlement." *Pacific Historical Review* 24 (November 1955): 369–77.

Singleton, Sara. *Constructing Cooperation: The Evolution of Institutions of Comanagement*. Ann Arbor: University of Michigan Press, 1998.

Smith, Barbara Sweetland, and Redmond J. Barnett, eds. *Russian America: The Forgotten Frontier*. Tacoma: Washington State Historical Society, 1990.

Smith, Dwight L. *A Tour of Duty in the Pacific Northwest: E. A. Porcher and H.M.S. "Sparrowhawk," 1865–1868*. Fairbanks: University of Alaska Press, 2000.

Smith, Marian L. "The Immigration and Naturalization Service (INS) at the U.S.-Canadian Border, 1893–1993: An Overview of Issues and Topics." *Michigan Historical Review* 26:2 (Autumn 2000): 127–47.

Smith, Marian W., ed. *Indians of the Urban Northwest*. New York: Columbia University Press, 1949.

———. "The Nooksack, the Chilliwack, and the Middle Fraser." *Pacific Northwest Quarterly* 41:4 (October 1950): 330–41.

Smith, Tim D. *Scaling Fisheries: The Science of Measuring the Effects of Fishing, 1855–1955*. Cambridge: Cambridge University Press, 1994.

Spence, Mark David. *Dispossessing the Wilderness: Indian Removal and the Making of the National Parks*. New York: Oxford University Press, 1999.

Sproat, Gilbert Malcolm. *Scenes and Studies of Savage Life*. London: Smith, Elder and Co., 1868.

Stacey, C. P. "Britain's Withdrawal from North America, 1864–1871." *Canadian Historical Review* 36:3 (September 1955): 185–98.

Stevens, Hazard. *The Life of Isaac Ingalls Stevens*. 2 vols. Boston: Houghton, Mifflin and Company, 1900.

Stewart, Hilary. *Indian Fishing: Early Methods on the Northwest Coast*. Vancouver: J. J. Douglas Ltd., 1977.

Strickland, Ron. *River Pigs and Cayuses: Oral Histories from the Pacific Northwest*. San Francisco: Lexikos, 1984.

Sturgis, William. *The Journal of William Sturgis*. Edited by S. W. Jackman. Victoria, B.C.: Sono Nis Press, 1978.

Suttles, Wayne. *Coast Salish Essays*. Seattle: University of Washington Press, 1987.

———. "The Economic Life of the Coast Salish of Haro and Rosario Straits." Ph.D. dissertation, University of Washington, 1951.

———. *Katzie Ethnographic Notes*. Edited by Wilson Duff. Anthropology in British Columbia. Memoir No. 2. Victoria: B.C. Provincial Museum, Department of Education, 1955.

———. "Post-Contact Culture Change among the Lummi Indians." *British Columbia Historical Quarterly* 18:1–2 (January–April 1954): 29–102.

———, with Cameron Suttles. *Native Languages of the Northwest Coast* (map). Portland: The Press of the Oregon Historical Society (Western Imprints), 1985.

Suttles, Wayne, ed. *Northwest Coast*. Vol. 7 of *Handbook of North American Indians*.

Series edited by William C. Sturtevant. Washington, D.C.: Smithsonian Institution, 1990.

Swan, James. *The Northwest Coast; Or, Three Years' Residence in Washington Territory.* New York: Harper & Brothers, 1857.

Taylor, Joseph E., III. "Boundary Terminology." *Environmental History* 13:3 (July 2008): 454- 81.

———. "El Niño and Vanishing Salmon: Culture, Nature, History, and the Politics of Blame." *Western Historical Quarterly* 29:4 (Winter 1998): 437–57.

———. *Making Salmon: An Environmental History of the Northwest Fisheries Crisis.* Seattle: University of Washington Press, 1999.

Thelen, David. "Rethinking History and the Nation-State: Mexico and the United States." *Journal of American History* 86:2 (September 1999): 439–52.

Thistle, John. "'As Free of Fish As a Billiard Ball Is of Hair': Dealing with Depletion in the Pacific Halibut Fishery, 1899–1924." *B.C. Studies* 142–43 (Summer–Autumn 2004): 105–25.

Thompson, E. P. *Whigs and Hunters: The Origins of the Black Act.* New York: Pantheon, 1975.

Thrush, Coll. *Native Seattle: Histories from the Crossing-Over Place.* Seattle: University of Washington Press, 2007.

Tolmie, William Fraser. *The Journals of William Fraser Tolmie: Physician and Fur Trader.* Editor unknown. Vancouver: Mitchell Press Limited, 1963.

Trimble, W. J. "American and British Treatment of the Indians in the Pacific Northwest." *Washington Historical Quarterly* 5:1 (January 1914): 32-54.

Truett, Samuel. "Neighbors by Nature: Rethinking Region, Nation, and Environmental History in the U.S.-Mexico Borderlands." *Environmental History* 2 (1997): 160–78.

Tyrrell, Ian R. "American Exceptionalism in an Age of International History." *American Historical Review* 96:4 (October 1991): 1031–55 and 1068–72.

Tyrrell, J. B., ed. *David Thompson's Narrative of His Explorations in Western America, 1784–1812.* 1916. Reprint, New York: Greenwood Press, 1968.

United Fishermen of the Pacific. "Constitution of the United Fishermen of the Pacific: Organized March 16, 1906." 1906[?].

United States. Court of Claims. *Duwamish et al. v. United States.* Printed copies available in University of Washington Special Collections.

United States. Department of Commerce and Labor. Bureau of the Census. *Fisheries of the United States, 1908.* Washington, D.C.: Government Printing Office, 1911.

United States. Department of Fish and Game. *Annual Report of the United States Commissioner of Fisheries.* Washington, D.C.: Government Printing Office, 1870–1938.

United States. Department of Indian Affairs. *Annual Report of the Commissioner of Indian Affairs.* Washington, D.C.: Government Printing Office, 1862–1918.

United States. Immigration and Naturalization Service. *Annual Report of the Commissioner General of Immigration.* Washington, D.C.: Government Printing Office, 1899–1918.

Vancouver, George. *A Voyage of Discovery to the North Pacific Ocean and around the World, 1791–1795.* 4 vols. Edited by W. Kaye Lamb. 2d series, nos. 163–66. London: Hakluyt Society, 1984.

Van Kirk, Sylvia. *"Many Tender Ties": Women in Fur-Trade Society in Western Canada, 1670–1870.* Winnipeg, Manitoba: Watson & Dwyer Publishing, 1980.

van Sittert, Lance. "The Other Seven Tenths." *Environmental History* 10:1 (January 2005): 106–9.

Vibert, Elizabeth. *Traders' Tales: Narratives of Cultural Encounters in the Columbia Plateau, 1807–1846.* Norman: University of Oklahoma Press, 1997.

Volpe, John P., Bradley R. Anholt, and Barry W. Glickman. "Competition among Juvenile Atlantic Salmon (*Salmo salar*) and Steelhead (*Oncorhynchus mykiss*): Relevance to Invasion Potential in British Columbia." *Canadian Journal of Fisheries and Aquatic Sciences* 58 (2001): 197–207.

Volpe, John P., Eric B. Taylor, David W. Rimmer, and Barry W. Glickman. "Evidence of Natural Reproduction of Aquaculture-Escaped Atlantic Salmon in a Coastal British Columbia River." *Conservation Biology* 14:3 (June 2000): 899–903.

Von Hesse-Wartegg, Ernst. "A Visit to Anglo-Saxon Antipodes (Chapter XVII of *Curiosa aus der Neuen Welt*, 1893)." Translated by John Maass. *B.C. Studies* 50 (Summer 1981): 29–38.

Wade, Jill. "The 'Gigantic Scheme': Crofter Immigration and Deep-Sea Fisheries Development for British Columbia (1887–1893)." *B.C. Studies* 53 (Spring 1982): 28–44.

Ward, W. Peter, and Robert A. J. McDonald, eds. *British Columbia: Historical Readings.* Vancouver: Douglas & McIntyre Ltd., 1981.

Ware, Reuben M. *Five Issues, Five Battlegrounds: An Introduction to the History of Indian Fishing in British Columbia, 1850–1930.* Chilliwack, B.C.: Coqualeetza Education Training Center for the Stò:lō Nation, 1983.

Warren, Louis S. *The Hunter's Game: Poachers and Conservationists in Twentieth-Century America.* New Haven, CT: Yale University Press, 1997.

Washington State Attorney General. *Biennial Report of the Attorney General, 1893–1936.*
———. *Report and Opinions of the Attorney General of the State of Washington, 1902–1910.*
———. *State Session Laws.*

Washington State. Department of Fish and Game. *Annual Report of the State Fish Commissioner to the Governor of the State of Washington, 1891–1938.*

Washington State. State Federation of Labor. *History of Washington State Federation of Labor from January 1902 to December 1924.* Seattle: Washington State Federation of Labor, 1924.

Wells, Oliver N. *The Chilliwacks and Their Neighbors.* Vancouver: Talonbooks, 1987.

White, Richard. *Land Use, Environment, and Social Change: The Shaping of Island County Washington.* Seattle: University of Washington Press, 1992.
———. "The Nationalization of Nature." *Journal of American History* 86:3 (December 1999): 976–86.
———. *The Organic Machine.* New York: Hill and Wang, 1995.

Wilcox, William A. "The Fisheries of the Pacific Coast." *Report of the Commissioner for the Year Ending June 30, 1893.* Washington D.C.: Government Printing Office, 1895.
———. "Notes on the Fisheries of the Pacific Coast in 1895." *Report of the Commissioner for the Year Ending June 30, 1896.* Washington D.C.: Government Printing Office, 1898.

Williams, Austin. "The Pacific Salmon Treaty: A Historical Analysis and Prescription for the Future." *Journal of Environmental Law and Litigation* 22:1 (Spring 2007): 153–95.

Williams, Glyndwr, ed. *London Correspondence Inward from Sir George Simpson, 1841–42.* London: Hudson's Bay Record Society, 1973.

Wilson, Robert M. *Seeking Refuge: Birds and Landscapes of the Pacific Flyway.* Seattle: University of Washington Press, 2010.

Wirth, John D. *Smelter Smoke in North America: The Politics of Transborder Pollution.* Lawrence: University Press of Kansas, 2000.

Worster, Donald. "World without Borders: The Internationalizing of Environmental History." *Environmental Review* 6 (Fall 1982): 8–13.

Index

der salmon sales, 93–94, 95, 140–42; conflicts with officials, 152–53, 156–57; cooperation among, 94, 106, 116–17, 140–41; monopoly of fishery by, 131–34; regulations proposed by, 160; salmon thefts by, 142–43, 206n15; transborder investments by, 119–20, 217n185; wasteful practices of, 138–39. *See also* trap owners

canneries: changing technology in, 98; diversity of workforce, 102; number in operation, 74–75, 95; production levels, 74–75, 199n91. *See also individual ethnic groups*

Cape Flattery, WA, 95

Cape Mudge, B.C., 26

Capitol City Canning and Packing Company, 132

Carlisle Packing Company, 142

Cascade Mountains, 12, 58

Cathlamet (people), 15, 42, 43

Chee Foo, 97

Chehalis (people), 15, 192n5

Chemakum (people), 15, 30

Cherry Point, WA, 136

Chileans, 102, 110

Chilliwack (people), 41

Chilliwack, B.C., 86

Chilliwack River, B.C., 41

China, 32, 97, 113

Chinatown (Vancouver, B.C.), 111

Chinese, 32, 141, 191n117; as cannery labor, 71, 73, 96–98, 101–2, 114, 120–21, 213n120, 218n188; illegal entry of, 98–100, 121, 209–10n69, 226n17; immigration laws against, 96–98, 148, 208n50; and Japanese, 113; numbers of, 96–98; protests by, 208n51; violence against, 103, 111, 112, 113. *See also* Asians; ethnic diversity

Chinook (people), 15, 17, 42, 49

Chinook jargon, 58, 69, 72

chinook salmon (also called spring), 4

chum salmon (also called dog), 4, 81, 128

Clatsop, 49

coho salmon (also called silver), 4, 163, 234n113

Collenson, W. T., 150

Columbia River, OR and WA, 8, 25, 35, 36, 40, 42, 43, 44, 45, 46, 79, 117, 146, 179–80n10; depleted runs on, 74, 170, 199n89; fishermen unions and, 111, 214n131, 214n132; fishing on, 17, 37, 73, 75, 81, 170, 189n94; salmon canneries on, 96, 97, 98; violence on, 103

Concomely (Chinook headman), 49, 50

confederation, 66, 195n38

Cook, James, 32, 33

Cowichan (people), 23, 40, 47, 49, 82, 86

Cowlitz (people), 15

Croatians, 107, 113

Cunningham, F. H., 86, 153, 163

Currie & McWilliams Cannery, 102

Custer, Red, 129, 136–37, 140

Daily British Colonist, 138

Dalles, The, 25

Dalmation Coast, 107

Darwin, L. H., 84–85, 163–64

Davidson, Florence Edenshaw, 48

de Laguna, Frederica, 45

Delenais, Louis, 49–50

Deming, E. B., 101, 139

Derby (people), 41

disease, 22, 30, 31, 33–34, 35, 40–41, 44, 185–86n12, 188n68; Indian concerns about, 45–47. *See also* venereal disease

Ditidaht (people), 15

Dominus (captain), 46

Douglas, James, 37, 38, 45, 49, 64, 65–66, 67, 69

Doyle, Henry, 93, 114, 235n129

Duwamish (people), 60, 61

ecological Indian, 7

Eells, Myron, 24

Elisha P. Ferry, 147

Elliot, Dave (Saanich), 88

Elliot Bay, WA, 60
Ellsperman, George, 92
Elwood, James, 92
Emma, 144, 156
Environmental Protection Agency (EPA), 173
ethnic diversity, 96, 106–16. *See also under* fishermen; *and individual ethnic groups*
exclusive economic zones, 170

Fairhaven, WA, 111
farming, 36, 57, 61
Fidalgo Island, WA, 69–70
Fidalgo Island Packing Company, 119, 123, 131, 132
Filipinos, 102
Findlay, Durham & Brodie, 125
Fingal, 91
Finkbonner, C. C., 61
Finns, 108. *See also* Scandinavians
First Nations. *See* Indians
fish farms, 172–73
fish pirates. *See* fish traps; piracy
fish traps, 83, 95, 103, 107, 111, 117, 155, 156, 157, 164, 199n98, 215n148, 218n4; in B.C., 76–77, 125, 162–63, 164, 199–200n98, 233n96, 234n112; Canadian transborder investments in, 119–20, 216n160; commercial fishery design of, 75–76; dispossession of Indian sites and, 76–79, 85, 86–87, 201n111, 204n157; Indian designs of, 17, 28; Indian restrictive access customs to, 26–27, 182n47; piracy of, 122–43, 145, 156, 222n56, 225n123; regulation of, 55, 83, 132–33, 142, 146, 159, 161–63; watchmen on, 125, 126–27, 131, 134, 135, 138, 140, 142, 162. *See also* border; fishery management; fishing; Indian fishing; piracy; trap owners
"fish wars," 170
fish wheels, 142
fishermen: income levels of, 220n37;

knowledge of marine environment, 107; negotiated nationality of, 99, 215n151; options available to, 207n29; protests of, 115–16, 168; violence among, 106–15, 133–34. *See also* banditry; border; ethnic diversity; piracy; *and individual ethnic groups*
fishery management: Canada's relaxation of regulations, 162–63, 166; lax law enforcement, 91, 135, 146–52, 159, 161–62; overfishing, 145, 165, 166, 169; patrols, 91, 125, 127, 140–41, 146–58, 170, 172, 173; regulations, 83–84, 117, 118, 133, 138, 139, 141–42, 145, 158–67, 169–74; violence in, 152–53. *See also* border; fish traps; fishing; Indian fishing; *and individual regulatory bodies*
fishing: contracts for, 7, 90, 92, 107, 116, 150; on the high seas, 9, 139, 169, 170, 172, 173, 236n8; illegal transborder, 71–72, 89–90, 91–95, 122–45, 153–54, 168, 174; industry's payment system for, 114–15. *See also* fish traps; fishery management; Indian fishing; *and individual ethnic groups*
Fitzhugh, E. C., 69
Fort Astoria, 36, 37, 39, 42, 44, 46, 49, 50
Fort George, 36, 44, 46, 50
Fort Langley, 18, 24, 36, 37, 38–39, 41, 42, 43, 44, 47, 49, 65
Fort McLoughlin, 36, 38, 49, 187n47
Fort Nisqually, 36, 46, 191n126
Fort Rupert, 65, 73, 187–88n48
Fort Simpson, 40, 44, 45
Fort Vancouver, 36, 37, 40, 43, 44, 49
Fort Victoria, 49, 187–88n48
Fraser, Simon, 17, 35
Fraser River, B.C., 12, 66, 117, 119, 164; canneries on, 70–74, 92, 93, 97, 100–1, 118; gold rush on, 65–66; hatcheries on, 165; Hell's Gate rockslide, 86, 145, 166–67, 169; Hudson's Bay Company and, 18, 36–37, 43; Indian complaints of encroachments on, 66–67, 81; Indian

settlements on, 26, 33, 40–41; Indian fishing of, 17, 23, 29, 85–87; illegal activity on, 92–95, 137, 141, 144; labor unions on, 109–16, 118; patrols on, 140, 149–53; pollution of, 138–39; regulations on, 158–59, 160, 163, 164; salmon fishery on, 8, 75, 79, 83, 92, 103–8, 116, 120, 127, 156, 158; salmon runs of, 4, 18, 47, 166, 168, 169, 170, 172, 174. *See also individual ethnic groups*

Fraser River Canners' Association, 94, 109, 118, 125, 127–28, 130

Fraser River Fishermen's Protective Association, 111

Friday Harbor, WA, 122

fur trade, 31–33, 34, 35–51

gaff hooks, 17, 156

Galbraith, William, 150, 153

George and Barker Cannery, 93

gill nets, 17, 22, 73, 79–81, 133, 134, 138, 162, 201n114; fishermen using, 81, 113, 127, 133; licenses for, 70–71, 133

Ginnett, Albert, 132, 139, 143

Gitxsan (people), 13

Gompers, Samuel, 113

Goodfellow, James, 119, 156

Governor John R. Rogers, 147

Grant, Ulysses, 61, 193n19

Gray, John, 100

Grays Harbor, WA, 146

Great Britain, 68, 75, 89; immigrants from, 108, 113, 114

Great Lakes region, 107, 158

Great Northern Cannery, 118

Greeks, 108

Green, C. F., 150

Guard, 148

Gunther, Erna, 27

Haida (people), 13, 21, 26, 45, 48, 69, 111

Haisla (people), 13

halibut, 232n89

Halq'eméylem, 11, 15, 23, 33, 40, 41, 67, 82

Hanford, C. H., 83

Hapgood, Andrew, 70

Harmon, Alexandra, 6

Haro Strait, 18

Harris, Douglas, 66

Harrison River, B.C., 138

Hawai'i, 32, 34, 37, 38, 101, 185n7; workers from, 38, 44, 49, 102

Hayashi Rintaro, 111

Heena, Paul (B.C. Indian headman), 88

Heiltsuk (people), 13

Hill, Nathan, 61

Hillside Cannery, 93

Hill-Tout, Charles, 46

"home guards," 35

Hood Canal, WA, 30

Hope, B.C., 67

Hudson's Bay Company (HBC), 18, 36–40, 42–51, 64, 65, 195n39, 197n68. *See also* disease; intermarriage; prostitution; venereal disease

Huestis, F. D., 147

Hume, George, 70

Hume, William, 70

immigrants. *See individual ethnic groups*

immigration regulations, 96; B.C. Natal Act (1900), 105–6. *See also individual ethnic groups*

Imperial Cannery, 102

India, 102; immigrants from, 105, 106, 210n85

Indian Affairs. *See* Canada Department of Marine and Fisheries; Indians; United States Bureau of Indian Affairs

Indian fishing: border crossings for salmon and, 71–73, 88, 91, 92, 93; competition from Asian workers and, 87–88, 111, 114; decline of, 86–88, 102, 198n72; discrimination against in B.C., 85–86, 87, 103; discrimination against in WA, 83–84; First Salmon ceremony and, 29; Indian protests against encroachments in B.C., 86; Indian protests against

LIBRARY OF CONGRESS CATALOGING-IN-PUBLICATION DATA

Wadewitz, Lissa K.

The nature of borders : salmon, boundaries, and bandits on the Salish Sea / Lissa K. Wadewitz.

   p. cm. — (Emil and Kathleen Sick series in Western history and biography)

Includes bibliographical references and index.

ISBN 978-0-295-99182-5 (pbk. : acid-free paper)

1. Salmon fisheries—Salish Sea (B.C. and Wash.)

2. Indians of North America—Fishing—Salish Sea (B.C. and Wash.)

3. Washington (State)—Boundaries—British Columbia.

4. British Columbia—Boundaries—Washington (State)

5. Borderlands—Salish Sea Region (B.C. and Wash.)

6. Pirates—Salish Sea (B.C. and Wash.)

7. Fishery law and legislation—Washington (State)

8. Fishery law and legislation—British Columbia.

9. Salish Sea (B.C. and Wash.)—Environmental conditions.

10. Salish Sea Region (B.C. and Wash.)—Ethnic relations.

I. Center for the Study of the Pacific Northwest.

II. Title.

SH348.W19 2012   333.95'656153—dc23   2012002569

Lightning Source UK Ltd.
Milton Keynes UK
UKOW03n0731270117
293010UK00005B/69/P